Lesson Plans

for

Dynamic Physical Education for Elementary School Children
Thirteenth Edition

Robert P. Pangrazi
Arizona State University

Allyn and Bacon
Boston London Toronto Sydney Tokyo Singapore

CONTENTS

Page Numbers for Individual Lesson Plans appear on pages 1-3, 95-98, and 193-196.

LESSON PLANS FOR DYNAMIC PHYSICAL EDUCATION
13TH EDITION

This edition of *Lesson Plans for Dynamic Physical Education* includes the activities and information necessary to plan a comprehensive lesson. The result should be less planning time and greater opportunity for contact with youngsters. The plans are designed to compliment the text *Dynamic Physical Education for Elementary School Children, 13th Edition. (DPE)*. Activities presented in the plans are covered in greater detail in the text. The lesson plans provide a guide for presenting movement experiences in a sequential and well-ordered manner. The lesson plans should be regarded as an aid for total curriculum planning. The lessons can be modified and shaped into a personalized curriculum that meets the needs of individual teachers.

Many teachers find it useful to take activities from the lesson plans and write major topics on 4" by 6" note cards. Lesson note cards relieve the burden of trying to remember the proper sequence of activities and the worry of forgetting key points of instruction.

Using the Lesson Plans

Three complete sets of lesson plans are included to cover three major developmental levels. Yearly plans for each of the three developmental levels are listed at the start of each set of lessons. The following is a brief description of the curriculum by developmental level:

Developmental Level I. For the majority of children, activities placed in developmental level I are appropriate for *kindergarten through 2nd-grade* children. Learner characteristics in developmental level I make it necessary to create a positive instructional learning environment. By stressing the joy and rewards of physical activity, behaviors can be developed that last a lifetime. The majority of activities for younger children are individual in nature and center on learning movement concepts through theme development. Children learn movement principles and body management skills at this level.

Developmental Level II. Developmental level II activities are appropriate for the majority of *3rd- and 4th-grade* children. However, because of ability and maturity differences, it is common to find youngsters who are performing at level I or level III. During developmental level II, refinement of fundamental skills and initial specialized skills is emphasized. Practicing a variety of manipulative skills enhances visual-tactile coordination. Children are given the opportunity to explore, experiment, and create activities without fear. Students are taught the how and why of activity patterns. Cooperation with peers is encouraged with more emphasis placed on group and team play. Initial instruction in sport skills begins in developmental level II. Sport lead-up activities are utilized so youngsters can apply newly learned skills in a small group setting.

Developmental Level III. Developmental level III activities shift toward specialized skills and sport activities. The majority of activities at this level are used with *5th- and 6th-grade* students. Football, basketball, softball, track and field, volleyball, and hockey are added to the sport offerings. Students continue learning and improving sport skills while participating in cooperative sport lead-up games. Less emphasis is placed on movement concept activities and a larger percentage of instructional time is devoted to manipulative activity. Adequate time is set aside for the rhythmic program, body management skills, and gymnastics. Fitness routines are offered with instruction focused on helping students make decisions about personal approaches to maintaining fitness levels.

Instructional Parts of the Lesson Plans

Each lesson plan is divided into four instructional parts as described in Chapter 3 of *DPE*. Each plan offers enough of activities for about one week of instruction. When more activities are needed, teachers should refer to *DPE*. Briefly, the four instructional parts of the lesson plan and major purposes of each are as follows:

1. **Introductory Activity**: Introductory activities change weekly and are used to physiologically prepare children for activity when entering the gymnasium or activity area. Activities used in this section demand little instruction and allow time to practice class management skills. Descriptions of all introductory activities can be found in *DPE*, Chapter 16.

2. **Fitness Development Activity**: Fitness activities utilize 7 to 8 minutes of a 30-minute lesson. The length of fitness modules varies depending on the developmental level of youngsters. Younger children need less structured routines while older children benefit by being able to personalize their fitness experiences. The activities should be progressive in nature and exercise all parts of the body. Allied to the workout should be discussions about the values of physical activity for a healthy lifestyle. A comprehensive discussion of fitness principles, physical activities, and routines is found in *DPE*, Chapter 12.

3. **Lesson Focus Activities**: The purpose of the lesson focus is to teach toward major program standards and objectives such as the development of eye-hand coordination, body management competency, and fundamental and specialized skills (e.g., folk dancing, shooting a basket, and catching an object). The lesson focus usually takes 15-20 minutes of the daily lesson depending on the length of the teaching period. Lesson focus activities are organized into units and vary in length depending on the developmental level of children. Lesson focus activities change weekly except when continuity of instruction demands longer units.

   Content in each lesson is organized in a developmentally appropriate sequence, with the first activity easiest and the last activity the most difficult. Instruction starts with the first activity. This progression assures each unit begins with success, since all children are capable of performing the beginning activities. It offers a proper sequence of activities for instruction. Developmentally mature children are allowed to progress further along the continuum of activities than less capable children.

4. **Game Activity**: This part of the lesson plan takes place at the closing of the lesson, utilizing the last 5-7 minutes of the period. Games can be used as a culminating activity for practicing skills emphasized in the lesson focus. At other times, games can be unrelated to the lesson focus and used to leave children with an enjoyable activity. The game should help children feel positive about activity so they look forward to the next lesson. If a lesson is physically demanding, a less active game can be played and vice versa. In some cases, a low key, relaxing activity might be used to help children unwind before returning to the classroom.

Contents of the Lesson Plans

The content of each lesson plan includes the following components.

1. **Objectives**: Student objectives are listed for each lesson. The objectives give direction to instructional goals and expected student outcomes.
2. **Equipment needed:** Specific equipment needed for each lesson is listed.
3. **Instructional Activities:** Instructional activities and skill experiences to be taught in the lesson are delineated in proper developmental sequence.
4. **Teaching hints:** This section includes organization tips and important learning cues. How equipment is arranged, how students are grouped, and proper technique cues are examples of information placed in this column.

A Note of Appreciation

Debbie Pangrazi, Elementary Physical Education Resource Teacher, Mesa (Arizona) Public Schools, continues to give direction and feedback about proper instructional sequences and has offered much input for improving the plans. Acknowledgments and appreciation go to Char Darst and Connie Orlowicz of the Mesa School District for their field-testing and numerous contributions. These teachers field-tested and improved the quality of the lesson plans. Donald Hicks, Supervisor of Physical Education for the Fort Worth (Texas) Country Day School continues to contribute with his professional insight into this edition. A warm note of thanks goes to Nicki Rippee, professor at University of Nevada, Reno and Carole Casten, professor at CSU - Dominguez Hills for their contributions to this edition. The professionalism of all these individuals is unparalleled.

SELF-EVALUATION GUIDE

The following points can be used to evaluate your instructional effectiveness.

1. Did you prepare ahead of time? Mental preparation prior to a lesson assures flow and continuity occur in a lesson.

2. Did you understand the "whys" of your lesson? Knowing why you are teaching something will give you greater strength and conviction in your presentation.

3. Was equipment arranged prior to your class? Proper equipment placement reduces management time and allows more time for instruction and practice.

4. Did you constantly move and reposition yourself during the lesson? Moving allows you to be close to more students so you can reinforce and help them. It usually reduces behavior problems.

5. Did you keep alert for children who are having trouble performing the activities? Youngsters want to receive relevant but subtle help.

6. Did you tell your class what your instructional goals were for the lesson? Students will be more focused when they know what they are supposed to learn.

7. Did you teach with enthusiasm and energy? Your energy and zest will rub off on students.

8. Did you use praise when youngsters made an effort or improved? Saying something positive to children increases their desire to perform at a higher level.

9. Did you give sufficient attention to the development of personalization and creativity?

10. Did you teach students to be responsible for learning? Students need to learn self-direction skills. Take time for such learning.

11. Did you teach for quality of movement or just offer a large quantity of activities in an attempt to keep students motivated? Repetition is an important part of skill learning and a component of quality instruction.

12. Did you bring closure to your lesson? This gives you feedback about the effectiveness of your instruction. Use methods of closure that give you information about all students.

13. Did you evaluate the utility of activities you presented? Try to find ways to modify activities to better contribute to educational outcomes.

14. Did you evaluate how you handled discipline problems? What are some ways you could handle situations differently or better in the future?

Try keeping a portfolio related to your instruction. Write down personal growth indicators and situations that make you feel your students are learning. Evaluation is a dynamic and ongoing process.

DYNAMIC PHYSICAL EDUCATION LESSON PLANS
Developmental Level I

Dynamic Physical Education for Elementary School Children
Orientation and Class Management Activities
Level I – Week 1

Objectives:
To learn and follow basic management activities necessary for participation in
  physical education classes

Equipment Required:
Tom-tom
Music for Fitness Challenges

Instructional Activities	Teaching Hints

Orientation Instructional Procedures

The first week of school should be used to teach students the system you are going to use throughout the year. The following are reminders you might find useful in establishing your expectations and routines.

1. Establish rules and expectations. Discuss your expectations with the class to assure students understand reasons for your guidelines. Explain what the consequences are when rules are not followed. Show where time-out boxes are located and how they will be used.

2. Explain to the class the method you will use to learn names. It might be helpful to ask classroom teachers to have students put their name on a piece of masking tape (nametag). Tell students that you will ask them their name on a regular basis until it is learned.

3. Develop entry and exit behaviors for students coming and leaving physical education classes. Students should know how to enter the instructional area and to leave equipment alone until told to use it. If squads are used for instruction, place students into squads and practice moving into formation on signal.

4. Decide how excuses for non-participation will be handled. If possible, set up a routine where the school nurse determines which students are excused for health reasons.

5. Safety is important. Children should receive safety rules to be followed on apparatus and playground equipment. Safety procedures to be followed in physical education classes should be discussed.

6. Illustrate how you will stop and start the class. In general, a whistle (or similar loud signal) and a raised hand is effective for stopping the class. A voice command should be used to start the class. Telling the class when before what (Chapter 5) will assure they do not begin before instructions are finished.

7. Discuss the issue, distribution, and care of equipment. Make students responsible for acquiring a piece of equipment and returning it at the end of the lesson. Place equipment around the perimeter of the teaching area to reduce the chance of students fighting over a piece of equipment.

8. Explain to the class that the format of the daily lesson will include an introductory activity, fitness development, lesson focus, and finish with a game activity.

9. Practice various teaching formations such as open-squad formation and closed-squad formation. Practice moving into a circle while moving (fall-in). Transitions between formations should be done while moving, i.e., jogging from scatter formation into a circular formation.

10. Refer to Chapters 3, 4, and 5 in the text for detailed information about planning, enhancing instructional effectiveness, and class management and discipline strategies.

Introductory Activity -- Move and Freeze on Signal

Have students move throughout the area using a variety of locomotor movements. On signal (whistle), they quickly freeze. Try to reduce the response latency by reinforcing students who stop quickly on signal.

The primary objective is to teach students the importance of moving under control (without bumping others or falling down) and quickly freezing.

Fitness Development Activity -- Fitness Challenges

1. Locomotor Movement: Walk for 30 seconds.

2. Flexibility and Trunk Development Challenges
   a. Bend in different directions.
   b. Stretch slowly and return quickly.
   c. Combine bending and stretching movements.
   d. Sway back and forth.
   e. Twist one body part; add body parts.

3. Locomotor Movement: Skip for 30 seconds.

4. Upper Body Strength Challenges
In a push-up position, do the following challenges:
   a. Lift one foot; the other foot.
   b. Wave at a friend; wave with the other arm.
   c. Scratch your back with one hand; use the other hand.
   d. Walk your feet to your hands.

5. Locomotor Movement: Jog for 30 seconds.

6. Abdominal Development Challenges
From a supine position:
   1. Lift your head and look at your toes.
   2. Lift your knees to your chest.
   3. Wave your legs at a friend.
From a sitting position;
   1. Slowly lay down with hands on tummy.
   2. Lift legs and touch toes.

7. Locomotor Movement: Run and leap for 30 seconds.

The goal should be to move students through a number of movement challenges. Emphasis should be placed on starting the fitness activities at a level where all students can feel successful.

Alternate the locomotor movements with the strength and flexibility challenges. Repeat the challenges as necessary.

Tape alternating segments (30 seconds in length) of silence and music to signal duration of exercise. Music segments indicate locomotor movements while intervals of silence announce doing the movement challenges.

Teach youngsters the different challenges and then allow them to select a challenge they can successfully perform.

The challenges should be enjoyable to perform.

Encourage students to focus on effort and feeling successful.

Workloads should be moderate with emphasis on success for all youngsters.

Lesson Focus – Orientation

Since much time during the first week is used for orientation procedures and management, no lesson focus activity is scheduled.

Game Activity -- Management Games

Play one or two management games to teach students how to move into partner and small group formation

Toe to Toe
Supplies: None
Skills: Fundamental locomotor movements

Youngsters perform a locomotor movement around the area. On signal, each child must find a partner and stand toe to toe (one foot only) with that person. An important skill is to take the nearest person for a partner without searching for a friend. Youngsters who can't find a partner within their immediate area must run quickly to the center of the area (use a marking spot or cone) to find a partner. The goal is to find a nearby partner as quickly as possible and avoid being the last pair formed. If the number of youngsters playing is uneven, the teacher can join in and play. Change locomotor movements often.

Whistle Mixer
Supplies: None
Skills: All basic locomotor movements

Children are scattered throughout the area. To begin, they walk around in any direction they wish. A whistle is blown a number of times in succession with short, sharp blasts. Children then form small groups with the number in each group equal to the number of whistle blasts. If there are four blasts, children form groups of four—no more, no less. When players have the correct number, they sit down immediately to signal that no one may leave the group and no one may enter the group. The goal is not to be left out or caught in a circle with the incorrect number of students. Encourage players to move toward the center of the area and raise their hands to facilitate finding others without a group. After the circles are formed, the teacher calls "Walk," and the game continues. In walking, children should move in different directions.

Dynamic Physical Education for Elementary School Children
Manipulative Skills Using Hoops
Level I – Week 2

Objectives:
To learn to move in an evasive fashion
To manipulate the hoop in a variety of challenges
To strike a ball with a bat

Equipment Required:
Music for Four Corners Movement
One hoop per child
Plastic bottle bat and ball
Batting tee (optional)

Instructional Activities	Teaching Hints
Introductory Activity -- Following Activity	
One partner leads and performs various kinds of movements. The other partner must move in a similar fashion. This can also be used with squads or small groups, allowing the captain to lead.	Student demonstration can be used to stimulate new ideas among students.
Fitness Development Activity --Four Corners Movement	
Outline a large rectangle with a cone at each corner. Place signs with movement tasks on both sides of the cones. Youngsters move around the outside of the rectangle and change movements as they pass each sign. The following movement activities are suggested:	Tape alternating segments of silence and music to signal duration of exercise. Music segments (30 seconds) indicate Four Corner aerobic activity while intervals of silence (45 seconds) announce performance of flexibility and strength development activities.

Corner 1. Skipping/Jumping/Hopping
    Corner 2. Sliding/Galloping
    Corner 3. Various animal movements
    Corner 4. Sport imitation movements
	Faster moving students should pass on the outside of the area.

Stop the class after 30 seconds of movement and perform fitness challenges (see Lesson Plan 1).	If signs are not used at the corners, teachers can specify by voice what movements are to be performed.

Lesson Focus -- Manipulative Skills Using Hoops

1. Hula-hoop using various body parts such as waist, neck, knees, arms and fingers.	Place the hoops around the perimeter of the area. Students move and pick up a hoop and begin practicing the assigned activity.
a. While hula-hooping on the arms, try to change the hoop from one arm to the other.	
b. Change hoop from one partner to another while hula-hooping around the waist.	
c. Try leg skippers--hula-hoop with one leg and jump the hoop with the other leg.	Encourage youngsters to find their personal space.
d. Hula-hoop around waist while on knees. While hooping, try to stand up and go back to knees.	
e. Exploratory activity.	When learning to hula-hoop, teach youngsters to move the body part back and forth rather than in a circle. The natural tendency is to move the body part in a circle, making it impossible to keep the hoop circling.
2. Place the hoops on the floor to create various patterns. Have the children perform various fundamental locomotor movements and animal walks in, out of and between the hoops. Create different challenges by having students go in and out of various color hoops and specify a certain number of hoops they must enter.	
3. Jump rope with the hoop--forward and backward. Begin with a back-and-forth pendulum swing. Try sideways jumping.	
4. Thread the needle. Balance the hoop on head and try to step through the hoop. Do it forward, backward and sideways.	Place the hoops on the floor when calling the class to attention. If students don't put the hoop on the floor, they will drop and disrupt the class.
5. Roll hoop and run alongside it. Run ahead of it. Cross in front of it. Go through the hoop.	
6. Spin the hoop like a top. How many times can you make it spin? How many times can you run around the spinning hoop before it falls?	The reverse spin can be taught by telling students to pull back and down toward the floor just prior to releasing the hoop.
7. Balance the hoop and then go through it before it falls.	

8. For a change-of-pace activity, put hoops on floor. Perform various locomotor movements around many hoops. On signal, curl up inside a hoop. For challenge, have fewer hoops than students.

Offer students a chance to perform their favorite activities.

9. Roll hoop with a reverse spin to make it return to the thrower.
10. Reverse spin, catch on arm, and hula-hoop it. Try catching on foot.

Game Activity

Animal Tag

Supplies: None

Skills: Imagery, running, dodging

Two parallel lines are drawn about 40 ft apart. Children are divided into two groups, each of which takes a position on one of the lines. Children in one group get together with their leader and decide what animal they wish to imitate. Having selected the animal, they move over to within 5 ft or so of the other line. There they imitate the animal, and the other group tries to guess the animal correctly. If the guess is correct, they chase the first group back to its line, trying to tag as many as possible. Those caught must go over to the other team. The second group then selects an animal, and the roles are reversed. If the guessing team cannot guess the animal, however, the performing team gets another try. To avoid confusion, children must raise their hands to take turns at naming the animal. Otherwise, many false chases will occur. If children have trouble guessing, the leader of the performing team can give the initial of the animal.

Bottle Bat Ball

Supplies: A plastic bottle bat, whiffle ball, batting tee (optional), home plate, base marker

Skills: Batting, retrieving balls

Formation: Scattered

A home plate is needed, and a batting tee can be used. Foul lines should be marked wide enough so as not to be restrictive. The batter gets three pitches (or swings) to hit a fair ball, or she is out. The pitches are easy (as in slow-pitch softball), so that the batter has a good chance to hit the ball. The batter hits the ball and runs around the base marker and back to home. If the ball is returned to the pitcher's mound before the batter reaches home, she is out. (A marker should designate the pitcher's mound.) Otherwise, the batter has a home run and bats again. One fielder other than the pitcher is needed, but another can be used. The running distance to first base is critical. It can remain fixed or can be made progressively (one step) longer, until it reaches such a point that the fielders are heavily favored.

Teaching suggestion: The game should make use of a plastic bottle bat and fun (whiffle) ball. A rotation system should be established when an out is made.

Variation: A batting tee can be used.

Dynamic Physical Education for Elementary School Children
Throwing Skills (1)
Level I – Week 3

Objectives:
To throw a ball using the overhand technique
To throw with velocity using side orientation and opposition
To learn the basic rules of simple game activities

Equipment Required:
Music and tape for Astronaut Exercises
Beanbags, whiffle balls, fleece balls, rag
   balls, and tennis balls
Hoops and/or mats for targets

Instructional Activities	Teaching Hints

Introductory Activity -- Group Over and Around

One-half of the class is scattered and is in a curled position. The other half of the class leaps or moves around the down children. On signal, reverse the groups quickly. In place of a curl, the down children can bridge as others go around. The down children can also alternate between curl and bridge, as well as move around the area while in bridge position.

Remind students not to touch the students who are in bridge or curl position.

Use different locomotor movements.

Fitness Development Activity -- Astronaut Exercises

Walk, do Arm Circles	30 seconds	Tape alternating segments of silence and music to signal duration of exercise.
Flexibility and Trunk Development Challenges	30 seconds	
Skip forward, backwards, and sideways	30 seconds	Music segments (30 seconds) indicate
Upper Body Strength Challenges	30 seconds	aerobic activity while intervals of silence
Slide; change lead leg	30 seconds	(30 seconds) signal flexibility and
Abdominal Development Challenges	30 seconds	strength development activities.
Jump like a Pogo Stick	30 seconds	
Upper Body Strength Challenges	30 seconds	See Chapter 12 for a description of how
Trot lightly in different directions	30 seconds	to perform challenge activities.
Flexibility and Trunk Development Challenges	30 seconds	
Gallop Backwards	30 seconds	Allow students to adjust the workload to an intensity that is consistent with their ability level.

Cool down with stretching and walking.

Lesson Focus --Throwing Skills (1)

Mimetics
1. "Pretend you:
   a. have to throw a rock across a big river!"
   b. want to throw a ball over a very tall building!"
   c. are a javelin thrower and you want to make the longest throw ever!"
   d. are a baseball pitcher and you are throwing a fast ball!"

Stand sideways to the target with the non-throwing side facing the target. Emphasize lifting the throwing arm and pointing at the target with the non-throwing arm.

Individual Activities
1. Throw beanbag or fleece ball against the wall. Concentrate on the following points:
   a. Feet together
   b. Foot opposite the throwing arm forward
   c. Start with non-throwing side toward the target area
2. Throw from one side of the gym and try to hit the other wall.

Use instructional cues:

"Raise your elbow to shoulder level."

"Start with your non-throwing side to the wall."

Mimetics
1. The teacher should cue students and model a good throw.
   a. Teacher should use terms such as "turn your non-throwing side to the target," "wind-up," "step toward the target," "follow through."
   b. Teacher can also use this time to observe and coach.
   c. *Encourage* students to throw as *hard as you can.*

"Reach up with your throwing arm like you are going to pick an apple"

"Take a step toward the target when you throw."

Individual Activities

1. Throwing yarn balls
   a. Throw against a wall or fence. Throw five balls, retrieve, and repeat.
   b. Teach the proper grip.
2. Throw rag balls or tennis balls against cardboard boxes near a wall or fence.
   a. Throw from 20-25 feet depending on skill level. Student should be able to hit the wall.
   b. Retrieve after all the balls have been thrown.
3. Throw at hoops leaning against a wall or fence.
   Throw from a distance so that children can hit the wall, but only with a forceful throw.

Focus on throwing form rather than accuracy.

Emphasize throwing hard! Proper form can only be learned when students try to throw as hard as possible.

Cue students to move their throwing hand behind their head before the throw.

Give each student 4 or 5 balls to throw. They can be placed in a frisbee to keep them from rolling around. When all balls have been thrown, students (on signal) retrieve the same number of balls they have thrown.

Game Activity

Aviator

Supplies: None

Skills: Running, locomotor movements, stopping

Players are parked (in push-up position) at one end of the playing area. The air traffic controller (ATC) is in front of the players and calls out, "Aviators aviators, take off!" Youngsters take off and move like airplanes to the opposite side of the area. The first person to move to the other side and land the plane (get into push-up position facing the ATC) is declared the new ATC.

If the ATC yells out some type of stormy weather, all planes must return to the starting line and resume the parked position. Examples of stormy weather commands are lightning, thunder, hurricane, and tornado. Each ATC is allowed to give stormy weather warnings once.

Sneak Attack

Supplies: None

Skills: Marching, running

Two parallel lines are drawn about 60 ft apart. Children are divided into two teams. One team takes a position on one of the lines, with their backs to the area. These are the chasers. The other team is on the other line, facing the area. This is the sneak team. The sneak team moves forward on signal, moving toward the chasers. When they get reasonably close, a whistle or some other signal is given, and the sneak team turns and runs back to their line, chased by the other team. Anyone caught before reaching the line changes to the chase team. The game is repeated, with the roles exchanged.

Dynamic Physical Education for Elementary School Children
Manipulative Skills Using Beanbags
Level I – Week 4

Objectives:
To move in a large group without bumping into others
To freeze on signal
To learn tossing and catching skills.
To cooperate in game activities

Equipment Required:
Tambourine or tom-tom
Music for Fitness Games & Challenges
One beanbag per student

Instructional Activities	Teaching Hints

Introductory Activity -- Bend, Stretch, and Shake

1. Bend various body parts individually and then bend various combinations of body parts.
2. Stretch the body in various levels. Encourage stretching from various positions such as standing, sitting, and prone position.
3. Practice shaking individual body parts when the tambourine is shaken. Progress to shaking the entire body.
4. Bend body parts while doing different locomotor movements. Bend limbs while shaking.

Use a tambourine to signal changes between bending, stretching and shaking.

Encourage smooth movements in bending and stretching activities.

Encourage creative responses.

Fitness Development Activity -- Fitness Games and Challenges

1. Stoop Tag - 45 seconds.
2. Freeze; perform stretching activities.
3. Back-to-Back Tag - 45 seconds.
4. Freeze; perform Abdominal Challenges using Curl-up variations.
5. Balance Tag - 45 seconds.
6. Freeze; perform Arm-Upper Body Strength Challenges using Push-up variations.
7. Elbow Swing Tag - 45 seconds.
8. Freeze; perform Trunk Development challenges.
9. Color Tag - 45 seconds.

Tape alternating segments of silence and music to signal duration of exercise. Music segments indicate fitness game activity while intervals of silence announce flexibility and strength development activities.

Choose any of the tag games. The names of the tag games indicate a "safe" position when one cannot be tagged, i.e., back to back with a partner or balancing on one foot.

Avoid getting caught up in rule infractions. The purpose of the tag games is to encourage locomotor movement.

Lesson Focus -- Manipulative Skills with Beanbags

Stand in place and practice tossing and catching
1. Toss and catch with both hands - right hand, left hand
2. Toss and catch with the back of hands. This will encourage children to catch with "soft hands."
3. Toss the beanbag to an increasingly high level, emphasizing a straight overhead toss. To encourage straight tossing, have the child sit down.

Stand in place, toss and catch while performing stunts
1. Toss overhead and perform the following stunts and catch the bag.
   a. 1/4 and 1/2 turns, right and left
   b. Full turn
   c. Touch floor
   d. Clap hands
   e. Clap hands around different parts of body, behind back, under legs.
   f. Heel click
   g. Sit down, get up
   h. Look between legs

Each student must have a beanbag for practice.

Give students two or three activities to practice so you have time to move and help individuals. Alternate activities from each of the categories so students receive a variety of skills to practice.

Emphasize tosses that are straight up and about 12 inches above the head.

Toss, move to a new spot and catch the beanbag
1. Toss overhead, move to another spot, and catch.
2. Toss, do a locomotor movement, and catch.
3. Toss and move from side to side.
4. Toss overhead behind self, move, and catch.

Balance the beanbag
1. Balance on the following body parts
    a. Head
    b. Back of hand
    c. Shoulder
    d. Knee
    e. Foot
    f. Elbow
    g. Exploratory activity
2. Balance and move as follows:
    a. Walk
    b. Run
    c. Skip
    d. Gallop
    e. Sit down
    f. Lie down
    g. Turn around
    h. Combinations of the above
    i. Exploratory activity

Beanbag challenge activities
1. Hold the beanbag between knees and play tag with a partner or small group.
2. Place the beanbag on tummy and shake it off.
3. Place the beanbag on back and Mule Kick it off.
4. Push the beanbag across the floor with different body parts.
5. Toss the beanbag up and touch specified body parts.
6. Put beanbags on floor. Rotate various body parts on a beanbag.
7. Beanbag Balance Tag - balance a beanbag on selected body parts. Announce a color to identify those who are it.

This is an excellent activity for teaching students to track (keep their eyes focused on) the beanbag. Remind them not to look away while tossing and catching.

Students should be encouraged to see how long they can balance the beanbag.

Movements should be controlled with as little bounce as possible.

These are body control activities. Students must be able to concentrate on moving slowly and keeping the beanbag in place.

Use the challenge to motivate students. These activities will be exciting and should be integrated throughout the lesson.

Hand-eye coordination is slowly learned after many repetitions. Encourage students to repeat their attempts.

Game Activities

Midnight
Supplies: None

Skills: Running, dodging

A safety line is established about 40 feet from a den in which two or three players, the foxes, are standing. The others stand behind the safety line and ask, "What time is it, Mr. Fox?" One of the foxes is designated to answer in various fashions, such as "one o' clock," "four o' clock," etc. When the fox says a certain time, the class walks forward that number of steps. For example, if the fox says, "six o'clock" the class has to move forward six steps. The fox continues to draw the players toward him. At some point, the fox answers the question by saying "Midnight," and chases the others back to the safety line. Any player who is caught becomes a fox in the den and helps to catch others.

Leap the Brook
Supplies: None

Skills: Leaping, jumping, hopping, turning

A brook is marked off on the floor for a distance of about 30 ft. For the first 10 ft, it is 3 ft wide; for the next 10 ft, it is 4 ft wide; for the last 10 ft, it is 5 ft wide. Children form a single file and jump over the narrowest part of the brook. They should be encouraged to do this several times, using different styles of jumping and leaping. After they have satisfactorily negotiated the narrow part, they move to the next width, and so on. The selection of the distances is arbitrary, and the distances can be changed if they seem unsuitable for any particular group of children.

Variation: Children can use different means of crossing the brook--leaping, jumping, hopping. They also can vary the kinds of turns to be made--right or left; or quarter, half, three quarter, or full. They should use different body shapes, different arm positions, and so on.

Dynamic Physical Education for Elementary School Children
Manipulative Skills Using Playground Balls
Level I – Week 5

Objectives:
To perform combinations of locomotor and non-locomotor movements
To bounce, toss, and catch a ball in a stationary position
To roll, bounce, and throw a ball to a partner.

Equipment Required:
Tom-tom
Music for Fitness Challenges
One 8½" playground or vinyl covered
   foam ball for each student

Instructional Activities	Teaching Hints
Introductory Activity -- Combination Movements	
1. Hop, turn around, and shake.	Use the tom-tom to signal movement
2. Jump, make a shape in the air, balance.	changes.
3. Skip, collapse, and roll.	
4. Curl, roll, jump with a half turn.	Challenge students to develop their
5. Whirl, skip, sink slowly.	personal combinations.
6. Hop, collapse, creep.	
7. Kneel, sway, jump to feet.	Create different movements using the
8. Lift, grin, and roll.	same words.

Fitness Development Activity – Fitness Challenges

Alternate locomotor movements with strength and flexibility challenges. Repeat the challenges as necessary.

Locomotor Movement: Walk for 30 seconds.

Flexibility and Trunk Development Challenges
  1. Bend in different directions.
  2. Stretch slowly and return quickly.
  3. Combine bending and stretching movements.
  4. Sway back and forth.
  5. Twist one body part; add body parts.
  6. Make your body move in a large circle.
  7. In a sitting position, wave your legs at a friend; make circles with your legs.

Locomotor Movement: Skip for 30 seconds.

Upper Body Strength Challenges
In a push-up position, do the following challenges:
  1. Lift one foot; the other foot.
  2. Wave at a friend; wave with the other arm.
  3. Scratch your back with one hand; use the other hand.
  4. Walk your feet to your hands.
  5. Turn over and face the ceiling; shake a leg; Crab Walk.

Locomotor Movement: Jog for 30 seconds.

Abdominal Development
From a supine position:
  1. Lift your head and look at your toes.
  2. Lift your knees to your chest.
  3. Wave your legs at a friend. From a sitting position:
  1. Slowly lay down with hands on tummy.
  2. Lift legs and touch toes.

Locomotor Movement: Run and leap for 30 seconds.

Teaching Hints (right column):

Tape alternating segments (30 seconds in length) of silence and music to signal duration of exercise. Music segments indicate doing the locomotor movements while intervals of silence announce performing the strength and flexibility challenges

Students select the fitness challenge they feel capable of performing. This implies that not all youngsters are required to do the same workload. Children differ and their ability to perform fitness workloads differs. Make fitness a personal challenge.

Since the range of activities is from easy to challenging, all youngsters can be successful. All youngsters should be able to do one of the fitness challenges.

Vary the locomotor movements as desired. Another alternative is to allow students to select the locomotor movement they would like to do.

Lesson Focus -- Manipulative Skills Using Playground Balls

1. Controlled Rolling and Handling in Place
   a. In a wide straddle position (other possible positions are seated with legs crossed or outstretched, and push-up position), place the ball on the floor, and roll it with constant finger guidance between and around the legs.
   b. Roll the ball in a figure-eight path in and out of the legs.
   c. Reach as far to the left as possible with the ball and roll it in front of you to the other side. Catch it as far to the right of the body as possible.
   d. Turn in place and roll the ball around with one hand in a large circle.
   e. Roll the ball around while lying on top of it. Roll the ball around the floor while on all fours, guiding it with the nose and forehead.
   f. With the back moderately bent, release the ball behind the head, let it roll down the back, and catch it with both hands.
   g. Make different kinds of bridges over the ball while using the ball as partial support for the bridge.

2. Bounce and Catch
   a. Two hands, one hand.
   b. Bounce at different levels.
   c. Bounce between legs.
   d. Close eyes and bounce.
   e. Dribble ball in a stationary and/or moving position.
   f. Dribble and follow the commands, such as move forward, backward, in a circle, or sideways, while walking, galloping, trotting, etc.

3. Toss and Catch
   a. Toss and catch, vary height.
   b. Add various challenges while tossing (i.e., touch floor, clap hands, turn, sit down, lie down).
   c. Toss and let bounce. Also add some challenges as above.
   d. Toss up and catch behind back--toss from behind back and catch in front of body.
   e. Create moving challenges (i.e., toss, run five steps and catch, toss and back up five hops and catch.)

4. Foot Skills
   a. Lift the ball up with both feet and catch. Both front and rear of body catch.
   b. From a sitting position with the ball between feet, toss it up, and catch with hands.
   c. Keep the ball in the air with feet and different body parts.

Give students two or three activities to practice so you have time to move and help youngsters. Alternate activities from each of the categories so students receive a variety of activities for practice.

Place emphasis on control of the ball. Students should be challenged to have "their ball under control."

An effective approach is to tell students to assume their feet are "glued to the floor." Tosses must be made directly overhead and caught without moving.

Tosses must begin at a low level and gradually be raised as students gain control of the ball. Little is gained by tossing the ball to a height where it can't be caught.

Game Activity

Teacher Ball

Supplies: A gray foam ball or rubber playground ball

Skills: Throwing, catching

One child is the teacher or leader and stands about 10 ft in front of three other students, who are lined up facing him. The object of the game is to move up to the teacher's spot by avoiding making bad throws or missing catches. The teacher throws to each child in turn, beginning with the child on the left, who must catch and return the ball. Any child making a throwing or catching error goes to the end of the line, on the teacher's right. Those in the line move up, filling the vacated space. If the teacher makes a mistake, he must go to the end of the line and the child at the head of the line becomes the new teacher. The teacher scores a point by remaining in position for three rounds (three throws to each child). After scoring a point, the teacher takes a position at the end of the line and another child becomes the teacher.

Scarecrow and the Crows

Supplies: None

Skills: Dodging, running

Children form a large circle representing the garden that is guarded by two or three players who are designated as scarecrows. Six to eight crows scatter on the outside of the circle, and the scarecrows assume a characteristic pose inside the circle. Players in the circle raise their joined hands and let the crows run through, into the garden, where they pretend to eat. The scarecrows try to tag the crows. The circle children help the crows by raising their joined hands and allowing them to leave the circle, but they try to hinder the scarecrows. If the scarecrows run out of the circle, all the crows immediately run into the garden and start to nibble at the vegetables while the circle children hinder the reentry of the scarecrows. After 15-20 seconds, new players are selected for the roles. If, after a reasonable period of time, the scarecrows have failed to catch any crows, change players.

Dynamic Physical Education for Elementary School Children
Movement Skills and Concepts (1)
Walking, Body Part Identification, and Personal Space
Level I – Week 6

Objectives:
To run rhythmically
To jump a self-turned rope
To perform walking variations
To understand the concept of personal space

Equipment Required:
Tom-tom
One jump rope for each student
One balloon or beachball for each student
Colored paper & shapes for game

Instructional Activities	Teaching Hints

Introductory Activity - European Running

1. Run and stop.
2. Run, and on signal make a full turn; continue in same direction. Turn the other way.
3. Run, and on signal run in general space. On next signal, re-form the original pattern.
4. Run and bend the upper body forward in four counts. Return to the upright position in four counts.
5. Run and clap the rhythm.

Stress personal space and moving without bumping into others.

Use a drum to accentuate the rhythm.

Start the rhythm slowly so students can hear and move easily. Accomplish a walking rhythm before moving to a trotting step.

Fitness Development Activity --Jump Rope Exercises

1. Jump rope – 45 seconds. If not able to jump, practice swinging the rope to the side while jumping
2. Place the rope on the floor and perform locomotor movements around and over the rope. Make different shapes and letters with the rope.
3. Jump rope – 45 seconds.
4. Hold the folded rope overhead. Sway from side to side. Twist right and left.
5. Jump rope – 45 seconds
6. Lie on back with rope held with outstretched arms toward ceiling. Bring up one leg at a time and touch the rope with toes. Lift both legs together. Sit up and try to hook the rope over the feet. Release and repeat.
7. Jump rope – 45 seconds
8. Touch toes with the folded rope.
9. Jump rope - 45 seconds.
10. Do Push-up variations with the rope folded and held between the hands.
11. Jump rope - 45 seconds.

Tape alternating segments (45 seconds in length) of silence and music (30 seconds) to signal duration of exercise. Music segments indicate aerobic activity with the jump ropes while intervals of silence announce using the jump ropes to enhance flexibility and strength development.

Space youngsters so they don't hit others with their rope.

Don't worry about non-jumpers. They will learn sooner or later. Give encouragement and keep them motivated.

Lesson Focus - Movement Skills and Concepts (1)

Fundamental Skill: Walking

1. Walk in different directions, changing direction on signal (90°).
2. While walking, bring up the knees and slap with the hands on each step.
3. Walk on heels, toes, side of the foot, Charlie Chaplin fashion (toes pointed way out).
4. Gradually lower the body while walking; gradually raise body.
5. Walk with a smooth gliding step.
6. Walk with a wide base on tip-toes; rock from side to side.
7. Clap hands alternately front and back. Clap hands under the thighs (slow walk).
8. Walk slowly. Accelerate. Decelerate.
9. Take long strides. Tiny steps.
10. Change levels on signal.
11. Walk quickly and quietly. Slowly and heavily. Quickly and heavily, etc.
12. Change direction on signal while facing the same way.
13. Walk angrily, then happily; add others.
14. Hold arms in different positions. Try different arm movements as you walk.
15. Walk different patterns: circle, square, rectangle, figure-eight, etc.

Select a few activities from each of the categories so students receive a variety of skills to practice. When possible, integrate the manipulative skills activities with fundamental skill activities.

Use the instructional cues to help students walk with proper form. "Head up; eyes forward. Swing the arms while walking. Keep the shoulders back and the tummy flat"

A drumbeat can be used to stimulate different walking speeds.

16. Walk through heavy mud, on ice of slick floor on a rainy day.
17. Walk like a soldier, a giant, a robot; add other.
18. Duck under trees or railings while walking.
19. Point toes out in different directions while walking--in, forward, and out.
20. Walk with high knees, stiff knees, one stiff knee, sore ankle.
21. Walk toward a spot, turn around in four steps. Move in a different direction.
22. Practice changing steps while walking.
23. Walk with a military goose step.

Skills: Working with Balloons or Beachballs

1. Keep your balloon in the air by rebounding it from the hand, fist, arm, elbow, knee, shoulder, head, and other body parts. Use one finger. Use the feet to keep balloon in the air.
2. Work out combinations of body parts, four different parts in succession.
3. Use contrasting terms while keeping the balloon in the air:
   a. close--far
   b. in front of--behind
   c. near--far
   d. right--left
   e. high--low
   f. sudden--smooth
4. Keep one foot in place, control balloon or beachball.
5. Play "let's pretend" we are volleyball players. Practice overhand, underhand, dig passes. Show serving.
6. All time for exploratory activity by individuals or partners.

Keep the balloons in control by tapping them into the area rather than striking them.

When first learning the skills, keep the feet in one place rather than moving.

As children master the skills, try performing some of the balloon skills while moving throughout the area.

Movement Concept: Identifying Body Parts

1. Children can be standing or seated. Touch the part of parts with both hands without looking at it. Children should repeat out loud the designated part touched by saying, "I am touching _____."
   a. Touch your shoulders
   b. Touch your ankles
   c. Touch your head
   d. Touch your toes
   e. Touch your ears
   f. Touch your knees
   g. Touch your eyes
   h. Touch your hips
   i. Touch your cheeks
   j. Touch your forehead
   k. Touch your thighs
   l. Touch your elbows
2. Thinking Activity
   Teacher touches the incorrect part of the body as commands are given. Students should touch the correct part and not be fooled by the teacher
3. As a part is named, form a pose and make this part the highest position of your body; the lowest.
4. Move about general space in any manner you wish. When a body part is called, stop and put both hands on the part(s).
5. Select a way you wish to move in general space. The signal to move will be the name of a body part. Move around the room with one hand on the body part. When another body part is called out, change the type of movement and hold the new body part.

Body part identification should be a "snappy" activity. Children should learn to respond quickly without much thought.

Practice combinations of body parts such as shoulders-ankles and knees.

Try the activities with the eyes closed.

Movement Concept: Exploring Personal Space

1. Keeping one foot in place on a spot, make a full arc with the other foot. Keep both one foot and one hand touching the spot, arc again with other foot.
2. Keeping your feet in place, sway and reach out as far as you can without losing balance or moving feet. Try with feet together and feet apart. Which is better for balance? Sit down and repeat movements. Do you need more or less space?

Place emphasis on understanding that most people have a personal space they don't want violated. Encourage youngsters to stay out of other's personal spaces.

3. Try some different types of movements in your personal space:
    a. Make yourself as wide as possible. Change to narrow. Experiment with narrow, small--large, high--low, etc. Try from other positions--kneeling, sitting balancing of seat, standing on one foot, lying on stomach, and other.
    b. In supine position, move arms and legs in different combinations out and back.
    c. Select one part of the body to keep in place. Make big circles with the rest of the body. Select other parts.
    d. Explore different positions where one foot is higher than any other body part.
    e. Pump yourself up like a balloon. Get bigger and bigger until I say, "Pop!"
    f. Let's pretend you are a snowman melting to the ground under a hot sun.
    g. With your feet in place, twist as far as you can one way and then the other (arms out to sides). Show me how a top spins.

Call out different movements and encourage students to respond quickly.

Offer the activities as challenges and allow students to do their best.

Game Activity

Change Sides

Supplies: None

Skill: Body management

Identify two parallel lines 30 feet apart with half of the class on each line. On signal, all players cross to the other line, face the center, and stand at attention. The first group to do all three things correctly wins a point. Children must be cautioned to use care when passing through the opposite group. They should be spaced well along each line; this allows room for them to move through each group. Vary the locomotor movements used by specifying skipping, hopping, long steps, sliding, and other varieties of movement. The position to be assumed at the finish can be varied also.

Where's My Partner?

Supplies: None

Skills: Fundamental locomotor movements

Children are in a double circle facing a partner. The inside circle has two or three more players than the outside. When the signal is given, the circles skip (or walk, run, hop, or gallop) to the right. This means that they are skipping in opposite directions. On the command "Halt," the circles face each other to find partners. The players left without a partner go to the mush pot (the center area of the circle) for one turn. The circles should be reversed after a time.

Variation: The game can also be played with music or a drumbeat. When the music stops, the players seek partners.

Colors

Supplies: Colored paper (construction paper) cut in circles, squares, or triangles for markers

Skills: Color or other perceptual concepts, running

Five or six different-colored markers should be used, with a number of children having the same color. Children are standing or seated in a circle with a marker in front of each child. The teacher calls out a color, and everyone having that color runs counterclockwise around the circle and back to place. The first one seated upright and motionless is declared the winner. Different kinds of locomotor movement can be specified, such as skipping, galloping, walking, and so on. After a period of play, the children leave the markers on the floor and move one place to the left.

Variation: Shapes (e.g., circles, triangles, squares, rectangles, stars, and diamonds) can be used instead of colors, as can numbers or other articles or categories, such as animals, birds, or fish. This game has value in teaching identification and recognition.

Dynamic Physical Education for Elementary School Children
Gymnastics Skills (1)
Level I – Week 7

Objectives:
To be able to perform animal walks
To balance body weight in a variety of positions
To be able to manage body weight in gymnastics activities

Equipment Required:
Music for Animal Movements
Tumbling Mats
8" foam rubber balls (6-8)
Cones

Instructional Activities	Teaching Hints
Introductory Activity – Countdown	
Standing with arms stretched overhead, students begin a countdown (10, 9, 8, 7, etc.) and gradually lower themselves into a crouched position with each count. On the words "blast off," they jump upwards and run in different directions. Students can run to a wall and return to their position. After students learn the activity, allow one of them to say, "Blast Off!"	Vary with challenges such as: 1. Different locomotor movements. 2. Various animal walks. 3. Change intervals of counting--slow, fast.
Fitness Development Activity --Animal Movements and Fitness Challenges	
1. Puppy Dog Walk --30 seconds. 2. Freeze; perform stretching activities. 3. Measuring Worm Walk--30 seconds 4. Freeze; perform abdominal development challenges. 5. Frog Jump--30 seconds. 6. Freeze; perform push-up position challenges. 7. Elephant Walk --30 seconds. 8. Freeze; perform stretching activities 9. Bear Walk--30 seconds. 10. Freeze; perform abdominal challenges. 11. Crab Walk--30 seconds. 12. Freeze and perform stretching and relaxing activities	Tape alternating segments (30 seconds in length) of silence and music to signal duration of exercise. Music segments indicate performing animal movements while intervals of silence announce doing the fitness challenges. A variation is to place animal movement signs throughout the area and instruct students to move from sign to sign performing the appropriate animal movement each time they reach a new sign.

Lesson Focus – Gymnastics Skills (1)

Animal Movements
Alligator Crawl
   Lie facedown on the floor with elbows bent. Move along the floor in alligator fashion, keeping the hands close to the body and the feet pointed out. First, use unilateral movements---that is, right arm and leg moving together---then change to cross-lateral movements.

Kangaroo Jump
   Carry the arms close to the chest with the palms facing forward. Place a beanbag or ball between the knees. Move in different directions by taking small jumps without dropping the object.

Puppy Dog Run
   Place the hands on the floor, bending the arms and legs slightly. Walk and run like a happy puppy. Look straight ahead. Keeping the head up, in good position, strengthens the neck muscles. Go sideward, backward, and so on. Turn around in place.

Tumbling and Inverted Balances
Rolling Log
   Lie on the back with arms stretched overhead. Roll sideways the length of the mat. The next time, roll with the hands pointed toward the other side of the mat. To roll in a straight line, keep the feet slightly apart.

Five groups of activities in this lesson ensure that youngsters receive a variety of experiences. Pick a few activities from each group and teach them alternately. For example, teach one or two animal movements, then a tumbling and inverted balance, followed by a balance stunt, etc. Give equal time to each group of activities

Variations of the Puppy Dog Run
   Cat Walk. Use the same position to imitate a cat. Walk softly. Stretch at times like a cat. Be smooth and deliberate.
   Monkey Run. Turn the hands and feet so that the fingers and toes point in (toward each other).

Place tumbling mats in the area so all youngsters are in view.

Side Roll

Start on the hands and knees, with one side toward the direction of the roll. Drop the shoulder, tuck both the elbow and the knee under, and roll over completely, returning to the hands-and-knees position. Momentum is needed to return to the original position. Practice rolling back and forth from one hand-and-knee position to another.

Forward Roll

Stand facing forward, with the feet apart. Squat and place the hands on the mat, shoulder width apart, with elbows against the insides of the thighs. Tuck the chin to the chest and make a rounded back. A push-off with the hands and feet provides the force for the roll. Carry the weight on the hands, with the elbows bearing the weight of the thighs. If the elbows are kept against the thighs and the weight is assumed there, the force of the roll is transferred easily to the rounded back. Try to roll forward to the feet. Later, try with the knees together and no weight on the elbows.

Balance Stunts

One-Leg Balance

Lift one leg from the floor. Later, bring the knee up. The arms should be free at first and then assume specified positions: folded across the chest, on the hips, on the head, or behind the back.

Double-Knee Balance

Kneel on both knees, with the feet pointed to the rear. Lift the feet from the ground and balance on the knees. Vary the position of the arms. Experiment with different arm positions.

Head Touch

On a mat, kneel on both knees, with feet pointed backward and arms outstretched backward for balance. Lean forward slowly and touch the forehead to the mat. Recover to position. Vary the arm position.

Individual Stunts

Directional Walk

For a left movement, begin in standing position. Do all of the following simultaneously: Take a step to the left, raise the left arm and point left, turn the head to the left, and state crisply "Left." Close with the right foot back to standing position. Take several steps left and then reverse.

Line Walking

Use a line on the floor, a chalked line, or a board. Walk forward and backward on the line as follows. First, take regular steps. Next, try follow steps---the front foot moving forward and the back foot moving up. The same foot always leads. Then do heel and toe steps, bringing the back toe up against the front heel on each step. Finally, hop along the line on one foot. Change to the other foot. The eyes should be focused ahead.

Fluttering Leaf

Keeping the feet in place and the body relaxed, flutter to the ground slowly, just as a leaf would do in autumn. Swing the arms back and forth loosely to accentuate the fluttering.

Elevator

With the arms out level at the sides, pretend to be an elevator going down. Lower the body a little at a time by bending the knees, but keep the upper body erect and the eyes forward. Return to position. Add a body twist to the downward movement. (A drum can be used.)

Don't force students to perform tumbling and inverted balances. If youngsters are fearful, gentle encouragement should be used.

The forward roll demands enough arm strength to keep the head off the mat. If youngsters lack strength, substitute the side roll for the forward roll.

Spotting the forward roll should rarely be used. If many children need to be spotted, the activity is probably too advanced. To spot the forward roll, the spotter should kneel alongside the child and place one hand on the back of the child's head and the other under the thigh. As the child moves through the roll, give an upward lift on the back of the neck to assure the neck does not absorb the weight of the body. This technique should be used for all forward roll variations.

Overweight children are at greater risk in stunts and tumbling activities. Allow them to avoid the tumbling activities if they so choose.

The Directional Walk is designed to aid in establishing right-left concepts. Definite and forceful simultaneous movements of the arm, head (turn), and leg (step) coupled with a crisp enunciation of the direction are the ingredients of this stunt.

Individual stunts are enjoyable challenges that all children can do. Place emphasis on form and balance.

Cross-Legged Stand

Sit with the legs crossed and the body bent partially forward. Respond appropriately to these six commands.

"Touch the right foot with the right hand."
"Touch the left foot with the right hand."
"Touch the right foot with the left hand."
"Touch the left foot with the left hand."
"Touch both feet with the hands."
"Touch the feet with crossed hands."

The commands should be given in varied sequences. The child must interpret that his right foot is on the left side, and vice versa. If this seems too difficult, have children start with the feet in normal position (uncrossed).

Variation: Do the stunt with a partner, one child giving the commands and the other responding as directed.

Partner and Group Stunts

Bouncing Ball

Toss a lively utility ball into the air and watch how it bounces lower and lower until it finally comes to rest on the floor. From a bent-knee position with the upper body erect, imitate the ball by beginning with a high bounce and gradually lowering the height of the jump to simulate the ball coming to rest. Children should push off from the floor with the hands to gain additional height and should absorb part of the body weight with their hands as well. Toss a real ball into the air and move with the ball.

Try this with a partner, one partner serving as the bouncer and the other as the ball. Reverse positions. Try having one partner dribble the ball in various positions.

Seesaw

Face and join hands with a partner. Move the seesaw up and down, one child stooping while the other rises. Recite the words to this version of "Seesaw, Margery Daw."

Seesaw, Margery Daw,
Maw and Paw, like a saw,
Seesaw, Margery Daw.

Variation: Jump upward at the end of the rise each time.

Game Activity

Circle Straddle Ball

Supplies: Two or more 8-in. foam balls
Skills: Ball rolling, catching

Children are in circle formation, facing in. Each stands in a wide straddle stance with the side of the foot against the neighbor's. The hands are on the knees. Two balls are used. The object of the game is to roll one of the balls between the legs of another player before he can get his hands down to stop the ball. Each time a ball goes between the legs of an individual, a point is scored. The players having the fewest points scored against them are the winners. Keep the circles small so students have more opportunities to handle the ball. Players must catch and roll the ball, rather than batting it. Children must keep their hands on their knees until a ball is rolled at them. After some practice, the following variation can be played.

Statues

Supplies: None
Skills: Body management, applying force, balance

Children are scattered in pairs around the area. One partner is the swinger and the other the statue. The teacher voices a directive, such as "Pretty," "Funny," "Happy," "Angry," or "Ugly." The swinger takes the statue by one or both hands, swings it around in a small circle two or three times (the teacher should specify), and releases it. The statue then takes a pose in keeping with the directive, and the swinger sits down on the floor. The statue must hold the position without moving or be disqualified. Reverse positions.

Variation: In the original game, the swinging is done until the directive is called. The swinger then immediately releases the statue, who takes the pose as called. This gives little time for the statue to react. Better and more creative statues are possible if the directive is given earlier.

Soap Bubbles

Supplies: Cones to delineate space, music
Skills: Body management

Each player is a soap bubble floating throughout the area. The teacher calls out the locomotor movement youngsters use to move in the area. The entire area is used to start the game. As the game progresses, the size of the area is decreased by moving the cones. Bubbles freeze on signal. Music can be used to stimulate movement. The object of the game is not to touch or collide with another bubble. When this occurs, both bubbles burst and sink to the floor and make themselves as small as possible. The space is made smaller until those who have not been touched are declared the winners. Those players who are broken bubbles may move to the unrestricted area and move.

Dynamic Physical Education for Elementary School Children
Movement Skills and Concepts (2)
Jumping, Tossing and Catching, and Moving in General Space
Level I – Week 8

Objectives:
To learn to evade or follow a partner while moving under control in general space
To learning a variety of jumping skills
To learn how forceful movements are generated

Equipment Required:
Music for Astronaut Exercises
One yarn ball for each student

Instructional Activities	Teaching Hints

Introductory Activity -- Run, Stop, and Pivot

Have the children run, and on signal, stop and pivot. Begin teaching a 90° pivot and move gradually to a 180° pivot. Relate the use of the pivot to various sport activities, such as basketball.

Encourage moving under control.

Bend the knees when stopping and place the weight on the pivot foot.

Fitness Development Activity --Astronaut Exercises

Walk, do Arm Circles	30 seconds	Tape alternating segments of silence and music to signal duration of exercise. Music segments (30 seconds) indicate aerobic activity while intervals of silence (30 seconds) signal flexibility and strength development activities.
Flexibility and Trunk Development Challenges	30 seconds	
Skip forward, backwards, and sideways	30 seconds	
Upper Body Strength Challenges	30 seconds	
Slide; change lead leg	30 seconds	
Abdominal Development Challenges	30 seconds	
Jump like a Pogo Stick	30 seconds	
Upper Body Strength Challenges	30 seconds	See Chapter 12 for a description of how
Trot lightly in different directions	30 seconds	to perform challenge activities.
Flexibility and Trunk Development Challenges	30 seconds	
Gallop Backwards	30 seconds	Allow students to adjust the workload to an intensity that is consistent with their ability level.

Cool down with stretching and walking.

Lesson Focus -- Movement Skills and Concepts (2)

Fundamental Skill--Jumping

1. Jump upward, trying for height.
2. Alternate low and high jumps.
3. Jump in various floor patterns--triangle, circle, square, letters, figure-eight, diamond shape.
4. Over a spot, jump forward, backwards, sideways, criss-cross.
5. Jump with the body stiff, like a pogo stick. Explore with arms in different positions.
6. Practice jump turns--quarter, half, three-quarter, full. Add heel clicks with turns.
7. Increase and decrease the speed of jumping. Increase the height of jumping.
8. Land with the feet apart sideways and together again. Try it forward and backward (stride).
9. Jump and land as quietly as possible.
10. Jump and criss-cross the feet sideways.
11. See how far you can jump in two, three, or four consecutive jumps.
12. Pretend you are a bouncing ball.
13. Clap hands or slap thighs when in the air.
14. Jump so the hands contact the floor.
15. Select a line. Proceed down it by jumping back and forth over the line. Add turns.

Select a few activities from each of the categories so students receive a variety of skills to practice. When possible, integrate the manipulative skill activities with fundamental skill activities. A common error is to teach all the activities from one category. The reason for multiple groups of activities is to provide variety and enhance motivation.

Use instructional cues such as:

"Swing your arms forward as you jump"

"Bend your knees"

"Land lightly by bending your knees"

"Jump as high as you can"

Manipulative Activity: Yarn Balls

Individual Activity

1. Toss and catch to self.
   a. Increase height gradually.
   b. Side to side.
   c. Front to back.
   d. Toss underneath the legs, around the body, etc.
   e. Toss and clap the hands. Clap around the body. Underneath the legs.
   f. Toss and make turns--quarter and half.
   g. Toss, perform the following, catch:
   Heel click
   Touch both elbows, knees, shoulders, and heels.
   h. Use contrasting tosses:
   High and low
   Near and far
   Front and back
2. Bat the ball upward as in volleyball, catch. Bat the ball, run forward and catch.
3. Toss forward, run and catch. Toss sideways and catch. Toss overhead, turn around, run and catch.

Partner Activity

1. Roll the ball back and forth.
2. Toss the ball back and forth, various ways.
3. Throw the ball back and forth.

Have the yarn balls placed around the perimeter of the area. On signal, ask students to jog to a ball, pick it up and practice tossing and catching.

Toss the ball to a height where it can be caught. Little is gained by a toss that is too high and out of control.

Encourage a successful toss to be one where the feet do not have to be moved to make a catch.

Partners should start close together and gradually move apart as they become successful.

Movement Concept: Moving in General Space

1. Run lightly in the area, changing direction as you wish without bumping or touching anyone. How many were able to do this? Try running zigzag fashion.
2. Run again in general space. On signal, change direction abruptly. Try again, only this time change both direction and the type of locomotor movement you are doing.
3. Run lightly and pretend you are dodging another runner. Run directly at another runner and dodge him or her.
4. Use a yarn ball to mark your personal space (spot); run in general space until the signal is given; return to your yarn ball and sit down.
5. We are going to do orienteering. Point to a spot on a wall, walk directly to the spot in a straight line. You may have to wait for other so as not to bump them. Pick another spot on a different wall and repeat. Return to home base on signal.
6. What happens when general space is decreased? Walk in general space. Now as space is decreased, walk again. Once more we are decreasing the space.
7. Run around your yarn ball until I Say, "Bang." Then explode in a straight direction until the stop signal is sounded. Return.
8. From your spot, take three (four or five) jumps (hops, skips, gallops, slides) in one direction, turn around and do the same back to home base. Try with long steps away and tiny steps back.
9. I am going to challenge you on right and left movements. First, let's walk in general space. When I say "right" (or "left") you change direction abruptly.
10. This time run rapidly toward another child. Stop and bow. Now stop and shake hands.

Place the yarn ball on the floor and used them as objects to move over and around.

Dodging demands running under control. Students should seldom run as fast as possible in physical education classes. Most activities demand controlled movement.

Explain simple orienteering activity.

Movement Concept: Use of Force

1. Show us how you do some forceful movements, such as chopping batting, hitting with a sledge, punching the punching bag. Try karate chops and kicks, kicking a soccerball, etc.
2. Show us a light movement you can make with the arm. Repeat the same movement more forcefully.
3. Make some movements that are light and sustained, heavy and sudden, heavy and sustained, light and sudden.

Help students understand how the amount of force varies.

Sport activities usually demand controlled force rather than doing something "as hard as possible."

4.   Make one part of the body move lightly, while another moves heavily.

Game Activity

Firefighter
Supplies: None

Skill: Running

A fire chief runs around the outside of a circle of children and taps a number of them on the back, saying "Firefighter" each time. After making the round of the circle, the chief goes to the center. When she says "Fire," the firefighters run counterclockwise around the circle and back to place. The one who returns first and is able to stand in place motionless is declared the winner and the new chief.

The chief can use other words to fool children, but they run only on the word Fire. This merely provides some fun, since there is no penalty for a false start. The circle children can sound the siren as the firefighters run.

Animal Tag
Supplies: None

Skills: Imagery, running, dodging

Two parallel lines are drawn about 40 ft apart. Children are divided into two groups, each of which takes a position on one of the lines. Children in one group get together with their leader and decide what animal they wish to imitate. Having selected the animal, they move over to within 5 ft or so of the other line. There they imitate the animal, and the other group tries to guess the animal correctly. If the guess is correct, they chase the first group back to its line, trying to tag as many as possible. Those caught must go over to the other team. The second group then selects an animal, and the roles are reversed. If the guessing team cannot guess the animal, however, the performing team gets another try. To avoid confusion, children must raise their hands to take turns at naming the animal. Otherwise, many false chases will occur. If children have trouble guessing, the leader of the performing team can give the initial of the animal.

Sneak Attack
Supplies: None

Skills: Marching, running

Two parallel lines are drawn about 60 ft apart. Children are divided into two teams. One team takes a position on one of the lines, with their backs to the area. These are the chasers. The other team is on the other line, facing the area. This is the sneak team. The sneak team moves forward on signal, moving toward the chasers. When they get reasonably close, a whistle or some other signal is given, and the sneak team turns and runs back to their line, chased by the other team. Anyone caught before reaching the line changes to the chase team. The game is repeated, with the roles exchanged.

Dynamic Physical Education for Elementary School Children
Kicking, Trapping, Bowling, and Rolling Skills
Level I – Week 9

Objectives:
To cooperatively play tag games and maintain body control
To change speeds and directions of movement
To practice kicking, trapping, bowling and rolling skills
To successfully participate in simple games

Equipment Required:
Music for Fitness Challenges
8" foam rubber ball (or 8½" partially
 deflated playground ball) for each
 student
15 bowling pins

Instructional Activities	Teaching Hints
Introductory Activity -- Tag Games	
Use a tag game youngsters enjoy to offer children immediate activity Many tag games can be found in Chapter 22. Some suggestions are: 1. Skunk 2. Stork 3. Stoop 4. Nose and Toe	Teach moving under control. Students should understand that they should seldom run as fast as possible in order to prevent collisions. Use different locomotor movements.

Fitness Development Activity --Fitness Challenges

Alternate locomotor movements with strength and flexibility challenges. Repeat the challenges as necessary.

Locomotor Movement: Walk for 30 seconds.

Flexibility and Trunk Development Challenges
1. Bend in different directions.
2. Stretch slowly and return quickly.
3. Combine bending and stretching movements.
4. Sway back and forth.
5. Twist one body part; add body parts.
6. Make your body move in a large circle.
7. In a sitting position, wave your legs at a friend; make circles with your legs.

Locomotor Movement: Skip for 30 seconds.

Upper Body Strength Challenges
In a push-up position, do the following challenges:
1. Lift one foot; the other foot.
2. Wave at a friend; wave with the other arm.
3. Scratch your back with one hand; use the other hand.
4. Walk your feet to your hands.
5. Turn over and face the ceiling; shake a leg; Crab Walk.

Locomotor Movement: Jog for 30 seconds.

Abdominal Development
From a supine position:
1. Lift your head and look at your toes.
2. Lift your knees to your chest.
3. Wave your legs at a friend. From a sitting position:
1. Slowly lay down with hands on tummy.
2. Lift legs and touch toes.

Locomotor Movement: Run and leap for 30 seconds.

Teaching Hints (right column):

Tape alternating segments (30 seconds in length) of silence and music to signal duration of exercise. Music segments indicate doing the locomotor movements while intervals of silence announce performing the strength and flexibility challenges

Students select the fitness challenge they feel capable of performing. This implies that not all youngsters are required to do the same workload. Children differ and their ability to perform fitness workloads differs. Make fitness a personal challenge.

Because students can select activities they feel able to do, there is little reason for not trying.

If students do not remember the various challenges, cue them by calling out a number of the activities. They can select one they enjoy.

Use different qualities of movement such as giant skips, quick gallops, tiny jogging steps, etc.

Animal walks can be substituted for locomotor movements.

Lesson Focus -- Kicking, Trapping, Rolling, and Bowling Skills

Kicking and Ball Control Skills

1. Inside of Foot Kick. Approach at 45° angle; inside of foot meets ball. Place non-kicking foot alongside ball.
2. Outside of Foot Kick. Short distance kick; keep toe down.
3. Long (instep) Pass. Contact the ball with the shoelaces. Not as accurate, but used for distance.
4. Sole of Foot Control. Use sole of foot to stop ball; make sure weight is placed on the non-receiving foot.
5. Inside of Foot Control. Use inside of foot and learn to "give" with leg so ball doesn't ricochet off foot.
6. The receiver can practice soccer skills. For example, the following skills are suggested:
   a. Toe Trap
   b. The Foot Pickup
   c. Bowl with Your Feet

Give each student a ball. The ball of preference is an 8" foam rubber ball since it will not be painful to kick and trap. Underinflated (they are easier to control) 8½" playground balls can be substituted.

Assign students two or three activities to practice so you have time to move and help youngsters. Alternate activities from each of the categories so students receive a variety of skills to practice.

Rolling and Bowling Skills

1. Two-handed roll; between the legs, with wide straddle stance.
2. Roll the ball with one hand. Use both left and right hands.
3. Roll the ball and put spin on the ball so it will curve to the left and right.
4. Roll the ball through human straddle targets:
   a. Start rolling at moderate stances and gradually increase as bowlers become more proficient.
   b. Use left and right hands.
   c. Scoring can be done giving two points for a ball that goes through the target without touching and one point for a ball going through, but touching a leg.
5. Use objects such as milk cartons, clubs, or bowling pins for targets. Various bowling games can be developed using the targets.
6. Stand with your back facing your partner. Bend over; look through your legs and bowl.

Work with a partner and practice rolling and bowling to each other.

When bowling through the legs of youngsters, students need to take turns. Encourage them to change position after three or four turns.

Game Activity

Change Sides

Supplies: None

Skill: Body management

Identify two parallel lines 30 feet apart with half of the class on each line. On signal, all players cross to the other line, face the center, and stand at attention. The first group to do all three things correctly wins a point. Children must be cautioned to use care when passing through the opposite group. They should be spaced well along each line; this allows room for them to move through each group. Vary the locomotor movements used by specifying skipping, hopping, long steps, sliding, and other varieties of movement. The position to be assumed at the finish can be varied also.

Musical Ball Pass

Supplies: Playground ball per group, music

Skills: Passing and handling

Break the class into a number of small groups (6-7 players) in circle formation facing the center. One ball is given to a player and is passed to the circle players when the music starts. The ball may not be passed to an adjacent person. When the music stops, the player who last passed the ball moves up to another circle. Another alternative is to go into the "well" in the center of the circle for one turn. To avoid arguments, a player must go to the center if the ball is on the way to her. More than one ball may be used.

Dynamic Physical Education for Elementary School Children
Fundamental Skills Using Parachute Activity
Level I – Week 10

Objectives:
To independently identify different locomotor movements
To independently travel the mini-challenge course
To cooperate with peers in parachute activities
To work cooperatively in low-organized game settings

Equipment Required:
Magic number cards
Music for fitness
Equipment for Mini-Challenge Course
Parachute
Colored paper in shapes for game
10-20 beanbags for game

Instructional Activities	Teaching Hints

Introductory Activity -- Magic Number Challenges

Students put together a series of movements based on the magic numbers given. For example, hold up a card with three numbers on it (10, 8, 14). Students respond by performing three different locomotor movements the specified number of times, respectively.

Encourage variety of response.

Use movements such as walking, running, jumping, hopping, galloping, sliding, leaping, and skipping.

Fitness Development Activity -- Mini-Challenge Course

Arrange four parallel courses with a group at each course. Students perform the challenges from a cone at the start to a finish cone and jog back to continuously repeat the course. On signal, groups rotate to a new course.

Course 1. Hop in and out of 5 hoops, Puppy Dog Walk around a cone for 5 seconds and skip to the finish cone.

Course 2. Weave in and out of four cones, Crab Walk around a cone for 5 seconds and gallop to finish cone.

Course 3. Do the Rolling Log the length of mat, do an agility run through 4 hoops, and slide to the finish cone.

Course 4. Jump over each of 5 cones, jump back and forth over a stretched out jump rope, run backwards around three cones; and hop to a cone.

Tape alternating segments (20 seconds in length) of silence and music to signal duration of exercise. Music segments indicate moving through the mini-challenge course while intervals of silence announce using the chute to enhance flexibility and strength development.

Students can set up their own mini-challenges.

Lesson Focus -- Fundamental Skills Using Parachute Activity

1. Circular movements.
   Move utilizing locomotor movements and holding the chute at various levels--walk, run, hop, jump, skip, slide, draw steps.
2. Shaking the Rug and Making Waves.
   Shaking the Rug should involve small, rapid movements, whereas Making Waves is large movements.
3. Making a Dome.
   Parachute should be on the floor and held with both hands. Make a dome by standing up and rapidly lifting the chute overhead.
4. Mushroom.
   Similar to the Dome except three or four steps toward the center are taken by each student.
   a. Mushroom Release--all students release the chute at its peak of inflation.
   b. Mushroom Run--Make a mushroom, students move toward center; a few selected students release grip, and run around the inside of the chute back to place.
5. Activities with Balls and Beanbags.
   a. Ball Circle--Use a basketball or cageball and make it circle around the outside of the chute. Add a second ball.
   b. Popcorn--Place six to ten whittle balls on the chute and shake them into the air.
   c. Giant Popcorn--Use beachballs instead of whiffle balls.

When performing locomotor movements with the chute, have students hold the chute with one hand. The direction of the movement can be stated by asking for a "right hand run," or a "left hand skip" etc.

When making a dome, have all students on one knee with both hands on the floor. On signal they make a strong movement upward.

Encourage all students to work together. Discuss how much easier it is when all students pull and lift together.

Try the activities holding the chute with both hands and with one hand.

d. Poison Snake--Place six to ten jump ropes on the chute. Divide the players in half. Try to shake the ropes so they touch a player on the opposing team.

6. Kite Run.

Half the class holds the chute on one side. They run in any direction together and as fast as possible. The parachute should trail like a kite.

7. Tug-of-War.

Divide the class into two equal halves. On signal, they pull and try to move each other.

8. Hole in One.

Use six or eight small balls of two different colors. The objects is to get the other team's balls to fall through the hole in the center.

9. Ocean Walk.

The class is on their knees, making waves with the chute. Three or four youngsters are selected to walk or jog "in the ocean" without falling.

Play the poison snake activity like a tag game. If the jump rope touches a player, they must release their grip and back away from the chute. Reset the game and start over with all players playing.

Playing hole in one is a challenge. Use many balls so the odds of a ball going into the center are increased.

Safety is important when walking on the parachute. The chute must not be lifted.

Game Activity

May I Chase You?

Supplies: None

Skills: Running, dodging

The class stands behind a line long enough to accommodate all. Two or three runners stand about 5 feet in front of the line. The class asks, "May I chase you?" One of the runners (designated by teacher) replies, "Yes, if you are wearing…" and names a color, an article of clothing, or a combination of the two. All who qualify immediately chase the runners until one is tagged. New runners are chosen and the game is repeated. Encourage players to think of other ways to identify those who run.

Tommy Tucker's Land

Supplies: About ten beanbags for each game

Skills: Dodging, running

Two or three youngsters, Tommy Tuckers (or Tammi Tuckers, if a girl), stand in the center of a 15-foot square where the beanbags are scattered. The Tuckers are guarding their land and treasure (beanbags). The other children chant,

I'm on Tommy Tucker's land,

Picking up gold and silver.

Children attempt to pick up as much of the treasure as they can while avoiding being tagged by the Tuckers. Any child who is tagged must return the treasure and retire from the game. The game is over when only one child is left or when all of the beanbags have been successfully filched. The teacher may wish to call a halt to the game earlier if a stalemate is reached. New Tuckers are selected.

Colors

Supplies: Colored paper (construction paper) cut in circles, squares, or triangles for markers

Skills: Color or other perceptual concepts, running

Five or six different-colored markers should be used, with a number of children having the same color. Children are standing or seated in a circle with a marker in front of each child. The teacher calls out a color, and everyone having that color runs counterclockwise around the circle and back to place. The first one seated upright and motionless is declared the winner.

Different kinds of locomotor movement can be specified, such as skipping, galloping, walking, and so on. After a period of play, the children leave the markers on the floor and move one place to the left.

Variation: Shapes (e.g., circles, triangles, squares, rectangles, stars, and diamonds) can be used instead of colors, as can numbers or other articles or categories, such as animals, birds, or fish. This game has value in teaching identification and recognition.

Dynamic Physical Education for Elementary School Children
Recreational Activities
Level I – Week 11

Objectives:
To be able to move continuously in moderately active activities
To learn the rules of recreational activities
To play in recreational activities independently without adult supervision

Equipment Required:
One hoop or beanbag per student for Ponies in the Stable
Music for Astronaut Exercises
Equipment for desired recreational activities

Instructional Activities	Teaching Hints

Introductory Activity -- Ponies in the Stable

A beanbag or hoop is used to mark each child's stable. On signal, youngsters gallop around the area and in and out of "stables." On a second signal, students return to the nearest stable.
Variations.
   1. Use different locomotor movements.
   2. Take different positions in the stable such as seated, balanced, collapsed.

To introduce excitement into the activity, remove a few stables and encourage students not to be left out.

Teach directions by asking students to move in a certain direction, i.e., north, south, etc.

Fitness Development Activity --Astronaut Exercises

Walk, do Arm Circles	30 seconds	Tape alternating segments of silence and music to signal duration of exercise.
Flexibility and Trunk Development Challenges	30 seconds	
Skip forward, backwards, and sideways	30 seconds	Music segments (30 seconds) indicate
Upper Body Strength Challenges	30 seconds	aerobic activity while intervals of silence
Slide; change lead leg	30 seconds	(30 seconds) signal flexibility and
Abdominal Development Challenges	30 seconds	strength development activities.
Jump like a Pogo Stick	30 seconds	
Upper Body Strength Challenges	30 seconds	See Chapter 12 for a description of how
Trot lightly in different directions	30 seconds	to perform challenge activities.
Flexibility and Trunk Development Challenges	30 seconds	
Gallop Backwards	30 seconds	Allow students to adjust the workload to an intensity that is consistent with their

Cool down with stretching and walking.

ability level.

Lesson Focus and Game Activity -- Recreational Activities

The purpose of this unit is to teach children activities that they can use for recreation outside of school or during recess. Suggested activities are:
1.   Shuffleboard
2.   Two Square
3.   Hopscotch
4.   Beanbag Horseshoes
5.   Jacks
6.   Marbles
7.   Sidewalk tennis
8.   Quoits
9.   Rubber Horseshoes
10. Four Square
11. Basketball, Soccer, and other seasonal sports
12. Any traditional and/or local area games

Teach students the rules of recreational activities so they are able to participate effectively during free-time.

Teach any games that are traditional to an area. Older youngsters may be a good source of advice for often-played games.

If desired, set up a number of stations and have youngsters rotate to different stations during the lesson.

Dynamic Physical Education for Elementary School Children
Walking and Jogging Skills
Level I – Week 12

Objectives:
To make a variety of shapes with the body
To walk and/or jog at a continuous and personalized pace
To understand the benefits of aerobic activity

Equipment Required:
Tom-tom or tambourine
Music for Walk, Trot, Jog
Equipment for games

Instructional Activities	Teaching Hints

Introductory Activity -- Run and Assume Shape

Place emphasis on making a variety of shapes and balances. Vary the locomotor movements.
1. Run and move to a prone (one drumbeat) or supine (two drumbeats) position on signal.
2. Run and move into a balance position.
3. Run and freeze in various shapes.

Place emphasis on running under control and assuming specified shape quickly.

Have students move into the activity area in scatter formation.

Fitness Development Activity --Walk, Trot, and Jog

Move to the following signals:
1. One drumbeat - walk.
2. Two drumbeats - trot.
3. Three drumbeats - jog.
4. Whistle - freeze and perform exercises.

Use strength and flexibility exercises between bouts of walk, trot, and jog to allow students to recover aerobically. Examples are:
1. Bend and Twist
2. Sitting Stretch
3. Push-up challenges
4. Abdominal Challenges
5. Body Twist
6. Standing Hip Bend

Tape alternating segments (20 seconds in length) of silence and music to signal duration of exercise. Music segments indicate walk, trot, and jog activity. Intervals of silence signal performance of the strength and flexibility exercises.

Encourage students to move around the area in the same direction.

See Chapter 12 for a description of how to perform the exercises. Any exercises can be substituted. Try to exercise all bodyparts.

Lesson Focus -- Walking and Jogging

The walking and jogging lesson offers emphasis on developing activity patterns that can be used outside of the school environment. An educational approach to this lesson teaches students that walking and jogging is a personal activity that offers excellent health benefits. It is an activity that can literally be done for a lifetime. The following are suggestions for implementing this unit of instruction:

1. Youngsters should be allowed to find a friend with whom they want to jog or walk. The result is usually a friend of similar ability level. A way to judge correct pace is to be able to talk with a friend without undue stress. If students are too winded to talk, they are probably running too fast. A selected friend will encourage talking and help assure that the experience is positive and within the student's aerobic capacity. *Pace, not race* is the motto.

2. Jogging and walking should be done in any direction so people are unable to keep track of the distance covered. Doing laps on a track can be discouraging for less able youngsters. They usually finish last and are open to chiding by the rest of the class.

3. Jogging and walking should be done for a specified time rather than a specified distance. All youngsters should not have to run the same distance. This goes against the philosophy of accompanying individual differences and varying aerobic capacities. Running or walking for a set amount of time will allow less able students to do the best they can without fear of ridicule.

4. Teachers should not be concerned about foot action, since the child selects naturally the means that is most comfortable. Arm movement should be easy and natural, with elbows bent. The head and upper body should be held up and back. The eyes look ahead. The general body position in walking and jogging should be erect but relaxed. Jogging on the toes should be avoided.

5. Jogging and walking should not be a competitive, timed activity. Each youngster should move at a self-determined pace. Racing belongs in the track program. Another reason to avoid speed is that racing keeps youngsters from learning to pace their running. For developing endurance and gaining health benefits, teach moving for a longer time at a slower speed rather than run at top speed for a shorter distance.

6. It can be motivating for youngsters if they run with a piece of equipment, i.e., beanbag or jump rope. They can play catch with a beanbag or roll a hoop while walking or jogging.

Game Activity

Low Organization Games

When the jogging activity is finished, students may be somewhat fatigued. Play games that do not place high demand on the cardiovascular system.

Dynamic Physical Education for Elementary School Children
Rhythmic Movement Skills (1)
Level I – Week 13

Objectives:
To be able to identify and perform animal movements
To march individually and in patterns
To be able to move rhythmically
To perform simple folk dances

Equipment Required:
Music for Parachute Fitness
Parachute
Music for rhythmic activities
Playground ball for game

Instructional Activities	Teaching Hints

Introductory Activity -- Simple Games

Use a game that youngsters learned earlier and contains ample gross motor activity. The following are suggested:

1. Toe to Toe, see Lesson Plan 1
2. Sneak Attack, see Lesson Plan 3
3. Change Sides, see Lesson Plan 6

Toe to Toe is excellent for teaching youngsters to find a partner quickly. Change Sides teaches youngsters to move across the teaching area without bumping into others.

Fitness Development Activity -- Parachute Fitness

1. Jog while holding the chute in the left hand. (music)
2. Shake the chute. (no music)
3. Slide while holding the chute with both hands. (music)
4. Sit and perform curl-ups. (no music)
5. Skip. (music)
6. Freeze, face the center, and stretch the chute tightly. Repeat five to six times. (no music)
7. Run in place while holding the chute taut at different levels. (music)
8. Sit with legs under the chute. Do a seat walk toward the center. Return to the perimeter. Repeat four to six times. (no music)
9. Place the chute on the ground. Jog away from the chute and return on signal. Repeat. (music)
10. Move into push-up position holding the chute with one hand. Shake the chute. (no music)
11. Shake the chute and jump in place. (music)
12. Lie on back with feet under the chute. Shake the chute with the feet. (no music)
13. Hop to the center of the chute and return. (music)
14. Sit with feet under the chute. Stretch by touching the toes with the chute. Relax with other stretches while sitting. (no music)

Tape alternating segments (20 seconds in length) of silence and music to signal duration of exercise. Music segments indicate aerobic activity with the parachute while intervals of silence announce using the chute to enhance flexibility and strength development.

Space youngsters evenly around the chute.

Use different hand grips (palms up, down, mixed).

All movements should be done under control. Some of the faster and stronger students will have to moderate their performance.

Lesson Focus - Rhythmic Movement Skills (1)

Marching

Try the following sequence.

1. Clap hands while standing in place to the beat of a tom-tom or record.
2. March in place; always start with the left foot.
3. March to the music in scatter formation, adding some of the following challenges;
   a. Be a big or small as you can.
   b. Count the rhythm.
   c. Change direction on signal.
   d. March backwards.
   e. March loudly or quietly.
   f. Make up a rhythmic poem like "Sound Off."
   g. Be a drum major leading the band.
   h. Play various instruments in the band while marching.
4. Try some simple patterns such as the following:
   a. Single-line formation.
   b. Double-line formation (with a partner).
   c. Two lines meet and go up the center.
   d. Two lines meet and split on signal.

Alternate activities from each of the categories so students receive a variety of skills to practice.

Use scatter formation during early learning stages.

When march in line, try to maintain spacing between individuals.

If desired, teach commands such as "about face, forward march, and halt."

Try saluting each other as they march past.

Parachute Rhythmic Routine

Perform rhythmic activities while holding or manipulating the parachute:

Beats	Movement
1-8	Eight walking steps to the left. Hold chute in both hands.
9-16	Eight backward steps to the right.
17-20	Raise parachute above head (up-2-3-4).
21-24	Lower chute to floor (Down-2-3-4).
25-32	Shake the chute (Up and Down).
33-36	Raise the chute overhead.
37-44	Lower chute quickly to floor and form a dome. Hold the dome for eight beats.

Practice the steps without the parachute when learning the movements.

Instead of holding to a specified number of beats, it might be easier to call out a change. This allows the teacher to continue the movement until most students have learned.

Rhythmic Activities

Make dances easy for students to learn by implementing some of the following techniques:

1. Teach the dances without using partners.
2. Allow youngsters to move in any direction without left-right orientation.
3. Use scattered formation instead of circles.
4. Emphasize strong movements such as clapping and stamping to increase involvement.
5. Play the music at a slower speed when first learning the dance.

Rhythms should be taught like other sport skills. Avoid striving for perfection so students know it is acceptable to make mistakes. Teach a variety of dances rather than one or two in depth in case some students find it difficult to master a specific dance.

Movin' Madness (American)

Music Source: WWCD-1044
Formation: Scattered
Skills: Keeping time, creativity
Directions:
Part I:
The tempo is slow, slow, fast-fast-fast. The children do any series of movements of their choice to fit this pattern, repeated four times. The movements should be large, gross motor movements.
Part II:
During the second part (chorus) of the music, the children do any locomotor movement in keeping with the tempo. The step-hop or a light run can be used with the tempo of Part II.
Teaching suggestions: Have the youngsters clap the rhythm. They should pay particular attention to the tempo in Part I. The music is Bleking, a dance presented later. The music for "I See You" is also suitable, but note that the movements in Part I are repeated twice instead of four times. The Part II music is suitable for skipping, sliding, or galloping.

Did You Ever See a Lassie? (Scottish)

Music Source: WWCD 7054; WWC-7054
Skills: Walking at 3/4 time, creativity
Formation: Single circle, facing halfway left, with hands joined; one child in the center
Verse
Did you ever see a lassie (laddie), a lassie, a lassie?
Did you ever see a lassie go this way and that?
Go this way and that way, and this way and that way?
Did you ever see a lassie go this way and that?
Directions:

Measures	Action
1--8	All walk (one step per measure) to the left in a circle with hands joined. (Walk, 2, 3, 4, 5, 6, 7, 8) The child in the center gets ready to demonstrate some type of movement.
9--16	All stop and copy the movement suggested by the child in the center.

When the verse starts over, the center child selects another to do some action in the center and changes places with her.

Ach Ja (German)

Music Source: WWC-0860
Skills: Walking, sliding
Formation: Double circle, partners facing counterclockwise, partners A on the inside, inside hands joined
Verse
When my father and my mother take the children to the fair,
Ach Ja! Ach Ja! Oh, they haven't any money, but it's little that they care,

Ach Ja! Ach Ja!
Tra la la, tra la la, tra la la la la la la la
Tra la la, tra la la, tra la la la la la la la
Ach Ja! Ach Ja!
Directions:
Explain that "Ach Ja" means "Oh yes."

Measures	Action
1--2	Partners walk eight steps in the line of direction. (Walk, 2, 3, 4, 5, 6, 7, 8)
3	Partners drop hands and bow to each other. (Bow)
4	Each A then bows to the B on the left, who returns the bow. (Bow)
5--8	Measures 1--4 are repeated.
9--10	Partners face each other, join hands, and take four slides in the line of direction. (Slide, 2, 3, 4)
11--12	Four slides are taken clockwise. (Slide, 2, 3, 4)
13	Partners bow to each other. (Bow)
14	A bows to the B on the left, who returns the bow. (Bow) To start the next dance, A moves quickly toward B, who is the next partner.

Bombay Bounce (American)

Music Source: Any record with a definite and moderately fast beat
Skills: Hesitation step, side step
Formation: Scattered, all facing forward
Directions:

Part I (16 counts): A hesitation step to the left is performed by taking a short step to the left followed by touching the right foot near the left while the weight remains on the left foot. A hesitation step to the right is similar except it begins with a step to the right. To begin the dance, eight hesitation steps are performed in place with a hand clap on each touch. (Left, touch and clap; right, touch and clap) Repeat 4 times.

Part II (16 counts): Take two side steps to the left, then two to the right. Clap on counts 4 and 8. (Left, close; Left, close and clap; Right, close; Right, close and clap). Repeat the pattern.

Part III (16 counts): Take four side steps left and four side steps right. Clap only on count 8. (Left, close, left, close, left, close, left, close and clap). Repeat to the right.

Part IV (16 counts): Take four steps forward and four steps backward, four steps forward and four steps backward. Clap on counts 4, 8, 12, and 16. (Forward, 2, 3, 4 and clap; Backward, 2, 3, 4 and clap; Forward, 2, 3, 4 and clap; Backward 2, 3, 4 and clap)

Teaching suggestions: Variations are possible (e.g., in Part IV, instead of four steps, use three steps and a kick [swing].)

Circassian Circle (English)

Music Source: WWCD-FDN
Skills: Walking, skipping, promenade
Formation: Large single circle of couples facing center with all hands joined
Directions:

Measures	Action
2	Introduction
1-2	All walk 4 steps toward center and back 4 steps to place (Walk 2, 3, 4; back, 2, 3, 4)
3-4	Repeat measures 1 and 2 (Walk 2, 3, 4; back, 2, 3, 4)
5-6	Girls walk 4 steps toward center and back 4 steps (Girls, 2, 3, 4; back, 2, 3, 4)
7-8	Boys walk 4 steps toward center, then turn a half-turn left and walk diagonally clockwise 4 steps to a new partner. (Boys, 2, 3, 4; move, to, new, partner)
9-10	Using a cross-arm grip, new partners lean away from each other and skip 8 steps clockwise once around each other. (Skip, 2, 3, 4, 5, 6, 7, 8)
11-12	Without dropping hands, couples promenade counterclockwise for 8 steps. Take the last two steps to stop and face the center to do the dance again. (Promenade, 2, 3, 4, 5, 6, face, center)

The dance is performed 4 times.

Danish Dance of Greeting (Danish)

Music Source: WWCD-1041; WWC-07042
Skills: Running or sliding, bowing
Formation: Single circle, all face center. Partner A stands to the left of partner B.
Directions:

Measures	Action
1	All clap twice and bow to partner. (Clap, clap, bow)
2	Repeat but turn back to the partner and bow to the neighbor. (Clap, clap, bow)
3	Stamp right, stamp left. (Stamp, stamp)
4	Turn around in four running steps. (Turn, 2, 3, 4)
5-8	Repeat the action of measures 1–4.
9-12	All join hands and run to the left for four measures. (Run, 2, 3, 4, ... 16)
13-16	Repeat the action of measures 9–12, taking light running steps in the opposite direction. (Run, 2, 3, 4, ... 16)

Variation: Instead of a running step, use a light slide.

Game Activity

Squirrel in the Trees

  Supplies: None

  Skills: Fundamental locomotor movements

  A number of trees are formed by two players facing each other and holding hands or putting hands on each other's shoulders. A squirrel is in the center of each tree, and one or two extra squirrels are outside. On signal, the trees open up and let the squirrels move around the area. The trees also stay together and move throughout the area. On signal, the trees freeze in place and the squirrels find any available tree. Only one squirrel is allowed in a tree.

Teaching Suggestion: Rotation is necessary so all students get to be a squirrel. Once the squirrels are in a tree, ask them to face one of the tree players. The person they are facing becomes their partner for a tree and the other person becomes a new squirrel.

Stop Ball

  Supplies: A ball

  Skills: Tossing, catching

  The class is divided into small circles with 5 to 7 players. One player, with their hands over their eyes, stands in the center of the circle. A ball is tossed clockwise or counterclockwise from player to player around the circle. Failing to catch the ball or making a bad toss incurs a penalty. That player takes one long step backward and stays out of the game for one turn. At a time of her own selection, the center player calls, "Stop." The player caught with the ball (or the ball coming to her) steps back and stays out for one turn. The center player should be allowed two or three turns and then changed.

Dynamic Physical Education for Elementary School Children
Fundamental Skills Using Long Jump Ropes
Level I – Week 14

Objectives:
To perform locomotor movements on cue
To choose fitness activities that assure personal success
To perform long jump roping skills
To know the difference between front and back door entry in long rope jumping
To pass and catch balls in a game setting

Equipment Required:
Circuit training music, signs, and cones
One long jump rope per 4-6 students (12-16 ft in length)
10 ft jump ropes for students who have trouble turning the 16 ft ropes
5 or 6 balls for game activities

Instructional Activities	Teaching Hints
Introductory Activity --Crossing the River	
Two lines about 40 feet apart designate a river. Each time the youngsters cross the river the must perform a different movement. For example: 1. Run, walk, hop, skip, leap. 2. Animal Walks such as bear, crab, and puppy dog. 3. Partner run, back to back, side by side.	Stress quality of movement rather than speed. Reinforce creativity and original movements.
Fitness Development Activity – Circuit Training	
Make signs, put them on cones and place around the perimeter of the teaching area. Students perform the exercise specified at each station while the music is playing. 1. Tortoise and Hare 2. Curl-up variations 3. Hula Hooping on arms 4. Standing Hip Bend 5. Agility run--run back and forth between two designated lines 6. Push-up variations 7. Crab Walk 8. Bend and Twist	Tape alternating segments of silence and music to signal duration of exercise. Music segments (begin at 30 seconds) indicate activity at each station while intervals of silence (10 seconds) announce it is time to stop and move forward to the next station.
Lesson Focus – Fundamental Skills Using Long Jump Ropes	

1. Jump a stationary rope, gradually raise the rope.
 2. Ocean Waves--Shake the rope with an up-and-down motion. Students try to jump a "low spot."
 3. Snake in the grass--Wiggle the rope back and forth on the grass. Jump without touching the rope.
 4. Pendulum swing--Move the rope back and forth like a pendulum. Jump the rope as it approaches the jumper.
 5. Practice turning the rope with a partner. The skill of turning *must* precede jumping skills. Standard 16 ft. long ropes are difficult for young children to turn. Substitute 8 to 12 ft ropes depending on the maturity of the youngsters.
 6. Practice turning the rope to rhythm. Music with a strong beat or a steady tom-tom beat is useful for developing rhythmic turning. Turning the rope to a steady rhythm *must* precede jumping skills.
 7. Run through a turning rope.
 8. Stand in the center of the turners and jump the rope as it is turned once. Add more jumps.
 9. Run in, jump once, and run out.
 10. Front door--turn the rope toward the jumper.
 11. Try the following variations:
   a Run in front door and out back door.
   b Run in back door and out front door.
   c. Run in back door and out back door.
   d. Run in front or back door, jump a specified number of times, and out.
 	
   e. Run in front or back door, jump, and do a quarter, half, and full turn in the air.
	Groups of four students work best because it allows students to rotate easily (two turners and two jumpers) without anyone being left out.
	
	 Use shorter jump ropes for students who have trouble learning to turn.
	
	 Teach turning by having students hold an end of the rope and standing as far apart as possible. Make small circles with the rope and gradually step toward each other, making large circles.
	
	 Rhythmic turning is important! Many students miss the jump because of erratic turning. Practice turning until it becomes a smooth even tempo.
	
	 Allow beginners to tell the turners what activity they want to do. Self-choice helps assure success.

f. Touch the ground while jumping.

g. Turn around while jumping.

12. Recite a chant while jumping.

Examples of chants:
Tick tock, tick tock,
What's the time by the clock?
It's one, two, [up to midnight].

I like coffee, I like tea,
How many people can jump like me?
One, two, three, [up to a certain number].

Game Activity

Ball Passing

Supplies: Five or six different kinds of balls for each circle

Skill: Object handling

Divide the class into two or more circles, with no more than 15 children in any one circle. Each circle consists of two or more squads, but squad members need not stand together. A ball is started around the circle and passed from player to player in the same direction. Introduce more balls until five or six are moving around the circle at the same time and in the same direction. If a child drops a ball, he must retrieve it, and a point is scored against his squad. After a period of time, a whistle is blown, and the points against each squad are totaled. The squad with the lowest score wins. Beanbags, large blocks, or softballs can be substituted for balls.

Hot Potatoes

Supplies: One to three balls or beanbags for each group

Skill: Object handling

Group players in small circles (8 to 12 per circle) so objects can be passed from one to another around the circle. Balls or beanbags or both are passed around the circle. The teacher or a selected student, who is standing with their back to the class randomly shouts, "stop!" The point of the game is to avoid being the person who passes the object to the person who caught it when the signal occurs. If this happens, the player(s) who passed the object gets up and moves to the next circle. Begin the game with one object and gradually add objects if the class is capable. Call out "Reverse" to signal a change in the direction the object is passed.

Aviator

Supplies: None

Skills: Running, locomotor movements, stopping

Players are parked (in push-up position) at one end of the playing area. The air traffic controller (ATC) is in front of the players and calls out, "Aviators aviators, take off!" Youngsters take off and move like airplanes to the opposite side of the area. The first person to move to the other side and land the plane (get into push-up position facing the ATC) is declared the new ATC.

If the ATC yells out some type of stormy weather, all planes must return to the starting line and resume the parked position. Examples of stormy weather commands are lightning, thunder, hurricane, and tornado. Each ATC is allowed to give stormy weather warnings once.

Dynamic Physical Education for Elementary School Children
Gymnastics Skills (2)
Level I – Week 15

Objectives:
To sustain moderate physical activity
To absorb the body weight on the hands
To balance the body in a variety of challenges

Equipment Required:
Music for Mini-Challenge Course
Equipment for Mini-Challenge Course
Tumbling mats
Beanbags for Partner Toe Toucher

Instructional Activities	Teaching Hints
Introductory Activity -- Popcorn	
Students pair up with one person on the floor in push-up position and the other standing ready to move. On signal, the standing students move over and under the persons on the floor. The person on the floor changes from a raised to a lowered push-up position each time the partner goes over or under her. On signal, reverse positions.	Caution to avoid touching others and respect personal space. Challenge students to see how many students they can move over and under.

Fitness Development Activity -- Mini-Challenge Course

Arrange four parallel courses with a group at each course. Students perform the challenges from a cone at the start to a finish cone and jog back to continuously repeat the course. On signal, groups rotate to a new course.

Course 1.   Hop in and out of 5 hoops, Puppy Dog Walk around a cone for 5 seconds and skip to the finish cone.

Course 2.   Weave in and out of four cones, Crab Walk around a cone for 5 seconds and gallop to finish cone.

Course 3.   Do the Rolling Log the length of mat, do an agility run through 4 hoops, and slide to the finish cone.

Course 4.   Jump over each of 5 cones, jump back and forth over a stretched out jump rope, run backwards around three cones; and hop to a cone.

Teaching Hints: Tape alternating segments (20 seconds in length) of silence and music to signal duration of exercise. Music segments indicate moving through the mini-challenge course while intervals of silence announce using the chute to enhance flexibility and strength development.

Students can set up their own mini-challenges.

Lesson Focus – Gymnastics Skills (2)

Animal Movements

Bear Walk

  Bend forward and touch the ground with both hands. Travel forward slowly by moving the hand and foot on the same side together (i.e., first the right hand and foot, then the left hand and foot). Make deliberate movements.

Gorilla Walk

  Bend the knees and carry the trunk forward. Let the arms hang at the sides. Touch the fingers to the ground while walking.

Rabbit Jump

  Crouch with knees apart and hands placed on the floor. Move forward by reaching out with both hands and then bringing both feet up to the hands. The eyes look ahead. Emphasize that this is a jump rather than a hop because both feet move at once.

Elephant Walk

  Bend well forward, clasping the hands together to form a trunk. The end of the trunk should swing close to the ground. Walk in a slow, deliberate, dignified manner, keeping the legs straight and swinging the trunk from side to side.

Tumbling and Inverted Balances

Forward Roll Review (See Lesson Plan 7)

Five groups of activities in this lesson ensure that youngsters receive a variety of experiences. Pick a few activities from each group and teach them alternately. For example, teach one or two animal movements, then a tumbling and inverted balance, followed by a balance stunt, etc. Give equal time to each group of activities.

Scatter tumbling mats throughout the area so that there is little standing in line waiting for a turn.

A major concern for safety is the neck and back region. Overweight children are at greater risk and might be allowed to avoid tumbling and inverted balances.

Backward Curl

Approach this activity in three stages. For the first stage, begin in a sitting position, with the knees drawn up to the chest and the chin tucked. The hands are clasped and placed behind the head with the elbows held out as far as possible. Gently roll backward until the weight is on the elbows. Roll back to starting position.

In stage two, perform the same action as before, but place the hands alongside the head on the mat while rolling back. The fingers are pointed in the direction of the roll, with palms down on the mat. (A good cue is, "Point your thumbs toward your ears and keep your elbows close to your body.")

For stage three, perform the same action as in stage two, but start in a crouched position on the feet with the back facing the direction of the roll. Momentum is secured by sitting down quickly and bringing the knees to the chest. This, like the Back Roller, is a lead-up to the Backward Roll. Teach children to push against the floor to take pressure off the back of the neck.

Climb-Up

Begin on a mat in a kneeling position, with hands placed about shoulder width apart and the fingers spread and pointed forward. Place the head forward of the hands, so that the head and hands form a triangle on the mat. Walk the body weight forward so that most of it rests on the hands and head. Climb the knees to the top of the elbows. (This stunt is a lead-up to the Headstand.)

Balance Stunts

Kimbo Stand

With the left foot kept flat on the ground, cross the right leg over the left to a position in which the right foot is pointed partially down and the toe is touching the ground.

Knee-Lift Stand

From a standing position, lift one knee up so that the thigh is parallel to the ground and the toe is pointed down. Hold. Return to starting position.

Stork Stand

From a standing position, shift all of the weight to one foot. Place the other foot so that the sole is against the inside of the knee and thigh of the standing leg. Hold. Recover to standing position.

Individual Stunts

Rubber Band

Get down in a squat position with the hands and arms clasped around the knees. On the command "Stretch, stretch, stretch," stretch as tall and as wide as possible. On the command "Snap," snap back to original position.

Pumping Up the Balloon

One child, the pumper, is in front of the other children, who are the balloons. The pumper pretends to use a bicycle pump to inflate the balloons. The balloons get larger and larger until the pumper shouts, "Bang," whereupon the balloons collapse to the floor. The pumper should give a "shoosh" sound every time a pumping motion is made.

Rising Sun

Lie on the back. Using the arms for balance only, rise to a standing position. Try with the arms folded over the chest.

Heel Click

Stand with the feet slightly apart, jump up, and click the heels, coming down with the feet apart.

Do not perform many repetitions of tumbling and inverted balances. For most children, limiting the number of forward or backward roll repetitions to four or five will prevent fatigue and injury.

The Backward Curl should be used to learn to roll back and forth. No youngster should be expected to roll over if it is difficult for them. In stunts and tumbling, it is important that the student decide if they are capable and confident enough to try the activity.

The Climb-up should only be performed by youngsters who have sufficient strength to support the body weight. Overweight children will find this to be a difficult activity.

Most children can accomplish balance stunts and this should be an area of accomplishment for all students.

Encourage students to hold the balance position for at least five counts.

An added challenge is to see how long the balance can be held with the eyes closed.

Emphasize a quick snapping back to position. Students can change their starting position as they desire.

Allow many children the chance to be a pumper.

Experiment with different positions of the feet. The feet can be crossed, spread wide, both to one side, and so on.

Try with a quarter turn right and left. Try clapping the hands overhead as the heels are clicked.

Partner and Group Stunts

Wring the Dishrag

Face and join hands with a partner. Raise one pair of arms (right for one and left for the other) and turn under, continuing a full turn until back to original position. Try in a reverse direction.

This an excellent opportunity to talk about cooperation and moving together. Emphasize form rather than doing it as fast as possible

Partner Toe Toucher

Partners lie on their backs with heads near each other and feet in opposite directions. Join arms with partner using a hand-wrist grip, and bring the legs up so that the toes touch partner's toes. Keep high on the shoulders and touch the feet high. Strive to attain the high shoulder position, as this is the point of most difficulty

One child carries a beanbag, a ball, or some other article between the feet, and transfers the object to the partner, who lowers it to the floor.

Game Activity

Where's My Partner?

Supplies: None

Skills: Fundamental locomotor movements

Children are in a double circle facing a partner. The inside circle has two or three more players than the outside. When the signal is given, the circles skip (or walk, run, hop, or gallop) to the right. This means that they are skipping in opposite directions. On the command "Halt," the circles face each other to find partners. The players left without a partner go to the mush pot (the center area of the circle) for one turn. The circles should be reversed after a time.

Variation: The game can also be played with music or a drumbeat. When the music stops, the players seek partners.

Change Sides

Supplies: None

Skill: Body management

Identify two parallel lines 30 feet apart with half of the class on each line. On signal, all players cross to the other line, face the center, and stand at attention. The first group to do all three things correctly wins a point. Children must be cautioned to use care when passing through the opposite group. They should be spaced well along each line; this allows room for them to move through each group. Vary the locomotor movements used by specifying skipping, hopping, long steps, sliding, and other varieties of movement. The position to be assumed at the finish can be varied also.

Dynamic Physical Education for Elementary School Children
Rhythmic Movement Skills (2)
Level I – Week 16

Objectives:
To be able to lead other students in simple locomotor movements
To learn the background of simple folk dances
To move rhythmically

Equipment Required:
Equipment for Mini-Challenge Course
Music for Mini-Challenge Course
Music for rhythmic activities

Instructional Activities	Teaching Hints

Introductory Activity -- Drill Sergeant

Designate a student to be a drill sergeant. The sergeant then gives commands such as:
1. Walk, jog, and halt.
2. March, jump twice, and freeze (pose).
3. March, about face, and halt.
4. March, double time, and march in place.

The teacher can serve as the initial sergeant and then appoint a student to call the group to attention, give directions, and commands to move.

Teach the marching commands of about face, double time, etc.

Fitness Development Activity -- Mini-Challenge Course

Arrange four parallel courses with a group at each course. Students perform the challenges from a cone at the start to a finish cone and jog back to continuously repeat the course. On signal, groups rotate to a new course.

Course 1. Hop in and out of 5 hoops, Puppy Dog Walk around a cone for 5 seconds and skip to the finish cone.
Course 2. Weave in and out of four cones, Crab Walk around a cone for 5 seconds and gallop to finish cone.
Course 3. Do the Rolling Log the length of mat, do an agility run through 4 hoops, and slide to the finish cone.
Course 4. Jump over each of 5 cones, jump back and forth over a stretched out jump rope, run backwards around three cones; and hop to a cone.

Tape alternating segments (20 seconds in length) of silence and music to signal duration of exercise. Music segments indicate moving through the mini-challenge course while intervals of silence announce using the chute to enhance flexibility and strength development.

Students can set up their own mini-challenges.

Lesson Focus--Rhythmic Movement Skills (2)
Carousel (Swedish)

Music Source: WWCD-1041
Skills: Draw step, sliding
Formation: Double circle, facing center. The inner circle, representing a merry-go-round, joins hands. The outer players, representing the riders, place their hands on the hips of the partner in front.

Verse
Little children, sweet and gay,
Carousel is running; it will run to evening.
Little ones a nickel, big ones a dime.
Hurry up, get a mate, or you'll surely be too late.

Chorus
Ha, ha, ha, happy are we,
Anderson and Peterson and Henderson and me,
Ha, ha, ha, happy are we,
Anderson and Peterson and Henderson and me.

Directions:

Measures	Verse Action
1--16	Moving to the left, children take 12 slow draw steps and stamp on the last three steps. (Step, together, 2, 3, . . . 12, stamp, stamp, stamp, rest)

Measures	Chorus Action
17--24	Moving left, speed up the draw step until it becomes a slide or gallop. Sing the chorus. (Slide, 2, 3, . . . 8)
25--32	Repeat measures 17--24 while moving to the right. (Slide, 2, 3, . . . 8)

During the chorus, the tempo is increased, and the movement is changed to a slide. Children should take short, light slides to prevent the circle from moving out of control.

Variation:

The dance can be done with youngsters holding the perimeter of a parachute.

Jolly Is the Miller (American)

Music Source: WWC-317

Skills: Marching

Formation: Double circle, partners facing counterclockwise, As on the inside, with inside hands joined. A Miller is in the center of the circle

Directions:

Verse

Jolly is the Miller who lives by the mill;

The wheel goes round with a right good will;

One hand on the hopper and the other on the sack;

The right steps forward and the left steps back.

Action

All sing. Youngsters march counterclockwise, with inside hands joined. During the second line when "the wheel goes round," the dancers turn their outside arm in a circle to form a wheel. Children change partners at the words "right steps forward and the left steps back." The Miller then has a chance to get a partner. The child left without a partner becomes the next Miller.

Hokey Pokey (American)

Music Source: WWCD-4903; WWC-9126

Skills: Body identification, nonlocomotor movements

Formation: Single circle, facing center

Verse

Line 1: You put your right foot in,

Line 2: You put your right foot out,

Line 3: You put your right foot in

Line 4: And you shake it all about;

Line 5: You do the hokey pokey

Line 6: And you turn yourself around.

Line 7: That's what it's all about.

Directions:

During the first four lines, the children act out the words. During lines 5 and 6, they hold their hands overhead with palms forward and do a kind of hula while turning around in place. During line 7, they stand in place and clap their hands three times. The basic verse is repeated by substituting, successively, the left foot, right arm, left arm, right elbow, left elbow, head, right hip, left hip, whole self, and backside. The final verse finishes off with the following:

   You do the hokey pokey,

   You do the hokey pokey,

   You do the hokey pokey.

   That's what it's all about

On each of the first two lines, the children raise their arms overhead and perform a bowing motion with the arms and upper body. On line 3, all kneel and bow forward to touch the hands to the floor. During line 4, they slap the floor five times, alternating their hands in time to the words.

Teaching suggestions:

Encourage the youngsters to make large and vigorous motions during the hokey pokey portions and during the turn around. This adds to the fun. The records all feature singing calls, but the action sequence of the different records varies. The children should sing lightly as they follow the directions given on the record.

Chimes of Dunkirk, Var. 1 (French-Belgian)

Music Source: WWCD-1042; WWC-07042

Skills: Turning in a small circle with a partner, changing partners

Formation: Double circle, partners facing

Directions:

Measures	Action
1--2	Stamp three times in place, right-left-right. (Stamp, 2, 3)
3--4	Clap hands three times above the head (chimes in the steeple). (Clap, 2, 3)
5--8	Partner A places both hands on partner B's hips; B places both hands on A's shoulders. Taking four steps, they turn around in place. (Turn, 2, 3, 4) On the next four counts, partner B (on the outside) moves one person to the left with four steps. (Change, 2, 3, 4) Repeat the sequence from the beginning.

How D'Ye Do, My Partner? (Swedish)

Music Source: WWCD-1041; WWC-07042

Skills: Bowing, curtsying, skipping

Formation: Double circle, partners facing, partner A on inside

Directions:

Measures	Action
1–2	Partners A bow to their partner. (Bow)
3–4	Partners B bow. (Bow)
5–6	A offers the right hand to B, who takes it with the right hand. (Join right hands) Both turn to face counterclockwise.
7–8	Couples join left hands in promenade position in preparation to skip when the music changes. (Join left hands)
9–16	Partners skip counterclockwise in the circle, slowing down on measure 15. (Skip) On measure 16, Bs stop and As move ahead to secure a new partner. (New partner)

The Hitch Hiker (American)

Music Source: WWCD-FDN

Skills: Chug step (a short backward jump with the feet together on the floor), skipping

Formation: Double circle, partners facing each other with boys inside facing out

Directions:

Measures	Action
2	Introduction
1-2	Take two chugs away from partner and clap hands on each step. Jerk right thumb over right shoulder while twisting right foot with heel on the floor. Repeat. (Chug chug, right, right).
3-4	Same as measures 1-2 except use left thumb and foot. (Chug, chug, left, left).
5-6	Same as measures 1-2 except use both thumbs and feet. (Chug, chug, both, both).
7-8	Skip diagonally forward and to the right toward a new partner with 4 skips; continue with four more skips around your new partner with right hands joined and get ready to repeat the dance. (Skip, 2, 3, 4, around, 2, 3, 4).

The sequence repeats eight times.

Looby Loo (English)

Music Source: WWCD-7054; WWC-7054

Skills: Skipping or running, body identification

Formation: Single circle, facing center, hands joined

Directions: The chorus is repeated before each verse. During the chorus, all children skip around the circle to the right. On the verse part of the dance, the children stand still, face the center, and follow the directions of the words. On the words "and turn myself about," they make a complete turn in place and get ready to skip around the circle again. The movements should be definite and vigorous. On the last verse, they jump forward and then backward, shake vigorously, and then turn about.

The dance can be made more fun and more vigorous by changing the tasks in the song. Try these tasks: Right side or hip, left side or hip, big belly, backside.

Nixie Polka (Nigarepolska) (Swedish)

Music Source: WWCD-1041; WWC-572
Skills: Bleking step
Formation: Single circle, all facing center, with one or more children scattered inside the circle

Measures	Part I Action
1–4	With hands joined, all spring lightly onto the left foot and extend the right foot forward, heel to ground, toe up. Next, spring lightly onto the right foot and extend the left foot forward. Repeat this action until four slow bleking steps are completed. (Slow, slow, slow, slow)
5–8	All clap hands once and shout "Hey!" The center child then runs around the inside of the circle, looking for a partner, finally selecting one. They join both hands and run lightly in place until the music is finished. This refrain is repeated, so the children have time to get back to the center of the circle. (Clap, run)

	Part II Action
1–4	The center dancer and partner, with both hands joined, repeat the action of measures 1–4. All dancers in the circle also repeat the action of measures 1–4. (Slow, slow, slow, slow)
5–8	On the first count, all clap hands, shouting "Hey!" The center dancer then about-faces and places both hands on the shoulders of partner, who now becomes the new leader. In this position, both shuffle around the inside of the circle, looking for a third person to dance with. The music is repeated again to allow ample time to return to the center. (Clap, run)

	Part III Action
1–4	The action of measures 1–4 is repeated, with the new dancer facing the circle and the two others facing the new dancer. (Slow, slow, slow, slow)
5–8	On the first count, all clap hands, shouting "Hey!" The two people in the center then about-face. All three now face the center to form a line of three dancers with a new leader, who looks for a fourth dancer. The music is repeated. (Clap, run)

The entire dance is thus repeated, accumulating dancers with each repetition. There should be one center dancer for each dozen dancers in the circle.

Game Activity

Skunk Tag

Supplies: None

Skills: Fundamental locomotor movements, dodging

Children are scattered about the area. One child is it and chases the others, trying to tag one of them. When a tag is made, she says, "You're it." The new it chases other children. Children are safe when they move into the skunk position which is assumed by kneeling and reaching one arm under a knee and holding their nose. The skunk position can only be held for five seconds; students are then eligible to be tagged.

Aviator

Supplies: None

Skills: Running, locomotor movements, stopping

Players are parked (in push-up position) at one end of the playing area. The air traffic controller (ATC) is in front of the players and calls out, "Aviators aviators, take off!" Youngsters take off and move like airplanes to the opposite side of the area. The first person to move to the other side and land the plane (get into push-up position facing the ATC) is declared the new ATC. If the ATC yells out some type of stormy weather, all planes must return to the starting line and resume the parked position. Examples of stormy weather commands are lightning, thunder, hurricane, and tornado. Each ATC is allowed to give stormy weather warnings once.

Right Angle

Supplies: Music

Skills: Rhythmic movement, body management

A tom-tom can be used to provide the rhythm for this activity. Some of the basic rhythm records also have suitable music. Children change direction at right angles on each heavy beat or change of music. The object of the game is to make the right-angle change on signal and not to bump into other players.

Dynamic Physical Education for Elementary School Children
Throwing Skills (2)
Level I – Week 17

Objectives:
To demonstrate a locomotor tasks
To know the cues for correct throwing
To throw a ball using the overhand technique
To throw with velocity using side orientation and opposition

Equipment Required:
Music and signs for Four Corners Fitness
Yarnballs, whiffle balls, rag balls or
 tennis balls
Hoops, boxes, pins, and mats for targets
Playground and foam balls for games

Instructional Activities	Teaching Hints

Introductory Activity -- Move, Perform Task on Signal

Do a locomotor movement; on signal, stop and perform a task. Suggested tasks are:
1. Seat Circles
2. Balances--foot, seat, and knee
3. Crab Kicks
4. Heel Clicks

Vary the locomotor movements by adding speed and level qualities.

Encourage students to perform their favorite task.

Fitness Development Activity --Four Corners Fitness

Outline a large rectangle with a cone at each corner. Place signs with movement tasks on both sides of the cones. Youngsters move around the outside of the rectangle and change movements as they pass each sign. The following movement activities are suggested for four signs:

Corner 1. Skipping/Jumping/Hopping
Corner 2. Sliding/Galloping
Corner 3. Various animal movements
Corner 4. Sport imitation movements

Stop the class after 30 seconds of movement and perform fitness challenges (see Lesson Plan 5).

Tape alternating segments of silence and music to signal duration of exercise. Music segments (30 seconds) indicate four corner aerobic activity while intervals of silence (45 seconds) announce performance of flexibility and strength development activities.

Faster moving students should pass on the outside of the rectangle.

Increasing or decreasing the size of the rectangle can vary the demands of the routine.

Lesson Focus -- Throwing Skills (2)

Mimetics
1. Cue students and model a good throw.
   a. Use terms such as "wind-up," "turn your non-throwing side to the target," "step toward the target, follow through."
   b. *Encourage* children to throw as *hard as possible*.
   c. Use skilled student throwers to model good throws.

Emphasize lifting the throwing arm and pointing at the target with the non-throwing arm.

Make a "T" with your arms in preparation to throw (both arms extended to sides at shoulder level).

Station Format
1. Activities emphasizing form.
   a. Standing on a tumbling mat
      Throwers stand on the edge of the mat and step off the mat (with the foot opposite the throwing arm) as they throw toward the wall. (The other foot remains on the mat.)
   b. Both feet in hoop.
      Throwers begin in a side-facing position to the target, with both feet inside the hoop; they then step outside of the hoop with the foot opposite the throwing arm and throw to the wall.
   c. Cone behind the student.
      The student must touch the cone with the throwing hand on the back-swing, then throw to the wall.

Focus on throwing form and the velocity of the throw rather than accuracy.

Emphasize throwing hard! Proper form can only be learned when students are encouraged to throw as hard as possible.

Cue students to move their throwing hand behind their head before the throw.

Using large targets (focus on velocity, not accuracy):
1. Throw at a wall or fence.
   a. Throw tennis or rag balls hard from 15-20 ft.
   b. Retrieve the balls after all have been thrown.
2. Throw at cardboard boxes near a fence (the noise from a good hit is reinforcing).

3. Throw at hoops leaning against a wall or fence.
4. Throw at bowling pins that make noise when they fall (audio reinforcement).
5. Throw for distance.
   Encourage students to throw as far as possible. Reinforce distance and throwing hard.

Give each student 4 or 5 balls to throw. They can be placed in a frisbee to keep them from rolling around. When all the balls have been thrown by all the students, students go retrieve the same number of balls they have thrown. Accuracy of throws should not be reinforced. When students throw for accuracy, they usually regress to an immature form of throwing. Reinforce distance, velocity, and throwing hard.

Game Activity

Charlie Over the Water

Supplies: A volleyball or playground ball

Skills: Skipping, running, stopping, bowling (rolling)

Place the class in circle formation. Two or more children are placed in the center of the circle, holding a ball. One of the center players is designated as Charlie (or Sally). The class skips around the circle to the following chant.

Charlie over the water,

Charlie over the sea,

Charlie caught a bluebird,

But can't catch me!

On the word me, the center players toss their balls in the air while the rest of the class runs and scatters throughout the area. When Charlie catches his ball, he shouts, "Stop!" All of the children stop immediately and must not move their feet. All of the center players roll their ball in an attempt to hit one of their scattered classmates. If a ball is rolled into a scattered player, that child becomes a new Charlie. If a center player misses, they remain in the center, and the game is repeated. If a center player misses twice, however, he picks another person to replace him.

Circle Straddle Ball

Supplies: Two or more 8-in. foam balls

Skills: Ball rolling, catching

Children are in circle formation, facing toward the center. Each player stands in a wide straddle stance with the side of their foot against their neighbor's. Their hands are placed on the knees. Two or more balls are used. The object of the game is to roll a ball between the legs of other players before they get their hands down to stop the ball. Keep the circles small so students have more opportunities to handle the ball. Players must catch and roll the ball rather than batting it. Hands must be kept on the knees until a ball is rolled at them. After some practice, the following variation can be played.

Variation: Two or more children are in the center, each with a ball. The other children are in the same formation as before. The center players try to roll the ball through the legs of any child, masking intent by using feints and changes of direction. Any child allowing the ball to go through becomes it.

Flowers and Wind

Supplies: None

Skill: Running

Two parallel lines long enough to accommodate the class are drawn about 30 feet apart. Children are divided into two groups. One group is the flowers and the other the wind. Each of the teams takes a position on one of the lines and faces the other team. The flowers secretly select the name of a common flower. When ready, they walk over to the other line and stand about 3 feet away from the wind. The players on the wind team begin to call out flower names—trying to guess the flower chosen. When the flower has been guessed, the flowers run to their goal line, chased by the players of the other team. Any player caught must join the other side. Reverse the roles and repeat the game. If one side has trouble guessing, give a clue about the color or size of the flower or the first letter of its name.

Dynamic Physical Education for Elementary School Children
Manipulative Skills--Basketball Related
Level I – Week 18

Objectives:
To be able to follow simple rules fitness games and demonstrate cooperative skills
To perform basketball related skills including:
  Chest and bounce pass
  Dribbling
  Shooting

Equipment Required:
One 8½" playground or foam rubber ball
  for each student
Hoops
Cardboard boxes for ball shooting
  practice
Wand or yardstick and blindfold

Instructional Activities	Teaching Hints
Introductory Activity -- Activity with Playground Balls	
Allow students to practice ball control skills. Encourage challenge by allowing them move if they are able to control the ball in place. Activities can range from tossing and catching to dribbling.	Place the balls around the perimeter of the area. On signal, students move throughout the area, acquire a ball and practice doing a favorite activity.
Fitness Development Activity --Fitness Games and Challenges	
1. Stoop Tag.	Alternate simple tag games with fitness challenge activities. Exercise all parts of the body including upper body and abdominal strength and flexibility.
2. Freeze; perform stretching activities.	
3. Back-to-Back Tag.	
4. Freeze; perform Abdominal Challenges using Curl-up variations.	
5. Balance Tag.	
6. Freeze; perform Arm-Upper Body Strength Challenges using Push-up variations.	
7. Elbow Swing Tag.	Any tag games can be used. Ask students what their favorite tag game is and play it.
8. Freeze; perform Trunk Development challenges.	
9. Color Tag.	
Lesson Focus -- Manipulative Skills (Basketball Related)	
1. Warm-up with informal passing back and forth between partners.	Have students get toe to toe with a partner. One partner gets a ball, returns, and starts passing to their partner.
2. Push (chest) pass--two handed. Emphasize one or two of the following points at a time depending on the skill level of students:	
a. Ball at chest level, face partner.	
b. Fingers spread above center of ball.	Reach for the ball when making the catch. As the ball is caught, bend the arms and bring the ball to the body to absorb the force.
c. Step toward partner and extend arms.	
d. Throw to chest level.	
e. Catch with finger tips.	
f. Thumbs together for high pass.	
g. Little fingers together for low pass.	
h. Hands relaxed, provide a little "give."	
i. Add the bounce pass—same technique.	The ball should be bounced slightly pass the midway point nearer the receiver and should bounce to chest level.
3. One-Handed Pass	
a. Side toward catcher.	
b. Ball back with both hands to side of head or above shoulder. Fingers spread, directly behind the ball.	
c. Release the forward hand and throw with a wrist snap.	Foam rubber balls (8") are lighter than playground balls. They are easier to catch and make students more confident and less fearful. Use them if they are available.
d. Practice both right and left.	
4. Birdie in the Cage	
a. Form circles of 7-8 children.	
b. Pass ball among the circle for practice. Be sure everyone handles the ball.	
c. Select "Birdie," put in center until he touches the ball, or there is a loose ball leaving the circle.	
5. Dribbling (each has a ball)	
a. Explain technique: wrist action, finger control, eyes ahead.	Practice dribbling in place before moving and dribbling.
b. Dribble in different directions. Use right and left in turn.	

6. One-Handed Shot
   a. Raise ball up to eye level, sight, and shoot to a partner (demonstrate).
   b. Shoot into cardboard boxes placed around the perimeter of the area
   b. Shoot at lowered baskets with partners alternating shooting and rebounding.
7. Add a short dribble and a shot.

Lower the baskets so students don't have to fling the ball. The important goal in shooting is correct form. Shooting at boxes and garbage cans allows students to use proper shooting "touch."

Game Activity

Blindfolded Duck

Supplies: A wand and blindfold

Skills: Fundamental locomotor movements

One child, designated the duck (Daisy if a girl, Donald if a boy), stands blindfolded in the center of a circle and holds a wand or similar article. She taps on the floor and tells the class to hop (or perform some other locomotor movement). Children in the circle act accordingly, all moving in the same direction. Daisy then taps the wand twice on the floor, which signals all children to stop. Daisy moves forward with her wand, still blindfolded, to find a child in the circle. She asks, "Who are you?" The child responds, "Quack, quack." Daisy tries to identify this person. If the guess is correct, the identified child becomes the new duck. If the guess is wrong, Daisy must take another turn. After two unsuccessful turns, another child is chosen to be the duck.

Cat and Mice

Supplies: None

Skills: Running, dodging

Form a large circle. One child is the cat and four others are the mice. The cat and mice cannot leave the circle. On signal, the cat chases the mice inside the circle. As they are caught, the mice join the circle. The last mouse caught becomes the cat for the next round. Start at one point in the circle and progress around the circle to select mice so each child gets a chance to be in the center.

Sometimes, one child has difficulty catching the last mouse or any of the mice. The point of the game is for all youngsters to be active. Change mice on a regular time interval rather than waiting until all mice are caught. Another variation is to gradually decrease the size of the circle ("take a step toward the center") so it becomes difficult to evade the cat.

Freeze

Supplies: Music or tom-tom

Skills: Locomotor movements to rhythm

Scatter the class throughout the room. When the music starts, players move throughout the area, guided by the music. They walk, run, jump, or use other locomotor movements, depending on the selected music or beat. When the music is stopped, players freeze and do not move. Players who freeze quickly are reinforced for their excellent work. A tom-tom or a piano is a fine accompaniment for this game, because the rhythmic beat can be varied easily and the rhythm can be stopped at any time. This game is useful for practicing management skills because it reinforces freezing on a stop signal.

Variations:

1. Specify the level at which children must freeze.

2. Have children fall to the ground or balance or go into a different position, such as the Push-Up, Crab, Lame Dog, or some other defined position.

Dynamic Physical Education for Elementary School Children
Movement Skills and Concepts (3)
Sliding, Galloping, Hoops, and Movement Combinations
Level I – Week 19

Objectives
To learn to move in an evasive fashion
To work cooperatively with others in the parachute activity
To perform a variety of gallop and slide steps
To demonstrate body management skills by performing a variety of movements
    through hoops

Equipment Required:
Music for Parachute Fitness
One hoop for each child
Parachute
10-12 beanbags or balls for the game

Instructional Activities	Teaching Hints
Introductory Activity -- Marking	

To teach marking, start by teaching partner tag. One partner moves whiles while the other partner attempts to tag him. Once tagged, the partners change roles and the other attempts to tag. Progress to marking which requires one of the partners to move in a desired fashion while the other attempts to stay near him. On signal, both partners freeze and cannot move their feet. The following partner tries to reach and touch (mark) the partner. If a mark is made, that partner receives a point. Resume the chase with the roles reversed.

The goal is not to play a chase game, but rather to dodge and change directions in order to evade their partner.

Remind students to run under control.

Fitness Development Activity --Parachute Fitness

1. Jog while holding the chute in the left hand. (music)
2. Shake the chute. (no music)
3. Slide while holding the chute with both hands. (music)
4. Sit and perform curl-ups. (no music)
5. Skip. (music)
6. Freeze, face the center, and stretch the chute tightly. Hold for 8-12 seconds. Repeat. (no music)
7. Run in place while holding the chute taut at different levels. (music)
8. Sit with legs under the chute. Do a seat walk toward the center. Return to the perimeter. Repeat four to six times. (no music)
9. Place the chute on the ground. Jog away from the chute and return on signal. Repeat. (music)
10. Move into push-up position holding the chute with one hand. Shake the chute. (no music)
11. Shake the chute and jump in place. (music)
12. Lie on back with feet under the chute. Shake the chute with the feet. (no music)
13. Hop to the center of the chute and return. Repeat. (music)
14. Sit with feet under the chute. Stretch by touching the toes with the chute. Relax with other stretches while sitting. (no music)

Tape alternating segments of silence and music to signal duration of exercise. Music segments indicate aerobic activity with the parachute while intervals of silence announce using the chute to enhance flexibility and strength development.

Space youngsters evenly around the chute.

Use different hand grips (palms up, down, mixed).

All movements should be done under control. Some of the faster and stronger students will have to moderate their performance.

Lesson Focus – Movement Skills and Concepts (3)

Fundamental Skill: Sliding
1. Slide in one direction, stop and slide in another.
2. Begin with short slides in crease slide length. Reverse.
3. Do a number of slides (3, 4, 5, 6), do a half turn, continue in the same direction, but leading with the other leg.
4. Slide with a 4-4 pattern.
5. Slide in a figure-eight pattern.
6. Change levels while sliding; touch the floor occasionally while sliding.
7. Slide lightly and noiselessly.
8. Pretend to be a defensive basketball player, sliding.
9. Slide with a partner.

Select a few activities from each of the categories so students receive a variety of skills to practice. When possible, integrate the manipulative skill activities with fundamental skill activities.

Use instructional cues:

"Move sideways"

"Don't cross the feet"

Fundamental Skill: Galloping

1. Form a circle. Slide in one direction (clockwise or counterclockwise). Gradually turn the body to face the line of direction; this is galloping.
2. Practice galloping freely in general space. Gallop backwards.
3. Gallop in a figure-eight and other patterns.
4. Change gallops (leading foot) on 8, 4 and 2 gallops.
5. Gallop with a partner.

Show the relationship between the slide and gallop steps. The gallop is simply a sliding step performed in a forward direction.

Show the uneven rhythm of the gallop.

Manipulative Skills: Hoop Activities

Each group uses four or five hoops and places them in a line on the floor.

1. Walk, hop, and jump through or on the sides of the hoops.
2. Leap over the hoops from the side.
3. Run around the hoops.
4. Jump astride the hoop and inside it alternately.
5. Jump through each center without touching the hoop.
6. Use different animal walks--Bunny Jump, Frog Jump, Crab Walk.
7. Jump down the line of hoops.
8. Using one hoop, take a push-up position. Keeping the hands on the hoop, circle with the feet. Then put the feet on the hoop and circle with the hands.
9. Jog through with high knees.
10. Do heel clicks in the center of each hoop.
11. Roll a hoop at a partner, who jumps over it as it approaches.

This is an excellent activity to teach cooperative skills. Youngsters should be encouraged to design their hoop patterns and to take turns performing through the hoops.

Near the end of the hoop activities, allow students time to pick up a hoop and perform individual activities.

Movement Concept: Movement Combinations

1. Run, leap, roll.
2. Shake (all over), gallop, freeze.
3. Hop, collapse, explode.
4. Whirl, skip, sink (melt) slowly.
5. Creep, pounce, curl.
6. Begin low, lift, grin, roll.
7. Kneel, sway, jump to feet.
8. Shrink, expand, slide.
9. On all fours, run, roll, jump.
10. Do a Jumping Jack (two or three times), slide, jump turn.

Encourage individual response. Use student demonstration to illustrate the breadth of responses.

Offer students the opportunity to demonstrate their response to a partner. Each partner then tries to imitate the other's combination.

Game Activity

Corner Spry

Supplies: Blindfold

Skills: Light, silent walking

One person is blindfolded and stands in the center of the square. The other players are scattered in the corner areas. On signal they travel as quietly as possible from corner area to corner area. The blindfolded person, when ready (less than 20 seconds), calls out "Corner Spry!" All players finish their trips to the corner nearest them. The blindfolded person then picks (by pointing) a corner, trying to select the one with the most players. Each time, select a new player to be blindfolded.

Variation: Number the corners 1, 2, 3, 4, and have the blindfolded person call out the corner number. The leader can start class movement by naming the locomotor movement to be used.

Hot Potatoes

Supplies: One to three balls or beanbags for each group

Skill: Object handling

Group players in small circles (8 to 12 per circle) so objects can be passed from one to another around the circle. Balls or beanbags or both are passed around the circle. The teacher or a selected student, who is standing with their back to the class randomly shouts, "stop!" The point of the game is to avoid being the person who passes the object to the person who caught it when the signal occurs. If this happens, the player(s) who passed the object gets up and moves to the next circle. Begin the game with one object and gradually add objects if the class is capable. Call out "Reverse" to signal a change in the direction the object is passed.

Popcorn

Supplies: None

Skills: Curling, stretching, jumping

Half of the class is designated as popcorn; these players crouch down in the center of a circle formed by the rest of the class. The circle children, also crouching, represent the heat. One of them is designated the leader, and his actions serve as a guide to the other children. The circle children gradually rise to a standing position, extend their arms overhead, and shake them vigorously to indicate the intensifying heat. In the meantime, the popcorn in the center starts to pop. This should begin at a slow pace and increase in speed and height as the heat is applied. In the final stages, children are popping up rapidly. After a time, the groups change places and the action is repeated.

Dynamic Physical Education for Elementary School Children
Fundamental Skills Using Benches
Level I – Week 20

Objectives:
To be able to lead other students in simple locomotor movements
To learn new exercises utilizing a jump rope
To pull one's body weight across a bench
To balance one's body while moving on a bench

Equipment Required:
Music for Jump Rope Exercises
One jump rope for each student
6 Benches
Plastic gallon jugs and 8" foam rubber balls

Instructional Activities	Teaching Hints

Introductory Activity -- New Leader Warm-Up

Place students in small groups (3-4). Groups move single file around the area, following a leader in the group. On signal, the last person moves to the head of the squad and become the leader. Various types of locomotor movements and exercises can be used by leaders to offer variety and challenge.

If students have trouble working small groups, teach the concept of leading and following by working with a partner.

Encourage variety of response.

Fitness Development Activity --Jump Rope Exercises

1. Jump rope – 45 seconds. If not able to jump, practice swinging the rope to the side while jumping
2. Place the rope on the floor and perform locomotor movements around and over the rope. Make different shapes and letters with the rope.
3. Jump rope – 45 seconds.
4. Hold the folded rope overhead. Sway from side to side. Twist right and left.
5. Jump rope – 45 seconds
6. Lie on back with rope held with outstretched arms toward ceiling. Bring up one leg at a time and touch the rope with toes. Lift both legs together. Sit up and try to hook the rope over the feet. Release and repeat.
7. Jump rope – 45 seconds
8. Touch toes with the folded rope.
9. Jump rope - 45 seconds.
10. Do Push-up variations with the rope folded and held between the hands.
11. Jump rope - 45 seconds.

Tape alternating segments (45 seconds in length) of silence and music (30 seconds) to signal duration of exercise. Music segments indicate aerobic activity with the jump ropes while intervals of silence announce using the jump ropes to enhance flexibility and strength development.

Space youngsters so they don't hit others with their rope.

Don't worry about non-jumpers. They will learn sooner or later. Give encouragement and keep them motivated.

Lesson Focus – Fundamental Skills Using Benches

Present activities from each of the categories so students receive a variety of skills to practice.

1. Animal walks on the bench:
   a. Seal walk
   b. Cat walk
   c. Lame dog walk
   d. Rabbit jump
   e. Choice activity
2. Locomotor movements:
   a. Skip on the bench.
   b. Gallop on the bench.
   c. Step on and off the bench.
   d. Jump on and off the bench.
   e. Hop on and off the bench.
   f. Choice activity
3. Pulls--Pull body along the bench in various positions.
   a. Prone position--head first, feet first.
   b. Supine position--head first, feet first.
   c. Side position--head first, feet first.
4. Pushes--same as above activity except push with the arms in all positions.

1. Mats should be placed at the ends of the benches to facilitate the dismount and various rolls and stunts executed after the dismount.

2. Four to five children is the maximum number that should be assigned to one bench.

3. The child next in turn should begin when the performer ahead is about three-quarters of the way across the bench.

4. All activities on the benches should be broken down into three distinct parts: the approach to and mounting of the bench, the actual activity on the bench, and the dismount from the bench.

5. Movements alongside the benches--proceed alongside the bench in the following positions. (Keep the limbs on the floor as far away as possible from the bench to achieve maximum effort.)
   a. Prone position--hands on bench.
   b. Supine position--hands on bench.
   c. Turn over--proceed along bench changing from prone to supine positions with hands on bench.
   d. All of the above positions performed with the feet on the bench.
6. Scooter movements--sit on bench and proceed along bench without using hands.
   a. Regular scooter--feet leading.
   b. Reverse scooter--legs trailing.
   c. Seat walk--walk on the buttocks.

5. When students have completed their movement across the bench, perform a jump dismount to complete the activity. Some examples of dismounts are:
   a. Single jump--forward or backward.
   b. Jump with turns--1/2 or 3/4 or full.
   c. Jackknife (Pike).
   d. Jackknife split (straddle).
   e. Jump and follow with a log or forward roll.

Game Activity

Bottle Kick Ball

Supplies: Plastic gallon jugs and 8-in. foam balls

Skills: Kicking, trapping

Players form a large circle around 10 to 12 plastic gallon jugs (bowling pins) standing in the middle of the circle. Players kick the balls and try to knock over the bottles. Use as many foam balls as necessary to keep all children active. If the group is large, make more than one circle of players.

Hill Dill

Supplies: None

Skills: Running, dodging

Two parallel lines are established 50 feet apart. Two or more players are chosen to be it and stand in the center between the lines. The remainder of the class stands on one of the parallel lines. The center player calls:

Hill Dill! Come over the hill,

Or else I'll catch you standing still!

Children run across the open space to the other line, while the one in the center tries to tag them. Anyone caught becomes a tagger. When children cross to the other line, they must wait for the next call. Start a new game when the majority of youngsters have been tagged.

Dynamic Physical Education for Elementary School Children
Movement Skills and Concepts (4)
Skipping, Catching with Scoops, Leading, and Body Support
Level I – Week 21

Objectives:

To perform locomotor movements

To be able to support the body weight with the arms.

To understand the concept of leading

To handle a ball with an implement

Equipment Required:

Music and tom-tom for Walk, Trot, & Jog

Scoops and balls

Instructional Activities	Teaching Hints

Introductory Activity -- Countdown

Standing with arms stretched overhead, students begin a countdown (10, 9, 8, 7, etc.) and gradually lower themselves into a crouched position with each count. On the words "blast off," they jump upwards and run in different directions. Students can run to a wall and return to their position. After students learn the activity, allow one of them to say, "Blast Off!"

Vary with challenges such as:
1. Different locomotor movements.
2. Change intervals of counting--slow, fast.

Fitness Development Activity --Walk, Trot, and Jog

Move to the following signals:
1. One drumbeat - walk.
2. Two drumbeats - trot.
3. Three drumbeats – jog.
4. Whistle - freeze and perform exercises.

Use various strength and flexibility exercises between bouts of walk, trot, and jog to allow students to recover aerobically. Examples are:
1. Bend and Twist
2. Sitting Stretch
3. Push-up challenges
4. Abdominal Challenges
5. Body Twist
6. Standing Hip Bend

Tape alternating segments (20 seconds in length) of silence and music to signal duration of exercise. Music segments indicate walk, trot, and jog activity. Intervals of silence signal performance of the strength and flexibility exercises.

Encourage students to move around the area in the same direction.

See Chapter 12 for a description of how to perform the exercises. Any exercises can be substituted. Try to exercise all bodyparts.

Lesson Focus -- Movement Skills and Concepts (4)

Fundamental Skill: Skipping
1. Skip in general space.
2. Vary the skip with exaggerated arm action and lifted knees; side-to-side motion; skip lightly; skip heavily.
3. Skip backward.
4. Clap as you skip.
5. Skip twice on the same side (double skip). Alternate double skips (two on each side).
6. Form a circle. Skip clockwise and counterclockwise.
7. Form by partners or by threes. Skip in general space.

Manipulative Skills: Scoop And Ball Activities
Individual Activities
1. Place the ball on the floor, scoop it up with the scoop.
2. Toss the ball upward and catch it with the scoop. Change scoop to the other hand and repeat.
3. Explore various ways of tossing the ball with the hand and catching in the scoop.
4. Throw the ball against a wall and catch with the scoop.
5. Throw the ball against the wall with the scoop and catch with the scoop.
6. Toss either with the hand or with the scoop and do a stunt before catching. Use heel click, quarter turn, touch scoop to floor.

Select a few activities from each of the categories so students receive a variety of skills to practice. When possible, integrate the manipulative skill activities with fundamental skill activities. A common error is to teach all the activities from one category. The reason for multiple groups of activities is to provide variety and enhance motivation.

For students having problems with skipping, be patient. To help them learn, slow down the movement to a step and hop on the same foot. Gradually speed it up to a skip.

Empty and washed plastic gallon jugs make excellent scoops. Cut out half of the bottle opposite the hand and a scoop remains.

Partner Activities
1. Roll the ball and pick up with the scoop.
2. Throw the ball back and forth, catching in the scoop.
3. Toss the ball on first bounce and catch in the scoop.
4. Repeat some of the previous activities and toss with the scoop.
5. Explore from other positions--sitting, kneeling, back to back, prone position.

Yarn balls are excellent with scoops when teaching control skill because they do not travel far when missed. Also, students can apply more force to the racquet which helps develop proper form.

Movement Concept: Supporting Body Weight with the Hands
1. Begin in all-fours position, practice taking the weight on the hands by kicking up the feet in a one-two fashion.
2. From standing position with the arms overhead, bring the hands to the floor and take the weight on the hands.
3. Take the weight successively on the hands by moving from the side as a preliminary to the cartwheel.
4. Have a partner hold your knees in a wheelbarrow position. Lift the legs as high as possible. May need to shift hands underneath.

If these activities are too difficult for some children, have them start on all fours and gently kick the feet off the floor.

When using partner activities that are weight bearing, match them so they are similar in weight.

Movement Concept: Leading with Different Body Parts
Children move across the space as indicated:
1. Move across with one arm leading.
2. Now a different movement with the other arm leading.
3. Repeat 1 with one foot leading.
4. Repeat 2 with other fool leading.
5. Move so one arm and one foot are leading.
6. Show us a movement where the shoulder leads.
7. How about a movement where one side leads?
8. Show a movement along the floor where the foot is leading.
9. Can you move so your head leads the movement?
10. What other kinds of leading parts can you show?

Use different locomotor movements.

Use different qualities of movement such as speed or force. Encourage use of general and personal space when moving.

Allow students to develop their personal movement and direction.

Movement Concept: Body Support
1. Make a bridge using five, four, three, and two parts of the body.
2. Select the number of body parts you wish to use and see how many different bridges you can make from this base.
3. Select three different bridges and go from one to the next smoothly in sequence (sustained flow).
4. Work with a partner and make different kinds of bridges.
5. Have your partner go under your bridge.

Bridges are an excellent way to begin learning about supporting body weight.

Emphasize creatively changing from one type of bridge to another.

When working with a partner, avoid touching each other.

Game Activity

Flowers and Wind
Supplies: None
Skill: Running

Two parallel lines long enough to accommodate the class are drawn about 30 feet apart. Children are divided into two groups. One group is the flowers and the other the wind. Each of the teams takes a position on one of the lines and faces the other team. The flowers secretly select the name of a common flower. When ready, they walk over to the other line and stand about 3 feet away from the wind. The players on the wind team begin to call out flower names—trying to guess the flower chosen. When the flower has been guessed, the flowers run to their goal line, chased by the players of the other team. Any player caught must join the other side. Reverse the roles and repeat the game. If one side has trouble guessing, give a clue.

Mousetrap
Supplies: None
Skills: Skipping, running, dodging

Half of the class forms a circle with hands joined, facing the center. This is the trap. The other half of the class is on the outside of the circle. These are the mice. Three signals are given for the game. These can be word cues or other signals. On the first signal, the mice skip around, outside the circle, playing happily. On the second signal, the trap is opened. (The circle players raise their joined hands to form arches.) The mice run in and out of the trap. The third signal signals the trap to snap shut. (The arms come down.) All mice caught in the trap join the circle. The game is repeated until most of the mice are caught. The players exchange places and the game begins anew.

Dynamic Physical Education for Elementary School Children
Movement Skills and Concepts (5)
Hopping, Hoop Activities, and Body Shapes/Letters
Level I – Week 22

Objectives:
To cooperatively play tag games and maintain body control
To hop continuously while performing a variety of challenges
To be able to recognize different shapes and make them with their body

Equipment Required:
Tape for Fitness Challenges
One hoop for each child
10-12 foam rubber balls (8")

Instructional Activities	Teaching Hints
Introductory Activity -- Tag Games	

Use a tag game youngsters enjoy to offer children immediate activity Some suggestions are:
1. Skunk
2. Stork
3. Stoop
4. Nose and Toe

Teach moving under control. Students should understand that they should seldom run as fast as possible in order to prevent collisions.

Use different locomotor movements.

Fitness Development Activity --Fitness Challenges

Alternate locomotor movements with strength and flexibility challenges. Repeat the challenges as necessary.

Locomotor Movement: Walk for 30 seconds.

Flexibility and Trunk Development Challenges
1. Bend in different directions.
2. Stretch slowly and return quickly.
3. Combine bending and stretching movements.
4. Sway back and forth.
5. Twist one body part; add body parts.
6. Make your body move in a large circle.
7. In a sitting position, wave your legs at a friend; make circles with your legs.

Locomotor Movement: Skip for 30 seconds.

Upper Body Strength Challenges
In a push-up position, do the following challenges:
1. Lift one foot; the other foot.
2. Wave at a friend; wave with the other arm.
3. Scratch your back with one hand; use the other hand.
4. Walk your feet to your hands.
5. Turn over and face the ceiling; shake a leg; Crab Walk.

Locomotor Movement: Jog for 30 seconds.

Abdominal Development
From a supine position:
1. Lift your head and look at your toes.
2. Lift your knees to your chest.
3. Wave your legs at a friend. From a sitting position:
1. Slowly lay down with hands on tummy.
2. Lift legs and touch toes.

Locomotor Movement: Run and leap for 30 seconds.

Tape alternating segments (30 seconds in length) of silence and music to signal duration of exercise. Music segments indicate doing the locomotor movements while intervals of silence announce performing the strength and flexibility challenges

Students select the fitness challenge they feel capable of performing. This implies that not all youngsters are required to do the same workload. Children differ and their ability to perform fitness workloads differs. Make fitness a personal challenge.

Because students can select activities they feel able to do, there is little reason for not trying.

If students do not remember the various challenges, cue them by calling out a number of the activities. They can select one they enjoy.

Use different qualities of movement such as giant skips, quick gallops, tiny jogging steps, etc.

Animal walks can be substituted for locomotor movements.

Fundamental Skill: Hopping

1. Hopping (Hopping is done on one foot only)
   a. Hop in place lightly, changing the feet at will.
   b. Hop numbered sequences, right and left: 1-1, 2-2, 3-3, 4-4, 5-5, 1-2, 2-1, 2-3, 3-2 (hop in place).
   c. Hop, increasing height, reverse.
   d. From your spot, take two, three, or four hops out, turn around and hop back on other foot. How much space can you cover?
   e. Hop on one foot, do a heel and toe pattern with the other. Can you change feet each time doing this?
   f. Pick two spots away from you. Hop in place, then move to one spot. Hop in place, then to the other. Return to spot.
   g. Hop forward, backward, sideways.
   h. Hop different patterns--square, triangle, circle, figure-eight, diamond, etc.
   i. Explore different positions in which you can hold the foot while hopping.
   j. Hold the free foot in different positions while hopping.
   k. Hop with the body in different leaning positions--forward, sideways, backward.
   l. Hop lightly, heavily.
   m. While hopping, touch the floor with either or both hands.
   n. Hop back and forth over a board or line, moving down the line.
   o. Trace out letters or numbers. Write your name hopping.
   p. Do quarter or half turns while hopping.

Manipulative Skills: Floor Targets and Hula Hooping

1. Jump in an out of the hoop.
2. Work with a partner and follow the leader through two hoops.
3. Jump in an out of a hoop held by a friend.
4. Hula hoop around the waist.
5. Hula hoop around the hands and arms, the neck, or legs (on back position).
6. Exploratory activity.

Movement Concept: Body Shapes

Possibilities include: Long or short; wide or narrow; straight or twisted; stretched or curled; large or small.

1. Show me a _____ (use terms above) shape.
2. When I say "change," go from a _____ shape to a _____ shape (vary these).
3. Explore symmetrical and asymmetrical. Take one of the above and make it symmetrical. Then change the same to an asymmetrical shape.
4. Explore other kinds of shapes.
5. Contrasting shapes. Do one kind of shape and its contrast. Or name a shape with its contrast or opposite.

Movement Concept: Letters with the Body

1. Make letters standing.
2. Make letters lying on the floor.
3. Divide class into two sets of groups: one group makes a letter and the other names it. Give only one guess. Change groups.
4. Make simple words of two letters or three letters, using one child per letter.
5. Form numbers of two digits.

Select a few activities from each of the categories so students receive a variety of skills to practice. When possible, integrate the manipulative skill activities with fundamental skill activities. A common error is to teach all the activities from one category. The reason for multiple groups of activities is to provide variety and enhance motivation.

Use instructional cues for hopping such as:

"Stay on your toes."

"Swing your arms upward."

"Use your arms for balance."

Change feet regularly so students learn to hop on both. Also, a little hopping goes a long ways. Children fatigue quickly.

Place the hoops around the perimeter of the area. On signal, students move to acquire a hoop and return performing a specified activity.

Teach what the shapes are like to make sure students know what they are. After they have been learned, start to encourage quick response to the shape commands.

Allow students time to think about the shapes of the letters and numbers.

Printing large letters on cards can help youngsters visualize the desired shape.

Rollee Pollee

Supplies: Many 8" foam balls

Skills: Ball rolling, dodging

Half of the class forms a circle; the other half is in the center. Balls are given to circle players. The circle players roll the balls at the feet and shoes of the center players, trying to touch them with a ball. The center players move around to avoid the balls. A center player who is touched leaves the center and joins the circle. After a period of time or when all of the children have been touched with a ball, teams trade places.

If a specified time limit is used, the team having the fewer players hit wins, or the team that puts out all of the opponents in the shorter time wins. Balls that stop in the center are dead and must be taken back to the circle before being put into play again. The preferable procedure is to have the player who recovers a ball roll it to a teammate rather than return to place

Stop Ball

Supplies: A ball

Skills: Tossing, catching

The class is divided into small circles with 5 to 7 players. One player, with their hands over their eyes, stands in the center of the circle. A ball is tossed clockwise or counterclockwise from player to player around the circle. Failing to catch the ball or making a bad toss incurs a penalty. That player takes one long step backward and stays out of the game for one turn. At a time of her own selection, the center player calls, "Stop." The player caught with the ball (or the ball coming to her) steps back and stays out for one turn. The center player should be allowed two or three turns and then changed.

Dynamic Physical Education for Elementary School Children
Movement Skills and Concepts Using Jump Rope Patterns (6)
Level I – Week 23

Objectives:
To understand and demonstrate the various factors of movement
To perform locomotor movements using a rope as a prop
To jump a self-turned rope
To make different letters, numbers, and shapes with a rope

Equipment Required:
Music for Circuit Training
One individual jump rope for each child

Instructional Activities	Teaching Hints

Introductory Activity -- Movement Varieties

Move using a basic locomotor movement (i.e., walking, jumping, hopping, skipping, galloping). Then add variety to the movement by asking students to respond to the following factors:
1. Level--low, high, in between.
2. Direction--straight, zigzag, circular, curved, forward, backward, upward, downward.
3. Size--large, tiny, medium movements.
4. Patterns--forming squares, diamonds, triangles, circles, figure-eights.
5. Speed--slow, fast, accelerate.

Use scatter formation.

Emphasize and reinforce creative responses.

Explain concepts of level, direction, size, and speed. Short explanations laced with activity allow students time to recover.

Fitness Development Activity –Circuit Training

Make signs, put them on cones and place around the perimeter of the teaching area. Students perform the exercise specified at each station while the music is playing.
1. Tortoise and Hare
2. Curl-up variations
3. Hula Hooping on arms
4. Standing Hip Bend
5. Agility run--run back and forth between two designated lines
6. Push-up variations
7. Crab Walk
8. Bend and Twist

Tape alternating segments of silence and music to signal duration of exercise. Music segments (begin at 30 seconds) indicate activity at each station while intervals of silence (10 seconds) announce it is time to stop and move forward to the next station.

Place an equal number of students at each station.

Use activities at the stations that students already know how to perform.

Lesson Focus - Movement Skills and Concepts Using Rope Patterns (6)

A. Rope Patterns
Lay rope lengthwise on floor.
1. Walk as on a balance beam.
   a. Forward
   b. Backward
   c. Sideways
2. Jump/hop down length and back.
   a. Vary time--slow, fast, accelerate, decelerate, even, uneven
   b. Vary levels and force--light, heavy, high to low.
3. Other locomotor movements.
   a. Crisscross
   b. Jumps with one-half turn
   c. Allow student choice
4. Imitate animals.
5. Crouch jumps.
   a. Various combinations; forward, backward, sideways.
   b. Allow exploration.
6. Put rope in shapes, letters, numbers.
   a. Move in and out of figures.
   b. Add movements, keeping the body inside figure.

Alternate rope pattern activities with rope jumping activities. This offers students time for recovery after rope jumping.

Encourage using both sides of the body. If hopping on the right foot, give equal time to the left foot.

If youngsters have trouble jumping or hopping over the rope, encourage them to step or leap over.

Select some children to demonstrate a movement shape or letter. When asking students to demonstrate, be sure they are capable to avoid embarrassment.

7. Partner work.
    a. Make figure with two ropes. Move in and out of figure.
    b. Using one rope, do follow activity. Take turns.

B. Rope Jumping
1. Hold rope. Jump in time.
2. Perform the slow-time and fast-time rhythm with the rope held in one hand and turned (propellers).
3. Jump the rope and practice slow to fast time.
4. Introduce a few basic steps.
    a. Two-step basic
    b. Alternating basic
    c. Backwards
    d. One foot

This lesson should introduce youngsters to rope jumping. It should not be too instructional, but should be used for the purpose of giving them a positive introduction to rope jumping. Instruction will come in a later lesson.

Game Activity

Change Sides
    Supplies: None
    Skill: Body management
    Identify two parallel lines 30 feet apart with half of the class on each line. On signal, all players cross to the other line, face the center, and stand at attention. The first group to do all three things correctly wins a point. Children must be cautioned to use care when passing through the opposite group. They should be spaced well along each line; this allows room for them to move through each group. Vary the locomotor movements used by specifying skipping, hopping, long steps, sliding, and other varieties of movement. The position to be assumed at the finish can be varied also.

Where's My Partner?
    Supplies: None
    Skills: Fundamental locomotor movements
    Children are in a double circle facing a partner. The inside circle has two or three more players than the outside. When the signal is given, the circles skip (or walk, run, hop, or gallop) to the right. This means that they are skipping in opposite directions. On the command "Halt," the circles face each other to find partners. The players left without a partner go to the mush pot (the center area of the circle) for one turn. The circles should be reversed after a time.
Variation: The game can also be played with music or a drumbeat. When the music stops, the players seek partners.

Colors
    Supplies: Colored paper (construction paper) cut in circles, squares, or triangles for markers
    Skills: Color or other perceptual concepts, running
    Use five or six different-colored markers with a number of children having the same color. Children start the game standing or seated in a circle each with a marker in front of them. The teacher (or another player) calls out a color. Everyone having that color runs counterclockwise around the circle and back to place. The first player seated upright and motionless is declared the winner. Different kinds of locomotor movement can be specified, such as skipping, galloping, walking, and so on. After a period of play, leave the markers on the floor and have the class move one place to the left so players have a different color.
Variation: Shapes (e.g., circles, triangles, squares, rectangles, stars, and diamonds) can be used instead of colors, as can numbers or other articles or categories, such as animals, birds, or fish.

Dynamic Physical Education for Elementary School Children
Partner Manipulative Activities Using Balls
Level I – Week 24

Objectives:
To catch a passed ball from a partner
To pass a ball to a partner (both chest and bounce pass)
To dribble a ball

Equipment Required:
Music for Astronaut Exercises
One 8½" playground ball for each pair of students
Bowling pins for targets (optional)

Instructional Activities	Teaching Hints

Introductory Activity -- Airplanes

Children pretend to be airplanes. They take off, zoom with arms out, swoop, turn, and glide. On signal, they drop to the floor in prone position. To takeoff again, they must "restart" their engines by doing a couple of push-up challenges while making a "vroom, vroom" engine sound.

Encourage creativity by naming different types of airplanes and helicopters.

Use different locomotor movements.

Fitness Development Activity --Astronaut Exercises

Walk, do Arm Circles	30 seconds
Flexibility and Trunk Development Challenges	30 seconds
Skip forward, backwards, and sideways	30 seconds
Upper Body Strength Challenges	30 seconds
Slide; change lead leg	30 seconds
Abdominal Development Challenges	30 seconds
Jump like a Pogo Stick	30 seconds
Upper Body Strength Challenges	30 seconds
Trot lightly in different directions	30 seconds
Flexibility and Trunk Development Challenges	30 seconds
Gallop Backwards	30 seconds

Cool down with stretching and walking.

Tape alternating segments of silence and music to signal duration of exercise. Music segments (30 seconds) indicate aerobic activity while intervals of silence (30 seconds) signal flexibility and strength development activities.

See Chapter 12 for a description of how to perform challenge activities.

Allow students to adjust the workload to an intensity that is consistent with their ability level.

Lesson Focus – Partner Manipulative Activities Using Balls

1. Rolling a ball back and forth to a partner.
   a. Practice different deliveries, i.e., two-handed, right and left.
   b. Roll at targets such as bowling pins or through the legs of a partner.
2. Dribbling and Passing Skills.
   a. One player guards and the other dribbles. Change on signal. Practice with both hands.
   b. Practice passing back and forth to a partner. Use the chest pass.
   c. Pass back and forth using the bounce pass.
   d. Combine passing and dribbling. Dribble the ball 3 times and pass to partner.
3. Rolling and Passing from different positions.
   a. Try rolling and passing skills from different positions, i.e., kneeling, sitting.
4. Passing and Moving
   a. One child remains in place and passes to the other child, who is moving. The moving child can trace different patterns, such as back and forth between two spots or in a circle around the stationary child.
   b. Practice different kinds of throws and passes as both children move in different patterns.
   c. Practice foot skills of dribbling and passing.
   d. Partners hold the ball between their bodies without using the hands or arms. Experiment with different ways to move together.
   d. Carrying a ball, run in different directions while partner follows. On signal, toss the ball upward so that the child following can catch it. Now change places and repeat the activity.
5. Try following activity; one partner leads a ball activity and the other follows.
6. Allow time for students to explore and create.

Encourage proper skill performance by using instructional cues such as:
"Keep your eyes on the ball."
"Catch the ball with the fingertips."
"Use opposition when passing the ball."

When catching, soft receipt of the ball is achieved by "giving" with the hands and arms. The hands should reach out somewhat to receive the ball and then cushion the impact by bringing the ball toward the body.

To catch a throw above the waist, the hands should be positioned so that the thumbs are together. To receive a throw below the waist, the little fingers should be kept toward each other and the thumbs kept out.

When throwing to a partner, unless otherwise specified, the throw should reach the partner at about chest height. At times, different target points should be specified---high, low, right, left, etc.

Game Activity

Animal Tag

Supplies: None

Skills: Imagery, running, dodging

Two parallel lines are drawn about 40 feet apart. Children are divided into two groups, each of which takes a position on one of the lines. Children in one group get together with their leader and decide what animal they wish to imitate. Having selected the animal, they move over to within 5 feet or so of the other line. There they imitate the animal, and the other group tries to guess the animal correctly. If the guess is correct, they chase the first group back to its line, trying to tag as many as possible. Those caught must go over to the other team. The second group then selects an animal, and the roles are reversed. If the guessing team cannot guess the animal, however, the performing team gets another try. To avoid confusion, children must raise their hands to take turns at naming the animal. Otherwise, many false chases will occur. If children have trouble guessing, the leader of the performing team can give the initial of the animal.

Aviator

Supplies: None

Skills: Running, locomotor movements, stopping

Players are parked (in push-up position) at one end of the playing area. The air traffic controller (ATC) is in front of the players and calls out, "Aviators aviators, take off!" Youngsters take off and move like airplanes to the opposite side of the area. The first person to move to the other side and land the plane (get into push-up position facing the ATC) is declared the new ATC. If the ATC yells out some type of stormy weather, all planes must return to the starting line and resume the parked position. Examples of stormy weather commands are lightning, thunder, hurricane, and tornado. Each ATC is allowed to give stormy weather warnings once.

Toe to Toe

Supplies: None

Skills: Fundamental locomotor movements

Youngsters perform a locomotor movement around the area. On signal, each child must find a partner and stand toe to toe (one foot only) with that person. An important skill is to take the nearest person for a partner without searching for a friend. Youngsters who can't find a partner within their immediate area must run quickly to the center of the area (use a marking spot or cone) to find a partner. The goal is to find a nearby partner as quickly as possible and avoid being the last pair formed. If the number of youngsters playing is uneven, the teacher can join in and play. Change locomotor movements often.

Dynamic Physical Education for Elementary School Children
Fundamental Skills Using Jumping Boxes
Level I – Week 25

Objectives:
To perform a variety of locomotor movements by choice
To perform balance skills while manipulating an object
To manage body weight in space
To absorb force when making contact with the floor

Equipment Required:
Secret Movement cards
Six 16" jumping boxes
Six 8" jumping boxes
Ball for game

Instructional Activities	Teaching Hints

Introductory Activity -- Secret Movement

Many different movements and/or combinations of movements are written on large flash cards. Without looking, the teacher or a student selects a card and directs the class to "show me" the secret movement. Youngsters select a movement and perform it until signaled to stop. The card is then revealed to the class to see which youngsters, by chance, guessed the secret movement.

Use the basic locomotor movements when first teaching Secret Movements.

Use a variety of movements such as animal walks, stunts, exercises, and sport imitation activities for variety.

Fitness Development Activity --Fitness Games and Challenges

1. Stoop Tag.
2. Freeze; perform stretching activities.
3. Back-to-Back Tag.
4. Freeze; perform Abdominal Challenges using Curl-up variations.
5. Balance Tag.
6. Freeze; perform Arm-Upper Body Strength Challenges using Push-up variations.
7. Elbow Swing Tag.
8. Freeze; perform Trunk Development challenges.
9. Color Tag.

Alternate simple tag games with fitness challenge activities. Exercise all parts of the body including upper body and abdominal strength and flexibility.

Assign many students to be it. Allow a student to quit being "it" if they so choose.

Lesson Focus – Fundamental Skills Using Jumping Boxes

Approaches to the Boxes
1. Basic movements such as skip, hop, jump, etc.
2. Various animal walks.
3. Stunts like heel clicks, half turns, and scooter movements can be used to approach the box.

Activities fall into three basic categories: approaching the box, mounting the box, and dismounting the box. Combining these variables can create a wide range of activities.

Mounting the Box
1. Step, jump, leap or hop onto the box.
2. Rabbit jump or leap frog onto the box.

Attention should be given to landing in proper form. Lightness, bent-knee action, balance, and body control should be stressed.

Dismounting
1. Jump off with a quarter, half and full turn.
2. Jump off forward, backward and sideways.
3. Jump off with different body shapes, i.e., stretch, curl, jack-knife.
4. Jump off followed by a forward or backward roll.
5. Change the above dismounts by substituting a hop or leap in place of the jump.
6. Hold a hoop in front of the box. Have the rest of the squad jump through the hoop.

Mats should be used to cushion the landing.

No more than four or five children should be assigned to each series of boxes.

The use of hoops, wands, and balls can create additional challenges.

Challenge Activities
1. Crouch jump over the boxes.
2. Use a beanbag, toss in air, dismount and catch.
3. Dribble a playground ball while mounting and dismounting boxes.
4. Hula-hoop to the box, mount and dismount without losing control of hoop.
5. Jump over a wand on the dismount.
6. Jump-rope to the box. Mount and dismount maintaining jumping rope.

Return activities work well with boxes. Children should strive for height and learn to relax as they go through space.

Squirrel in the Trees

Supplies: None

Skills: Fundamental locomotor movements

A number of trees are formed by two players facing each other and holding hands or putting hands on each other's shoulders. A squirrel is in the center of each tree, and one or two extra squirrels are outside. On signal, the trees open up and let the squirrels move around the area. The trees also stay together and move throughout the area. On signal, the trees freeze in place and the squirrels find any available tree. Only one squirrel is allowed in a tree. Rotation is necessary so all students get to be a squirrel. Once the squirrels are in a tree, ask them to face one of the tree players. The person they are facing becomes their partner for a tree and the other person becomes a new squirrel.

Stop Ball

Supplies: A ball

Skills: Tossing, catching

The class is divided into small circles with 5 to 7 players. One player, with their hands over their eyes, stands in the center of the circle. A ball is tossed clockwise or counterclockwise from player to player around the circle. Failing to catch the ball or making a bad toss incurs a penalty. That player takes one long step backward and stays out of the game for one turn. At a time of her own selection, the center player calls, "Stop." The player caught with the ball (or the ball coming to her) steps back and stays out for one turn. The center player should be allowed two or three turns and then changed.

Dynamic Physical Education for Elementary School Children
Movement Skills and Concepts (7)
Twisting, Turning, Stretching and Relaxing Movements
Level I – Week 26

Objectives:

To apply movement concepts such as body and space awareness, relationships, and qualities of movement to a variety of locomotor and body management skills

To combine locomotor and non-locomotor skills into movement themes, e.g., supporting body weight, bridges, receiving and transferring weight.

Equipment Required:

Music for Animal Movements

Teacher's choice of equipment for introductory activity and manipulative skills in the lesson focus

Instructional Activities	Teaching Hints

Introductory Activity -- Creative and Exploratory Opportunities

Put out enough equipment for all children to have a piece. Allow them to explore and create activities while moving. Another alternative is to have students work with a piece of equipment with a partner or small group.

Ask students to move and be active without being told what to do. Encourage independent thinking.

Fitness Development Activity -- Animal Movements and Fitness Challenges

1. Puppy Dog Walk --30 seconds.
2. Freeze; perform stretching activities.
3. Measuring Worm Walk--30 seconds
4. Freeze; perform abdominal development challenges.
5. Frog Jump--30 seconds.
6. Freeze; perform push-up position challenges.
7. Elephant Walk --30 seconds.
8. Freeze; perform stretching activities
9. Bear Walk--30 seconds.
10. Freeze; perform abdominal challenges.
11. Crab Walk--30 seconds.
12. Freeze and perform stretching and relaxing activities

Tape alternating segments (30 seconds in length) of silence and music to signal duration of exercise. Music segments indicate performing animal movements while intervals of silence announce doing the fitness challenges.

A variation is to place animal movement signs throughout the area and instruct students to move from sign to sign performing the appropriate animal movement each time they reach a new sign.

Lesson Focus Movement Skills and Concepts (7)

Fundamental Skill: Twisting

1. Glue your feet to the floor. Can you twist your body to the right and to the left? Can you twist slowly, quickly? Can you bend and twist at the same time? How far can you twist your hands back and forth?
2. Twist two parts of the body at the same time. Try three. More?
3. Can you twist one part of the body in one direction and another in a different direction?
4. Is it possible to twist the upper half of your body without twisting the lower part? How about the reverse?
5. Seated on the floor, what parts of the body can you twist?
6. Can you twist one part of the body around another? Why or why not?
7. Balance on one foot and twist your body. Can you bend and twist in this position?
8. Show different shapes that can be made using twisted body parts.

Fundamental Skill: Turning

1. Turn your body left and right with quarter and half turns. Turn clockwise and counterclockwise.
2. Post compass directions on the walls--north, south, east, and west. Have children face the correct direction on call. Introduce some in-between directions--northwest, southeast, etc.
3. Can you stand on one foot and turn around slowly, quickly, with a series of small hops?

Select a few activities from each of the categories so students receive a variety of skills to practice. When possible, integrate the manipulative skill activities with fundamental skill activities. A common error is to teach all the activities from one category. The reason for multiple groups of activities is to provide variety and enhance motivation.

Teach youngsters the difference between a twist and turn. Twisting is rotating a selected body part around it own long axis. Twisting involves movement around the body part itself while turning focuses on the space in which the body turns. Turning here involves movement of the entire body.

Emphasize maintaining balance while performing turning activities.

4. Show me how you can cross your legs with a turn and then sit down. Can you get up without moving your feet too much.

5. When you hear the signal, turn completely around one. Next time turn the other way. Now try with two full turns; three.

6. Lie on your tummy and turn yourself around in an arc. Try seated position.

Perform twisting and turning movements in both directions. Also, try the movements in sitting or on tummy.

Fundamental Skill: Rocking

1. How many different ways can your rock? Which part of the body is used to rock the highest?

2. Select a part of the body and show me how you ca rock smoothly and slowly. How about quickly and smoothly?

3. Can you rock like a rocking chair?

4. Lie on your back and rock. Point both hands and feet toward the ceiling and rock on the back.

5. Lie on your tummy and rock. Rock as high as you can. Can you hold your ankles and make giant rocks?

6. Can you rock in a standing position? Try forward, sideways and diagonal rocking directions.

7. Select a position where you can rock and twist at the same time.

8. Who can lie on his or her back, with knees up and rock side to side?

Make rocking a smooth and steady rhythm. It should be a controlled movement.

Rocking is usually best done when the body surface is rounded. Discuss how the body can be rounded to make rocking easier.

Manipulative Skill: Student's Choice

Select one or more manipulative activities that need additional developing with respect to the children's needs and progress. During the week's work, a different activity might be scheduled each individual day.

Since equipment was placed out for the introductory activity, use it for the manipulative skill.

Movement Concept: Stretching and Curling

1. While on your feet, show us a stretched position. A curled position.

2. Go very slowly from your stretched position to the curled one you select. Go rapidly.

3. Keeping one foot in place (on a spot), show how far you can stretch in different directions.

4. Show us a straight (regular) curled position. A twisted curled position. A tight curled position.

5. Select three different curled positions. On signal, go from one to the other rapidly. Repeat with stretch positions.

6. Explore and show the different ways that the body can support itself in curled positions.

Stretching and curling are somewhat opposite movements.

Encourage stretching through the full range of movement. The stretch is done slowly and smoothly.

Encourage holding the stretch for 6-10 seconds.

Movement Concept: Tension and Relaxation

1. Make yourself as tense as possible. Now relax.

2. Take a deep breath, hold it tight. Expel the air and relax.

3. Tense and reach as high as you can; slowly relax and droop to the floor.

4. Show how you can tense different parts of the body.

5. Tense one part of the body and relax another. Shift the tenseness to the relaxes part and vice-versa.

6. Press your fingers hard against your tensed abdominal muscles. Take your fists and best lightly against the tensed position. Relax. Repeat.

7. Move forward, stop suddenly in a tensed position. Relax. Repeat.

Relaxation activities are an excellent way to finish the lesson. Help youngsters learn to recognize when a limb and muscles are relaxed.

A quiet atmosphere facilitates relaxing. Soft voices encourage students to "wind down."

Midnight

Supplies: None

Skills: Running, dodging

A safety line is established about 40 feet from a den in which two or three players, the foxes, are standing. The others stand behind the safety line and ask, "What time is it, Mr. Fox?" One of the foxes is designated to answer in various fashions, such as "one o' clock," "four o' clock," etc. When the fox says a certain time, the class walks forward that number of steps. For example, if the fox says, "six o'clock" the class has to move forward six steps. The fox continues to draw the players toward him. At some point, the fox answers the question by saying "Midnight," and chases the others back to the safety line. Any player who is caught becomes a fox in the den and helps to catch others.

Twins (Triplets)

Supplies: None

Skills: Body management

Youngsters are scattered throughout the area with a partner (twin). Commands are given such as "Take three hops and two leaps" or "Walk backward four steps and three skips." When the pairs are adequately separated, the leader calls out, "Find your twin!" Players find their twin and stand frozen toe to toe. The goal is to not be the last pair to find each other and assume the frozen position. Assure students move away from each other during the movements. One alternative is to find a new twin each time. Another variation is to separate twins in opposite ends of the playing area.

Variation: The game is more challenging when played in groups of three (triplets). When using this variation, new partners should be selected each time.

Dynamic Physical Education for Elementary School Children
Rhythmic Movement Skills (3)
Level I – Week 27

Objectives:
To be able to lead other students in simple locomotor movements
To perform a variety of exercises using jump ropes
To move rhythmically and learn simple folk dances

Equipment Required:
Music for Jump Rope Exercises
Tom-tom
Music for rhythms
Equipment for mini-challenge course

Instructional Activities	Teaching Hints

Introductory Activity -- New Leader Warm-Up

Place students in small groups (3-4). Groups move single file around the area, following a leader in the group. On signal, the last person moves to the head of the squad and become the leader. Leaders can use various types of locomotor movements and/or exercises to offer variety and challenge.

If students have trouble working small groups, teach the concept of leading and following by working with a partner.

Encourage variety of response.

Fitness Development Activity --Jump Rope Exercises

1. Jump rope – 45 seconds. If not able to jump, practice swinging the rope to the side while jumping
2. Place the rope on the floor and perform locomotor movements around and over the rope. Make different shapes and letters with the rope.
3. Jump rope – 45 seconds.
4. Hold the folded rope overhead. Sway from side to side. Twist right and left.
5. Jump rope – 45 seconds
6. Lie on back with rope held with outstretched arms toward ceiling. Bring up one leg at a time and touch the rope with toes. Lift both legs together. Sit up and try to hook the rope over the feet. Release and repeat.
7. Jump rope – 45 seconds
8. Touch toes with the folded rope.
9. Jump rope - 45 seconds.
10. Do Push-up variations with the rope folded and held between the hands.
11. Jump rope - 45 seconds.

Tape alternating segments (45 seconds in length) of silence and music (30 seconds) to signal duration of exercise. Music segments indicate aerobic activity with the jump ropes while intervals of silence announce using the jump ropes to enhance flexibility and strength development.

Space youngsters so they don't hit others with their rope.

Don't worry about non-jumpers. They will learn sooner or later. Give encouragement and keep them motivated.

Lesson Focus -- Rhythmic Movement Skills (3)

Make dances easy for students to learn by implementing some of the following techniques:
1. Teach the dances without using partners.
2. Allow youngsters to move in any direction without left-right orientation.
3. Use scattered formation instead of circles.
4. Emphasize strong movements such as clapping and stamping to increase involvement.
5. Play the music at a slower speed when first learning the dance.
Teach a variety of dances rather than one or two in depth in case some students find it difficult to master a specific dance.

Shortnin' Bread (American)

Music Source: WWCD-7050; WWC-7050
Skills: Sliding, turning with a partner
Formation: Scattered with partner
Directions:

Measures	Action
1–2	Clap own hands
3–4	Pat partner's hands
5–6	Clap own hands
7–8	Slap own thighs
9–16	Repeat measures 1–8
17–20	Couples slide to the right holding hands.
21–24	Circle holding hands.
25–32	Repeat measures 17–24 moving to the left.

Children's Polka (German)

Music Source: WWCD-07042; WWC-07042

Formation: Single circle of couples, partners facing

Skill: Step-draw

Directions:

Measures	Action
1–2	Take two step-draw steps toward the center of the circle, ending with three steps in place. (Draw, draw, step, 2, 3)
3–4	Take two step-draw steps away from the center, ending with three steps in place. (Draw, draw, step, 2, 3)
5–8	Repeat the pattern of measures 1–4.
9	Slap own knees once with both hands; clap own hands once. (Slap, clap)
10	Clap both hands with partner three times. (Clap, 2, 3)
11–12	Repeat the pattern of measures 9 and 10.
13	Hop, placing one heel forward, and shake the forefinger at partner three times. (Scold, 2, 3)
14	Repeat the "scolding" pattern with the other foot and hand. (Scold, 2, 3)
15–16	Turn once around in place with four running steps and stamp three times in place. (Turn, 2, 3, 4; Stamp, 2, 3)

Jump Jim Jo (American)

Music Source: WWCD-1041

Skills: Jumping, running, draw step

Formation: Double circle, partners facing, both hands joined

Directions:

Measures	Action
1–2	Do two jumps sideward, progressing counterclockwise, followed by three quick jumps in place. (Slow, slow, fast, fast, fast)
3–4	Release hands and turn once around in place with four jumps (two jumps per measure). Finish facing partner and rejoin hands. (Jump, turn, 3, 4)
5	Take two sliding steps sideward, progressing counterclockwise. (Slide, slide)
6	Partners face counterclockwise with inside hands joined and tap three times with the toe of the outside foot. (Tap, tap, tap)
7–8	Take four running steps forward, then face partner, join both hands, and end with three jumps in place. (Run, 2, 3, 4; Jump, 2, 3)

Jingle Bells, Var. 1 (Dutch)

Music Source: Any version of Jingle Bells

Skills: Elbow swing, skipping, sliding

Formation: Double circle, partners facing, with both hands joined.

Directions:

Measures	Action
1–2	Partners take eight slides counterclockwise. (Slide, 2, 3, ... 8)
3–4	Partners turn so they are standing back to back, and take eight more slides in the line of direction. This move is best made by dropping the front hands and swinging the back hands forward until the dancers are standing back to back. They rejoin the hands that are now in back. Make this move with no loss of rhythm. (Slide, 2, 3, ... 8)
5–6	Repeat the action of measures 1 and 2. To get back to the face-to-face position, let go of the back hands and swing the front hands backward, allowing the bodies to pivot and face again. (Slide, 2, 3, ... 8)
7–8	Repeat measures 3 and 4. (Slide, 2, 3, ... 8)

Chorus	Action
1	Clap own hands three times. (Clap own, 2, 3)
2	Clap both hands with partner three times. (Clap both, 2, 3)
3	Clap own hands four times. (Clap own, 2, 3, 4)
4	Clap both hands with partner once. (Clap both)
5–8	Right elbow swing with partner. Partners hook right elbows and swing clockwise with eight skips. (Swing, 2, 3, 4, 5, 6, 7, 8)
9–12	Repeat the clapping sequence of measures 1–4.
13–16	Left elbow swing with partner for eight skips, finishing in the original starting position, ready to repeat the entire dance with the same partner; or do a left elbow swing with partner for four skips, which is once around, then all children in the inner circle skip forward to the outer dancer ahead and repeat the entire dance from the beginning with a new partner. (Swing, 2, 3, 4, 5, 6, 7, 8)

Seven Steps (Austrian)

Music Source: WWCD-FDN
Skills: Running, hopping
Formation: Double circle with couples facing counterclockwise with inside hands joined
Directions:

Measures	Action
2	Introduction
1-2	Start with outside foot and run 7 steps forward counterclockwise, and then pause with weight on outside foot on 8th count. (Run, 2, 3, 4, 5, 6, 7, pause)
3-4	Start with inside foot and run 7 steps backward (clockwise), and then pause with weight on inside foot on 8th count. (Run, back, 3, 4, 5, 6, 7, pause)
5	Release hands, turn away from partner and starting with the outside foot, run 3 steps away from partner and hop on the outside foot on the 4th count. (Away, 2, 3, hop)
6	Turn and face partner and starting with the inside foot, run 3 steps toward partner and then hop on the inside foot on the 4th count (Back, 2, 3, hop)
7-8	Partner with right hands joined run once around each other with 8 running steps clockwise to the right. (Swing, 2, 3, 4, 5, 6, 7, 8)
9	Release hands, turn away from partner and starting with the outside foot, run 3 steps away from partner; on the 4th count hop and turn on the outside foot to face diagonally toward new partner. (Apart, 2, 3, hop)
10	Take 3 running steps to a new partner (inside partner moves counterclockwise forward diagonally toward new partner and outside partner moves clockwise backward diagonally to next partner. Then hop on the 4th count
11-12	New partners run once around each other with 8 running steps counterclockwise with left hands joined. Finish in starting position with inside hands joined.

Perform the dance a total of 5 times.

Skip to My Lou (American)

Music Source: WWCD-7054; WWC 7054
Skills: Skipping, changing partners
Formation: Scattered with a partner
Directions: During the chorus, partners skip around the area. At the verse, everyone finds a new partner and continues skipping.

Game Activity

Jack Frost and Jane Thaw

Supplies: Any type of marker to distinguish Jack Frost, and Jane Thaw

Skills: Running, dodging, holding position

The class is scattered and moves to avoid being frozen (tagged) by 2 or 3 Jack Frosts, who carry a blue pinnie or streamer in one hand. Frozen children remain immobile until touched (thawed) by the Jane Thaws who are identified by a red streamer or pinnie.

Marching Ponies

Supplies: None

Skills: Marching, running

Two or three children are ringmasters and crouch in the center of a circle of ponies formed by the rest of the class. Two goal lines on opposite sides of the circle are established as safe areas. The ponies march around the circle counting out loud with each step. At a predetermined number of steps (whispered to the ringmasters by the teacher), the ringmasters jump up and attempt to tag the others before they can reach the safety lines. Anyone tagged joins the ringmaster in the center and helps catch others. Reorganize the game after six to eight children have been caught. Try other characterizations, such as lumbering elephants, jumping kangaroos, and the like.

Tag Games

Supplies: None

Skills: Fundamental locomotor movements, dodging

Tag is played in many ways. Children are scattered about the area. One child is it and chases the others, trying to tag one of them. When a tag is made, she says, "You're it." The new it chases other children. The following are suggested:

1. Object Tag. Touching a specified type of object (e.g., wood, iron) or the floor or an object of a specified color makes the runner safe.

2. Mimic Tag. Children can be safe by mimicking a particular action or pose.

3. Locomotor Tag. The child who is it specifies how the others should move--skipping, hopping, jumping. The tagger must use the same kind of movement.

Dynamic Physical Education for Elementary School Children
Gymnastics Skills (3)
Level I – Week 28

Objectives:
To identify and place body parts on an objects
To work cooperatively with others in the parachute activity
To understand safety considerations related to tumbling and inverted balances
To balance the body in a variety of situations
To perform individual self-testing stunts

Equipment Required:
One beanbag for each student
Music and parachute for fitness
Tumbling mats
Foam balls (8") for games

Instructional Activities	Teaching Hints

Introductory Activity -- Body Part Identification

Each student stands near a beanbag placed on the floor. Students are instructed to move over and around the beanbags on the floor. When a body part is called, students place the body part on the nearest beanbag.
Variations:
1. Use different movements.
2. Use different body parts
3. Call combinations of movements and body parts.

Students should be encouraged to move over and around as many beanbags as possible.

Challenge students by calling out a color. They then must avoid moving over and around all beanbags of that color.

Fitness Development Activity --Parachute Fitness

1. Jog while holding the chute in the left hand. (music)
2. Shake the chute. (no music)
3. Slide while holding the chute with both hands. (music)
4. Sit and perform curl-ups. (no music)
5. Skip. (music)
6. Freeze, face the center, and stretch the chute tightly. Hold for 8-12 seconds. Repeat. (no music)
7. Run in place while holding the chute taut at different levels. (music)
8. Sit with legs under the chute. Do a seat walk toward the center. Return to the perimeter. Repeat four to six times. (no music)
9. Place the chute on the ground. Jog away from the chute and return on signal. Repeat. (music)
10. Move into push-up position holding the chute with one hand. Shake the chute. (no music)
11. Shake the chute and jump in place. (music)
12. Lie on back with feet under the chute. Shake the chute with the feet. (no music)
13. Hop to the center of the chute and return. Repeat. (music)
14. Sit with feet under the chute. Stretch by touching the toes with the chute. Relax with other stretches while sitting. (no music)

Tape alternating segments of silence and music to signal duration of exercise. Music segments indicate aerobic activity with the parachute while intervals of silence announce using the chute to enhance flexibility and strength development.

Space youngsters evenly around the chute.

Use different grips (palms up, down, mixed).

All movements should be done under control. Some of the faster and stronger students will have to moderate their performance.

Lesson Focus – Gymnastics Skills (3)

Animal Movement
Siamese Twin Walk
  Stand back to back with a partner. Lock elbows. Walk forward, backward, and sideward in unison.

Tightrope Walk
  Select a line, board, or chalked line on the floor as the high wire. Pretend to be on the high wire and do various tasks with exaggerated loss and control of balance. Add tasks such as jumping rope, juggling balls, and riding a bicycle. Pretend to hold a parasol or a balancing pole while performing.

Lame Dog Walk
  Walk on both hands and one foot. Hold the other foot in the air as if injured. Walk a distance and change feet. The eyes should look forward. Move backward also and in other combinations. Try to move with an injured front leg.

Five groups of activities in this lesson ensure that youngsters receive a variety of experiences. Pick a few activities from each group and teach them alternately. For example, teach one or two animal movements, then a tumbling and inverted balance, followed by a balance stunt, etc. Give equal time to each group of activities

Crab Walk

Squat down and reach back, putting both hands on the floor without sitting down. With head, neck, and body level, walk forward, backward, and sideward.

Tumbling and Inverted Balances

Forward and Backward Roll review
   See previous Lessons Plans 7 and 15

Mountain Climber

This activity is similar to the exercise known as the Treadmill. The weight is taken on the hands with one foot forward and one foot extended back, similar to a sprinter's start. When ready, the performer switches foot position with both feet moving simultaneously.

Switcheroo

This Handstand lead-up activity begins in the front lunge position with the arms overhead. In one continuous movement, bend forward at the hips, place the hands on the mat, and invert the legs over the head. Scissor the legs in the air, and then reverse the position of the feet on the mat. Repeat in a smooth and continuous motion.

Balance Stunts

Forward Balance

Extend one leg backward until it is parallel to the floor. Keeping the eyes forward and the arms out to the sides, bend forward, balancing on the other leg. Hold for 5 seconds without moving. Reverse legs. (This is also called a Forward Scale.)

Hand-and-Knee Balance

Get down on all fours, taking the weight on the hands, knees, and feet, with toes pointed backward. Lift one hand and the opposite knee. Keep the free foot and hand from touching during the hold. Reverse hand and knee positions.

Single-Knee Balance

Perform the same action as in the previous stunt, but balance on one knee (and leg), with both arms outstretched to the sides. Use the other knee.

Individual Stunts

Turn-Over

From a front-leaning rest position, turn over so that the back is to the floor. The body should not touch the floor. Continue the turn until the original position is reassumed. Reverse the direction. Turn back and forth several times.

Thread the Needle

Touch the fingertips together in front of the body. Step through with one foot at a time while keeping the tips in contact. Step back to the original position. Next, lock the fingers in front of the body, and repeat the stunt. Finally, step through the clasped hands without touching the hands.

Heel Slap

From an erect position with hands at the sides, jump upward and slap both heels with the hands.

Pogo Stick

Pretend to be on a pogo stick by keeping a stiff body and jumping on the toes. Hold the hands in front as if grasping the stick. Progress in various directions.

Stunts and tumbling activities are self-testing activities in that each student has to overcome personal fear to accomplish many of the activities. This means that students should be encouraged to perform rather than forced.

Use many tumbling mats to avoid standing in line (3 or 4 students per mat).

Tumbling and inverted balances demand upper body strength. Therefore, students without adequate strength will not be able to safely complete the activities. Allow students to judge their ability.

This activity is a lead-up to the Handstand and teaches children to support the body weight briefly with the arms.

Overweight children are often at a disadvantage in this unit. Have empathy and patience for all students.

Balance activities are excellent activities to teach because all students are capable of performing them.

Encourage students to see how long they can hold the balances.

The body should be kept as rigid as possible throughout the turn.

Stress upward propelling action by the ankles and toes, with the body kept stiff, particularly at the knee joints.

Partner and Group Stunts
Double Top
  Face partner and join hands. Experiment to see which type of grip works best. With straight arms, lean away from each other and at the same time move the toes close to partner's. Spin around slowly in either direction, taking tiny steps.

Try a variation of the Double Top by doing it standing right side to right side.

Game Activity

Charlie Over the Water
  Supplies: A volleyball or playground ball
  Skills: Skipping, running, stopping, bowling (rolling)
  Place the class in circle formation. Two or more children are placed in the center of the circle, holding a ball. One of the center players is designated as Charlie (or Sally). The class skips around the circle to the following chant:

    Charlie over the water,
    Charlie over the sea,
    Charlie caught a bluebird,
    But can't catch me!

On the word me, the center players toss their balls in the air while the rest of the class runs and scatters throughout the area. When Charlie catches his ball, he shouts, "Stop!" All of the children stop immediately and must not move their feet. All of the center players roll their ball in an attempt to hit one of their scattered classmates. If a ball is rolled into a scattered player, that child becomes a new Charlie. If a center player misses, they remain in the center, and the game is repeated. If a center player misses twice, however, he picks another person to replace him.

Circle Straddle Ball
  Supplies: Two or more 8-in. foam balls
  Skills: Ball rolling, catching
  Children are in circle formation, facing toward the center. Each player stands in a wide straddle stance with the side of their foot against their neighbor's. Their hands are placed on the knees. Two or more balls are used. The object of the game is to roll a ball between the legs of other players before they get their hands down to stop the ball. Keep the circles small so students have more opportunities to handle the ball. Players must catch and roll the ball rather than batting it. Hands must be kept on the knees until a ball is rolled at them. After some practice, the following variation can be played.
  Variation: Two or more children are in the center, each with a ball. The other children are in the same formation as before. The center players try to roll the ball through the legs of any child, masking intent by using feints and changes of direction. Any child allowing the ball to go through becomes it.

Flowers and Wind
  Supplies: None
  Skill: Running
  Two parallel lines long enough to accommodate the class are drawn about 30 feet apart. Children are divided into two groups. One group is the flowers and the other the wind. Each of the teams takes a position on one of the lines and faces the other team. The flowers secretly select the name of a common flower. When ready, they walk over to the other line and stand about 3 feet away from the wind. The players on the wind team begin to call out flower names—trying to guess the flower chosen. When the flower has been guessed, the flowers run to their goal line, chased by the players of the other team. Any player caught must join the other side. Reverse the roles and repeat the game. If one side has trouble guessing, give a clue about the color or size of the flower or the first letter of its name.

Dynamic Physical Education for Elementary School Children
Individual Rope Jumping Skills
Level I – Week 29

Objectives:
To perform locomotor movements over a rope
To perform fitness development activities
To jump a self-turning rope
To identify body changes during jump roping activities

Equipment Required:
Music for Four Corners Fitness
One jump rope for each student
Four cones and signs for four corners
 fitness
10 beanbags

Instructional Activities	Teaching Hints

Introductory Activity -- Locomotor Movements with Equipment

Each student is given a jump rope and moves around the area using various basic locomotor movements. On signal, they drop the rope, and jump, hop, or leap over as many ropes as possible.

Any piece of equipment can be used.

If desired, students can turn and jump the rope.

Fitness Development Activity – Four Corners Fitness

Outline a large rectangle with a cone at each corner. Place signs with movement tasks on both sides of the cones. Youngsters move around the outside of the rectangle and change movements as they pass each sign. The following movement activities are suggested:

  Corner 1. Skipping/Jumping/Hopping
  Corner 2. Sliding/Galloping
  Corner 3. Various animal movements
  Corner 4. Sport imitation movements

Stop the class after 30 seconds of movement and perform fitness challenges (see Lesson 5).

Tape alternating segments of silence and music to signal duration of exercise. Music segments (30 seconds) indicate four corner aerobic activity while intervals of silence (45 seconds) announce performance of flexibility and strength development activities.

Allow students to select a fitness challenge they feel capable of performing. This implies that not all youngsters are required to do the same workload. Children differ and their ability to perform fitness workloads differs. Make fitness a personal challenge.

Lesson Focus -- Individual Rope Jumping Skills

The following are lead-up activities for beginning jumpers:
1. Clap hands to a tom-tom beat.
2. Jump in place to a beat without rope. Jump back and forth over rope on floor.
3. Hold both ends of the jump rope in one hand and turn it so a steady rhythm can be made through a consistent turn. Just before the rope hits the ground, the student should practice jumping.
4. Count the rhythm out loud to cue students when to jump.
5. Start jumping the rope one turn at a time--gradually increase the number of turns.
6. Try jogging and jumping rope. The even rhythm of running often makes it easier for some youngsters to jump the rope.

Introduce the two basic jumps:
1. Slow time. Jump twice each time the rope turns. One of the jumps is performed when the rope is overhead and serves as a preparatory jump.
2. Fast time. One jump each time the rope makes a complete turn. No preparatory jump is allowed.

Since rope is a physically taxing activity, it is suggested that time be allowed for recovery. One way to do this is to play less active games between bouts of rope jumping.

Background music with a strong beat can be motivating for youngsters.

Rope jumping is difficult to master. Be patient and understand that it may take some students a year or two to learn the activity.

Another way to rest students is to have them make shapes, letter, and names with their rope. Tail tag (fold the rope and place it in the waistband) requires trying to pull out the tail of others.

Tommy Tucker's Land

Supplies: About ten beanbags for each game

Skills: Dodging, running

Two or three youngsters, Tommy Tuckers (or Tammi Tuckers, if a girl), stand in the center of a 15-foot square where the beanbags are scattered. The Tuckers are guarding their land and treasure (beanbags). The other children chant:

I'm on Tommy Tucker's land,

Picking up gold and silver.

Children attempt to pick up as much of the treasure as they can while avoiding being tagged by the Tuckers. Any child who is tagged must return the treasure and retire from the game. The game is over when only one child is left or when all of the beanbags have been successfully filched. The teacher may wish to call a halt to the game earlier if a stalemate is reached. New Tuckers are selected.

Change Sides

Supplies: None

Skill: Body management

Identify two parallel lines 30 feet apart with half of the class on each line. On signal, all players cross to the other line, face the center, and stand at attention. The first group to do all three things correctly wins a point. Children must be cautioned to use care when passing through the opposite group. They should be spaced well along each line; this allows room for them to move through each group. Vary the locomotor movements used by specifying skipping, hopping, long steps, sliding, and other varieties of movement. The position to be assumed at the finish can be varied also.

Dynamic Physical Education for Elementary School Children
Movement Skills and Concepts (8)
Bending, Stretching, and Weight Transfer
Level I – Week 30

Objectives:
To understand the difference between bending and stretching
To bend and stretch in many different ways
To be able to transfer weight from one body part to another

Equipment Required:
One hoop for each student
Music for Walk, Trot, and Jog
Tom-tom or tambourine
Parachute

Instructional Activities	Teaching Hints
Introductory Activity -- Activity Using Hoops	
Issue a hoop for each child and encourage creative activity. If necessary, suggest some of the following challenges:	Have the class start moving upon entry into teaching area.
1. Run or hop with hoop, stop and jump the hoop.	Place the hoops around the perimeter of the area.
2. Run and roll the hoop like a tire.	
3. Spin the hoop and see how many times you can run around it.	
4. Roll the hoop and go through it.	While the class is moving, ask students to acquire a hoop and practice jumping in and out of it. Reverse the procedure to put the hoops away.
5. Combine two hoop activities with two locomotor movements.	
6. Try some of the activities learned in the previous hoop lesson focus.	

Fitness Development Activity -- Walk, Trot, and Jog	
Move to the following signals:	Tape alternating segments (20 seconds in length) of silence and music to signal duration of exercise. Music segments indicate walk, trot, and jog activity. Intervals of silence signal performance of the strength and flexibility exercises.
1. One drumbeat - walk.	
2. Two drumbeats - trot.	
3. Three drumbeats - jog.	
4. Whistle - freeze and perform exercises.	
Perform various strength and flexibility exercises between bouts of walk, trot, and jog. Examples are:	See Chapter 12 for a description of how to perform the exercises. Any exercises can be substituted. Try to maintain the balance of exercising all bodyparts.
1. Bend and Twist	
2. Sitting Stretch	
3. Push-up Challenges	
4. Abdominal Challenges	
5. Body Twist	
6. Standing Hip Bend	

Lesson Focus -- Movement Skills and Concepts (8)	
Fundamental Skill: Bending	Select a few activities from each of the categories so students receive a variety of skills to practice. When possible, integrate the manipulative skill activities with fundamental skill activities. A common error is to teach all the activities from one category. The reason for multiple groups of activities is to provide variety and enhance motivation.
1. Can you bend forward and up?	
2. Show how far you can bend backward. Can you see behind you on your backward bend?	
3. Combine a forward bend with a backward bend.	
4. Bend right and left. Try with your hands out to the sides. Overhead.	
5. Explore different ways the body can bend in a standing position.	
6. Sit down. How does this affect the bending possibilities of the body? Can you bend forward so your chin touches the floor?	
7. How many body parts (joints) can you bend below the waist? Above the waist?	
8. Who can lie down and bend two, three, four, five, six parts?	
9. Pick two similar parts. Bend one part while unbending the other.	Teach the various joints that are bent with different movements.
10. Pick two body parts (joints). Beginning at the same time, bend one quickly and one slowly. Bend one smoothly and one with jerks.	
11. Make a familiar shape by bending two body parts.	Explain the difference between bending and stretching.
12. Show how you can bend to look funny, happy, sad, slow, and quick.	

Fundamental Skill: Stretching

1. Stretch as many body parts as you can.
2. Stretch your arms, legs and feet in as many ways as possible.
3. At the same time stretch your feet in one direction and your arms in another.
4. Stretch one body part quickly, slowly, smoothly. Try another. Repeat.
5. Bend a body part and tell me which muscles or muscle groups are being stretched.
6. How many ways can you stretch while sitting on the floor?
7. Lie on the floor (prone or supine) and stretch two parts at once. Add others up to five.
8. From any position you like, see if you can at the same time stretch one part quickly (but smoothly) and one part slowly. Try one part quickly and two parts slowly.
9. From a kneeling position, set a mark on the floor where you can reach (stretch) without losing balance. Increase the distance.
10. Stretch your one arm while your other curls (bends). Reverse.
11. Can you stretch as tall as a giraffe? As wide as an elephant? As long as a snake?
12. Can you stretch the muscles in your chest, back, ankles, wrist, and fingers? Is this easy?

Encourage smooth controlled stretching. Use cues such as smoothly, gently, without jerking, etc.

Help youngsters understand what muscles are being stretched. They can tell by feeling which muscles are tight and hard.

Discuss why people stretch - to maintain flexibility and be able to have a full range of motion in all joints.

Discuss how adults stretch their muscles prior to vigorous activity.

Manipulative Skill: Parachute Activities

Use locomotor activities with the parachute as the prior activities (bending and stretching) are non-moving activities. See the previous Lesson Plan 10 for parachute activities.

The parachute activity should place emphasis on locomotor movements since the other parts of the lesson are somewhat inactive.

Movement Concept: Receiving and Transferring Weight

1. Project yourself high into the air and land. Try to land now with as little noise as possible.
2. Practice projecting yourself into the air and landing in different fashions.
3. Experiment with different landings where one or both hands touch the floor at the completion of the landing.
4. Experiment with turns as you land.
5. Begin your movement through the air with a short run and practice landings.
6. Take a position with the body balanced on two different parts. Transfer the weight to another two parts. Go from three to three.
7. Transfer the weight from a rounded part of the body to the hands and/or the feet. Go back to the rounded part.
8. Jump and land under control. Transfer the weight to another two body parts.
9. Explore different combinations of transferring the weight from various parts to others.

Weight transfer is used in movement to create force. Use throwing as an example of transferring the weight from the rear foot to the forward foot.

Bend the knees when absorbing force from weight transfer. Bent joints are like springs and reduce the chance of injury to joints.

Game Activity

Marching Ponies

Supplies: None
Skills: Marching, running

Two or three children are ringmasters and crouch in the center of a circle of ponies formed by the rest of the class. Two goal lines on opposite sides of the circle are established as safe areas. The ponies march around the circle counting out loud with each step. At a predetermined number of steps (whispered to the ringmasters by the teacher), the ringmasters jump up and attempt to tag the others before they can reach the safety lines. Anyone tagged joins the ringmaster in the center and helps catch others. Reorganize the game after six to eight children have been caught. Try other characterizations, such as lumbering elephants, jumping kangaroos, and the like.

Cat and Mice

Supplies: None
Skills: Running, dodging

Form a large circle. One child is the cat and four others are the mice. The cat and mice cannot leave the circle. On signal, the cat chases the mice inside the circle. As they are caught, the mice join the circle. The last mouse caught becomes the cat for the next round. Start at one point in the circle and progress around the circle to select mice so each child gets a chance to be in the center. Sometimes, one child has difficulty catching the last mouse or any of the mice. The point of the game is for all youngsters to be active. Change mice on a regular time interval rather than waiting until all mice are caught.

Dynamic Physical Education for Elementary School Children
Movement Skills and Concepts (9)
Leaping, Jump Rope Targets, and Levels/Speed
Level I – Week 31

Objectives:
To perform combinations of running and leaping steps
To move at different levels and speeds
To understand the concepts of acceleration and deceleration

Equipment Required:
Music and signs for Animal Movements
One jump rope for each child
Tom-tom
Colored paper shapes for game

Instructional Activities	Teaching Hints

Introductory Activity --Locomotor Movement Variations

Using the basic locomotor movements and try the following variations:
1. Changes in speed
2. Weight bearing on different parts of foot (toes, heels, sides of feet)
3. Change directions
4. Making different patterns (triangles, squares, etc.)

The locomotor movements are walking, running, galloping, skipping, hopping jumping, leaping, and sliding.

Encourage students to put together sequences of various locomotor movements.

Fitness Development Activity --Animal Movements and Fitness Challenges

1. Puppy Dog Walk --30 seconds.
2. Freeze; perform stretching activities.
3. Measuring Worm Walk--30 seconds
4. Freeze; perform abdominal development challenges.
5. Frog Jump--30 seconds.
6. Freeze; perform push-up position challenges.
7. Elephant Walk --30 seconds.
8. Freeze; perform stretching activities
9. Bear Walk--30 seconds.
10. Freeze; perform abdominal challenges.
11. Crab Walk--30 seconds.
12. Freeze and perform stretching and relaxing activities

Tape alternating segments (30 seconds in length) of silence and music to signal duration of exercise. Music segments indicate performing animal movements while intervals of silence announce doing the fitness challenges.

A variation is to place animal movement signs throughout the area and instruct students to move from sign to sign performing the appropriate animal movement each time they reach a new sign.

Lesson Focus -- Movement Skills and Concepts (9)

Fundamental Skill: Leaping (taking off on one foot and landing on the other)
1. Run in different directions and practice your leaping. Alternate the leading foot.
2. As you run, try a leap for good height; for distance; for both.
3. Explore the different arm positions you can use in leaping. Which is best? Try sailing through the air like an airplane.
4. Leap with a quarter or half turn.
5. If there are benches or other obstacles present, leap over these. Put several in succession for consecutive leaps.
6. Put one-half the children down scattered in curled position, face to the floor. The others leap over as many as possible.
7. Practice making two or three leaps in succession.
8. Practice Leap the Brook.

Select a few activities from each of the categories so students receive a variety of skills to practice. When possible, integrate the manipulative skill activities with fundamental skill activities. A common error is to teach all the activities from one category. The reason for multiple groups of activities is to provide variety and enhance motivation.

Use instructional cues to stimulate correct movement:
"Leap as far as possible."
"Lift with your arms."

Movement Concept: Levels and Speed
Find an area to move and explore the following:
1. Show me a slow, low level movement down and back.
2. What other ways can you go down and back at a slow, low level?
3. Change to a high level, fast movement.
4. What other ways can you do a high level, fast movement?
5. Combine a low, fast movement down with a high, slow movement back.
6. Explore other ways to move at different levels and speeds.

Explain the terms of speed and levels so children learn the concepts of altering movements.

Movement Concept: Partner Activity and Jump Rope Floor Targets

1. Jumping, hopping, cross-steps, scissors steps, heel clicks, etc.
2. Add quarter and half-turns, levels.
3. Take the weight partially on the hands; crouch jumps, bunny jump, cartwheel, etc.
4. Form a selected shape with the rope. Repeat 1, 2, 3. Form the same shape with your body.
5. Matching activity. One partner performs and the other matches the movement.
6. Partner activity. Join hands in some way; hop, jump, or use other movements down the rope or figure. Wheelbarrow or use partner-support activities and move down the rope.

Begin with the rope laid in a straight line along the floor and perform movements down the rope:

Emphasize not touching the rope while moving.

Movement Concept: Acceleration and Deceleration

Teach students what accelerate and decelerate mean.

1. Begin a movement and accelerate.
2. Begin with a fast movement and decelerate.
3. Accelerate to a fast speed and decelerate the same movement.
4. Accelerate with one movement to fast speed, shift to another movement, and decelerate.
5. Can you accelerate one movement of the body while decelerating another at the same time?

Suggested movements for practicing acceleration and deceleration: Stepping in place, running in place, circling body parts, arm thrust movements, jumping, hopping, changing stride, arm and leg movement while lying on back, pretending to be a locomotive engine of a railroad train.

Game Activity

Mix and Match

Supplies: None

Skills: Fundamental locomotor movements

A dividing line is established through the middle of the area. Half of the children are on one side and half are on the other. Two or three extra persons are placed on one side of the area. A signal is given for youngsters to move as directed on their side of the line. They can be told to run, hop, skip, or make some other movement. On signal, players run to the dividing line and reach across to join hands with a player on the opposite side. The goal is to find a partner and not be left out. Children may reach over but not cross the line. The players left out move to the opposite side so that players without a partner are from alternating sides.

Colors

Use five or six different-colored markers with a number of children having the same color. Children start the game standing or seated in a circle each with a marker in front of them. The teacher (or another player) calls out a color. Everyone having that color runs counterclockwise around the circle and back to place. The first player seated upright and motionless is declared the winner. Different kinds of locomotor movement can be specified, such as skipping, galloping, walking, and so on. After a period of play, leave the markers on the floor and have the class move one place to the left so players have a different color.

Variation: Shapes (e.g., circles, triangles, squares, rectangles, stars, and diamonds) can be used instead of colors, as can numbers or other articles or categories, such as animals, birds, or fish.

Dynamic Physical Education for Elementary School Children
Rhythmic Movement Skills (4)
Level I – Week 32

Objectives:
To move rhythmically in simple folk dances
To accept the outcomes of game activities
To show consideration for others in a variety of situations

Equipment Required:
Hoop or beanbag for each student
Parachute
Music for Parachute Fitness & rhythms
Wand and blindfold for game

Instructional Activities	Teaching Hints

Introductory Activity -- Ponies in the Stable

A beanbag or hoop is used to mark each child's stable. On signal, youngsters gallop around the area and in and out of "stables." On a second signal, students return to the nearest stable.

Variations.
1. Use different locomotor movements.
2. Take different positions in the stable such as seated, balanced, collapsed.

To introduce excitement into the activity, remove a few stables and encourage students not to be left out.

Teach directions by asking students to move in a certain direction, i.e., north, south, etc.

Fitness Development Activity -- Parachute Fitness

1. Jog while holding the chute in the left hand. (music)
2. Shake the chute. (no music)
3. Slide while holding the chute with both hands. (music)
4. Sit and perform curl-ups. (no music)
5. Skip. (music)
6. Freeze, face the center, and stretch the chute tightly. Repeat five to six times. (no music)
7. Run in place while holding the chute taut at different levels. (music)
8. Sit with legs under the chute. Do a seat walk toward the center. Return to the perimeter. Repeat four to six times. (no music)
9. Place the chute on the ground. Jog away from the chute and return on signal. Repeat. (music)
10. Move into push-up position holding the chute with one hand. Shake the chute. (no music)
11. Shake the chute and jump in place. (music)
12. Lie on back with feet under the chute. Shake the chute with the feet. (no music)
13. Hop to the center of the chute and return. Repeat. (music)
14. Sit with feet under the chute. Stretch by touching the toes with the chute. Relax with other stretches while sitting. (no music)

Tape alternating segments (20-25 seconds in length) of silence and music to signal duration of exercise. Music segments indicate aerobic activity with the parachute while intervals of silence announce using the chute to enhance flexibility and strength development.

Space youngsters evenly around the chute.

Use different hand grips (palms up, down, mixed).

All movements should be done under control. Some of the faster and stronger students will have to moderate their performance.

Lesson Focus -- Rhythmic Movement Skills (4)

Make dances easy for students to learn by implementing some of the following techniques:
1. Teach the dances without using partners.
2. Allow youngsters to move in any direction without left-right orientation.
3. Use scattered formation instead of circles.
4. Emphasize strong movements such as clapping and stamping to increase involvement.
5. Play the music at a slower speed when first learning the dance.

Rhythms should be taught like other sport skills. Avoid striving for perfection so students know it is acceptable to make mistakes. Teach a variety of dances rather than one or two in depth in case some students find it difficult to master a specific dance.

The Muffin Man (American)

Music Source: WWCD-YR002; WWC-YR002

Formation: Single circle, facing center, hands at sides. One child, the Muffin Man, stands in front of another child.

Verses:

1. Oh, have you seen the Muffin Man,
The Muffin Man, the Muffin Man?
Oh, have you seen the Muffin Man,
Who lives on _____Street?

2. Oh, yes, we've seen the Muffin Man,
The Muffin Man, the Muffin Man.
Oh yes, we've seen the Muffin Man,
Who lives on _____Street.

Directions:

Verse 1: The children stand still and clap their hands lightly, with the exception of the Muffin Man and his partner. These two join hands and jump lightly in place while keeping time to the music. On the first beat of each measure, a normal jump is taken, followed by a bounce in place (rebound) on the second beat.

Verse 2: The Muffin Man and his partner then skip around the inside of the circle individually and, near the end of the verse, each stands in front of a child, their new partner.

Verse 1 is then repeated, with two sets of partners doing the jumping. During the repetition of verse 2, four children skip around the inside of the circle and choose partners. This procedure continues until all children have been chosen.

Seven Jumps (Danish)

Music Source: WWCD-1043; WWC-3528

Formation: Single circle, hands joined

Directions:

There are seven jumps to the dance. Each jump is preceded by the following action.

Measures	Action
1--8	The circle moves to the right with seven step-hops, one to each measure. On the eighth measure, all jump high in the air and reverse direction. (Step-hop, 2-hop, 3-hop, . . . 7-hop, change direction)
9--16	Circle to the left with seven step-hops. Stop on measure 16 and face the center. (Step-hop, 2-hop, 3-hop, . . . 7-hop, face center)
17	All drop hands, place their hands on hips, and lift the right knee upward with the toes pointed downward. (Knee up)
18	All stamp the right foot to the ground on the signal note, then join hands on the next note. (Stamp)
1--18	Repeat measures 1--18, but do not join hands.
19	Lift the left knee, stamp, and join hands.
1--19	Repeat measures 1--19, but do not join hands.
20	Put the right toe backward and kneel on the right knee. Stand and join hands.
1--20	Repeat measures 1--20; do not join hands.
21	Kneel on the left knee. Stand and join hands.
1--21	Repeat measures 1--21; do not join hands.
22	Put the right elbow to the floor with the cheek on the fist. Stand and join hands.
1--22	Repeat measures 1--22; do not join hands.
23	Put the left elbow to the floor with the cheek on the fist. Stand and join hands.
1--23	Repeat measures 1--23; do not join hands.
24	Put the forehead on the floor. Stand and join hands.
1--16	Repeat measures 1--16.

To increase motivation, the dance can be done with a parachute. The dancers hold the parachute taut with one hand during the step-hops. The chute is kept taut with both hands for all jumps except the last, during which the forehead touches the chute on the floor.

Yankee Doodle (American)

Music Source: WWCD-FCN

Formation: Scattered or open circle facing counterclockwise

Directions:

Measures	Action
1--4	All gallop 8 steps (Gallop, 2, . . . 8)
5--8	All stop, face center, point to cap and bow on word "macaroni." (Stop, point, bow)
9--12	All join hands and take six slides to the right and stamp feet two times on word "dandy." (Slide, 2, 3, . . . 6; Stamp, stamp)
13--16	All slide six times to the left and clap hands two times on the word "candy." (Slide, 2, 3, . . . 6; Clap clap)

Change the locomotor movements to fit the age and interest of the group. Have the class create new movement patterns.

Eins Zwei Drei (German)

Music Source: HLP-4026
Formation: Single circle of couples (partner B to partner A's right) facing the center and numbered alternately couple 1, 2, 1, 2
Directions:
Explain that "Eins, Zwei, Drei" means "one, two, three" in German.

Measures	Part I Action
1—2	Couples 1 take three steps toward the center of the circle as they clap their hands by brushing them vertically like cymbals. (Forward, 2, 3, pause)
3--4	Couples 1 repeat measures 1--2, walking backward to place. (Back, 2, 3, pause)
5—8	Couples 1 face, join both hands, and take four slides toward the center of the circle and four slides back to place. Partner A starts with the left foot, partner B with the right. (Slide, 2, 3, 4)
9--16	Couples 2 repeat measures 1--8.

Measures	Part II Action
17	Partner A turns and touches the right heel sideward while shaking the right index finger at partner. Partner B does the same with the left heel and left index finger. (Scold, 2, 3)
18	Repeat measure 17 with the corner, reversing footwork and hands. (Scold, 2, 3)
19--20	Repeat measures 17 and 18.
21--24	All join hands and circle left with eight slides. (Slide, 2, 3, . . . 8)
25--32	Repeat measures 17--24, reversing the direction of the slides. (Slide, 2, 3, . . . 8)

Rhythm Sticks – It's a Small, Small World (American)

Music Source: WWC-2015
Skills: Rhythmic tapping and manipulation of sticks
Formation: Children sitting cross-legged individually scattered around the area

Rhythm sticks or lummi sticks are 12 – 15 inches in length. Activities may be done individually or in partners. This routine is done individually. The sticks are held in the thumb and the forefinger at about the bottom third of the stick.

Measures	Call	Action
1-2	Down, cross, down, cross	Tap ends of both sticks on the floor, and then cross the arms over tapping the sticks on the floor again.
3-4	Down, cross, down, cross	Repeat
5-6	Down, cross, down, cross	Repeat
7-8	Chorus: It's a small, small world.	Lean forward touching head to knees (curl forward).
9-10	Tap, tap, knees, knees	Tap sticks two times in front of the chest, and then lightly tap the knees twice.
11-12	Tap, tap, knees, knees	Repeat
13-14	Tap, tap, knees, knees	Repeat
15-16	Chorus: It's a small, small world.	Lean forward touching head to knees (curl forward).

The sequence above repeats a number of times with touches to the toes, shoulders, head, and nose. As a variation, youngsters can face a partner and tap both of their sticks to their partner's sticks.

Shoemaker's Dance (Danish)

Music Source: WWCD-1042; WWC-07042
Skills: Skipping, heel and toe
Formation: Double circle, partners facing, with partner A's back to the center of the circle
Directions:

Measures	Part I Action
1	With arms bent and at shoulder height, and with hands clenched to form fists, circle one fist over the other in front of the chest. (Wind the thread)
2	Reverse the circular motion and wind the thread in the opposite direction. (Reverse direction)
3	Pull the elbows back vigorously twice. (Pull and tighten the thread)
4	Clap own hands three times. (Clap, 2, 3)
5–7	Repeat the pattern of measures 1–3.
8	Tap own fists together three times to drive the nails. (Tap, 2, 3)
	Part II Action
9–16	Partners face counterclockwise, inside hands joined. Skip counterclockwise, ending with a bow. (Skip, 2, 3, ... 15, bow)

Variation of Part II Action

9	Place the heel of the outside foot forward (counts 1 and), and point the toe of the outside foot in back (2 and).
10	Take three running steps forward, starting with the outside foot and pausing on the last count.
11–12	Repeat the pattern of measures 9–10, starting with the inside foot.
13–16	Repeat the pattern of measures 9–12, entire "heel and toe and run, run, run" pattern dance, four times singing Part II verse.

Bleking (Swedish)

Music Source: WWCD_1044; WWC-07042

Skills: Bleking step, step-hop

Formation: Single circle, partners facing, both hands joined. Partners A face counterclockwise and partners B clockwise.

Directions:

Part I—The Bleking Step: Cue by calling "Slow-slow, fast-fast-fast."

Measures Action

1	Hop on the left foot and extend the right heel forward with the right leg straight. At the same time, thrust the right hand forward. Hop on the right foot, reversing the arm action and extending the left foot to rest on the heel. (Slow, slow)
2	Repeat the action with three quick changes—left, right, left. (Fast, fast, fast)
3–4	Beginning on the right foot, repeat the movements of measures 1 and 2. (Slow, slow, fast, fast, fast)
5–8	Repeat measures 1–4.

Part II—The Windmills: Partners extend their joined hands sideways at shoulder height.

Measures Action

9–16	Partners turn in place with a repeated step-hop. At the same time, the arms move up and down like a windmill. The turning is done clockwise, with A starting on the right foot and B on the left. At the completion of the step-hops (16), the partners should be in their original places ready for Part I again. (Step-hop, 2-hop, 3-hop, ... 16-hop)

Variations:

Change from original positions to a double circle, partners facing, As with back to the center. Part I is as described. For Part II, all face counterclockwise, and partners join inside hands. Partners do the basic schottische of "step, step, step, hop" throughout Part II.

Another excellent variation is to do the dance with partners scattered in general space. Part I is as described. For Part II, the children leave their partners and step-hop in various directions around the dancing area. When the music is about to change back to Part I, performers find a partner wherever they can, and the dance is repeated.

Game Activity

Circle Stoop

Supplies: Music or tom-tom

Skills: Moving to rhythm

Children are in a single circle, facing counterclockwise. A march or similar music, or a tom-tom beat, can be used to signal movement. The class marches until the music stops. When the music stops, players stoop and touch both hands to the ground without losing balance. The last person to touch both hands to the ground and those children who lost their balance pay a penalty by going into the mush pot (the center of the circle) for one turn. The music intervals should be varied so youngsters don't anticipate the signal

Blindfolded Duck

Supplies: A wand and blindfold

Skills: Fundamental locomotor movements

One child, designated the duck (Daisy if a girl, Donald if a boy), stands blindfolded in the center of a circle and holds a wand or similar article. She taps on the floor and tells the class to hop (or perform some other locomotor movement). Children in the circle act accordingly, all moving in the same direction. Daisy then taps the wand twice on the floor, which signals all children to stop. Daisy moves forward with her wand, still blindfolded, to find a child in the circle. She asks, "Who are you?" The child responds, "Quack, quack." Daisy tries to identify this person. If the guess is correct, the identified child becomes the new duck. If the guess is wrong, Daisy must take another turn. After two unsuccessful turns, another child is chosen to be the duck.

Dynamic Physical Education for Elementary School Children
Fundamental Skills Using Individual Mats
Level I – Week 33

Objectives:
To be able to identify the eight locomotor movements
To perform fitness challenges independently
To manage the body in space and on the floor

Equipment Required:
Music for Fitness Challenges
One individual mat for each student

Instructional Activities	Teaching Hints
Introductory Activity --Locomotor Movements and Freeze	
Perform the locomotor movements below; freeze quickly on signal with a wide base of support. A suggestion is to tape alternating segments of silence and music to signal duration of the locomotor movements. Segments of silence to indicate the "freeze" position can be decreased in duration until the desired response latency is reached.	Ask class to start moving upon entry into teaching area.
	If necessary, demonstrate how to perform the movements.
1. Walk 2. Run 3. Jump 4. Hop 5. Skip 6. Gallop 7. Leap 8. Slide	Reinforce stopping without falling.

Fitness Development Activity --Fitness Challenges	
1. Locomotor Movement: Walk for 30 seconds.	Alternate the locomotor movements with the strength and flexibility challenges. Repeat the challenges as necessary.
2. Flexibility and Trunk Development Challenges a. Bend in different directions. b. Stretch slowly and return quickly. c. Combine bending and stretching movements. d. Sway back and forth. e. Twist one body part; add more body parts.	Tape alternating segments (30 seconds in length) of silence and music to signal duration of exercise. Music segments indicate locomotor movements while intervals of silence announce doing the movement challenges.
3. Locomotor Movement: Skip for 30 seconds.	
4. Upper Body Strength Challenges In a push-up position, do the following challenges: a. Lift one foot; the other foot. b. Wave at a friend; wave with the other arm. c. Scratch your back with one hand; use the other hand. d. Walk your feet to your hands. e. Turn over and face the ceiling; shake a leg; crab walk.	Teach youngsters the different challenges and then allow them to select a challenge they can successfully perform.
5. Locomotor Movement: Jog for 30 seconds.	The challenges should be enjoyable to perform.
6. Abdominal Development Challenges From a supine position: 1.Lift your head and look at your toes. 2.Lift your knees to your chest. 3.Wave your legs at a friend. From a sitting position; 1.Slowly lay down with hands on tummy. 2.Lift legs and touch toes.	Encourage students to focus on trying and feeling successful. Workloads should be moderate with emphasis on success for all youngsters.
7. Locomotor Movement: Run and leap for 30 seconds.	

Lesson Focus – Fundamental Skills Using Individual Mats	
Non Locomotor Movements 1. Stretch a. Different directions. b. Different parts of body.	*Give students two or three activities to practice so you have time to move and help. Alternate activities from each of*

82

2. Curl
3. Balance
   a. Balance on different body parts.
   b. Balance on different number of parts.
   c. Go from one balance to another.
4. Bridge
   a. Bridge across the short width, long width.
   b. Different parts or number of parts.
   c. Bridge to a full arch.
5. Reach
   a. Keep toes on mat, reach as far as possible.
   b. Keep hand on mat, reach as far as possible.
   c. Keep hand on mat, reach as far as possible with a foot.
6. Rock
   a. On different parts
7. Roll
   a. Different types of rolls.
   b. Roll up in the mat.
8. Twist
   a. Full twist, held.
   b. Moving twists
   c. Twist and untwist.
9. Use other Terms
   a. Straight, curved, narrow, wide, prone melt, shake, fall, collapse.
10. Combination Movements

On and off the Mats
1. Different locomotor movements- hop, jump, leap.
2. Weight on the hands. Crouch jumps, forward and backward.
3. Animal imitations, i.e., Rabbit, Frog, etc.

Over the Mat
1. Locomotor movements: Add turns, secure height.
2. Weight on the hands.
3. Combinations: Over one way and back another way.
4. How many mats can you jump over in 10 seconds? Change the movements over the mat.
5. Hop over fine blue mats. Change the movement, number, and color of the mats.

Movements around the Mats
1. Different locomotor movements.
2. Animal Walks, i.e., Dog, Bear, Cat, Rabbit.
3. Keep hands on the mat.
4. Keep feet on the mat.

Mats as a Base
1. Use different magic numbers.
   a. A number of movements out and back.
   b. Different number combinations.
   c. Animal imitations.

Challenge Activities
1. Try some individual and partner stunts with the mats as a base.
   a. Coffee Grinder
   b. Chinese Get-up
   c. Wring the Dishrag
2. Jump from mat to mat without touching the floor. Can you move across the area? Skip from mat to mat.
3. Play "Ring around the Mat." Skip around the mat and all fall down.

youngsters the categories so students receive a variety of skills to practice.

Each student needs a mat. Carpet squares can be used. Indoor-outdoor carpet with rubber backing is best because it doesn't slide.

Encourage students to create as many different varieties of each non locomotor movement.

To develop a clear understanding of the movements, challenge the students by changing to different movements quickly.

Combine sequences of the different non locomotor movements, i.e., rock, bridge, and curl.

Encourage youngsters to manage their body when performing the activities. This is an excellent opportunity to encourage moving with falling.

4. Move between five mats and cartwheel over two mats. Use different movements and tumbling activities.
5. Put your mat together with a partner and make different shapes, numbers, and letters. Do the same thing in small groups.
6. Magic Carpet Ride - one person pulls a partner sitting on the mat.

Game Activity

Sneak Attack

Supplies: None

Skills: Marching, running

Two parallel lines are drawn about 60 feet apart. The class is divided into two teams. One team takes a position on one of the lines, with their backs to the area. These are the chasers. The other team is on the other line, facing the area. This is the sneak team. The sneak team moves forward on signal, moving toward the chasers. When they get reasonably close, a signal is given, and the sneak team turns and runs back to their line, chased by the other team. Anyone tagged before reaching the line changes to the chase team. The game is then repeated, with the roles exchanged.

Mat Games

Supplies: Individual Mats

Skills: Running, jumping

Each child is seated on a mat. On signal, each rises and jumps over as many different mats as possible. On the next signal, each child takes a seat on the nearest mat. The last child to be seated can pay a penalty. The game can also be played by eliminating one or two mats so that one or two children are left without a home base. The teacher can stand on a mat or turn over mats to put them out of the game. To control roughness, the rule should be that the first child to touch a mat gets to sit on it.

A variation of this game is to have each child touch at least ten mats and then sit cross-legged on his own mat, or a child can be required to alternate touching a mat and jumping over the next mat until a total of ten is reached. "See how many mats you can cartwheel or jump over in 10 seconds." Change the challenge and try again.

Dynamic Physical Education for Elementary School Children
Fundamental Skills Using Balance Beams
Level I – Week 34

Objectives:
To know the names of fitness activities in Astronaut Exercises
To learn to balance the body while walking a beam
To manipulate an object while walking a beam

Equipment Required:
Music for Astronaut Exercises
Six balance beam benches or 2"x4"
    boards (8 ft long)
Hoops, wands, and beanbags for beam
    activities

Instructional Activities	Teaching Hints

Introductory Activity -- Airplanes

Children pretend to be airplanes. They take off, zoom with arms out, swoop, turn, and glide. On signal, they drop to the floor in prone position. To takeoff again, they must "restart" their engines by doing a couple of push-up challenges while making a "vroom, vroom" engine sound.

Encourage creativity by naming different types of airplanes and helicopters.

Use different locomotor movements.

Fitness Development Activity --Astronaut Exercises

Walk, do Arm Circles	30 seconds	Tape alternating segments of silence and
Flexibility and Trunk Development Challenges	30 seconds	music to signal duration of exercise.
Skip forward, backwards, and sideways	30 seconds	Music segments (30 seconds) indicate
Upper Body Strength Challenges	30 seconds	aerobic activity while intervals of silence
Slide; change lead leg	30 seconds	(30 seconds) signal flexibility and
Abdominal Development Challenges	30 seconds	strength development activities.
Jump like a Pogo Stick	30 seconds	
Upper Body Strength Challenges	30 seconds	See Chapter 12 for a description of how
Trot lightly in different directions	30 seconds	to perform challenge activities.
Flexibility and Trunk Development Challenges	30 seconds	
Gallop Backwards	30 seconds	Allow students to adjust the workload to

Cool down with stretching and walking.

an intensity that is consistent with their ability level.

Lesson Focus -- Fundamental Skills Using Balance Beams

Balance beam activities should be done using controlled walking movements. Speed of movement should always be avoided.

Dismounts

All moves across the balance beam should end with a dismount. The following dismounts are examples.
1. Single jump (forward or backward)..
2. Jump with turns (half turn, three-quarter turn, or full turn).
3. Jackknife. Jump, kick the legs up, and touch the toes with the fingertips. Keep the feet together.
4. Jackknife Split. Same as the Jackknife, but spread the legs as far as possible.
5. Jump, land and do a Forward Roll.
6. Backward jump, land and do a Backward Roll.
7. Side jump to a Side Roll.

Balance Beam Activities
1. Practice walking on floor lines to establish qualities of controlled movement and not looking at feet.
2. Walk length of beam.
   a. Walk forward.
   b. Walk backward.
   c. Walk sideways--lead with both left and right sides of body.
   d. Try other steps--follow steps, heel and toe, on toes, etc.
3. Walk different directions and vary arm and body positions.

If balance beams are not available, use 2" X 4" boards placed on the floor. This will give students some elevation off the floor and offer balance challenges.

Place the beams parallel to each other and have a similar number of students lined up behind each one. Students progress down the beam.

After moving the length of the beam, have students do a locomotor movement to the end of the teaching area and return. This will offer students both balance activities and the chance to practice locomotor movements. It also keeps students engaged in activity for a longer period of time and reduces standing and waiting time. Specified movements can be placed on return activity signs.

If a student steps off the beam, have them get back on and progress. Sometimes, students stop walking the beam and

a. Hands on hips.
b. Hand on head.
c. Arms folded across chest.
d. Lean to one side or the other.
e. Body bent forward or backward.
f. Hands on knees or feet.
4. Perform animal movements across the balance beam.
   a. Puppy dog walk
   b. Bear Walk
   c. Crab Walk
5. Use manipulative equipment while walking the beam.
   a. Balance objects such as beanbags or wands while walking across beam.
   b. Step over a wand or through a hoop while walking the beam.
   c. Toss and catch a beanbag while walking the beam
   d. Twirl a hoop while walking the beam.
   e. Bounce a ball while walking a beam.
   f. Play catch with a partner while walking the beam.
6. Try do a stork stand in the middle of the beam (on one foot)

receive little practice.
Move with controlled, deliberate movements across the beam. Speed is not a goal.

Game Activity

Toe to Toe

Supplies: None

Skills: Fundamental locomotor movements

Youngsters perform a locomotor movement around the area. On signal, each child must find a partner and stand toe to toe (one foot only) with that person. An important skill is to take the nearest person for a partner without searching for a friend. Youngsters who can't find a partner within their immediate area must run quickly to the center of the area (use a marking spot or cone) to find a partner. The goal is to find a nearby partner as quickly as possible and avoid being the last pair formed. If the number of youngsters playing is uneven, the teacher can join in and play. Change locomotor movements often.

Mousetrap

Supplies: None

Skills: Skipping, running, dodging

Half of the class forms a circle with hands joined, facing the center. This is the trap. The other half of the class is on the outside of the circle. These are the mice. Three signals are given for the game. These can be word cues or other signals. On the first signal, the mice skip around, outside the circle, playing happily. On the second signal, the trap is opened. (The circle players raise their joined hands to form arches.) The mice run in and out of the trap. The third signal signals the trap to snap shut. (The arms come down.) All mice caught in the trap join the circle. The game is repeated until most of the mice are caught. The players exchange places and the game begins anew.

Aviator

Supplies: None

Skills: Running, locomotor movements, stopping

Players are parked (in push-up position) at one end of the playing area. The air traffic controller (ATC) is in front of the players and calls out, "Aviators aviators, take off!" Youngsters take off and move like airplanes to the opposite side of the area. The first person to move to the other side and land the plane (get into push-up position facing the ATC) is declared the new ATC. If the ATC yells out some type of stormy weather, all planes must return to the starting line and resume the parked position. Examples of stormy weather commands are lightning, thunder, hurricane, and tornado. Each ATC is allowed to give stormy weather warnings once.

Dynamic Physical Education for Elementary School Children
Movement Skills and Concepts (10)
Running, Racquet Skills, Moving in Different Ways
Level I – Week 35

Objectives:
To recognize variety within locomotor movements
To work independently at circuit training stations
To understand movement concepts of over and under/different ways of moving
To handle a racquet and ball

Equipment Required:
Music and signs for Circuit Training
One racquet and ball for each child
Hoops (4-6)
8" foam balls (5-7)

Instructional Activities	Teaching Hints

Introductory Activity -- Movement Varieties

Move using a basic locomotor movement (i.e., walking, jumping, hopping, skipping, galloping). Then add variety to the movement by asking students to respond to the following factors:
1. Level--low, high, in between.
2. Direction--straight, zigzag, circular, curved, forward, backward, upward, downward.
3. Size--large, tiny, medium movements.
4. Patterns--forming squares, diamonds, triangles, circles, figure-eights.
5. Speed--slow, fast, accelerate.

Use scatter formation.

Emphasize and reinforce creative responses.

Explain concepts of level, direction, size, and speed. Short explanations laced with activity allow students time to recover.

Fitness Development Activity --Circuit Training

Make signs, put them on cones and place around the perimeter of the teaching area. Students perform the exercise specified at each station while the music is playing.
1. Tortoise and Hare
2. Curl-up variations
3. Hula Hooping on arms
4. Standing Hip Bend
5. Agility run--run back and forth between two designated lines
6. Push-up variations
7. Crab Walk
8. Bend and Twist

Tape alternating segments of silence and music to signal duration of exercise. Music segments (begin at 30 seconds) indicate activity at each station while intervals of silence (10 seconds) announce it is time to stop and move forward to the next station.

Place an equal number of students at each station.

Use activities at the stations that students already know how to perform.

Lesson Focus -- Movement Skills and Concepts (10)

Fundamental Skill: Running
1. Run lightly around the area; stop on signal.
2. Run lightly and change directions on signal.
3. Run, turn around with running steps on signal and continue in a new direction.
4. Pick a spot away from you. Run to it and return without bumping anyone.
5. Run low, gradually increase the height. Reverse.
6. Run patterns. Run inside and around objects.
7. Run with high knee action. Add a knee slap with the hand as you run.
8. Run with different steps—tiny, long, light, heavy, criss-cross, wide and others.
9. Run with arms in different positions--circling, overhead, stiff at sides and others (choice).
10. Free running. Concentrate on good knee lift.
11. Run at different speeds.
12. Touch the ground at times with either hand as you run.
13. Run backwards, sideways.
14. Run with exaggerated arm movements and/or high bounce.
15. Practice running, crossing from one line to another.
    a. Cross your feet as you run.
    b. Touch the ground with one and both hands as you run.

Select a few activities from each of the categories so students receive a variety of skills to practice. When possible, integrate the manipulative skill activities with fundamental skill activities. A common error is to teach all the activities from one category. The reason for multiple groups of activities is to provide variety and enhance motivation.

Encourage running under control. Falling down or collisions should be discouraged. Reinforce students who do run under control.

c. Run forward, looking backward over your right shoulder.
d. Same, but look over the left shoulder.
e. Change direction every few steps.
f. Run to the center, stop completely, then continue.
g. Make two stops going across--first with the right side forward and then with the left side forward as you stop.
h. Run forward and stop. Come back three steps and stop. Continue in forward direction.
i. Do a two-count stop on the way.
j. Run sideways across, leading with one side. Next time lead with the other.
k. Run forward halfway and then backward the rest.
l. Run backward halfway and then forward the rest.
m. Make a full turn in the center and continue. Do this right and left.
n. Provide for student choice.

Use instructional cues:

"Look ahead when running"

"Bend the arms at the elbows and gently move them back and forth"

When teaching running skills, couple them with stopping skills. Encourage effective stopping by bending the knees and lowering the center of gravity.

Manipulative Activity--Racquets and Balls
Individual Activity
1. Place the ball on the racquet face. Roll it around the face.
2. Hit the ball into the air with the racquet. Retrieve and repeat.
3 Bounce the ball into the air, using the racquet, specify number.
4 Bounce the ball into the air, decreasing the height of the bounce until it rests on the face of the racquet.
5 Bounce the ball on the floor.
6 Alternate bouncing upward and to the floor.
7 Dribble the ball and move while dribbling.
8 Choice activity.

Other pieces of manipulative equipment can be used if racquets and balls are not available.

Place the racquets and balls around the perimeter of the area. On signal, students move and pick up a racquet and ball and begin rolling it around the face of the racquet.

Partner Activity
1. One partner tosses the other hits it back.
2. Try batting it back and forth. If using a tennis ball, let it bounce between hits.
3. Place ball on floor and roll it back and forth.

Partners should be close to each other so control of the ball is maintained.

Movement Concept: Over and Under
1. One partner is an obstacle and the other goes over, under, and around the "obstacle." Reverse positions.
2. Copying action. One partner takes a position and the other goes over and under the first. Reverse positions, but try to copy the same sequence.
3. Progressive sequencing. The first child does a movement (over, under, or around). The second child repeats the movement and adds another. The first child repeats the first two movements and adds a third. The second child repeats and adds a forth.

The goal is to **not** touch the partner who is the obstacle.

Encourage creativity and reinforce new ideas.

Movement Concept: Moving in Different Ways
1. Show me different ways to move when your body is in the air part of the time; when your body is always in contact with the floor.
2. Show me different ways you can progress along the floor without using your hands or feet. Can you "walk" using your seat?
3. What are the different ways you can roll and move?
4. What ways can you move sideways? How can you move on all fours?
5. Move across the floor halfway with one movement and the other half with a decidedly different movement.
6. Explore the different ways you can move when leading with selected parts of the body.

Use student demonstration to encourage variety and creativity. Discuss the many ways of solving a movement problem.

Rollee Pollee

Supplies: Many 8" foam balls

Skills: Ball rolling, dodging

Half of the class forms a circle; the other half is in the center. Balls are given to circle players. The circle players roll the balls at the feet and shoes of the center players, trying to touch them with a ball. The center players move around to avoid the balls. A center player who is touched leaves the center and joins the circle. After a period of time or when all of the children have been touched with a ball, teams trade places. Balls that stop in the center are dead and must be taken back to the circle before being put into play again. The preferable procedure is to have players who recovers balls roll them to a teammate rather than return to place with the ball.

Mix and Match

Supplies: None

Skills: Fundamental locomotor movements

A dividing line is established through the middle of the area. Half of the children are on one side and half are on the other. Two or three extra persons are placed on one side of the area. A signal is given for youngsters to move as directed on their side of the line. They can be told to run, hop, skip, or make some other movement. On signal, players run to the dividing line and reach across to join hands with a player on the opposite side. The goal is to find a partner and not be left out. Children may reach over but not cross the line. The players left out move to the opposite side so that players without a partner are from alternating sides.

Dynamic Physical Education for Elementary School Children
Movement Skills and Concepts (11)
Pushing, Pulling, Rope Jumping, and Balancing the Body
Level I – Week 36

Objectives:
To make a variety of shapes with the body
To know the difference between pushing and pulling
To know the mechanics of effective pushing and pulling
To understand the difference between making circles with body parts and twisting

Equipment Required:
Tom-tom & music for Walk, Trot, and Jog
One jump rope for each student
Plastic bottle bat and ball
Batting tee

Instructional Activities	Teaching Hints
Introductory Activity -- Run and Assume Shape	
Place emphasis on making a variety of shapes and balances. Vary the locomotor movements.	Place emphasis on running under control and assuming specified shape quickly.
1. Run and move to a prone (one drumbeat) or supine (two drumbeats) position on signal.	
2. Run and move into a balance position.	Have students move into the activity area
3. Run and freeze in various shapes.	in scatter formation.

Fitness Development Activity --Walk, Trot, and Jog

Move to the following signals:
  1.One drumbeat - walk.
  2.Two drumbeats - trot.
  3.Three drumbeats - jog.
  4.Whistle - freeze and perform exercises.

Tape alternating segments (20 seconds in length) of silence and music to signal duration of exercise. Music segments indicate walk, trot, and jog activity. Intervals of silence signal performance of the strength and flexibility exercises.

Use various strength and flexibility exercises between bouts of walk, trot, and jog to allow students to recover aerobically. Examples are:
  1. Bend and Twist
  2. Sitting Stretch
  3. Push-up challenges
  4. Abdominal Challenges
  5. Body Twist
  6. Standing Hip Bend

Encourage students to move around the area in the same direction.

See Chapter 12 for a description of how to perform the exercises. Any exercises can be substituted. Try to exercise all bodyparts.

Lesson Focus - Movement Skills and Concepts (11)

Fundamental Skill: Pushing
1. Push against a wall first in an erect position and then with knees bent and one foot braced behind the other. Which is better
2. Push an imaginary object that is very light. Now try pushing a very heavy object.
3. Try to push a partner who is sitting on the floor
4. Can you push an object with your feet without using your arms and hands? Try with the hands braced behind you.
5. Put your back against an object and push with your feet.
6. Explore different ways to push your object.
7. Find a friend to explore different ways to push him or her over a line.
8. Sit down back to back with your partner and see whether you can move him or her.
9. Lie on the floor and push yourself backward, forward, sideways. Which is easiest?
10. Lie on the floor and push yourself forward with one hand and one foot. Which hand-foot combination is best?
11. Show how you can push a ball to a friend. Push slowly and steadily.

Select a few activities from each of the categories so students receive a variety of skills to practice. When possible, integrate the manipulative skill activities with fundamental skill activities. A common error is to teach all the activities from one category. The reason for multiple groups of activities is to provide variety and enhance motivation.

Use instructional cues such as:
    "Use a wide stance"
    "Bend your knees and lower your center of gravity"
    "Place all of your body behind your hands while pushing"

Fundamental Skill: Pulling

1. Reach for an imaginary object near the ceiling and pull the object toward you quickly. Now slowly and smoothly.
2. Clasp your hands together and pull against each hand as hard as you can. Vary the positions of the arms.
3. Hold hands with your partner and try to pull against each other balancing on one foot.
4. Hold hands with partner, drop low, and pull hard against each other.
5. Have partner sit down. Pull partner slowly by the feet.
6. Pretend to pull a heavy object while you are lying on the floor.
7. With partner seated on the floor, pull him or her to his or her feet.

Use instructional cues to enhance pulling skills:
"Lower your body and widen your base of support"
"Lean away from the source of pull"

Use slow controlled pulling. Remind youngsters to ask their partner to stop if the hand grip is slipping.

Manipulative Skills: Rope Jumping

Encourage children to work on needed skill areas. Suggest working first without music and then with music.

Allow students time to practice new jumping skills. Find students who can demonstrate different skills if necessary.

Movement Concepts: Circles in the Body

1. How many joints of the body can do circular motion (circles)?
2. How many different ways can you make the arms circle, using both arms at once?
3. Lie on your back, lift your legs. Can you make the arms and legs go in circles? Can you make them go in different circles?
4. In a standing position, show arm circles in horizontal, vertical and diagonal direction using one arm at a time.
5. Repeat item 4, using both arms.
6. Lie on back and lift the legs. Make circles with the feet first singly and then together.
7. Explore different ways to make two different body parts make circles in different directions.
8. Make a large circle with one part of the body and a small one with another.
9. What joints can twist as well as circle?

Explain that a joint is where different body parts are connected.

Explain the terms horizontal, vertical, and diagonal.

Encourage students to make different size circles in many different directions.

Explain the difference between twisting and circling.

Movement Concept: Balancing the Body

1. On different parts of the body.
2. On different number of body parts, varying from one through five. Different combinations.
3. Balancing on different levels.
4. Work out a sequence of three or four balance poses. Flow from one to the next.
5. Try to balance on both hands.
6. With a partner, form different balances.

Balance skills should emphasize smooth movements that are held 3 to 5 seconds. Students will always try to speed up the balance activity if they are having trouble maintaining balance.

Share balance innovations with peers.

Movement Concept: Sports Imitation Activities

1. Pretend you are a football player --kicking the ball, passing the ball, making a tackle, centering the ball.
2. Pretend you are a basketball player--shooting a basket, dribbling, guarding, jump ball, a free throw shot.
3. Let's pretend you are a track and field star performing at: the shot-put, the javelin throw, or the discus. Move like a hurdler.
4. Pretend you are a baseball player--pitching, catching a fly ball, fielding a grounder and throwing to first, batting, bunting, sliding into a base.

If desired, pictures of athletes can be used to motivate movement.

Place emphasis on performing the activities with speed and authenticity. Some students may need to see demonstrations of how the skills should be performed.

Change Sides

Supplies: None

Skill: Body management

Identify two parallel lines 30 feet apart with half of the class on each line. On signal, all players cross to the other line, face the center, and stand at attention. The first group to do all three things correctly wins a point. Children must be cautioned to use care when passing through the opposite group. They should be spaced well along each line; this allows room for them to move through each group. Vary the locomotor movements used by specifying skipping, hopping, long steps, sliding, and other varieties of movement. The position to be assumed at the finish can be varied also.

Bottle Bat Ball

Supplies: A plastic bottle bat, whiffle ball, batting tee (optional), home plate, base marker

Skills: Batting, retrieving balls

Batters get three pitches (or swings if a batting tee is used) to hit a fair ball or they are out. The pitches are easy (as in slow-pitch softball) so the batter has a chance to hit the ball. The batter hits the ball and runs around the base marker and back to home plate. If the ball is returned to the pitcher's mound before the batter reaches home, the batter is out. (A marker should designate the pitcher's mound.) Otherwise, the batter has a home run and earns a run for her team. One fielder other than the pitcher is needed, but another can be used. The running distance to first base is critical. It can remain fixed or can be made progressively (one step) longer, until it reaches such a point that the fielders are heavily favored.

Dynamic Physical Education for Elementary School Children
Fundamental Skills Using Climbing Ropes
Level I – Alternate Lesson Plan

Objectives:
To be able to recite safety rules for rope climbing
To be able to hang on a climbing rope for 5 seconds
To be able to swing on a climbing rope

Equipment Required:
Climbing Ropes
Tumbling mats placed under ropes
Benches or Jumping Boxes

Instructional Activities	Teaching Hints

Introductory Activity

Substitute from a selected Lesson Plan

Fitness Development Activity

Substitute from a selected Lesson Plan

Lesson Focus – Fundamental Skills Using Climbing Ropes

Supported Pull-Ups

In supported Pull-Up activities, a part of the body remains in contact with the floor. The Pull-Up is hand-over-hand and the return is hand-under-hand.
1. Kneel directly under the rope. Pull up to the tiptoes and return to kneeling position.
2. Start in a sitting position under the rope. Pull up; the legs are supported on the heels. Return to sitting position.
3. Start in a standing position. Grasp the rope, rock back on the heels, and lower the body to the floor. Keep a straight body. Return to standing position.

Hangs

In a hang, the body is pulled up in one motion and held up for a length of time (5, 10, or 20 seconds). Progression is important.
1. From a seated position, reach up as high as possible and pull the body from the floor, except for the heels. Hold.
2. Same as the previous stunt, but pull the body completely free of the floor. Hold.
3. From a standing position, jump up, grasp the rope, and hang. This should be a Bent-Arm Hang with the hands about even with the mouth. Hold.
4. Repeat the previous stunt, but add leg movements---one or both knees up, bicycling movement, Half Lever (one or both legs up, parallel to the floor), Full Lever (feet up to the face).

Pull-Ups

In the Pull-Up, the body is raised and lowered repeatedly. The initial challenge should be to accomplish one Pull-Up in the defined position. The number of repetitions should be increased with care. All of the activities described for hangs are adaptable to Pull-Ups. The chin should touch the hands on each Pull-Up.

Swinging and Jumping

For swinging and jumping, a bench, box, or stool can serve as a takeoff point. To take off, the child reaches high and jumps to a bent-arm position. Landing should be with bent knees.
1. Swing and jump. Add half turns and full turns.
2. Swing and return to the perch. Add single- and double-knee bends.
3. Jump for distance, over a high-jump bar or through a hoop.
4. Swing and pick up a bowling pin and return to the perch.
5. Carry objects (e.g., beanbags, balls, deck tennis rings). A partner, standing to the side away from the takeoff bench, can put articles to be carried back on the takeoff perch by placing each article between the knees or feet.
6. Not using a takeoff device, run toward a swinging rope, grasp it, and gain momentum for swinging.

Climbing the Rope

1. *Scissors Grip*. For the Scissors Grip, approach the rope and reach as high as possible, standing with the right leg forward of the left. Raise the back leg, bend at the knee, and place the rope inside the knee and outside the foot. Cross the forward

1. Mats should be placed under all ropes.

2. The hand-over-hand method should be used for climbing and the hand-under-hand method for descending.

3. Caution the children not to slide; sliding can cause rope burns on the hands and legs.

4. A climber who becomes tired should stop and rest. Proper rest stops should be taught as part of the climbing procedure.

5. Children also should be taught to leave enough margin for a safe descent. No children should go higher than their strength allows.

6. Spotters should be used initially for activities in which the body is inverted.

leg over the back leg, and straighten the legs with the toes pointed down. This should give a secure hold. To climb using the Scissors Grip, raise the knees up close to the chest, the rope sliding between them, while supporting the body with the hand grip. Lock the rope between the legs and climb up, using the hand-over-hand method and stretching as high as the hands can reach. Bring the knees up to the chest and repeat the process.

2. *Leg-Around Rest*. Wrap the left leg completely around the rope, keeping the rope between the thighs. The bottom of the rope then crosses over the instep of the left foot from the outside. The right foot stands on the rope as it crosses over the instep, providing pressure to prevent slippage. To provide additional pressure, release the hands and wrap the arms around the rope, leaning away from the rope at the same time. To climb using the Leg-Around Rest, proceed as in climbing with the Scissors Grip, but loosen the grip each time and re-grip higher.

Descending the Rope

There are four methods to descend the rope. The only differences are in the use of the leg locks, as the hand-under-hand is used for all descents.

1. *Scissors Grip*. From an extended scissors grip position, lock the legs and lower the body with the hands until the knees are against the chest. Hold with the hands, and lower the legs to a new position.

2. *Leg-Around Rest*. From the leg-around rest position, lower the body until the knees are against the chest. Lift the top foot, and let the feet slide to a lower position. Secure with the top foot and repeat.

3. *Instep Squeeze*. Squeeze the rope between the insteps by keeping the heels together. Lower the body while the rope slides against the instep.

4. *Stirrup Descent*. Place the rope on the outside of the right foot and carry it over the instep of the left. Pressure from the left foot holds the position. To get into position, let the rope trail along the right leg, reach under, and hook it with the left instep. When the pressure from the left leg is reduced, the rope slides smoothly while the descent is made with the hands.

7. Rosin in powdered form and magnesium chalk aid in gripping. It is particularly important that they be used when the rope becomes slippery.

8. Children swinging on the ropes should be instructed to make sure that other children are out of the way.

9. Marks to limit the climb can be put on the rope with adhesive tape. A height of 8 to 10 feet above the floor is reasonable until a child demonstrates proficiency.

10. If the ceiling is higher than 15 or 16 feet, a bright piece of tape should be wrapped around the rope to limit climbing height.

Game Activity

Substitute from a selected Lesson Plan

DYNAMIC PHYSICAL EDUCATION LESSON PLANS
Development Level II

WEEK	INTRODUCTORY ACTIVITY	FITNESS DEVELOPMENT ACTIVITY	LESSON FOCUS ACTIVITY	GAME ACTIVITY	PAGE
12	Fastest Tag in West	Astronaut Exercises	Walking and Jogging Skills	Recreational Activities	126
13	Jumping & Hopping Patterns	Challenge Course Fitness	Rhythmic Movement Skills (1)	Whistle March Arches Home Base	128
14	Group Tag	Walk Trot, & Jog	Long Rope Jumping Skills	Fly Trap Trades Fox Hunt	132
15	Addition Tag	Challenge Course	Gymnastics Skills (2)	Partner Stoop Crows & Cranes	134
16	High Fives	Challenge Course	Rhythmic Movement Skills (2)	Fox Hunt Steal the Treasure Addition Tag	137
17	Partner Leaping	Aerobic Fitness & Partner Resistance	Basketball Related Skills (1)	Birdie in the Cage Dribblerama Captain Ball Basketball Tag	141
18	Bridges by Three	Aerobic Fitness and Partner Resistance	Basketball Related Skills (2)	Captain Ball Five Passes Around the Key	144
19	Locomotor & Manipulative activity	Exercises to Music	Throwing Skills (2)	In the Prison Snowball Center Target Throw Target Ball Throw	147
20	Yarnball Fun	Exercises to Music	Fundamental Skills Using Benches	Cageball Kickover Squad Tag	149
21	Movement Varieties	Continuity Drills	Hockey Related Skills (1)	Circle Keepaway Star Wars Hockey Lane Hockey Circle Staddleball	151
22	Run, Stop, and Pivot	Continuity Drills	Hockey Related Skills (2)	Modified Hockey Lane Hockey	154

WEEK	INTRODUCTORY ACTIVITY	FITNESS DEVELOPMENT ACTIVITY	LESSON FOCUS ACTIVITY	GAME ACTIVITY	PAGE
23	Moving to Music	Aerobic Fitness	Gymnastics Skills (3)	Steal the Treasure Trees	156
24	Stretching and Jogging	Stretching and Jogging	Track & Field Related Skills (1)	Potato Shuttle Relay Shuttle Relays	159
25	Stretching and Jogging	Stretching and Jogging	Track & Field Related Skills (2)	Circular Relays Shuttle Relays One on one contests	162
26	Move & Perform Task	Walk, Trot, & Jog	Manipulative Skills Using Beanbags	Crows & Cranes Galloping Lizzie	164
27	Long Rope Routine	Parachute Fitness	Rhythmic Movement Skills (3)	Jump the Shot Beachball Batball Club Guard	166
28	Squad Leader Movement	Parachute Fitness	Manipulative Skills Using Paddles & Balls	Trades Bounce Ball	170
29	European Running w/ Equipment	Exercise to Music	Individual Rope Jumping Skills	Loose Caboose Wolfe's Beanbag Exchange Tag	172
30	Marking	Circuit Training	Volleyball Related Skills (1)	Beachball Volleyball Informal Volleyball	174
31	Home Base	Hexagon Hustle	Volleyball Related Skills (2)	Beachball Volleyball Informal Volleyball Shower Service Ball	176
32	Combination Movement Patterns	Continuity Drills	Rhythmic Movement Skills Using Equipment (4)	Alaska Baseball Addition Tag	178
33	European Running w/ variations	Aerobic Fitness	Manipulative Skills Using Frisbees	Frisbee Keep Away Frisbee Golf	182
34	Tortoise & Hare	Aerobic Fitness	Fundamental Skills Using Balance Beams	Hand Hockey Nonda's Car Lot	184

Dynamic Physical Education for Elementary School Children
Orientation and Class Management Activities
Level II – Week 1

Objectives:
To learn and follow basic management activities necessary for participation in physical education classes

Equipment Required:
Tom-tom
Music for Fitness Challenges

Instructional Activities	Teaching Hints

Orientation Instructional Procedures

The first week of school should be used to teach students the system you are going to use throughout the year. The following are reminders you might find useful in establishing your expectations and routines.

1. Establish rules and expectations. Discuss your expectations with the class to assure students understand reasons for your guidelines. Explain what the consequences are when rules are not followed. Show where time-out boxes are located and how they will be used.

2. Explain to the class the method you will use to learn names. It might be helpful to ask classroom teachers to have students put their name on a piece of masking tape (nametag). Tell students that you will ask them their name on a regular basis until it is learned.

3. Develop entry and exit behaviors for students coming and leaving physical education classes. Students should know how to enter the instructional area and to leave equipment alone until told to use it. If squads are used for instruction, place students into squads and practice moving into formation on signal.

4. Decide how excuses for non-participation will be handled. If possible, set up a routine where the school nurse determines which students are excused for health reasons.

5. Safety is important. Children should receive safety rules to be followed on apparatus and playground equipment. Safety procedures to be followed in physical education classes should be discussed.

6. Illustrate how you will stop and start the class. In general, a whistle (or similar loud signal) and a raised hand is effective for stopping the class. A voice command should be used to start the class. Telling the class when before what (Chapter 5) will assure they do not begin before instructions are finished.

7. Discuss the issue, distribution, and care of equipment. Make students responsible for acquiring a piece of equipment and returning it at the end of the lesson. Place equipment around the perimeter of the teaching area to reduce the chance of students fighting over a piece of equipment.

8. Explain to the class that the format of the daily lesson will include an introductory activity, fitness development, lesson focus, and finish with a game activity.

9. Practice various teaching formations such as open-squad formation and closed-squad formation. Practice moving into a circle while moving (fall-in). Transitions between formations should be done while moving, i.e., jogging from scatter formation into a circular formation.

10. Refer to Chapters 3, 4, and 5 in the text for detailed information about planning, developing an effective learning environment, and class management strategies.

Introductory Activity -- Move and Freeze on Signal

Have students move throughout the area using a variety of locomotor movements. On signal (whistle), they quickly freeze. Try to reduce the response latency by reinforcing students who stop quickly on signal.

The primary objective is to teach students the importance of moving under control (without bumping others or falling down) and quickly freezing.

Fitness Development Activity -- Teacher Leader Movement Challenges

1. Locomotor Movement: Walk for 30 seconds.

2. Flexibility and Trunk Development Challenges
   a. Bend in different directions.
   b. Stretch slowly and return quickly.
   c. Combine bending and stretching movements.
   d. Sway back and forth.
   e. Twist one body part; add body parts.

3. Locomotor Movement: Skip for 30 seconds.

4. Shoulder Girdle Challenges
   In a push-up position, do the following challenges:
   a. Lift one foot; the other foot.
   b. Wave at a friend; wave with the other arm.
   c. Scratch your back with one hand; use the other hand.
   d. Walk your feet to your hands.

5. Locomotor Movement: Jog for 30 seconds.

6. Abdominal Development Challenges
   From a supine position:
   1. Lift your head and look at your toes.
   2. Lift your knees to your chest.
   3. Wave your legs at a friend.
   From a sitting position;
   1. Slowly lay down with hands on tummy.
   2. Lift legs and touch toes.

7. Locomotor Movement: Run and leap for 30 seconds.

The goal should be to move students through a number of movement challenges. Emphasis should be placed on starting the fitness activities at a level where all students can feel successful.

Alternate the locomotor movements with the strength and flexibility challenges. Repeat the challenges as necessary.

Tape alternating segments (30 seconds in length) of silence and music to signal duration of exercise. Music segments indicate locomotor movements while intervals of silence announce doing the movement challenges.

Teach youngsters the different challenges and then allow them to select a challenge they can successfully perform.

The challenges should be enjoyable to perform.

Encourage students to focus on effort and feeling successful.

Workloads should be moderate with emphasis on success for all youngsters.

Lesson Focus -- Orientation

Since much time during the first week is used for orientation procedures and management, no lesson focus activity is scheduled.

Game Activity -- Management Games

Play one or two management games to teach students how to move into partner and small group formation

Toe to Toe
   Supplies: None
   Skills: Fundamental locomotor movements
   Youngsters perform a locomotor movement around the area. On signal, each child must find a partner and stand toe to toe (one foot only) with that person. An important skill is to take the nearest person for a partner without searching for a friend. Youngsters who can't find a partner within their immediate area must run quickly to the center of the area (use a marking spot or cone) to find a partner. The goal is to find a nearby partner as quickly as possible and avoid being the last pair formed. If the number of youngsters playing is uneven, the teacher can join in and play. Change locomotor movements often.

Whistle Mixer
   Supplies: None
   Skills: All basic locomotor movements
   Children are scattered throughout the area. To begin, they walk around in any direction they wish. A whistle is blown a number of times in succession with short, sharp blasts. Children then form small groups with the number in each group equal to the number of whistle blasts. If there are four blasts, children form groups of four—no more, no less. When players have the correct number, they sit down immediately to signal that no one may leave the group and no one may enter the group. The goal is not to be left out or caught in a circle with the incorrect number of students. Encourage players to move toward the center of the area and raise their hands to facilitate finding others without a group. After the circles are formed, the teacher calls "Walk," and the game continues. In walking, children should move in different directions.

Dynamic Physical Education for Elementary School Children
Manipulative Skills Using Wands & Hoops
Level II – Week 2

Objectives:
To stop quickly and under control
To maintain the fitness development activity
To toss and catch an object in a variety of situations

Equipment Required:
Music tape for exercises
One wand & hoop for each child
Beanbags or fleece balls

Instructional Activities	Teaching Hints

Introductory Activity -- Fundamental Movements and Stopping

Use the locomotor movements (run, walk, hop, jump, leap, slide, gallop and skip) to move throughout the instructional area. On signal, students stop and freeze without falling. Teach proper stopping form, lowering the center of gravity, spreading the feet for a wide base of support, and keeping the body weight over the feet (minimize leaning). This is an excellent activity for teaching students to move in their own space (as far away from others as possible).

Tape alternating segments of silence and music to signal duration of the locomotor movements. Segments of silence that indicate the "freeze" position can be decreased in duration until the desired response latency is reached.

Fitness Development Activity -- Teacher Leader Exercises

Arm Circles	25 seconds
Bend and Twist	25 seconds
Treadmill	25 seconds
Abdominal Challenges	25 seconds
Single-Leg Crab Kick	25 seconds
Knee to Chest Curl	25 seconds
Run in Place	25 seconds
Trunk Twister	25 seconds

Follow each exercise with 25 seconds of aerobic activity.

Tape alternating segments (25 seconds) of silence and music. The music signals aerobic activity. During the silent segments the exercises are performed

Allow students to adjust the workload to their personal ability and fitness level. This means that some students may perform more repetitions than others.

Move and help students with the exercises.

Lesson Focus -- Manipulative Skills Using Wands and Hoops

Select activities from the each of the exercises and challenges groups.

Strength Exercises with Wands
1. Pull the Wand Apart. Place the hands 6 inches apart near the center of the wand. With a tight grip to prevent slippage and with arms extended, pull the hands apart. Change grip and position.
2. Push the Wand Together. Hold the wand as previously, except push the hands together.
3. Wand Twist. Hold the wand with both hands about 6 inches apart. Twist the hands in opposite directions.
4. Bicycle. Holding the wand horizontally throughout and using an overhand grip, extend the wand outward and downward. Bring it upward near the body, completing a circular movement. On the downward movement, push the wand together, and on the upward movement, pull the wand apart.
5. Arm Spreader. Hold the wand overhead with hands spread wide. Attempt to compress the stick. Reverse force, and attempt to pull the stick apart.
6. Dead Lift. Partially squat and place the wand under the thighs. Place the hands between the legs and try to lift. Try also with hands on the outside of the legs.
7. Abdominal Tightener. From a standing position, place the wand behind the buttocks. With hands on the ends of the wand, pull forward and resist with the abdominal muscles.

Stretching Exercises with Wands
1. Side Bender. Grip the wand and extend the arms overhead with feet apart. Bend sideways as far as possible, maintaining straight arms and legs. Recover, and bend to the other side.

Wands can be made from ¾ inch maple dowels or from a variety of broom and mop handles. They should be cut to a length of 36 inches. Wands are noisy when they hit the floor. Putting rubber crutch tips on the ends of a wand alleviates most of the noise and makes them easier to pick up.

The isometric exercises with wands presented can be performed with a variety of grips. With the wand horizontal, use either the overhand or underhand grip. With the wand in vertical position, grip with the thumbs pointed up, down, or toward each other.

Repeat each exercise with a different grip. Exercises can also be repeated with the wand in different positions: in front of the body (either horizontal or vertical), overhead, or behind the back. Hold each exercise for 8 to 12 seconds.

2. Body Twist. Place the wand behind the neck, with arms draped over the wand from behind. Rotate the upper body first to the right as far as possible and then to the left. The feet and hips should remain in position. The twist is at the waist.

3. Body Twist to Knee. Assume body twist position. Bend the trunk forward and twist so that the right end of the wand touches the left knee. Recover, and touch the left end to the right knee.

4. Shoulder Stretcher. Grip the wand at the ends in a regular grip. Extend the arms overhead and rotate the wand, arms, and shoulders backward until the stick touches the back of the legs. The arms should be kept straight. Those who find the stretch too easy should move their hands closer to the center of the wand.

5. Toe Touch. Grip the wand with the hands about shoulder width apart. Bend forward, reaching down as far as possible without bending the knees. The movement should be slow and controlled. Try the same activity from a sitting position.

6. Over the Toes. Sit down, flex the knees, place the wand over the toes, and rest it against the middle of the arch. Grip the stick with the fingers at the outside edge of the feet. Slowly extend the legs forward, pushing against the stick and trying for a full extension of the legs.

Be gentle when stretching. Reach and stretch the muscles, hold the stretch for a few seconds and relax. Repeat a number of times.

Because wands are noisy when dropped, youngsters should hold their wands with both hands or put them on the floor during instruction.

Wand Challenges

1. Can you reach down and pick up your wand without bending your knees?
2. Try to balance your wand on different body parts. Watch the top of the wand to get cues on how to retain the balance.
3. Can you hold your stick against the wall and move over it? Gradually raise the height of the wand.
4. Let's see whether you can hold the stick at both ends and move through the gap.
5. Can you twirl the wand and keep it going like a windmill?
6. Let's see how many different ways you can move over and around your wand when it is on the floor.
7. Put one end of the wand on the floor and hold the other end. How many times can you run around your wand without getting dizzy?
8. Place one end of the wand against a wall. Holding the other end and keeping the wand against the wall, duck underneath. Place the wand lower and lower on the wall and go under.
9. Place the wand between your feet and hop around as though you are on a pogo stick.
10. Toss the wand from one hand to the other.
11. Hold the wand vertically near the middle. Can you release your grip and catch the wand before it falls to the floor?
12. Have a partner hold a wand horizontally above the floor. Jump, leap, and hop over the wand. Gradually raise the height of the wand.
13. Put your wand on the floor and try making different kinds of bridges over it.
14. Place the wand on the floor. Curl alongside it, just touching it. Curl at one end of the wand.
15. Balance the wand vertically on the floor. Release the wand and try to complete different stunts--clapping the hands, doing a heel click, touching different body parts—before the wand falls to the floor.
16. Put the wand on the floor and see how many ways you can push it, using different body parts.

An adequate amount of space is needed for each individual because wand stunts demand room.

Children may easily be injured using wands improperly. Teach children proper use of wands. Emphasize the need to use care when handling wands to avoid injury to self and others. Do not allow any improper use of wands.

Hoop Activities

1. Hula-hoop using various body parts such as waist, neck, knees, arms and fingers.
   a. While hula-hooping on the arms, try to change the hoop from one arm to the other.
   b. Change hoop from one partner to another while hula-hooping.
   c. Try leg-skippers--hula-hoop with one leg and jump the hoop with the other leg.
2. Jump-rope with the hoop--forward, sideways, and backward. Begin with a back-and-forth swing.

Hoops produce noisy activity. The teacher may find it helpful to have the children lay their hoops on the floor when they are to listen.

In activities that require children to jump through hoops, instruct the holder to grasp the hoop lightly, so as not to cause an awkward fall if a performer hits it.

3. Roll hoop and run alongside it. Run in front of it.
4. Roll hoop with a reverse spin to make it return to the thrower.
5. Roll with a reverse spin and see how many times partner can go through it.
6. Balance the hoop on your head, try to walk through it ("thread the needle") forward, backward and sideways.
7. Try partner activities:
   a. Play catch with hoop.
   b. Hula-hoop on one arm, toss to partner who catches it on one arm.
   c. Use two hoops for catching.
   d. Hoop with one hoop and play catch with other.
   e. Move through a hoop held by a partner.

Hoops can serve as a "home" for various activities. For instance, children might leave their hoops to gallop in all directions and then return quickly to the hoop on command.

When teaching the reverse spin with hoops, have the students throw the hoop up, in place, rather than forward along the floor. After they learn the upward throw, they can progress to the forward throw for distance.

Game Activity

Galloping Lizzie

Supplies: A beanbag or fleece ball

Skills: Throwing, dodging, running

Two or more players are it and have a beanbag or fleece ball. The other players are scattered around the playground. The players with the bag or ball run after the others and attempt to hit other players below the waist with the object. The person hit becomes it, and the game continues. The tagger must throw the bag or ball, not merely touch another person with it.

Crows and Cranes

Supplies: None

Skills: Running, dodging

Establish two goal lines on opposite sides of the area. The class is divided into two groups—the crows and the cranes. The groups face each other at the center of the area, about 5 feet apart. The leader calls out either "Crows" or "Cranes," using a cr-r-r-r-r-r sound at the start of either word to mask the result. If "Crows" is the call, the crows chase the cranes to the goal line. If "Cranes" is the call, the cranes chase. Any player caught goes over to the other side and becomes a member of that group. The team that has the most players when the game ends is the winner.

Dynamic Physical Education for Elementary School Children
Throwing Skills (1)
Level II – Week 3

Objectives:
To recognize a variety of shapes and move the body into the correct shape
To perform continuous fitness activity
To know the elements of proper throwing
To throw with maximum velocity

Equipment Required:
Music for Teacher Leader Exercises
Many types of balls for throwing
Throwing targets; hoops, mats, bowling
    pins and/or cageball
Whistle

Instructional Activities	Teaching Hints

Introductory Activity -- Move and Assume Shape

Have students move using a variation of a basic movement. Freeze on signal and assume a designated shape. Some suggestions are:
  a. Balance
  b. Stretch
  c. Curl
  d. Bridge

Encourage creativity in movements and poses.

Reinforce moving under control.

Use scatter formation.

Fitness Development Activity -- Teacher Leader Exercises

Arm Circles	25 seconds
Bend and Twist	25 seconds
Treadmill	25 seconds
Abdominal Challenges	25 seconds
Single-Leg Crab Kick	25 seconds
Knee to Chest Curl	25 seconds
Run in Place	25 seconds
Trunk Twister	25 seconds

Follow each exercise with 25 seconds of aerobic activity.

Tape alternating segments (25 seconds) of silence and music. The music signals aerobic activity. During the silent segments the exercises are performed

Allow students to adjust the workload to their personal ability and fitness level. This means that some students may perform more repetitions than others.

Move and help students with the exercises.

Lesson Focus -- Throwing Skills (1)

Individual activities
1. Throw balls against the wall. Emphasize the following points:
  a. Start with the feet together.
  b. Start with non-throwing side to the wall.
  c. Lift both the throwing and non-throwing arm (to form a "T" in order to assure the throwing arm elbow is lifted and the non-throwing arm points at the target.
  d. Begin the throw with a step forward with the foot opposite the throwing arm.
  e. Throw as hard as possible.
2. Throw from one side of the gym and try to hit the other wall.
3. If outside, throw as hard and far as possible.

Throwing takes a great deal of practice to master. Two major issues to consider when teaching throwing are:
1. How can I arrange my class so students receive the most opportunity to throw?
2. How can I arrange my class so students get to throw with maximum velocity. A mature pattern of throwing cannot be learned if students are not allowed to throw with maximum force.

Throwing for form
1. Arrange activities to emphasize proper throwing form. Some suggestions are:
  a. Throwing off a tumbling mat. The slight step down off the mat helps some students develop the forward step with the non-throwing side foot. The student stands on the edge of the mat and steps to the floor with the non-throwing side foot as the throw begins. (The other foot remains on the mat). Use the cues, "step, elbow leads, and throw.
  b. Starting a throw with both feet in a hoop. The thrower must lift the front foot to step out of the hoop. Begin with the non-throwing side of the body facing the target and both feet inside the hoop. As the throw begins, a forward step is taken with the non-throwing foot out of the hoop.

Proper form and velocity of throws are closely related. A reason for practicing form is to encourage students to think about technique.

Give each student 4 or 5 balls to throw. They can be placed in a frisbee to keep them from rolling around. When all students are done throwing, they retrieve the same number of balls they have thrown.

c. Touching a cone behind the thrower. The thrower lines up with a cone about an arms-length away and near the throwing side (away from the target). As the throwing arm is extended on the backswing, a slight backward reach is made to encourage reaching back in preparation to throw.

Throwing for velocity is exciting for youngsters. It can also increase the activity level of the lesson as youngsters retrieve the thrown objects.

Throwing for velocity
1. Throw at mats on the wall
   a. Throw fleece balls hard from 15 to 20 feet
   b. Retrieve only if the balls roll behind the throwing line.
2. Throw at hoops leaning against the wall and try to knock them down.
3. Throw at bowling pins
4. Throw outside for distance.

A cageball is an excellent target for encouraging throwing velocity. When it is hit, it will move slightly. A goal can be made to move the cageball across a goal line.

Game Activity

Whistle Mixer
Supplies: A whistle
Skills: All basic locomotor movements

Children are scattered throughout the area. To begin, they walk around in any direction they wish. A whistle is blown a number of times in succession with short, sharp blasts. Children then form small groups with the number in each group equal to the number of whistle blasts. If there are four blasts, children form groups of four—no more, no less. When players have the correct number, they sit down immediately to signal that no one may leave the group and no one may enter the group. The goal is not to be left out or caught in a circle with the incorrect number of students. Encourage players to move toward the center of the area and raise their hands to facilitate finding others without a group. After the circles are formed, the teacher calls "Walk," and the game continues. In walking, children should move in different directions.

Variation: A fine version of this game is done with the aid of a tom-tom. Different beats indicate different locomotor movements--skipping, galloping, slow walking, normal walking, running. The whistle is still used to set the number for each circle.

Couple Tag
Supplies: None
Skills: Running, dodging

Establish two goal lines on opposite sides of the area. Players run in pairs, with inside hands joined. All pairs, except two, line up on one of the goal lines. The pairs in the center are it. They call "Come," and the children, keeping hands joined, run to the other goal line. The pairs in the center, also retaining joined hands, try to tag any other pair. As soon as a couple is caught, they help the center couple. The game continues until all are caught. The last couple caught is it for the next game.

Variation: *Triplet Tag*. The game can be played with sets of threes. Tagging is done with any pair of joined hands. If a triplet breaks joined hands, that group is considered caught.

Partner Stoop
Supplies: Music
Skills: Marching rhythmically

The game follows the same basic principle of stooping as in Circle Stoop, but is played with partners. The group forms a double circle in one direction with one partner on the inside and one on the outside. When the music begins, all march in the line of direction. After a short period of marching, a signal (whistle) is sounded, and the inside circle reverses direction and marches the other way. The partners are thus separated. When the music stops, the outer circle stands still, and the partners making up the inner circle walk (or run) in any direction to rejoin their respective outer circle partners. As soon as players reach their partner, they get toe to toe and stoop without losing balance. The last couple to stoop and those who lose their balance go to the center of the circle and wait out the next round. Start the game walking and gradually pick up the speed of the movements when the class moves under control.

Dynamic Physical Education for Elementary School Children
Football Related Activities
Level II – Week 4

Objectives:
To lead other students in New Leader activities
To independently perform hustle activities
To be able to throw and catch a football
To be able to center a football

Equipment Required:
Signs and music for Hexagon Hustle
One foam rubber junior football for each
  two students
Pinnies to identify teams

Instructional Activities	Teaching Hints

Introductory Activity -- New Leader

Make groups of 3-4 students, assigning one of the students to be a leader. The groups move around the area, following the leader. On signal, the last person moves to the head of the squad and become the leader. Various types of locomotor movements and/or exercises should be used.

Movement should be continuous unless an exercise is being performed.

Encourage students to design their personal movement patterns

Fitness Development Activity -- Hexagon Hustle

Hustle	20 seconds	
Push-Up from Knees	30 seconds	
Hustle	20 seconds	
Bend and Twist (8 counts)	30 seconds	
Hustle	20 seconds	
Jumping Jacks (4 counts)	30 seconds	
Hustle	20 seconds	
Abdominal Challenges (2 counts)	30 seconds	
Hustle	20 seconds	
Double Leg Crab Kick	30 seconds	
Hustle	20 seconds	
Sit and Stretch (8 counts)	30 seconds	
Hustle	20 seconds	
Power Jumper	30 seconds	
Hustle	20 seconds	
Squat Thrust (4 counts)	30 seconds	

Outline a large hexagon with six cones. Place signs with directions on both sides of the cones. The signs identify the hustle activity students are to perform as they approach a cone. Tape alternating segments of silence and music to signal duration of exercise. Music segments indicate aerobic activity while intervals of silence announce flexibility and strength development activities.

See Chapter 12 for a description of exercises and activities.

Lesson Focus -- Football-Related Activities

Skills

Practice the following skills:

1. Forward Passing

The ball should be gripped lightly behind the middle with the fingers on the lace. The thumbs and fingers should be relaxed. In throwing, the opposing foot should point in the direction of the pass, with the body turned sideways. In preparation for the pass, the ball is raised up and held over the shoulders. The ball is delivered directly forward with an overhand movement of the arm and with the index finger pointing toward the line of flight.

2. Catching

When making a catch, the receiver should keep both eyes on the ball and catch it in the hands with a slight give. As soon as the ball is caught, it should be tucked into the carrying position. The little fingers are together for most catches.

3. Centering

Centering involves transferring the ball, on a signal, to the quarterback. In elementary school, the shotgun formation is most often used. This requires snapping the ball a few yards backward to the quarterback. A direct snap involves placing the hands under the buttocks of the center. The ball is then lifted, rotated a quarter turn, and snapped into the hands of the quarterback.

Use instructional cues to improve throwing techniques:
1. Turn the non-passing side toward the direction of the target.
2. Pass the ball with an overhand motion.
3. Step toward the pass receiver.

The following instructional cues will focus on catching technique:
1. Thumbs together for a high pass (above shoulder level).
2. Thumbs apart for a low pass (below shoulder level).
3. Reach for the ball, give, and bring the ball to the body.

The centering player takes a position with the feet well spread and toes pointed straight ahead. Knees are bent and close enough to the ball to reach it with a slight stretch. The right hand takes about the same grip as is used in passing. The other hand is on the side near the back of the ball and merely acts as a guide. On signal from the quarterback, the center extends the arms backward through the legs and centers the ball to the quarterback.

Instructional cues for centering include the following:
1. Reach forward for the ball.
2. Snap the ball with the dominant hand.
3. Guide the ball with the nondominant hand.

Drills
Set up stations for skill practice. Rotate students to each station.

Station 1 - Stance Practice
Students work with a partner and practice getting into the proper stance position. When stance form is mastered, partners can practice getting into position and racing to cones five yards away.

Station 2 - Centering to a Partner
Students work in pairs and practice centering to each other.

Station 3 - Passing and Receiving with a Partner
Students work in pairs and practice passing and receiving the ball. Place emphasis on proper throwing and catching technique.

Station 4 - Pass Defense Drill
Work in groups of three. One player is the passer, one the receiver, and one the defensive player. The passer takes the ball, calls the signal for the receiver to run a pattern, and passes to the receiver who is covered by the defensive player

Signs that describe key points for each skill should be placed on cones at each station. Instructional cues should also be placed on the signs so students can analyze their form and performance.

Use foam rubber footballs with third and fourth graders. This helps students learn the skills without fear of being hurt by the ball.

Game Activity

Football End Ball
Supplies: Foam rubber junior footballs
Skills: Passing, catching

The court is divided in half by a centerline. End zones are marked 3 feet wide, completely across the court at each end. Players on each team are divided into three groups: forwards, guards, and ends. The object is for a forward to throw successfully to one of the end-zone players. End-zone players take positions in one of the end zones. Their forwards and guards then occupy the opposite half of the court farthest from this end zone. The forwards are near the centerline, and the guards are back near the end zone in their half of the court. When a team gets the ball, the forwards try to throw over the heads of the opposing team to an end-zone player. To score, an end-zone player must have both feet inside the zone and catch the ball. No moving with the ball is permitted by any player. After each score, the ball is immediately turned over to the other team.

A penalty results in loss of the ball to the other team. Penalties are assessed for the following.
1. Holding a ball for more than 5 seconds
2. Stepping over the end line or stepping over the centerline into the opponent's territory
3. Pushing or holding another player

In case of an out-of-bounds ball, the ball belongs to the team that did not cause it to go out. The nearest player retrieves the ball at the sideline and returns it to a player of the proper team. Fast, accurate passing is encouraged. Players in the end zones must practice jumping high to catch the ball while still landing with both feet inside the end-zone area. A system of rotation is desirable. Each time a score is made, players on that team can rotate one person. To outline the end zones, tumbling mats (4 by 7 feet or 4 by 8 feet) can be used. Three or four mats forming each end zone delineate a definite area and eliminate the problem of defensive players (guards) stepping into the end zone.

Five Passes
Supplies: Foam rubber junior footballs, pinnies or other identification
Skills: Passing, catching

Players scatter on the field. The object of the game is for one team to make five consecutive passes to five different players without losing control of the ball. This scores 1 point. The defense may play the ball only and may not make personal contact with opposing players. No player can take more than three steps when in possession of the ball. Taking more than three steps is traveling and the ball is awarded to the other team.

The ball is given to the opponents at the nearest out-of-bounds line for traveling, minor contact fouls, after a point has been scored, and for causing the ball to go out of bounds. No penalty is assigned when the ball hits the ground. It remains in play, but the five-pass sequence is interrupted and must start again. Jump balls are called when the ball is tied up or when there is a pileup. The official should call out the pass sequence.

Dynamic Physical Education for Elementary School Children
Manipulative Skills Using Playground Balls
Level II – Week 5

Objectives:

To sequence a series of locomotor movements

To participate in physical activity that exercises all body parts

To throw and catch a playground ball

To control a playground ball with the feet

To appreciate differences in ability among peers

Equipment Required:

Six cones for Hexagon Hustle

Signs and music for Hexagon Hustle

One 8½" playground ball or foam rubber ball for each student

Instructional Activities	Teaching Hints

Introductory Activity – Following Activity

One partner leads and performs combinations of locomotor and non-locomotor movements. The other partner follows and performs the same movements. This can also be used with groups of 3-4 students following a leader.

Change the leaders often so all students get a chance to create some movements.

Fitness Development Activity – Hexagon Hustle

Hustle	25 seconds	Outline a large hexagon with six cones.
Push-Up from Knees	30 seconds	Place signs with directions on both sides
Hustle	25 seconds	of the cones. The signs identify the hustle
Bend and Twist (8 counts)	30 seconds	activity students are to perform as they
Hustle	25 seconds	approach a cone. Tape alternating
Jumping Jacks (4 counts)	30 seconds	segments of silence and music to signal
Hustle	25 seconds	duration of exercise. Music segments
Abdominal Challenges (2 counts)	30 seconds	indicate aerobic activity while intervals
Hustle	25 seconds	of silence announce flexibility and
Double Leg Crab Kick	30 seconds	strength development activities.
Hustle	25 seconds	
Sit and Stretch (8 counts)	30 seconds	Encourage students to do their best.
Hustle	25 seconds	Workloads should be personalized by
Power Jumper	30 seconds	each student by performing activities they
Hustle	25 seconds	feel able to do.
Squat Thrust (4 counts)	30 seconds	

Lesson Focus -- Manipulative Skills Using Playground Balls

Individual Activities

Controlled rolling and handling

1. Sit, stand, or on back--roll ball around and handle it between legs, behind back to develop a proper "feel" of the ball.

Give students two or three activities to practice so you have time to move and help youngsters. Alternate activities from each of the categories so students receive a variety of skills to practice.

Bounce and catch

1. Two hands, one hand.
2. Bounce at different levels.
3. Bounce between legs.
4. Close eyes and bounce.
5. Dribble ball in a stationary and/or moving position.
6. Dribble and follow the commands, such as: move forward, backward, in a circle, sideways, while walking, galloping, trotting, etc.

When catching, soft receipt of the ball is achieved by "giving" with the hands and arms. The hands should reach out somewhat to receive the ball and then cushion the impact by bringing the ball in toward the body in a relaxed way.

Toss and catch

1. Toss and catch, vary height.
2. Add various challenges while tossing (i.e., touch floor, clap hands, turn, make body turns, sit down, lie down).
3. Toss and let bounce. Also add some challenges as above.
4. Toss up and catch behind back--toss from behind back and catch in front.
5. Create moving challenges (i.e., toss, run five steps, catch, toss, back up five hops, and catch).

Toss high as you can and still maintain control.

To catch a throw above the waist, the hands should be positioned so that the thumbs are together. To receive a throw below the waist, the little fingers should be kept toward each other and the thumbs kept out.

Bat the ball (as in volleyball) to self (teach a low-controlled bat).
1. Bat the ball--use palm, back, and side of hand.
2. Bat the ball using different body parts.

Foot skills
1. Pick the ball up with both feet and catch. Both front and rear of body catch.
2. From a sitting position, ball between feet, toss ball up and catch with hands.
3. While sitting, toss ball up with hands and catch with feet.
4. Put ball between feet or knees and play tag games.
5. Keep ball in air by using feet, knees, head. How many times can you bounce it in succession.

Partner Activities
Passing skills
1. Two-handed, right and left.
2. Throw to various targets--high, low, right and left.
3. Odd throws—under leg, around body, football center, shot-put, windmill, discus.
4. Push-shot types. Straight push, arch.
5. Roll the ball to partner. Flick it in the air with foot and catch.
6. Have one partner dribble and the other attempt to take it away without fouling.

Laterality is an important consideration. Right and left members of the body should be given practice in turn.

When throwing to a partner, unless otherwise specified, the throw should reach the partner at about chest height. At times, different target points should be specified---high, low, right, left, at the knee, and so on.

Distance between partners should be short at first and should be lengthened gradually.

Control the passes. Move closer together if necessary.

Game Activity

Bounce Ball

Supplies: Volleyballs or rubber playground balls of about the same size
Skills: Throwing, ball rolling

The court is divided into halves. The class is divided into two teams and each team occupies one half of the court and is given a number of balls. Two players from each team should be assigned to retrieve balls that go behind their end lines. The object of the game is to bounce or roll the ball over the opponents' end line. A ball thrown across the line on a fly does not count. Two scorers are needed, one at each end line. Players can move wherever they wish in their own area but cannot cross the centerline. After the starting signal, the balls are thrown back and forth at will.

One Step

Supplies: A ball or beanbag for each pair of children
Skills: Throwing, catching

Two players stand facing each other about 3 feet apart. One has a ball or beanbag. The object of the game is to throw or toss the item so that the partner can catch it without moving her feet. When the throw is completed successfully, the thrower takes one step backward and waits for a throw from her partner. Players try to increase the distance one step at a time until they reach an established line. When either player misses or moves their feet, the partners move forward and start over.

Variables that provide interest and challenge are types of throws, types of catches, and different steps. Throwing can be underhand, overhand, two-handed, under one leg, around the back, and so on. Catching can be two-handed, left-handed, right-handed, to the side, and so on. The step can be a giant step, a tiny step, a hop, a jump, or a similar movement.

Dynamic Physical Education for Elementary School Children
Fundamental Skills Using Tug-of-War Ropes & Relays
Level II – Week 6

Objectives:
To be able to lead and follow peers performing activity
To perform fitness activities independently
To learn cooperative skills required in performing relay activities
To know how to generate maximum force in pulling activities
To demonstrate personal responsibility skills when competing

Equipment Required:
Signs and music for circuit training
5-6 hoops
One tug-of-war rope for each set of
partners
Beanbags and playground balls for relays

Instructional Activities	Teaching Hints

Introductory Activity – Four Corners Movement

Lay out a rectangle with a cone at each corner. As the child passes each corner, he changes to a different locomotor movement.

Challenge students to perform various qualities of movement (i.e., soft, heavy, slow, fast).

Fitness Development Activity -- Circuit Training

Students do the best they can at each station within the time limit. This implies that not all youngsters are required to do the same workload. Children differ and their ability to perform fitness workloads differs. Make fitness a personal challenge.
Rope Jumping
Triceps Push-Ups
Agility Run
Body Circles
Hula Hoop
Knee Touch Curl-Ups
Crab Walk
Tortoise and Hare
Bend and Twist

Conclude circuit training with 2-4 minutes of walking, jogging, rope jumping or other aerobic activity.

Tape alternating segments of silence and music to signal duration of exercise. Music segments (begin at 30 seconds) indicate activity at each station while intervals of silence (10 seconds) announce it is time to stop and move forward to the next station.

Use signals such as start, stop, and move up to ensure rapid movement to the next station.

Ask students to do the best they can. Expect workloads to differ.

Fundamental Skills Using Partner Tug-of-War Ropes and Relays

Partner Tug-of-War Ropes
   Alternate tug-of-war rope activities with relays for complete physical development. Relays stimulate the cardiovascular system while tug-of-war activities develop the muscular system. Try different ways of pulling. Let students try to devise ways other than those mentioned for pulling against each other.
1. Pull with the right hand only, the left hand only, both hands.
2. Grasp with the right hand, with the body supported on three points (the left hand and the feet). Change hands.
3. Pull with backs toward each other, with the rope between the legs, holding with one hand only.
4. Opponents get down on all fours, with feet toward each other. Hook the loops around one foot of each opponent and pull with both hands and the foot that remains on the floor.
5. Opponents get into crab position and pull the rope by hooking a foot through the loop.
6. Opponents face each other and stand on one foot only. Contestants try to pull each other off balance without losing their own balance. If the raised foot touches the floor, the other person is declared the winner.
7. Contestants stand with opposite sides toward each other. They hold a tug-of-war rope with opposite hands and move apart until the rope is taut. The goal is to make the other person move the feet by pulling and giving on the rope. The legs must be kept straight, and only the arms can be used in the contest.

Contests should be between opponents of comparable ability. Each child should have a chance to win.

Plan a system of rotation so children meet different opponents.

Caution students to not let go of the rope. If the grip is slipping, they should inform the other student, renew the grip, and start over.

Individual ropes are excellent for partner resistance activities. A few of these activities should be practiced each time the children use the ropes.

8. Students stand 10 feet away from the rope, which is on the floor. On signal, they run to the rope, pick it up, and have a tug-of-war. Contestants can start from different positions, such as push-up, curl-up, or Crab.

9. Instead of opponents pulling each other across a line, each tries to pull the other toward a peg or bowling pin placed behind them so that they can pick up the objects.

10. Two individual ropes are tied together at the center so that four loops are available for pulling. Four cones form a square, and four children compete to see who can pick up a cone first.

11. Two children pull against two others. The rope loops should be made big enough so that both can secure handholds on each end. They can use right hands only or left hands only.

12. Frozen Tug-of-War. Two children take hold of a rope, each with both hands on a loop. The children are positioned close enough together so that there is some slack in the rope. A third child grasps the rope to make a 6-inch bend at the center, and the contestants then pull the rope taut so that there is no slack. On the signal "Go," the third child drops the loop, and the opponents try to pull each other off balance. The feet are "frozen" to the floor; if the position of either foot is moved, that player loses.

13. Hawaiian Tug-of-War is an exciting game activity for youngsters. Two parallel lines are drawn about 20 feet apart. The game is between two people, but as many pairs as are in a class can play. A partner tug-of-war rope is laid on the floor at right angles to, and midway between, the two parallel lines. The players position themselves so that each is standing about 1 foot from one of the loops of the rope. They are in position to pick up the rope and pull against each other on signal. The object of the game is to pull the other child far enough to be able to touch the line behind. The magic word is "Hula." This is the signal to pick up the rope and begin to pull. Children must not reach down and pick up the rope until "Hula" is called. The teacher can use other commands, such as "Go" and "Begin," to deceive the children.

Relays

Beanbag Pass Relay

Players are in a line, standing side by side. The player on the right starts the beanbag, which is passed from one player to the next down the line. When it gets to the end of the line, the relay is over. The teacher should be sure that each player handles the bag. Children should rotate positions in line.

In the next stage, a revolving relay can be developed in which each member of the team rotates from the right of the squad to the left. When each child has had an opportunity to be the lead member of the group, the relay is finished. This relay can be varied with an underleg pass. The child passes the beanbag underneath one leg to the next player.

Circle Beanbag Pass Relay

Players stand in a circle, facing out, but close enough so that the beanbag can be handed from player to player. One circuit begins and ends with the same player. The underleg pass can be used in this formation also.

Carry-and-Fetch Relay

Players are in closed squad formation, with a hoop or circle positioned up to 30 feet in front of each team. The first runner on each team has a beanbag. On the command "Go," this player carries the beanbag forward and puts it inside the hoop, then returns and tags off the next runner. The second runner goes forward, picks up the beanbag, and hands it off to the third runner. One runner carries the beanbag forward and the next runner fetches it back. Different locomotor movements can be specified.

Make the starting routine clear so that each contestant understands. Make definite rules about what constitutes a win and how long a contest must endure to be called a tie.

A line on the floor perpendicular to the direction of the rope makes a satisfactory goal for determining a win. One child pulls the other forward until the second child is over the line. If the distance seems too short, two parallel lines can be drawn 8 to 10 feet apart, with the object now being to pull the opponent out of the area between the lines. Another criterion for a win could be for children to pick up objects placed behind them.

Restrict teams to four or five players. Too many on a team increases the amount of time spent waiting for a turn.

Change teams regularly so all youngsters have a chance to be on a winning team. You should reserve the right to change team makeup and the order in which the students are placed on individual teams.

Try changing teams after each new relay. Placing less skilled players in the first or last position of the relay team will force these students to perform in front of the class and reveal to others that they are inferior. Place less skilled students in the middle of the team. Use discretion when moving players to avoid labeling them as unskilled performers.

Beanbag Circle Change Relay

Players are in lane formation. Two hoops or circles are about 15 and 30 feet in front of each team. A beanbag is in the far hoop. The first runner runs forward, picks up the beanbag, and moves it to the inner hoop. The next player picks it up and takes it back to the other hoop. The beanbag must rest inside the hoop.

The Farmer and the Crow Relay

Runners are in lane formation. A line is drawn about 20 feet in front of the teams. The first runner of each team is the farmer, the second runner the crow, and so on. The farmer has five beanbags. On the signal "Go," the farmer hops forward and drops the five beanbags in a reasonably spaced fashion, with the last beanbag placed beyond the drawn line. The farmer then runs back and tags the next player, the crow. The crow runs to the farthest beanbag, begins hopping, picking up the beanbags. The crow hands the five beanbags to the third runner, another farmer, who puts the objects out again. Whenever players have a beanbag, they hop; when they have no beanbags, they run. The last beanbag should be placed beyond the far line, because this determines how far each player has to move. The relay can be done with only hopping allowed.

Bounce Ball Relay

A circle is drawn 10 to 15 feet in front of each team. The first player runs to the circle, bounces the ball once, runs back to the team, and gives the ball to the second player, who repeats the routine. Each player has a turn, and the team whose last child carries the ball over the finish line first wins. To vary the relay, players can bounce the ball more than once.

Kangaroo Relay

The first player in each lane holds a ball between the knees. He jumps forward, retaining control of the ball, rounds the turning point, jumps back to the head of the file, and hands the ball to the next player. If a player loses the ball from between the knees, she must stop and replace it. Slightly deflated balls are easier to retain.

Infractions of rules should be discussed. Relays are a social learning experience. Children are in a situation where they must conform to rules if the experience is going to be enjoyable for all students. Use this time to discuss how cooperation precedes competition; it is impossible to compete if players choose not to cooperate.

Designate a deceleration area with a cone or spot to prevent running into a wall.

Place the marker 10 feet from the wall. Too much emphasis on winning makes the skilled resent losing and intimidates those of lesser ability. This is an excellent time to discuss the idea of winning at any cost.

A trial run should always be made so each team clearly understands the procedures. If a new relay does not start properly, stop the activity and review the instructions. Practice the relay first before embarking on a serious competitive run.

Traffic rules should be clear. In most cases, the way to the right governs. When runners go around the turning point, they do it from the right (counterclockwise), returning past the finish line on the right side. Some procedures to ensure a fair tagging off of the next runner should be instituted. Runners should not leave the restraining line before being tagged. Exchanging a baton or a beanbag also restrains runners from leaving too early.

Game Activity

Relaxation Activities

Relays are active and exciting. Try some relaxation activities to calm the class before they return to the classroom.

1. Use the progressive relaxation technique. Tense a muscle or muscle group and then relax it slowly and smoothly. Progressive relax all the major body parts by moving from head to toes. For example: "Frown and squinch up your face, making many wrinkles, and then slowly relax your face and smooth it out." Each time the muscle group is relaxed, exhale completely.
2. Hold an isometric contraction at the elbow joint. With the other hand, feel the contraction in the biceps and triceps. Do the same with other joints and muscles.
3. While standing, slowly take a deep breath, and expel the air as completely as possible, while simultaneously dropping the head and collapsing the chest.

Dynamic Physical Education for Elementary School Children
Gymnastics Skills (1)
Level II – Week 7

Objectives:
To move rhythmically to a drumbeat
To support the body weight in a variety of tumbling and stunt activities
To control the body weight in a variety of tumbling and stunt activities
To enjoy participation in group games

Equipment Required:
Tom-tom or tambourine
Circuit training music and signs
5-6 hoops and individual jump ropes
Tumbling mats
Balls & bowling pins for game activities

Instructional Activities	Teaching Hints

Introductory Activity -- European Rhythmic Running

To introduce a group of children to Rhythmic Running, have them clap to the beat of the drum. Next, as they clap, have them walk in place, keeping time. Following this, have them run in place, omitting the clapping. Finally, the class can run in single-file formation, develop the ability to follow a leader, maintain proper spacing and move to the rhythm of the tom-tom.

A variation is to have a leader move in different shapes and designs. Have class freeze and see if they can identify the shape or formation.

Fitness Development Activity -- Circuit Training

Rope Jumping
Triceps Push-Ups
Agility Run
Body Circles
Hula Hoop
Knee Touch Curl-Ups
Crab Walk
Tortoise and Hare
Bend and Twist

Conclude circuit training with 2-4 minutes of walking, jogging, rope jumping or other aerobic activity.

Tape alternating segments of silence and music to signal duration of exercise. Music segments (begin at 30 seconds) indicate activity at each station while intervals of silence (10 seconds) announce it is time to stop and move forward to the next station.

Use signals such as start, stop, and move up to ensure rapid movement to the next station.

Ask students to do the best they can. Expect workloads to differ.

Lesson Focus – Gymnastics Skills (1)

Animal Movements
Cricket Walk
  Squat. Spread the knees. Put the arms between the knees and grasp the outside of the ankles with the hands. Walk forward or backward. Chirp like a cricket. Turn around right and left. See what happens when both feet are moved at once!

Frog Jump
  From a squatting position, with hands on the floor slightly in front of the feet, jump forward a short distance, landing on the hands and feet simultaneously. Note the difference between this stunt and the Rabbit Jump. Emphasis eventually should be on both height and distance. The hands and arms absorb part of the landing impact to prevent excessive strain on the knees.

Seal Crawl
  Start in the front-leaning rest position, the weight supported on straightened arms and toes. Keeping the body straight, walk forward, using the hands for propelling force and dragging the feet. Keep the body straight and the head up.

Reverse Seal Crawl
  Do the Seal Crawl with the tummy facing up and dragging the heels.

Six groups of activities in this lesson ensure that youngsters receive a variety of experiences. Pick a few activities from each group and teach them alternately. For example, teach one or two animal movements, then a tumbling and inverted balance, followed by a balance stunt, etc. Give equal time to each group of activities

Scatter tumbling mats throughout the area so that there is little standing in line waiting for a turn. No more than 3-4 students per mat.

Youngsters can do the animal walks around their mats. Many of the activities in this unit do not have to be performed on the mat.

Tumbling and Inverted Balances
Forward Roll

Stand facing forward, with the feet apart. Squat and place the hands on the mat, shoulder width apart, with elbows against the insides of the thighs. Tuck the chin to the chest and make a rounded back. A push-off with the hands and feet provides the force for the roll. Carry the weight on the hands, with the elbows bearing the weight of the thighs. If the elbows are kept against the thighs and the weight is assumed there, the force of the roll is transferred easily to the rounded back. Try to roll forward to the feet. Later, try with the knees together and no weight on the elbows.

Forward Roll to a Walkout

Perform the Forward Roll as described previously, except walk out to a standing position. The key to the Walkout is to develop enough momentum to allow a return to the feet. The leg that first absorbs the weight is bent while the other leg is kept straight.

Review the Backward Curl (taught in grades K-2)

Approach this activity in three stages. For the first stage, begin in a sitting position, with the knees drawn up to the chest and the chin tucked. The hands are clasped and placed behind the head with the elbows held out as far as possible. Gently roll backward until the weight is on the elbows. Roll back to starting position.

In stage two, perform the same action as before, but place the hands alongside the head on the mat while rolling back. The fingers are pointed in the direction of the roll, with palms down on the mat. (A good cue is, "Point your thumbs toward your ears and keep your elbows close to your body.")

For stage three, perform the same action as in stage two, but start in a crouched position on the feet with the back facing the direction of the roll. Momentum is secured by sitting down quickly and bringing the knees to the chest.

Backward Roll (Handclasp Position)

Clasp the fingers behind the neck, with elbows held out to the sides. From a crouched position, sit down rapidly, bringing the knees to the chest for a tuck to secure momentum. Roll completely over backward, taking much of the weight on the forearms. With this method, the neck is protected.

Climb-Up (taught in grades K-2)

Begin on a mat in a kneeling position, with hands placed about shoulder width apart and the fingers spread and pointed forward. Place the head forward of the hands, so that the head and hands form a triangle on the mat. Walk the body weight forward so that most of it rests on the hands and head. Climb the knees to the top of the elbows. (This stunt is a lead-up to the Headstand.)

Balance Stunts
One-Leg Balance Reverse

Assume a forward balance position by balancing on one leg, bending over at the waist until the chest is parallel with the floor, and extending the arms. In a quick movement, to give momentum, swing the free leg down and change to the same forward balance position facing in the opposite direction (a 180-degree turn). No unnecessary movement of the supporting foot should be made after the turn is completed. The swinging foot should not touch the floor.

Tummy Balance

Lie prone on the floor with arms outstretched forward or to the sides, with palms down. Raise the arms, head, chest, and legs from the floor and balance on the tummy. The knees should be kept straight.

Leg Dip

Extend both hands and one leg forward, balancing on the other leg. Lower the body to sit on the heel and return without losing the balance or touching the floor with any part of the body. Try with the other foot.

A major concern for safety is the neck and back region. Overweight children are at greater risk and might be allowed to avoid tumbling and inverted balances.

Do not perform many repetitions of tumbling and inverted balances. For most children, limiting the number of forward or backward roll repetitions to four or five will prevent fatigue and injury. The Backward Curl should be used to learn to roll back and forth. No youngster should be expected to roll over if it is difficult. In stunts and tumbling, it is important that the student decide if they are capable and confident enough to try the activity.

The Backward Curl is a lead-up to the Backward Roll. Teach children to push against the floor to take pressure off the back of the neck.

The handclasp position backward roll should be learned before the traditional backward roll. The handclasp method, in contrast to the traditional backward roll, does not require adequate arm strength to lift the body off the floor and release the head.

The Climb-Up should only be performed by youngsters who have sufficient strength to support the body weight. Overweight children will find this to be a difficult activity.

With the exception of the tumbling and inverted balances group, all the activities in this unit can be performed by all youngsters. If in doubt about an activity in the tumbling and inverted balances group, avoid teaching it.

This activity is excellent for back strength. It also reinforces students who are flexible in the back area.

When doing the Leg Dip, another student can assist from the back by applying upward pressure to the elbows.

Individual Stunts

Reach-Under

Take a position with the feet pointed ahead (spaced about 2 feet apart) and toes against a line or a floor board. Place a beanbag two boards in front of, and midway between, the feet. Without changing the position of the feet, reach one hand behind and between the legs to pick up the beanbag. Now pick up with the other hand. Repeat, moving the beanbag a board farther away each time.

If a beanbag is unavailable, youngsters can see how far they can gradually reach and note the distance in relationship to a tile, piece of grass, or board in the floor.

Stiff Person Bend

Place the feet about shoulder width apart and pointed forward. Place a beanbag a few inches behind the right heel. Grasp the left toes with the left hand, thumb on top. Without bending the knees, reach the right hand outside the right leg and pick up the beanbag without releasing the hold on the left toes

These are enjoyable challenges for youngsters. Increase the challenge by gradually increasing the distance of the reach. Reverse sides of the body.

Coffee Grinder

Put one hand on the floor and extend the body to the floor on that side in a side-leaning rest position. Walk around the hand, making a complete circle and keeping the body straight.

The Coffee Grinder should be done slowly, with controlled movements. The body should remain as straight as possible throughout the circle movement.

Scooter

Sit on the floor with legs extended, arms folded in front of the chest, and chin held high. To scoot, pull the seat toward the heels, using heel pressure and lifting the seat slightly. Extend the legs forward again and repeat the process.

Partner and Group Stunts

Partner Hopping

Partners coordinate hopping movements for short distances and in different directions and turns. Three combinations are suggested.

Find a partner who is similar in ability.

1. Stand facing each other. Extend the right leg forward to be grasped at the ankle by partner's left hand. Hold right hands and hop on the left leg.
2. Stand back to back. Lift the leg backward, bending the knee, and have partner grasp the ankle. Hop as before.
3. Stand side by side with inside arms around each other's waist. Lift the inside foot from the floor and make progress by hopping on the outside foot.

If either partner begins to fall, the other should release the leg immediately. Reverse foot positions.

Partner Twister

Partners face and grasp right hands as if shaking hands. One partner swings the left leg over the head of the other and turns around, taking a straddle position over partner's arm. The other swings the right leg over the first partner, who has bent over, and the partners are now back to back. First partner continues with the right leg and faces in the original direction. Second partner swings the left leg over the partner's back to return to the original face-to-face position.

Partners need to duck to avoid being kicked by each other's feet as the legs are swung over.

Partner Pull-Up

Partners sit facing each other in a bent knee position, with heels on the floor and toes touching. Pulling cooperatively, they come to a standing position.

The goal is to *simultaneously* come to the standing position, instead of one standing and pulling the other to their feet.

Game Activity

Whistle Mixer

Supplies: A whistle

Skills: All basic locomotor movements

Children are scattered throughout the area. To begin, they walk around in any direction they wish. A whistle is blown a number of times in succession with short, sharp blasts. Children then form small groups with the number in each group equal to the number of whistle blasts. If there are four blasts, children form groups of four—no more, no less. When players have the correct number, they sit down immediately to signal that no one may leave the group and no one may enter the group. The goal is not to be left out or caught in a circle with the incorrect number of students. Encourage players to move toward the center of the area and raise their hands to facilitate finding others without a group. After the circles are formed, the teacher calls "Walk," and the game continues. In walking, children should move in different directions.

Circle Contests

    Supplies: Volleyballs or 8-in. foam rubber balls, two bowling pins

    Skills: Throwing, catching

    Two teams arranged in independent circles compete against each other. The circles should be the same diameter; lines can be drawn on the floor to ensure this. The players of each team are numbered consecutively so each player in one circle corresponds to a player in the other circle. Two numbered players, in sequence, go to the center of the opponents' circle to compete for their team in either of the following activities.

1. *Circle Club Guard.* The two center players guard a bowling pin. The ball is rolled at the club. The circle that knocks down the club first wins a point.

2. *Touch Ball.* The circle players pass the ball from one to another while the two center players try to touch it. The center player who touches the ball first wins a point for the respective team. In case neither player is able to touch the ball in a reasonable period of time, the action should be cut off without awarding a point.

    After all players have competed, the team with the most points wins. For *Circle Club Guard*, there must be three passes to different people before the ball can be rolled at the club. Establishing circle lines may be necessary to regulate throwing distance.

Alaska Baseball

    Supplies: A volleyball or soccer ball

    Skills: Kicking, batting, running, ball handling

    Players are divided into two teams; one is at bat while the other is in the field. A straight line provides the only out-of-bounds line, and the team at bat is behind this line midway between the ends of the line. The other team is scattered around the fair territory. One player propels the ball, either batting a volleyball or kicking a stationary soccer ball. Her teammates are in a close file behind her. As soon as the batter sends the ball into the playing area, she starts to run around her own team. Each time the runner passes the head of the file, the team gives a loud count.

    There are no outs. The first fielder to get the ball stands still and starts to pass the ball back overhead to the nearest teammate, who moves directly behind to receive it. The remainder of the team in the field must run to the ball and form a file behind the fielder. The ball is passed back overhead, with each player handling the ball. When the last field player in line has a firm grip on it, she shouts "Stop." At this signal, a count is made of the number of times the batter ran around her team. To score more accurately, half rounds can be counted. Five batters or half of the team should bat; then the teams should change places. This is better than allowing an entire team to bat before changing to the field, because players in the field fatigue from many consecutive runs.

Dynamic Physical Education for Elementary School Children
Soccer Related Activities (1)
Level II – Week 8

Objectives:
To strike a foam rubber soccer ball with a variety of body parts
To dribble a foam rubber soccer ball with the feet
To trap a foam rubber ball with a variety of body parts
To play a soccer lead-up activity and understand the joy of participation

Equipment Required:
Music tape for Astronaut Exercises
8" foam rubber or 8½" playground ball
  for each student
Pinnies (optional)
Cones for marking the drill areas and
  goals

Instructional Activities	Teaching Hints

Introductory Activity -- Magic Number Challenges

Students are challenged to put together a combination of locomotor movements corresponding to the magic numbers designated (e.g., 10, 8 and 7). Students would have to do three different movements 10, 8 and 7 time, respectively. Use cards with specified numbers. Think of new activities for each series of numbers.

The number of movements, the repetitions and the types of movements can be changed to offer a wide variety of challenges.

Fitness Development Activity -- Astronaut Exercises

Walk, do Arm Circles	35 seconds
Crab Full-Leg Extension	30 seconds
Skip sideways	35 seconds
Body Twist	30 seconds
Slide; change lead leg	35 seconds
Jumping Jack variations	30 seconds
Crab Walk	35 seconds
Curl-Ups with Twist	30 seconds
Hop to center and back	35 seconds
Four Count Push-Ups	30 seconds
Gallop Backwards	35 seconds
Bear Hugs	30 seconds
Grapevine Step (Carioca)	35 seconds
Trunk Twisters	30 seconds
Power Jumper	35 seconds

Cool down with stretching and walking.

Tape alternating segments of silence (30 seconds) and music (35 seconds) to signal the duration of exercise. Music segments indicate aerobic activity while intervals of silence announce flexibility and strength development activities.

See Chapter 12 for a description of how to perform the exercises.

Allow students to adjust the workload to an intensity that is consistent with their ability level.

Use scatter formation; ask students to change directions from time to time in order to keep spacing.

Lesson Focus -- Soccer Related Activities (1)

Skills
Practice the following skills:
1. Dribbling
   Dribbling is moving the ball with a series of taps or pushes to cover ground and still retain control. It allows a player to change direction quickly and to avoid opponents. The best contact point is the inside of the foot, but the outside of the foot will be used at faster running speeds. The ball should be kept close to the player to maintain control.
2. Inside-of-the-Foot Pass (Push Pass)
   The inside-of-the-foot pass is used for accurate passing over distances of up to 15 yards. Because of the technique used, this pass is sometimes referred to as the push pass. The non-kicking foot is placed well up, alongside the ball. As the kicking foot is drawn back, the toe is turned out. During the kick, the toe remains turned out so that the inside of the foot is perpendicular to the line of flight. The sole is kept parallel to the ground. At contact, the knee of the kicking leg should be well forward, over the ball, and both knees should be slightly bent.

When teaching students beginning skills, have them place their hands behind their back to avoid the temptation of touching the ball with the hands.

Keep the ball near the body so it can be controlled. (Don't kick it too far in front of the body.) Dribble the ball with a controlled tap.

Place the non-kicking foot alongside the ball. Keep the head down and eyes focused on the ball during contact.

Make contact with the outside or inside of the foot rather than with the toe.

3. Inside-of-the-Foot Trap

This is the most common method of control, and is used when the ball is either rolling along the ground or bouncing up to knee height. The full surface of the foot, from heel to toe, should be presented perpendicular to the ball.

Move in line with the path of the ball and reach with the foot to meet the ball. Give when ball contact is made to absorb force.

Drills

Use the following partner drills to practice the skills above:

1. Dribbling, marking, and ball recovery. Pairs are scattered, with one player in each pair having a soccer ball. That player dribbles in various directions, and the second player attempts to stay close to the first (marking). As skill development occurs, the defensive player can attempt to recover the ball from the dribbler. If successful, roles are reversed.

Each student should practice dribbling and handling the ball individually. Use drills after students have had time to practice the skills individually. Working with a partner increases the motivational level.

2. Dribbling, Passing, and Trapping. One player of the pair has a ball and dribbles in different directions. On signal, she passes to her partner, who traps the ball and begins dribbling, continuing until another signal is given.

Emphasize controlled activity. The goal is not to see how far or hard the ball can be kicked.

Game Activity -- Soccer Lead-Up Games

Circle Kickball

Supplies: Two soccer balls or 8-in. foam rubber balls

Skills: Kicking, controlling

Players are in circle formation. Using the side of the foot, players kick the balls back and forth inside the circle. The object is to kick a ball out of the circle beneath the shoulder level of the circle players. A point is scored against each of the players where a ball leaves the circle between them. If, however, a lost ball is clearly the fault of a single player, then the point is scored against that player only. Any player who kicks a ball higher than the shoulders of the circle players has a point scored against him. Players with the fewest points scored against them win. A player is not penalized if he leaves the circle to recover a ball and the second ball goes through the vacated spot.

Soccer Touch Ball

Supplies: A soccer ball

Skills: Kicking, controlling

Players are spaced around a circle 10 yards in diameter with two players in the center. The object of the game is to keep the players in the center from touching the ball. The ball is passed back and forth as in soccer. If a center player touches the ball with a foot, they are awarded a point. Implement a rule that no player may contain or hold the ball longer than 3 seconds to keep the game moving. Rotate two new players into the center after 15 to 30 seconds.

Diagonal Soccer

Supplies: A soccer ball, pinnies (optional)

Skills: Kicking, passing, dribbling, some controlling, defending, blocking shots

Two corners are marked off with cones 5 feet from the corners on both the sides, outlining triangular dead areas. Each team lines up and tries to protect two adjacent sides of the square. To begin competition, three players from each team move into the playing area in their own half of the space. These are the active players who may roam anywhere in the square. The other players act as goalkeepers.

The object of the game is for active players to kick the ball through the opposing team's line (beneath shoulder height) to score. After 30 to 45 seconds, active players rotate to the sidelines and new players take their place. Players on the sidelines may block the ball with their bodies and use their hands. The team against whom the point was scored starts the ball for the next point. Only active players may score. Scoring is much the same as in Circle Kickball in that a point is awarded for the opponents when any of the following occur:

1. A team allows the ball to go through its line below the shoulders.
2. A team touches the ball illegally.
3. A team kicks the ball over the other team above shoulder height.

Soccer Take-Away

Supplies: A soccer ball for each student

Skills: Dribbling and defensive skills

Four or five players are designated as defensive players. Each of the rest of the students have a soccer ball and dribble it around the area. The defensive players try to take away a ball from the offensive players. When a successful steal is made, the player losing control of the ball becomes a defensive player.

Dynamic Physical Education for Elementary School Children
Soccer Related Activities (2)
Level II – Week 9

Objectives:
To strike a foam rubber soccer ball with a variety of body parts
To dribble a foam rubber soccer ball with the feet
To trap a foam rubber ball with a variety of body parts
To play a soccer lead-up activity and understand the joy of participation

Equipment Required:
6 marking spots
Music tape for Astronaut Exercises
One 8" foam rubber or 8½" playground
   ball for each student
Pinnies for games (optional)
Cones for marking the drill areas and
   goals

Instructional Activities	Teaching Hints

Introductory Activity – Home Base

The class is divided in to teams of 5-6 players. One player in each group is designated the captain. Rubber spots are placed throughout the teaching area equal to the number of teams. Each spot serves as a home base for one of the squads. The teams begin in a straight line with the captain standing on a spot and the rest of the team lined up behind her. The teacher calls out a locomotor movement that the players use to move throughout the area. When the teacher calls "home base!" each team lines up in starting formation with the captain first in line. The first team to return to proper position is awarded wins that round.

This is an excellent game to teach youngsters how to get in small group formations quickly.

If desired, use the call "find your home" to assemble the class in pre-assigned squads. Some teachers use squads for station teaching and dividing the class into teams.

Fitness Development Activity -- Astronaut Exercises

Walk, do Arm Circles	35 seconds
Crab Full-Leg Extension	30 seconds
Skip sideways	35 seconds
Body Twist	30 seconds
Slide; change lead leg	35 seconds
Jumping Jack variations	30 seconds
Crab Walk	35 seconds
Curl-Ups with Twist	30 seconds
Hop to center and back	35 seconds
Four Count Push-Ups	30 seconds
Gallop Backwards	35 seconds
Bear Hugs	30 seconds
Grapevine Step (Carioca)	35 seconds
Trunk Twisters	30 seconds
Power Jumper	35 seconds

Cool down with stretching and walking.

Tape alternating segments of silence (30 seconds) and music (35 seconds) to signal the duration of exercise. Music segments indicate aerobic activity while intervals of silence announce flexibility and strength development activities.

See Chapter 12 for a description of how to perform the exercises.

Allow students to adjust the workload to an intensity that is consistent with their ability level.

Use scatter formation; ask students to change directions from time to time in order to keep spacing.

Lesson Focus -- Soccer-Related Activities (2)

Skills
Divide the skills into four stations and place necessary equipment at each station. Students can practice skills they learned in last week's lesson.
1. Review and practice the long pass. Set up a station with plenty of room and students with a partner. They long pass back and forth to each other.
2. Review the inside-of-the foot pass and trapping: Work with a partner and practice passing and trapping.
3. Practice dribbling skills: Give each student a ball and have them practice dribbling. Move the ball with a series of taps. Start slowly and keep the ball in front of the body.
4. Dribbling and Passing: Students work with a partner. One dribbles the ball a short distance and then pass it to their partner.

Make signs that tell students the skills they are to practice at each station. Set the signs on cones in the areas where students are to practice.

The foam training balls are best for teaching introductory soccer skills. They don't hurt students when kicked or when they are struck by a ball.

Drills Using Three Players

With one ball for three players, many of the possibilities suggested for pair practice are still possible. An advantage of drills for three players is that fewer balls are needed.

1. Passing and controlling. The trio of players set up a triangle with players about 10 yards apart. Controlled passing and practice in ball control should occur.
2. Dribbling and passing. A shuttle-type drill can be structured where players keep going back and forth continuously. Player 1 has the ball and dribbles to player 2, who dribbles the ball back to player 3, who in turn dribbles to player 1. Players can dribble the entire distance or dribble a portion of the distance and then pass the ball to the end player. Obstacles can be set up to challenge players to dribble through or around each obstacle.
3. Dribbling and stopping the ball. Three dribblers are in line, each with a ball. The leader moves in various directions, followed by the other two players. On signal, each player controls her ball. The leader circles around to the back ball, and the other two move one ball forward. The dribbling continues for another stop. A third stop puts the players back in their original positions.
4. Passing. Players stand in three corners of a 10-yard square. After a player passes, he must move to the empty corner of the square, which is sometimes a diagonal movement.
5. Passing and defense. One player is the feeder and rolls the ball to either player. As soon as she rolls the ball, she attempts to block or tackle the player receiving the ball to prevent a pass to the third player, who, if the pass is completed, attempts to pass back.

Grids with areas that are approximately 10 yards square can be marked off with marking spots or cones. The drills are then conducted with a threesome in each area.

The drills can also be set up as individual stations where students rotate after a specified time.

Many of the drills are simple game activities. Students enjoy the opportunity to play with friends.

Emphasis should be on form and practicing the skills. If students are unable to control the ball, drills may not work and students should be given time to practice individually.

Game Activity -- Soccer Lead-Up Activities

Diagonal Soccer

Supplies: A soccer ball, pinnies (optional)

Skills: Kicking, passing, dribbling, some controlling, defending, blocking shots

Two corners are marked off with cones 5 feet from the corners on both the sides, outlining triangular dead areas. Each team lines up and tries to protect two adjacent sides of the square. To begin competition, three players from each team move into the playing area in their own half of the space. These are the active players who may roam anywhere in the square. The other players act as goalkeepers.

The object of the game is for active players to kick the ball through the opposing team's line (beneath shoulder height) to score. After 30 to 45 seconds, active players rotate to the sidelines and new players take their place. Players on the sidelines may block the ball with their bodies and use their hands. The team against whom the point was scored starts the ball for the next point. Only active players may score. Scoring is much the same as in Circle Kickball in that a point is awarded for the opponents when any of the following occur:

1. A team allows the ball to go through its line below the shoulders.
2. A team touches the ball illegally.
3. A team kicks the ball over the other team above shoulder height.

Soccer Touch Ball

Supplies: A soccer ball

Skills: Kicking, controlling

Players are spaced around a circle 10 yards in diameter with two players in the center. The object of the game is to keep the players in the center from touching the ball. The ball is passed back and forth as in soccer. If a center player touches the ball with a foot, they are awarded a point. Implement a rule that no player may contain or hold the ball longer than 3 seconds to keep the game moving. Rotate two new players into the center after 15 to 30 seconds.

Dribblerama

Supplies: One soccer ball for each player

Skills: Dribbling, protecting the ball

The playing area is a large circle or square, clearly outlined. All players dribble within the area. The game is played on two levels.

Level 1: Each player dribbles throughout the area, controlling the ball so it does not touch another ball. If a touch occurs, both players go outside the area and dribble around the area. Once youngsters have completed dribbling one lap, they may reenter the game.

Level 2: Two equal playing areas are delineated. All players start in one of the areas. While dribbling and controlling the ball, each player attempts to kick any other ball out of the area. When a ball is kicked out, the player owning that ball takes it to the other area and dribbles. As more players move to the second area, a second game ensues. Players in this area move back to the opposite side. This keeps all players actively involved in the games.

Bull's Eye

Supplies: One soccer ball per player

Skills: Dribbling, protecting the ball

The playing area is a large outlined area--circle, square, or rectangle. One player holds a ball in her hands, which serves as the bull's-eye. The other players dribble within the area. The player with the bull's-eye attempts to throw her ball (basketball push shot) at any other ball. The ball that is hit now becomes the new bull's-eye. The old bull's-eye becomes one of the dribblers. A new bull's-eye cannot hit back immediately at the old bull's-eye. If the group is large, have two bull's-eyes. No score is kept and no one is eliminated.

Dynamic Physical Education for Elementary School Children
Fundamental Skills Using Parachute Activities
Level II – Week 10

Objectives:
To perform a variety of fitness activities rhythmically
To work together with peers to accomplish parachute activities
To develop strength through parachute activities

Equipment Required:
Music and signs for Aerobic Fitness
Parachute, beanbags, jump ropes, and
  cageball
Box and 4 balls

Instructional Activities	Teaching Hints

Introductory Activity -- Group Over and Around

One half of the class is scattered. Each is in a curled position. The other half of the class leaps or jumps over the down children. On signal, reverse the group quickly. In place of a curl, the down children can bridge while the other youngsters move around them.

The down children can also alternate between curl and bridge, as well as move around the area while in a bridged position.

Fitness Development Activity -- Aerobic Fitness

1. Rhythmic run with clap
2. Bounce turn and clap
3. Rhythmic 4-count curl-ups (knees, toes, knees, back)
4. Rhythmic Crab Kicks (slow time)
5. Jumping Jack combination
6. Double knee lifts
7. Lunges (right, left, forward) with single-arm circles (on the side lunges) and double-arms circles (on the forward lunge)
8. Rhythmic trunk twists
9. Directional run (forward, backward, side, turning)
10. Rock side to side with clap
11. Side leg raises (alternate legs)
12. Rhythmic 4-count push-ups (If these are too difficult for students, substitute single-arm circles in the push-up position.)

Use music to stimulate effort. Any combination of movements can be used.

Keep the steps simple and easy to perform. Some students will become frustrated if the learning curve is steep.

Signs that explain the aerobic activities will help students remember performance cues.

Don't stress or expect perfection. Allow students to perform the activities as best they can.

Alternate bouncing and running movements with flexibility and strength development movements.

Lesson Focus -- Parachute Activities

Parachute Warm-Up Activities. These activities are useful for starting children on the parachute. They are demanding activities that allow students to use excess energy.

Shaking the Rug and Making Waves
   Shaking the Rug involves rapid movements of the parachute, either light or heavy. Making Waves involves large movements to send billows of cloth up and down.

Chute Crawl
   Half of the class, either standing or kneeling, stretches the chute at waist level parallel to the ground. The remaining children crawl under the chute to the opposite side from their starting position.

Kite Run
   The class holds the chute on one side with one hand. The leader points in the direction they are to run while holding the chute aloft like a kite.

Running Number Game
   The children around the chute count off by fours; then they run lightly, holding the chute in one hand. The teacher calls out one of the numbers. Children with that number immediately release their grip on the chute and run forward to the next place vacated. They must put on a burst of speed to move ahead.

One parachute is generally sufficient for a class of 30 children. Parachutes come in different sizes, but those with diameters ranging from 24 to 32 feet are suitable for a regular class. The size with most utility is the 28-foot parachute. Each parachute has an opening near the top to allow trapped air to escape and to keep the parachute shaped properly. Most parachutes are constructed of nylon. A parachute should stretch tight and not sag in the middle when it is pulled snug by children spaced around it.

Parachute Exercise Activities. Exercises should be done vigorously and with enough repetitions to challenge the children. In addition to the exercises presented, others can be adapted to parachute play.

Toe Toucher

Sit with feet extended under the parachute and hold the chute taut with a two-hand grip, drawing it up to the chin. Bend forward and touch the grip to the toes. Return parachute to stretched position.

Curl-Up

Extend the body under the parachute in curl-up position, so that the chute comes up to the chin when held taut. Do Curl-Ups, returning each time to the stretched chute position.

Dorsal Lift

Lie prone, with head toward the parachute and feet pointed back, away from it. Grip the chute and slide toward the feet until there is some tension on it. Raise the chute off the ground with a vigorous lift of the arms, until head and chest rise off the ground. Return.

V-Sit

Lie supine, with head toward the chute. Do V-Ups by raising the upper and lower parts of the body simultaneously into a V-shaped position. The knees should be kept straight.

Backward Pull

Face the parachute and pull back, away from its center. Pulls can be made from a sitting, kneeling, or standing position.

Parachute Activities with Equipment

Ball Circle

Place a basketball or a cageball on the raised chute. Make the ball roll around the chute in a large circle, controlling it by raising or lowering the chute. Try the same with two balls. A beach ball is also excellent.

Popcorn

Place a number of beanbags (from six to ten) on the chute. Shake the chute to make them rise like corn popping.

Team Ball

Divide the class in half, each team defending half of the chute. Using from two to six balls of any variety, try to bounce the balls off the opponents' side, scoring 1 point for each ball.

Poison Snake

Divide into teams. Place from 6 to 10 jump ropes on the chute. Shake the chute and try to make the ropes hit players on the other side. For each rope that touches one team member, that team has a point scored against it. The team with the lower score is the winner.

Parachute Dome Activities To make a dome, children begin with the parachute on the floor, holding with two hands and kneeling on one knee. To trap air under the chute, children stand up quickly, thrusting their arms above the head, and then return to starting position.

Students under the Chute

Tasks for under the chute can be specified, such as turning a certain number of turns with a jump rope, throwing and catching a beanbag, or bouncing a ball a number of times. The needed objects should be under the chute before the dome is made.

Number Exchange

Children are numbered from one to four. The teacher calls a number as the dome is made, and those with the number called must change position to be under the dome before the chute comes down. Locomotor movements can be varied.

Punching Bag

Children make a dome and stand on the edges. They then punch at the chute while slowly and gently walking the edges of the chute toward the center.

The grips used in handling the parachute are comparable to those employed in hanging activities on an apparatus. Grips can be with one or two hands, overhand (palms facing away), underhand (palms facing toward), or mixed (one hand underhand and the other overhand).

For preliminary explanations, the parachute can be stretched out on the ground in its circular pattern, with the children seated so that they cannot touch the parachute during instructions. When the children hold the parachute during later explanations, they should retain their hold lightly, letting the center of the parachute drop to the ground. Children must be taught to exercise control and not to manipulate the parachute while explanations are in progress.

Walking on the parachute should be discouraged, since it is a slippery surface and may increase the chance of falls.

Teach the proper technique of lifting the parachute. Youngsters should start with one knee on the floor; as the hands lift upward, stand and make the legs do the work. As the stand occurs, take a step toward the center of the chute and lift upward. Lifting should be done with the legs and arms.

Blooming Flower

Children make a dome and kneel with both knees on the edge of the chute. Youngsters hold hands around the chute and lean in and out to represent a blooming flower opening.

Lights Out

While making a dome, the children take two steps toward the center and sit inside the chute. The chute can be held with the hands at the side or by sitting on it.

Mushroom Activities

To form a mushroom, students begin with the chute on the ground, kneeling on one knee and holding with two hands. They stand up quickly, thrusting the arms overhead. Keeping the arms overhead, each walks forward three or four steps toward the center. The arms are held overhead until the chute is deflated.

Mushroom Release

All children release at the peak of inflation and either run out from under the chute or move to the center and sit down, with the chute descending on top of them.

Mushroom Run

Children make a mushroom. As soon as they move into the center, they release holds and run once around the inside of the chute, counterclockwise, back to place.

Game Activity

Indianapolis 500

Supplies: None

Skills: Running, tagging

Players start in a large circle and are numbered off in threes or fours. A race starter says "Start your engines," and then calls out a number. Those players with the corresponding number run in the same direction around the circle and try to tag players in front of them. If the leader yells "Pit stop," all runners have to stop and return to their original position. If "Car crash" is called by the leader, all runners change direction and continue running. Change starters often.

Box Ball

Supplies: A sturdy box, 2 ft square and about 12 in. deep; four volleyballs (or similar balls)

Skills: Running, ball handling

The class is divided into four even teams, with 6 to 10 players per team. Each team occupies one side of a square at an equal distance from the center. Players face inward and number off consecutively from right to left. A box containing four balls is put in the center. A number is called and the player from each team who has that number runs forward to the box, takes a ball, and runs to the head of her line, taking the place of player 1. In the meantime, players in the line move to the left just enough to fill in the space left by the runner. On reaching the head of the line, the runner passes the ball to the next person and so on down the line to the end person. The last player runs forward and returns the ball to the box. The first team to return the ball to the box scores a point.

The runner must not pass the ball down the line until she is in place at the head of the line. The ball must be caught and passed by each child or risk team disqualification. Runners stay at the head of the line and retain their original number. The lines are not kept in consecutive number sequence.

Dynamic Physical Education for Elementary School Children
Playground and Recreational Activities
Level II – Week 11

Objectives:
To learn the rules of games that are common on local playgrounds
To learn the etiquette of games that are common on local playgrounds
To understand the recreational and self-directed nature of playground games

Equipment Required:
Tambourine
Signs and music for Aerobic Fitness
Equipment needed for playground games

Instructional Activities	Teaching Hints

Introductory Activity -- Bend, Stretch and Shake

Students should alternate between various bending and stretching activities. On signal, students shake and relax various body parts. Teach a variety of bending and stretching activities.

Use a tambourine to signal changes in bending and stretching. Shake it to signal shaking activities.

Fitness Development Activity -- Aerobic Fitness

The following aerobic movements are suggestions only. Also, stop the aerobic fitness movements and do flexibility and strength development activity to allow students time to recover aerobically.

1. Rhythmic run with clap
2. Bounce turn and clap
3. Rhythmic 4-count curl-ups (knees, toes, knees, back)
4. Rhythmic Crab Kicks (slow time)
5. Jumping Jack combination
6. Double knee lifts
7. Lunges (right, left, forward) with single-arm circles (on the side lunges) and double-arms circles (on the forward lunge)
8. Rhythmic trunk twists
9. Directional run (forward, backward, side, turning)
10. Rock side to side with clap
11. Side leg raises (alternate legs)
12. Rhythmic 4-count push-ups (If these are too difficult for students, substitute single-arm circles in the push-up position.)

Use music to stimulate effort. Any combination of movements can be used.

Keep the steps simple and easy to perform. Some students will become frustrated if the learning curve is steep.

Signs that explain the aerobic activities will help students remember performance cues.

Don't stress or expect perfection. Allow students to perform the activities as best they can.

Alternate bouncing and running movements with flexibility and strength development movements.

Lesson Focus and Game Activity – Playground and Recreational Activities

Playground and Recreational Activities

The objective of this lesson should be to teach youngsters the rules and methods for playing games during their free time. Emphasis should be on self-direction so students do not need supervision.

1. Tetherball
2. Four Square
3. Two Square
4. Volley Tennis
5. Basketball
   a. Around the Key
   b. Twenty One
   c. Freeze Out
6. Hopscotch
7. Jump Rope
8. Soccer (2 on 2)
9. Frisbee Golf
10. Wall Handball
11. Any playground and recreational activities played at your school.

The focus of this lesson is to teach students the rules and etiquette required to play recreational activities. Take time to discuss questions students might have about the activities.

These playground games listed here are just examples. Most schools have a number of games that are popular and played by the majority of youngsters. Ask youngsters what games are popular and allow some selected upper grade students to teach them.

If desired, set up stations and divide students into four groups. All students to rotate to each group during the lesson focus time. Use signs on cones that explain the activities to be done at each station.

Dynamic Physical Education for Elementary School Children
Walking and Jogging Skills
Level II – Week 12

Objectives:
To travel throughout the area and be able to avoid or catch another individual
To understand the differences in aerobic capacities among classmates
To find a running or walking pace that is comfortable for an extended time

Equipment Required:
Recreational and individual equipment desired
Music for Astronaut Exercises

Instructional Activities	Teaching Hints
Introductory Activity -- Fastest Tag in the West	
All students are it. On signal, they try to tag each other. If they are tagged, they must freeze, but they are eligible to tag other students who pass near them. If two or more players tag each other simultaneously, they are both/all "frozen."	The focus of this game is activity. Don't overemphasize rules. When about half of the class is frozen, start the game over.

Fitness Development Activity -- Astronaut Exercises

Walk, do Arm Circles	35 seconds	Tape alternating segments of silence (30 seconds) and music (35 seconds) to signal the duration of exercise. Music segments indicate aerobic activity while intervals of silence announce flexibility and strength development activities.
Crab Full-Leg Extension	30 seconds	
Skip sideways	35 seconds	
Body Twist	30 seconds	
Slide; change lead leg	35 seconds	
Jumping Jack variations	30 seconds	
Crab Walk	35 seconds	
Curl-Ups with Twist	30 seconds	See Chapter 12 for a description of how to perform the exercises.
Hop to center and back	35 seconds	
Four Count Push-Ups	30 seconds	
Gallop Backwards	35 seconds	Allow students to adjust the workload to an intensity that is consistent with their ability level.
Bear Hugs	30 seconds	
Grapevine Step (Carioca)	35 seconds	
Trunk Twisters	30 seconds	
Power Jumper	35 seconds	Use scatter formation; ask students to change directions from time to time in order to keep spacing.

Cool down with stretching and walking.

Lesson Focus -- Walking and Jogging Skills

The walking and jogging lesson should be a relaxed lesson with emphasis on developing activity patterns that can be used outside of the school environment. An educational approach to this lesson teaches students that walking and jogging are done without equipment and offer excellent health benefits. It is an activity that can literally be done for a lifetime. The following are suggestions for implementing this unit of instruction:

1. Youngsters should be allowed to find a friend with whom they want to jog or walk. The result is usually a friend of similar ability level. A way to judge correct pace is to be able to talk with a friend without undue stress. If students are too winded to talk, they are probably running too fast. A selected friend will encourage talking and help assure that the experience is positive and within the student's aerobic capacity. *Pace, not race* is the motto.

2. Jogging and walking should be done in any desired direction so others are unable to keep track of the distance covered. Doing laps on a track is one of the surest ways to discourage less able youngsters. They always finish last and are open to chiding by the rest of the class.

3. Jogging and walking should be done for a specified time rather than a specified distance. All youngsters should not have to run the same distance. This goes against the philosophy of accompanying individual differences and varying aerobic capacities. Running or walking for a set amount of time will allow the less able child to move without fear of ridicule.

4. Teachers should not be concerned about foot action, since the child selects naturally the means that is most comfortable. Arm movement should be easy and natural, with elbows bent. The head and upper body should be held up and back. The eyes look ahead. The general body position in walking and jogging should be erect but relaxed.

5. Jogging and walking should not be a competitive, timed activity. Each youngster should move at a self-determined pace. Racing belongs in the track program. Another reason to avoid speed is that racing keeps youngsters from learning to pace themselves. For health benefits, it is best to move for a longer time at a slower speed than to run at top speed for a shorter distance.

6. It is motivating for many youngsters to run with a piece of equipment, i.e., beanbag or jump rope. They can play catch with a beanbag or roll a hoop while walking or jogging.

Game Activity -- Individual or Recreational Activity

When youngsters are finished jogging, allow them the opportunity to participate in a choice of individual or recreational activities.

Dynamic Physical Education for Elementary School Children
Rhythmic Movement Skills (1)
Level II – Week 13

Objectives:
To perform a locomotor movement and manipulate an object simultaneously
To perform rhythmic movements in folk dances
To appreciate the origin of folk dances
To understand the cultural differences among students from different backgrounds

Equipment Required:
Equipment for the Challenge Course
Music for games
Music for rhythmic activities

Instructional Activities	Teaching Hints
Introductory Activity -- Jumping and Hopping Patterns	
Students jump or hop to a target area and return with a different pattern. Many combinations can be devised with the basic idea being to develop a pattern to get to the target and another to return to home spot. An example is: Jump in all directions and hop back to place; or three jumps forward and a half twist, three jumps back to place and a half twist.	Encourage students to develop personal combinations of movement. Increase the distance of movement as the patterns are developed.

Fitness Development Activity – Challenge Course

Design a course around the perimeter of the area using the following ideas:

1. Step on jumping box, dismount to tumbling mat and do a forward roll.
2. Run and weave through four wands held upright by cones.
3. Handwalk across a horizontal ladder or do a flexed-arm hang from a climbing rope for 5 seconds.
4. Step on and off three jumping boxes (small-large-small).
5. Agility run through hoops.
6. Perform jump turns.
7. Leap over a magic rope held taut with two chairs or jumping boxes.
8. Hop on one foot.
9. Do a Log Roll across a tumbling mat.
10. Alternate going over and under six obstacles (cones and wands or hoops).
11. Crouch jump or scooter movements the length of a balance-beam bench.
12. Slide through a parallel tumbling mat maze (mats stood on their sides).

Move through the Challenge Course with quality movements rather than speed.

Distribute youngsters throughout the course instead of starting them at one common point.

Stop the class at regular intervals to perform flexibility and strength development activities.

Change directions periodically. This helps prevent a build-up of students at slower moving stations.

Lesson Focus -- Rhythmic Movement Skills (1)

Make dances easy for students to learn by implementing some of the following techniques:
Rhythms should be taught like other sport skills. Avoid striving for perfection so students know it is acceptable to make mistakes. Teach a variety of dances rather than one or two in depth in case some students find it difficult to master a specific dance.

1. Teach the dances without using partners.
2. Allow youngsters to move in any direction without left-right orientation.
3. Use scattered formation instead of circles.
4. Emphasize strong movements such as clapping and stamping to increase involvement.
5. Play the music at a slower speed when first learning the dance.

The Bird Dance (Chicken Dance)

Music Source: WWCD-4903; WWC-9126
Formation: Circle or scatter formation, partners facing
Directions:

Measures	Part I Action
1	Four snaps---thumb and fingers, hands up
2	Four flaps---arms up and down, elbows bent
3	Four wiggles---hips, knees bent low
4	Four claps
5--16	Repeat action of measures 1--4 three times

Measures	Part II Action
1--8	With a partner, either do a right-hand star with 16 skips or 16 walking steps, or do an elbow swing. (Skip, 2, 3, . . . 15, change hands)
9--16	Repeat with the left hand. On the last four counts of the last swing, everyone changes partners. If dancing in a circle formation, partners B advance forward counter-clockwise to the next partner A. If dancing in a scattered formation, everyone scrambles to find a new partner. (Skip, 2, 3, . . . 12, change partners)

Csebogar (Hungarian)

Music Source: WWCD 1042;
Formation: Single circle, partners facing center, hands joined with partners B on the right
Directions:

Measures	Part I Action
1--4	Take seven slides to the left. (Slide, 2, 3, 4, 5, 6, 7, change)
5--8	Take seven slides to the right. (Back, 2, 3, 4, 5, 6, 7, stop)
9—12	Take three skips to the center and stamp on the fourth beat. Take three skips backward to place and stamp on the eighth beat. (Forward, 2, 3, stamp; Backward, 2, 3, stamp)
13--16	Hook right elbows with partner and turn around twice in place, skipping. (Swing, 2, 3, 4, 5, 6, 7, 8)

Measures	Part II Action (Partners face each other in a single circle with hands joined.)
17--20	Holding both of partner's hands, take four draw steps (step, close) toward the center of the circle. (Step-close, 2-close, 3-close, 4-close)
21--24	Take four draw steps back to place. (Step-close, 2-close, 3-close, 4-close)
25--26	Go toward the center of the circle with two draw steps. (In-close, 2-close)
27--28	Take two draw steps back to place. (Out-close, 2-close)
29--32	Hook elbows and repeat the elbow swing, finishing with a shout and facing the center of the circle in the original formation. (Swing, 2, 3, 4, 5, "Csebogar")

Crested Hen (Danish)

Music Source: WWCD-1042
Formation: Sets of three. One child is designated the center child.
Directions:

Measures	Part I Action
1—4	Dancers in each set form a circle. Starting with a stamp with the left foot, each set circles to the left, using step-hops. (Stamp and, 2 and, 3 and, 4 and, 5, 6 and, 7 and, stop)
5—8	The figure is repeated. Dancers reverse direction, beginning again with a stamp with the left foot and following with step-hops. The change of direction should be vigorous and definite, with the left foot crossing over the right. At the end of the sequence, two dancers release each other's hands to break the circle and stand on either side of the center person, forming a line of three while retaining joined hands with the center dancer. (Stamp and, 2 and, 3 and, 4 and, 5 and, 6 and, 7 and, line)

Measures	Part II Action (During this part, the dancers use the step-hop continuously while making the pattern figures)
9—10	The dancer on the right moves forward in an arc to the left and dances under the arch formed by the other two. (Under and, 2 and, 3 and, 4 and)
11—12	After the right dancer has gone through, the two forming the arch turn under (dishrag), to form once again a line of three. (Turn and, 2 and, 3 and, 4 and)
13—16	The dancer on the left then repeats the pattern, moving forward in an arc under the arch formed by the other two, who turn under to unravel the line. (Under and, 2 and, 3 and, 4 and; Turn and, 2 and, 3 and, circle)

   As soon as Part II is completed, dancers again join hands in a small circle. The entire dance is repeated. Another of the three can be designated the center dancer.

Bingo (American)

Music Source: WWCD-FDN
Skills: Walking, right-and-left grand
Formation: Double circle, partners side by side and facing counterclockwise, partners A on the inside and inside hands joined.
Note: Bingo is a favorite of young people. The singing must be brisk and loud. The dance is in three parts.
Directions:
Part I: Partners walk counterclockwise around the circle, singing the following refrain. (Walk, 2, 3, ... 15, face center)
Part II: All join hands to form a single circle, partner B on partner A's right. They sing (spelling out) with these actions.

Action

All take four steps into the center.

All take four steps backward.

All take four steps forward again.

Take four steps backward, drop hands, and face partner.

Part III: Shake right hands with the partner, calling out B on the first heavy note. All walk forward, passing their partner, to meet the oncoming person with a left handshake, calling out I on the next chord. Continue to the third person with a right handshake, sounding out the N. Pass on to the fourth person, giving a left handshake and a G. Instead of a handshake with the fifth person, face each other, raise the arms high above the head, shake all over, and sound out a long, drawn-out O. The fifth person becomes the new partner, and the dance is repeated.

Variation: The dance can be adapted to the use of a parachute. At the end of Part II (the end of the line "And Bingo was his name") partners A face the chute and hold it with both hands, lifting it to shoulder level. Partners B drop their hands from the parachute and get ready to move clockwise. On each of the letters B-I-N-G-O, they move inside the first A, outside the next, and so on, for five changes. They then take a new place as indicated and get ready to repeat the dance. The next sequence can have partners B remaining in place, holding the chute, while partners A move counterclockwise.

Grand March (American)

Music Source: WWCD-WOF2 or any good march or square dance record

Skills: Controlled walking, marching, grand march figures

Formation: Partners B are on the left side of the room, facing the end, and partners A are on the right side, facing the same end. This is the foot of the hall. The teacher or caller stands at the other end of the room, the head of the hall. An alternative formation is to put half of the class on each side of the room and to designate each half with different colored pinnies.

Directions:

Call	Action
Down the center by twos.	The lines march forward to the foot of the hall, turn the corner, meet at the center of the foot of the hall, and march in couples toward the caller, with inside hands joined. The Bs' line should be on the proper side so that, when the couples come down the center, A is on B's left. Odd couples are numbered 1, 3, 5, and so on. Even couples are numbered 2, 4, 6, and so on.
Twos left and right.	The odd couples go left and the even couples go right around the room and meet at the foot of the hall.
Down the center by fours.	The couples walk down the center, four abreast.
Separate by twos.	When they approach the caller, odd couples go left and even couples right. They meet again at the foot of the hall.
Form arches.	Instead of coming down the center, odd couples form arches and even couples tunnel under. Each continues around the sides of the hall to meet at the head.
Other couples arch.	Even couples arch, and odd couples tunnel under. Each continues around the sides of the room to the foot.
Over and under.	The first odd couple arches over the first even couple, then ducks under the second even couple's arch. Each couple goes over the first couple and under the next. Continue around to the head of the hall.
Pass right through.	As the lines come toward each other, they mesh and pass through each other in the following fashion: All drop handholds. Each B walks between the A and B of the opposite couple and continues walking to the foot of the hall.
Down the center by fours.	Go down the center four abreast.
Fours left and right.	The first four go left around the room, and the second four go right. The fours meet at the foot of the hall.
Down the center by eights.	Go eight abreast down the center.
Grapevine.	All persons in each line join hands and keep them joined. The leader takes either end of the first line and starts around the room with the line trailing. The other lines hook on to form one long line.
Wind it up.	The leader winds up the group in a spiral formation, like a clock spring. The leader makes the circles smaller and smaller until he or she is in the center.
Reverse (unwind).	The leader turns and faces in the opposite direction and walks between the lines of winding dancers. The leader unwinds the line and leads it around the room.
Everybody swing.	After the line is unwound, everybody does a square dance swing.

Apat Apat (Philippines)

Music Source: WWCD-RM4; WWC-572
Skills: Walking; star hold
Formation: Double circle of partners facing counterclockwise with inside hands joined
Directions:

Measures	Action
	Introduction
1	All face counterclockwise with inside hands joined and walk forward 4 steps. On count 4, release hands and execute a ½ turn right to face clockwise. (Walk, 2, 3, turn)
2	Take 4 walking steps forward clockwise. Release hands on the fourth step and face partner. (Walk, 2, 3, face)
3	Walk 4 steps backward away from partner. (Away, 2, 3, 4)
4	Walk 4 steps forward toward partner with each partner taking a ¼ turn to the right on the 4th count. Partners will be facing in opposite directions. (Forward, 2, 3, right turn)
5	Walk forward 4 steps with partners moving in opposite directions. (Forward, 2, 3, 4)
6	Walk backward 4 steps to meet partner. (Backward, 2, 3, 4)
7	Face partner. With right hand star (join right hands with elbows bent) walk clockwise around partner 4 steps in place. (Star, 2, 3, 4)
8	Release hands, inside circle youngsters walk forward 4 steps counterclockwise to meet next partner. Outside circle youngsters turn ½ turn in place to wait for new partner.

Repeat the dance.

Game Activity

Whistle March

Supplies: Music
Skill: Moving rhythmically

Brisk marching music is useful for this game. Children are scattered around the room, walking in various directions and keeping time to the music. A whistle is blown a number of times. On this signal, lines are formed of that precise number of children, no more and no fewer. To form the lines, children stand side by side with elbows touching. As soon as a line of the proper number is formed, they begin to march to the music around the room. Any children left over go to the center of the room and remain there until the next signal. On the next whistle signal (a single blast), the lines break up, and all walk individually around the room in various directions. When forming new lines, it may be helpful to stipulate that players must group with different players each time.

Arches

Supplies: Music
Skills: Moving rhythmically

The game is similar to London Bridge. An arch is placed in the playing area. (To form an arch, two players stand facing one another with hands joined and arms raised.) When the music starts, the other players move in a circle, passing under the arch. Suddenly, the music stops, and the arch is brought down by dropping the hands. All players caught in an arch immediately pair off to form other arches, keeping in a general circle formation. If a caught player does not have a partner, he waits in the center of the circle until one is available. The last players caught (or left) form arches for the next game.
Variation: Different types of music can be used, and children can move according to the pattern of the music.

Home Base

Supplies: Cones to delineate the area, four pinnies
Skills: Reaction time, locomotor movements, body management

Place a number of marking spots on the floor throughout the area. Divide the class into groups of 5 or 6. Ask each group to quickly line up with one person on a marking spot and the rest of the players behind in single file. The person on the spot is designated as the team captain. A locomotor movement is called and all players do this movement throughout the area. When "Home base," is called, the captains quickly find the closest spot and their respective squad members line up behind them. The first team to return to proper position (standing in a straight line) is declared the winner. Avoid calling "Home base" until the students are thoroughly mixed. A number of different formations can be specified that students must assume upon return to their home base.

Dynamic Physical Education for Elementary School Children
Long-Rope Jumping Skills
Level II – Week 14

Objectives:
To travel throughout the area and be able to avoid or catch another individual
To jump a rope turned by others
To know the difference in long-rope jumping between entering front and back doors

Equipment Required:
Music for Walk, Trot, and Jog
Long-jump ropes (two for each group of four children)

Instructional Activities	Teaching Hints

Introductory Activity -- Group Tag

A number of players are designated to be it. On signal, they try to tag other players. If a player is tagged, that player becomes it and must try to tag another. In other words, each person who is it tags only one player. If players want to be "safe," they must stand toe-to-toe in a group of three or more students.

Encourage students to say "you're it" when they tag someone.

If students can't catch someone, they can give up being it.

Fitness Development Activity -- Walk, Trot, and Jog

Move to the following signals:
1. One drumbeat - walk.
2. Two drumbeats - trot.
3. Three drumbeats - jog
4. Whistle - freeze and perform exercises.

Perform various strength and flexibility exercises between bouts of walk, trot and jog. Examples are:
1. Bend and Twist
2. Sitting Stretch
3. Push-Up Challenges
4. Abdominal Challenges
5. Trunk Twister
6. Body Circles
7. Crab Walk

Tape alternating segments of silence and music to signal duration of exercise. Music segments indicate aerobic activity (30-45 seconds) while intervals of silence announce flexibility and strength development activities (30 seconds).

Assure that students run under control (not as fast as they can) and in the same direction.

Allow students to perform at a level they feel comfortable. Youngsters are genetically different and should not be expected to do the same amount of exercise repetitions.

Lesson Focus -- Long-Rope Jumping Skills

1. Run through turning rope from front door approach.
2. Run through turning rope from back door approach.
3. Try different approaches, a few jumps and varied exits
   a. Run in front door, out back door.
   b. Run in front door and out front door.
   c. Run in back door and out back door.
   d. Run in back door and out front door.
   e. Run in front or back door, jump and do a quarter, half and full turn.
   f. Add individual rope.
4. Hot Pepper: *Gradually* increase the speed of the rope
5. High Water: *Gradually* raise the height of the rope while it is turned.
6. Have more than one child jump at a time. Students can enter in pairs or any other combination. Have jumpers change positions while jumping.
7. Have jumper attempt to jump while holding a beanbag or playground ball between the knees.
8. Have one of the turners jump the long rope.
9. Play catch with a partner while jumping the rope.
10. Egg Beater: Two long ropes are turned simultaneously with four turners.
11. Double Dutch: Requires two long ropes turned alternately. Rope near jumper is turned back door and far rope front door. To start turning, begin with the ropes held tight. Start turning in small circles and gradually move together.

Turning the rope is a difficult skill for young children. It must be practiced regularly until children can maintain an even, steady rhythm. Effective turning is requisite to successful jumping. If turning is not rhythmic, skilled jumpers will have problems. Youngsters must be taught: Learn to turn first, then learn to jump.

Front door means entering from the side where the rope is turning forward and toward the jumper after it reaches its peak. Back door means entering from the side where the rope is turning backward and away from the jumper. To enter front door, the jumper follows the rope in and jumps when it completes the turn. To enter back door, the jumper waits until the rope reaches its peak and moves in as the rope moves downward.

Fly Trap

Supplies: None

Skills: Fundamental locomotor movements

Half of the class is scattered around the playing area, sitting on the floor in cross-legged fashion. These children form the trap. The rest of the players are flies and they buzz around the seated children. When a whistle is blown, the flies must freeze where they are. If any of the trappers can touch a fly, that fly sits down at that spot and becomes a trapper. The trappers must keep their seats glued to the floor. The game continues until all of the flies are caught. Some realism is given to the game if the flies make buzzing sounds and move their arms as wings. Some experience with the game enables the teacher to determine how far apart to place the seated children. After most of the flies have been caught, the groups trade places. Change the method of locomotion.

Trades

Supplies: None

Skills: Imagery, running, dodging

Designate two lines at opposite ends of the area. The class is divided into two teams of equal number. One team, the chasers, stands on one of the lines. The other team, the runners, starts on the other line. The runners move toward the chasers while reciting the following dialogue:

Runners: *Here we come.*

Chasers: *Where from?*

Runners: *New Orleans.*

Chasers: *What's your trade?*

Runners: *Lemonade.*

Chasers: *Show us some.*

The runners move close to the other team's goal line and proceed to act out an occupation or a specific task that they have chosen previously. The opponents try to guess what the pantomime represents. When a correct guess is made, the chasers try to tag the running team before they reach the goal line. Any runner tagged must join the chasers. The game is repeated with roles reversed. The team ending with the greater number of players is the winner. If a team has trouble guessing the pantomime, the other team should provide hints. Teams also should be encouraged to have a number of activities selected so that little time is consumed in choosing the next activity to be pantomimed.

Fox Hunt

Supplies: None

Skills: Running, dodging

Two players form trees by facing each other and holding hands. The third member of the group is a fox and stands between the hands of the trees. Three players are identified as foxes without trees and three players are designated as hounds. The hounds try to tag the foxes that are not in trees. The extra foxes may move to a tree and displace the fox that is standing in the tree. In addition, the foxes in trees may leave the safety of their trees at any time. If the hound tags a fox, their roles are reversed immediately, the fox becoming the hound. The game should be stopped at regular intervals to allow the players who are trees to change places with the foxes and hounds. Different locomotor movements can be specified to add variety to the game.

Dynamic Physical Education for Elementary School Children
Gymnastics Skills (2)
Level II – Week 15

Objectives:
To hear and move to different rhythms
To support and control body weight in a variety of stunts and tumbling activities
To participate in game activities in a cooperative manner

Equipment Required:
Equipment for Challenge Course
Tumbling mats
Music for game

Instructional Activities	Teaching Hints
Introductory Activity -- Addition Tag	
Two couples are it, and each stands with inside hands joined. These are the taggers. The other children run individually. The couples move around the playground, trying to tag with the free hands. The first person tagged joins the couple, making a trio. The three then chase until they catch a fourth. Once a fourth person is caught, the four divide and form two couples, adding another set of taggers to the game. This continues until all children are tagged.	The game moves faster if started with two couples. A tag is legal only when the couple or group of three keeps their hands joined.

Fitness Development Activity – Challenge Course

Design a course around the perimeter of the area using the following ideas:
1. Step on jumping box, dismount to tumbling mat and do a forward roll.
2. Run and weave through four wands held upright by cones.
3. Handwalk across a horizontal ladder or do a flexed-arm hang from a climbing rope for 5 seconds.
4. Step on and off three jumping boxes (small-large-small).
5. Agility run through hoops.
6. Perform jump turns.
7. Leap over a magic rope held taut with two chairs or jumping boxes.
8. Hop on one foot.
9. Do a Log Roll across a tumbling mat.
10. Alternate going over and under six obstacles (cones and wands or hoops).
11. Crouch jump or scooter movements the length of a balance-beam bench.
12. Slide through a parallel tumbling mat maze (mats stood on their sides).

Teaching Hints:
Move through the Challenge Course with quality movements rather than speed.

Distribute youngsters throughout the course instead of starting them at one common point.

Stop the class at regular intervals to perform flexibility and strength development activities.

Change directions periodically. This helps prevent a build-up of students at slower moving stations.

Lesson Focus – Gymnastics Skills (2)

Animal Movements

Measuring Worm

From a front-leaning rest position, keeping the knees stiff, inch the feet up as close as possible to the hands. Regain position by inching forward with the hands. Keep the knees straight, with the necessary bending occurring at the hips.

Mule Kick

Stoop down and place the hands on the floor in front of the feet. The arms are the front legs of the mule. Kick out with the legs while the weight is supported momentarily on the arms. Taking the weight on the hands is important. The stunt can be learned in two stages. First, practice taking the weight momentarily on the hands. Next, add the kick.

Walrus Walk

Begin in a front-leaning rest position, with fingers pointed outward. Make progress by moving both hands forward at the same time. Try to clap the hands with each step.

Tumbling and Inverted Balances

Frog Handstand (Tip-Up)

Squat down on the mat, placing the hands flat, with fingers pointing forward and elbows inside and pressed against the inner part of the knees. Lean forward, using the leverage of the elbows against the knees, and balance on the hands. Hold

Six groups of activities in this lesson ensure that youngsters receive a variety of experiences. Pick a few activities from each group and teach them alternately. For example, teach one or two animal movements, then a tumbling and inverted balance, followed by a balance stunt, etc. Give equal time to each group of activities.

Scatter tumbling mats throughout the area so that there is little standing in line waiting for a turn.

Youngsters can do the animal walks around their mats. Many of the activities in this unit do not have to be performed on the mat.

A major concern for safety is the neck and back region. Overweight children are at greater risk and might be allowed to for 5 seconds. Return to position. The head does not touch the mat at any time. The hands may be turned in slightly if this makes better contact between the elbows and the insides of the thighs.

avoid tumbling and inverted balances.

Half Teeter-Totter

This is continued lead-up activity for the Handstand. Begin in the lunge position and shift the weight to the hands. Kick the legs up in the air to a 135-degree angle, then return to the feet. This activity is similar to the Switcheroo, except that the feet are kicked higher without switching foot position.

All tumbling and inverted balances should be done on tumbling mat.

Cartwheel

Start with the body in an erect position, arms outspread and legs shoulder width apart. Bend the body to the right and place the right hand on the floor. Follow this, in sequence, by the left hand, the left foot, and the right foot. Perform with a steady rhythm. Each body part should touch the floor at evenly spaced intervals. The body should be straight and extended when in the inverted position. The entire body must be in the same plane throughout the stunt, and the feet must pass directly overhead.

Children who have difficulty with the Cartwheel should be instructed to concentrate on taking the weight of the body on the hands in succession (like the spokes of a wheel). They need to get the feel of the weight support and later can concentrate on getting the body into proper position. After the class has had some practice in doing Cartwheels, a running approach with a skip can be added before takeoff.

Balance Stunts

Leg Dip

Extend both hands and one leg forward, balancing on the other leg. Lower the body to sit on the heel and return without losing the balance or touching the floor with any part of the body. Try with the other foot.

Balance Jump

With hands and arms out to the sides and body parallel to the ground, extend one leg back and balance the weight on the other leg. Quickly change balance to the other foot, maintaining the initial position but with the feet exchanged. Keep the body parallel to the ground during the change of legs. Try with arms outstretched forward.

Working in pairs can be helpful. One student critiques the other's performance to make sure that the key performance and safety areas are addressed.

Seat Balance

Sit on the floor, holding the ankles in front, with elbows inside the knees. The feet are flat on the floor, and the knees are bent at approximately a right angle. Raise the legs (toes pointed) so that the knees are straight, and balance on the seat for 5 seconds.

After the activities are learned, place emphasis on correct performance emphasizing three phases:
1. Starting position
2. Execution
3. Finishing position

Individual Stunts

Heelstand

Begin in a full-squat position with the arms dangling at the sides. Jump upward to full leg extension with the weight on both heels and fling the arms out diagonally. Hold momentarily, then return to position. Several movements can be done rhythmically in succession.

Wicket Walk

Bend over and touch the floor with the weight evenly distributed on the hands and feet, thus forming a wicket. Walk the wicket forward, backward, and sideward.

Keep the arms and legs as nearly vertical as possible when doing the Wicket Walk. A common error in the execution of this stunt is to keep the hands positioned too far forward of the feet.

Knee Jump to Standing

Kneel, with seat touching the heels and toes pointing backward (shoelaces against the floor). Jump to a standing position with a vigorous upward swing of the arms. It is easier to jump from a smooth floor than from a mat, because the toes slide more readily on the floor.

Partner and Group Stunts

Rowboat

Partners sit on the floor or on a mat, facing each other with legs apart and feet touching. Both grasp a wand with both hands. Pretend to row a boat. Seek a wide range of movement in the forward-backward rowing motion.

The stunt can be done without a wand by having children grasp hands.

Leapfrog

One student forms a back. A leaper takes a running start, lays hands flat on the back at the shoulders, and vaults over the low student. Backs are formed at various heights. To form a low back, crouch down on the knees, curling into a tight ball with the head tucked well down. To form a medium back, reach down the outside of the legs from a standing position and grasp the ankles. The feet should be reasonably spread and the knees straight.

The position must be stable in order to absorb the shock of the leaper. To form a high back, stand stiff-legged, bend over, and brace arms against the knees. The feet should be spread, the head down, and the body braced to absorb the vault.

Wheelbarrow

One partner gets down on the hands with feet extended to the rear and legs apart. The other partner (the pusher) grasps partner's legs about halfway between the ankles and the knees. The wheelbarrow walks forward on the hands, supported by the pusher. Movements should be under good control.

Children have a tendency to grasp the legs too near the feet. The pusher must not push too fast. The wheelbarrow should have the head up and look forward. The pusher should carry the legs low and keep the arms extended.

Game Activity

Partner Stoop

Supplies: Music

Skills: Marching rhythmically

The game follows the same basic principle of stooping as in Circle Stoop, but is played with partners. The group forms a double circle in one direction with one partner on the inside and one on the outside. When the music begins, all march in the line of direction. After a short period of marching, a signal (whistle) is sounded, and the inside circle reverses direction and marches the other way. The partners are thus separated. When the music stops, the outer circle stands still, and the partners making up the inner circle walk (or run) in any direction to rejoin their respective outer circle partners. As soon as players reach their partner, they get toe to toe and stoop without losing balance. The last couple to stoop and those who lose their balance go to the center of the circle and wait out the next round. Start the game walking and gradually pick up the speed of the movements when the class moves under control.

Crows and Cranes

Supplies: None

Skills: Running, dodging

Establish two goal lines on opposite sides of the area. The class is divided into two groups—the crows and the cranes. The groups face each other at the center of the area, about 5 feet apart. The leader calls out either "Crows" or "Cranes," using a cr-r-r-r-r sound at the start of either word to mask the result. If "Crows" is the call, the crows chase the cranes to the goal line. If "Cranes" is the call, the cranes chase. Any player caught goes over to the other side and becomes a member of that group. The team that has the most players when the game ends is the winner.

Dynamic Physical Education for Elementary School Children
Rhythmic Movement Skills (2)
Level II – Week 16

Objectives:
To control body movements while moving through the Challenge Course
To perform a variety of locomotor movements in a rhythmic setting
To understand the difference between compliance and non-compliance of rules

Equipment Required:
Equipment for Challenge Course
Music for Rhythmic Activities
Bowling pins and balls for game

Instructional Activities	Teaching Hints
Introductory Activity -- High Fives	
Students move in different directions throughout the area. On signal, they are challenged to run toward a partner, jump, and give a "high five" (slap hands) while moving. Emphasis should be placed on timing so that the "high five" is given at the top of the jump.	Change the type of high fives, i.e., low, under leg, roundhouse. High fives should be given gently. No hard slapping.
Fitness Development Activity – Challenge Course	
Design a course around the perimeter of the area using the following ideas:	Move through the Challenge Course with quality movements rather than speed.
1. Step on jumping box, dismount to tumbling mat and do a forward roll.	
2. Run and weave through four wands held upright by cones.	
3. Handwalk across a horizontal ladder or do a flexed-arm hang from a climbing rope for 5 seconds.	Distribute youngsters throughout the course instead of starting them at one common point.
4. Step on and off three jumping boxes (small-large-small).	
5. Agility run through hoops.	
6. Perform jump turns.	Stop the class at regular intervals to perform flexibility and strength development activities.
7. Leap over a magic rope held taut with two chairs or jumping boxes.	
8. Hop on one foot.	
9. Do a Log Roll across a tumbling mat.	
10. Alternate going over and under six obstacles (cones and wands or hoops).	Change directions periodically. This helps prevent a build-up of students at slower moving stations.
11. Crouch jump or scooter movements the length of a balance-beam bench.	
12. Slide through a parallel tumbling mat maze (mats stood on their sides).	

Lesson Focus -- Rhythmic Movement Skills (2)

Begin each lesson with a review of one or two dances youngsters know and enjoy. Review dances from lesson plan #13 as desired before teaching new ones.

Rhythms should be taught like other sport skills. Avoid striving for perfection so students know it is acceptable to make mistakes. Teach a variety of dances rather than one or two in depth in case some students find it difficult to master a specific dance. Make dances easy for students to learn by implementing some of the following techniques:
  1. Teach the dances without using partners.
  2. Allow youngsters to move in any direction without left-right orientation.
  3. Use scattered formation instead of circles.
  4. Emphasize strong movements such as clapping and stamping to increase involvement.
  5. Play the music at a slower speed when first learning the dance.

Wild Turkey Mixer (American)

Music Source: WWC-FFD or any music with a definite rhythm
Formation: Trios abreast facing counterclockwise around the circle
Directions:

Measures	Action
1--8	In lines of three, with the right and left person holding the near hand of the center person, all walk 16 steps forward. (Walk, 2, 3, . . . 16)
9--12	The center person (Wild Turkey) turns the right-hand person once around with the right elbow. (Turn, 2, 3, 4, 5, 6, 7, 8)
13--16	The Wild Turkey turns the left-hand person with the left elbow, and then moves forward to repeat the dance with the two new people ahead. (Turn, 2, 3, 4; Forward, 2, 3, 4)

This dance can be adapted to other pieces of music. With a faster tempo, the elbow swings are done with a skip instead of a walk.

Patty Cake (Heel and Toe) Polka (International)

Music Source: WWCD-FDN

Formation: Double circle, partners facing, A in the inner circle with back to the center. Both hands are joined with partner. A's left and B's right foot are free.

Directions:

Measures	**Part I Action**
1--2	Heel-toe twice with A's left and B's right foot. (Heel, toe, heel, toe)
3--4	Take four slides sideward to A's left, progressing counterclockwise. Do not transfer the weight on the last count. Finish with A's right and B's left foot free. (Slide, 2, 3, 4)
5--8	Repeat the pattern of measures 1--4, starting with A's right and B's left foot, progressing clockwise. Finish with the partners separated and facing. (Heel, toe, heel, toe; slide, 2, 3, 4)

Measures	**Part II Action**
9	Clap right hands with partner three times. (Right, 2, 3)
10	Clap left hands with partner three times. (Left, 2, 3)
11	Clap both hands with partner three times. (Both, 2, 3)
12	Slap own knees three times. (Knees, 2, 3)
13--14	Right elbow swing with partner. Partners hook right elbows and swing once around with four walking steps, finishing with A's back to center. (Swing, 2, 3, 4)
15--16	Progress left to a new partner with four walking steps. (Left, 2, 3, 4)

Repeat the entire dance with the new partner.

Oh, Susanna (American)

Music Source: WWCD-1043

Formation: Single circle, all facing center, partner B on the right

Directions:

Measures	**Part I Action**
1--4	Partners B walk forward four steps and back four, as partners A clap hands. (Forward, 2, 3, 4; Back, 2, 3, 4)
5--8	Reverse, with As walking forward and back, and Bs clapping time. (Forward, 2, 3, 4; Back, 2, 3, 4)

Measures	**Part II Action**
1--8	Partners face each other, and all do a grand right and left by grasping the partner's right hand, then passing to the next person with a left-hand hold. Continue until reaching the seventh person, who becomes the new partner. (Face, 2, 3, 4, 5, 6, 7, 8)

Measures	**Chorus**
1--16	All join hands in promenade position with the new partner and walk counterclockwise around the circle for two full choruses singing: "Oh Susanna, oh don't you cry for me, For I come from Alabama with my banjo on my knee." (Promenade, 2, 3, . . . 16)

Repeat the dance from the beginning, each time with a new partner. For variety in the chorus, skip instead of walk, or walk during the first chorus and swing one's partner in place during the second chorus.

Troika (Russian)

Music Source: WWCD-3528; WWC-3528

Formation: Trios face counterclockwise. Start with hands joined in a line of three. The body weight is on the left foot; the right foot is free.

Directions:

Measures	**Part I Action**
1	Take four running steps diagonally forward right, starting with the right foot. (Diagonal, 2, 3, 4)
2	Take four running steps diagonally forward left, starting with the right foot. (Diagonal, 2, 3, 4)
3--4	Take eight running steps in a forward direction, starting with the right foot. (Forward, 2, 3, 4, 5, 6, 7, 8)
5--6	The center dancer and the left-hand partner raise joined hands to form an arch and run in place. Meanwhile, the right-hand partner moves counterclockwise around the center dancer with eight running steps, goes under the arch, and back to place. The center dancer unwinds by turning under the arch. (Under, 2, 3, 4; Turn, 2, 3, 4)
7--8	Repeat the pattern of measures 5 and 6, with the left-hand partner running under the arch formed by the center dancer and the right-hand partner. (Under, 2, 3, 4; Turn, 2, 3, circle)

Measures	**Part II Action**
9--11	The trio joins hands and circles left with 12 running steps. (Run, 2, 3, 4, 5, 6, 7, 8, 9, 10, 11, 12)
12	Three stamps in place (counts 1--3), pause (count 4). (Stamp, 2, 3, pause)

13--15   The trio circles right with 12 running steps, opening out at the end to re-form in lines of three facing counterclockwise. (Run, 2, 3, 4, 5, 6, 7, 8, open, 10, 11, 12)

16   The center dancer releases each partner's hand and runs under the opposite arch of joined hands to advance to a new pair ahead.

Right- and left-hand partners run in place while waiting for a new center dancer to join them in a new trio. (Stamp, 2, line, pause)

Green Sleeves (English)

Music Source: WWCD-1042
Skills: Walking, star formation, over and under
Formation: Double circle with couples in sets of four, facing counterclockwise. Two couples form a set and are numbered 1 and 2. Inside hands of each couple are joined.
Directions:

Measures	Call	Action
1–8	Walk	Walk forward 16 steps.
9–12	Right-hand star	Each member of couple 1 turns individually to face the couple behind. All join right hands and circle clockwise (star) for eight steps
13–16	Left-hand star	Reverse direction and form a left-hand star. This should bring couple 1 back to place facing in the original direction.
17–20	Over and under	Couple 2 arches and couple 1 backs under four steps while couple 2 moves forward four steps. Couple 1 then arches and couple 2 backs under (four steps for each).
21–24	Over and under	Repeat the action of measures. 17–20

La Raspa (Mexican)

Music Source: WWCD-05117
Skills: Bleking step, running, elbow swing
Formation: Partners are facing, couples scattered around the room.
Directions: La raspa means "the rasp" or "the file," and the dance movements are supposed to represent a rasp or file in action. Directions are the same for both partners.
Part I: To begin, the partners face each other, partner B with hands at sides and partner A with hands behind the back.

Measures   Action
1–4   Beginning right, take one bleking step. (Slow, slow, fast, fast, fast)
5–8   Turn slightly counterclockwise away from partner (right shoulder to right shoulder) and, beginning with a jump on the left foot, repeat measures 1–4. (Slow, slow, fast, fast, fast)
9–12   Repeat action of measures 1–4, facing opposite direction (left shoulder to left shoulder). (Slow, slow, fast, fast, fast)
13–16   Repeat action of measures 1–4, facing partner. (Slow, slow, fast, fast, fast)

Part II: Partners hook right elbows; left elbows are bent and left hands are pointed toward the ceiling.

Measures   Action
1–4   Do a right elbow swing, using eight running or skipping steps. Release and clap the hands on the eighth count. (Swing, 2, 3, 4, 5, 6, 7, clap)
5–8   Do a left elbow swing, using eight running or skipping steps. Release and clap the hands on the eighth count. (Swing, 2, 3, 4, 5, 6, 7, clap)
9–16   Repeat the actions of measures 1–8.

Variations:

Face partner (all should be in a single-circle formation for this version) and do a grand right and left around the circle. Repeat Part I with a new partner.

All face center or face a partner and do the Bleking step. On each pause, clap own hands twice.

Pata Pata (African)

Music Source: WWCD-3528; WWC-3528
Skills: Toe touches, knee lift, quarter turns
Formation: Single lines facing in one direction
Directions:

Measures	Action
1-2	Start with feet together; touch right foot sideward right and return next to left foot. (Right touch, together)
3-4	Same as above with left foot. (Left touch, together)
5	With feet together, move toes out keeping heels on the ground. (Toes out)
6	Turn heels out keeping toes on the ground (Heels out)
7	Turn heels in keeping toes on the ground (Heels in)

8	Turn toes in keeping heels on the ground. The feet should now be together. (Toes in)
9-12	Raise right knee diagonally in front of the body and then touch right foot next to left foot. Repeat for counts 11-12. (Lift, touch, lift, touch)
13-16	Kick left foot forward while turning a ¼ turn to the right with weight on the right foot. Step backward left, right, left. Feet should be together at the end of count 16. (kick, left, right, left)

Repeat the dance.

Variation: When youngsters learn the footwork, it is enjoyable to add some arm movements to the dance. At count 5, with elbows close to the body, raise hands up and straight out palms up. Count 6 turn palms down with elbows out. Count 7, turn palms up. Count 8, turn palms down.

Game Activity

Fox Hunt

Supplies: None

Skills: Running, dodging

Two players form trees by facing each other and holding hands. The third member of the group is a fox and stands between the hands of the trees. Three players are identified as foxes without trees and three players are designated as hounds. The hounds try to tag the foxes that are not in trees. The extra foxes may move to a tree and displace the fox that is standing in the tree. In addition, the foxes in trees may leave the safety of their trees at any time. If the hound tags a fox, their roles are reversed immediately, the fox becoming the hound. The game should be stopped at regular intervals to allow the players who are trees to change places with the foxes and hounds. Different locomotor movements can be specified to add variety to the game.

Steal the Treasure

Supplies: A bowling pin

Skill: Dodging

A playing area about 20 feet square is outlined, with a small circle in the center. A bowling pin placed in the small circle (hula hoop) as the treasure. Two guards are selected to protect the treasure. The guards can move as far from the treasure as they like to tag a player. Anyone tagged must retire and wait for the next game. To successfully steal the treasure, a player must pick it up cleanly without getting tagged. The guards tag them when they come too near. If the treasure is knocked over by a player trying to steal it, that player must also wait out a turn. There is a delicate balance for the guards between being too far from the treasure and staying too near the treasure and never tagging anyone. If the guards tag all players, they are declared billionaires.

Addition Tag

Supplies: None

Skills: Running, dodging

Two or more couples are it and each stands with inside hands joined. These are the taggers. The rest of the class runs individually. The couples move around the area, trying to tag with the free hands. The first person tagged joins the couple, making a trio. The three then chase until they catch a fourth. Once a fourth person is caught, the four divide and form two couples, adding another set of taggers to the game. This continues until the majority of the players are tagged. The game moves faster if started with two couples. A tag is legal only when the couple or group of three keeps their hands joined. The game can be used as an introductory activity, since all children are active.

Dynamic Physical Education for Elementary School Children
Basketball Related Skills (1)
Level II – Week 17

Objectives:
To understand the basic rules of basketball
To dribble, pass and shoot a basketball with proper form
To participate in basketball lead-up games

Equipment Required:
Music for Aerobic Fitness
One junior basketball or playground ball per student
8 hoops or individual mats
Pinnies

Instructional Activities	Teaching Hints

Introductory Activity -- Partner Leaping

Two youngsters work together. One partner leaps over the other, moves forward 5 to 10 steps, and curls on the floor. The other partner now leaps over their partner and repeats the pattern. Increase the distance students must run before assuming the curled position on the floor.

Add some locomotor movements or stunts that youngsters must perform before leaping over their partner.

Fitness Development Activity -- Aerobic Fitness and Partner Resistance Exercises

Students find a partner and lead each other in aerobic activities. Partners switch leader and follower roles after each partner resistance exercise. This routine assumes that students have previous aerobic fitness experience. If not, the aerobic activities will have to be led by the teacher.

Bounce and Clap	25 seconds
Arm Curl-Up	45 seconds
Jumping Jack Variations	25 seconds
Camelback	45 seconds
Lunge Variations	25 seconds
Fist Pull Apart	45 seconds
Directional Runs	25 seconds
Scissors	45 seconds
Rhythmic Running	25 seconds
Butterfly	45 seconds
Bounce with Body Twist	25 seconds
Resistance Push-Up	45 seconds

Walk, stretch, and relax for a minute or two.

Tape alternating segments of silence and music to signal duration of exercise. Music segments indicate aerobic activity (25 seconds) while intervals of silence announce partner resistance exercises (45 seconds).

Teach the exercises first; See Chapter 12 in the text for complete descriptions. A sign with aerobic activities on one side and partner resistance exercises on the other help students remember the activities. The signs can be held upright by cones and shared by 2-4 students.

Take 6-10 seconds to complete a resistance exercise.

Lesson Focus -- Basketball-Related Skills (1)

Skills
Practice the following skills:
1. Chest (or Two-Hand) Pass
   For the chest, or two-hand, pass, one foot is ahead of the other, with the knees flexed slightly. The ball is released at chest level, with the fingers spread on each side of the ball. The elbows remain close to the body, and the ball is released by extending the arms and snapping the wrists as one foot moves toward the receiver.
2. Catching
   Receiving the ball is a most important fundamental skill. Many turnovers involve failure to handle a pass properly. The receiver should move toward the pass with the fingers spread and relaxed, reaching for the ball with elbows bent and wrists relaxed. The hands should give as the ball comes in.
3. Dribbling
   Dribbling is used to advance the ball, break for a basket, or maneuver out of a difficult situation. The dribbler's knees and trunk should be slightly flexed, with hands and eyes forward. The fingertips propel the ball with the hand cupped and relaxed. There is little arm motion. Younger children tend to slap at the ball rather than push it. The dribbling hand should be alternated, and practice in changing hands is essential.

Instructional cues help students focus on proper performance of passing.
1. Fingers spread with thumbs behind the ball.
2. Elbows in; extend through the ball.
3. Step forward, extend arms, and rotate hands slightly inward.
4. Throw at chest level to the receiver.
5. For bounce passes, bounce the ball past the halfway point nearer the receiver.

Instructional cues for catching include the following:
1. Move into the path of the ball.
2. Reach and give with the ball (absorb the force of the ball by reaching and bringing the ball to the chest).

4. Shooting - One-Hand (set) Push Shot

The one-hand push shot is used as a set shot for young children. The ball is held at shoulder-eye level in the supporting hand with the shooting hand slightly below center and behind the ball. As the shot begins, the supporting (non-shooting) hand remains in contact as long as possible. The shooting hand then takes over with fingertip control, and the ball rolls off the center three fingers. The hand and wrist follow through, finishing in a flexed position. Vision is focused on the hoop during the shot. Proper technique should be emphasized rather than accuracy.

Drills

Passing and Catching Drills

1. Slide Circle Drill

In the slide circle drill, a circle of four to six players slides around a person in the center. The center person passes to and receives from the sliding players. After the ball has gone around the circle twice, another player takes the center position.

2. Circle-Star Drill

With only five players, a circle-star drill is particularly effective. Players pass to every other player, and the path of the ball forms a star. The star drill works well as a relay. Any odd number of players will cause the ball to go to all participants, assuring that all receive equal practice.

Dribbling Drills

3. Random Dribbling

Each child has a ball. Dribbling is done in place, varied by using left and right hands. Develop a sequence of body positions (i.e., standing, kneeling, lying on the side, on two feet and one hand). Encourage players to develop a sequence by dribbling a certain number of times in each selected position. Dribble with each hand.

4. One-Hand Control Drill

Begin with the right hand holding the ball. Make a half circle around the right leg to the back. Bounce the ball between the legs (back to front) and catch it with the right hand and move it around the body again. After continuing for a short time, switch to the left hand.

Shooting Drills

5. Basic Shooting Drill

In one simple shooting drill, players form files of no more than four people, and take turns shooting a long and a short shot or some other prescribed series of shots.

6. Set-Shot Drill

In the set-shot drill, players are scattered around a basket in a semicircle, with a leader in charge. Players should be close enough to the basket so that they can shoot accurately. The leader passes to each in turn to take a shot. The leader chases the ball after the shot. A bit of competition can be injected by allowing a successful shooter to take one step back for the next shot, or a player can shoot until he misses.

Instructional cues for dribbling include the following:
1. Push the ball to the floor. Don't slap it.
2. Push the ball forward when moving.
3. Eyes forward and head up.

Shooting instructional cues focus on proper form:
1. Keep the shooting elbow near the body.
2. Bend the knees and use the legs.
3. Release the ball off the fingertips.

Baskets should be lowered to 8 or 9 feet, depending on the size of the youngsters.

Lowered baskets help students shoot with proper form. Shooting is not a throw. If students have to throw the ball at the basket, it is too high.

Practice the skills in an individual manner as much as possible. The best alternative is a ball for every student to shoot and dribble. Reduce taking turns as much as possible when practicing skills.

Use junior basketballs or smaller for third and fourth grade students. It is difficult for students to learn skills with regulations size balls. They are too heavy and too large in diameter for youngsters.

Game Activity

Birdie in the Cage

Supplies: A soccer ball, basketball, or volleyball

Skills: Passing, catching, intercepting

Players are placed in circle formation with two or more children in the center of the circle. The object of the game is for the center players to try to touch the ball while circle players are passing it. After a brief time (15-20 seconds) choose new players to enter the circle. If scoring is desired, center players can count the number of touches they made. The ball should move rapidly. Passing to a neighboring player is not allowed. Play can be limited to a specific type of pass (bounce, two-hand, push).

Dribblerama

Supplies: One basketball for each player

Skills: Dribbling and protecting the ball

Dribblerama can be played at two levels of difficulty. Level 1: All players dribble throughout the area, controlling their ball so that it does not touch another ball. If a touch occurs, both players go outside the area and dribble around the area. Once youngsters have completed dribbling around the area, they reenter the game.

Level 2: The area is divided in half and all players move to one of the halves. While dribbling and controlling a ball, each player attempts to cause another player to lose control of his ball. When control is lost, that player takes his/her ball and moves to the opposite half of the area. Play continues against other players who have lost control. When 5 or 6 players remain, bring all players back into the game and start over.

Captain Ball

Supplies: A basketball, pinnies, eight hoops or individual mats

Skills: Passing, catching, guarding

Two games can be played crosswise on a basketball court. A centerline is needed; otherwise, normal boundary lines are used. Carpet squares or marking spots delineate where forwards and the captains must stay. A team is composed of a captain, three or more forwards, and three or more guards. The guards are free to move in their half of the playing area and try to throw the ball to their captain. The captain and forwards are each assigned to respective spots and must always keep one foot on their assigned carpet square or marking spot. Guarding these four circle players are three guards.

The game is started by a jump at the centerline with two guards from opposing teams. The guards can rove in their half of the court but may not touch the opposing forwards. After a made basket, an opposing guard immediately puts the ball into play with an inbounds throw. Guards try to throw the ball to their forwards, who maneuver to be open. The forward then tries to throw it to the other forwards or into the captain. Three points are scored when three forwards handle the ball and it is passed to the captain. Two points are scored when the ball is passed to the captain but has not been handled by three forwards.

Stepping over the centerline is a foul. It is also a foul if a guard steps on a forward's spot or mat or makes personal contact with a player on a mat or spot. The penalty for a foul is a free throw. For a free throw, the ball is given to an unguarded forward, who has 5 seconds to get the ball successfully to the guarded captain. If the throw is successful, one point is scored. If it is not successful, the ball is in play. Rotate free throw shooting among all the forwards.

As in basketball, when the ball goes out of bounds, it is awarded to the team that did not cause it to go out. If a forward or a captain catches a ball without one a foot touching their mat or spot, the ball is taken out of bounds by the opposing guard. For violations such as traveling or kicking the ball, the ball is awarded to an opposing guard out of bounds. No score may be made from a ball that is thrown in directly from out of bounds.

An effective offensive formation places guards spaced along the centerline. By passing the ball back and forth among the guards, the forwards have more opportunity to be open, since the passing makes the guards shift position. The guards may dribble, but are restricted to three dribbles for the purpose of advancing the ball. The forwards and captain should shift back and forth to become open for passes. They must keep one foot on the mat or spot. Short and accurate passing uses both chest and bounce passes. Forwards and centers may jump for the ball but must come down with one foot on the mat or spot.

Variations:

1. Four guards can be used, but scoring is then more difficult.

2. A five-circle formation can be used, forming a five spot like that on a die. Nine players are needed on each team: four forwards, four guards, and one captain.

3. A platform 6 to 8 in. high and 20 in. square can elevate the captain to make reception of the ball easier.

Basketball Tag

Supplies: A foam rubber basketball, pinnies

Skills: Catching, passing, dribbling, guarding

Designate three to five students to be it and wear a pinny. The rest of the class passes the ball and tries to tag one of the students who is it with the ball. If desired, more than one ball can be used. More than one ball can be used and more than one player per team can be identified as it.

Dynamic Physical Education for Elementary School Children
Basketball Related Skills (2)
Level II – Week 18

Objectives:
To cooperatively resist a partner performing exercises
To perform defensive skills
To shoot the lay-up shot
To participate as a team member in basketball leadup games

Equipment Required:
Music for Aerobic Fitness
One junior basketball or playground ball
  per student
8 hoops or individual mats
Pinnies

Instructional Activities	Teaching Hints

Introductory Activity – Bridges by Three

Form groups of three. Two of the children make bridges, and the third child goes around both bridges and sets up a bridge. Each child in turn goes around the bridges of the other two. Different kinds of bridges can be specified. To assure adequate activity, specify how many steps the youngster must run after going around both bridges. For example, "do 10 skips before making your bridge."

Encourage students to develop personal combinations of movement.

Increase the distance of movement students move after going through both bridges.

Fitness Development Activity -- Aerobic Fitness and Partner Resistance Exercises

Students find a partner and lead each other in aerobic activities. Partners switch leader and follower roles after each partner resistance exercise. This routine assumes that students have previous aerobic fitness experience. If not, the aerobic activities will have to be led by the teacher.

Bounce and Clap	25 seconds
Arm Curl-Up	45 seconds
Jumping Jack variations	25 seconds
Camelback	45 seconds
Lunge variations	25 seconds
Fist Pull apart	45 seconds
Directional Runs	25 seconds
Scissors	45 seconds
Rhythmic Running	25 seconds
Butterfly	45 seconds
Bounce with Body Twist	25 seconds
Resistance Push-Up	45 seconds

Walk, stretch, and relax for a minute or two.

Tape alternating segments of silence and music to signal duration of exercise. Music segments indicate aerobic activity (25 seconds) while intervals of silence announce partner resistance exercises (45 seconds).

Teach the exercises first; See Chapter 12 in the text for complete descriptions. A sign with aerobic activities on one side and partner resistance exercises on the other help students remember the activities. The signs can be held upright by cones and shared by 2-4 students.

Take 6-10 seconds to complete a resistance exercise.

Lesson Focus -- Basketball-Related Skills (2)

Skills:
Review skills from the previous lesson plan which include passing, catching, dribbling, set shot. Introduce new skills:
1. Defending
    Defending involves bending the knees slightly, spreading the feet, and facing the opponent at a distance of about 3 feet. The weight should be distributed evenly on both feet to allow for movement in any direction. Sideward movement is done with a sliding motion. The defender should wave one hand to distract the opponent and to block passes and shots.
2. Lay-Up Shot
    The lay-up is a short shot taken when going in toward the basket either after receiving a pass or at the end of a dribble. In a shot from the right side, the takeoff is with the left foot, and vice versa. The ball is carried with both hands early in the shot and then shifted to one hand for the final push. The ball, guided by the fingertips, should be laid against the backboard with a minimum of spin.

Instructional cues for proper defending are as follows:

1. Keep the knees bent.
2. Keep the hands up.
3. Don't cross the feet when moving.

Instructional cues for the lay-up shot are:
1. Take off on the foot opposite the shooting hand

2. Lay the ball on the backboard above the basketball.
3. Jump upward and slightly forward on the takeoff.

Drills:
Review previous drills learned in the previous lesson and introduce the following:
1. Group Defensive Drill

For the group defensive drill, the entire class is scattered on a basketball floor, facing one of the sides. The instructor or the student leader stands on the side, near the center. The leader points in one direction (forward, backward, or to one side) and gives the command "Move." When the students have moved a short distance, the leader commands, "Stop." Players keep good defensive position throughout.
2. Lay-Up Drill

Two short lines of players are placed; one to the left of the basket and the other on the right side of the basket. One line passes to the other line for lay-up shots. Shooters come in from the right side first (this is easier), then from the left, and finally from the center. Each player goes to the end of the other line.

Commands can be changed so that movement is continuous. Commands are "Right," "Left," "Forward," "Backward," and "Stop." The leader must watch that movement is not so far in any one direction that it causes players to run into obstructions. Commands can be given in order, and pointing can accompany commands.

Game Activity

Captain Ball

Supplies: A basketball, pinnies, eight hoops or individual mats

Skills: Passing, catching, guarding

Two games can be played crosswise on a basketball court. A centerline is needed; otherwise, normal boundary lines are used. Carpet squares or marking spots delineate where forwards and the captains must stay. A team is composed of a captain, three or more forwards, and three or more guards. The guards are free to move in their half of the playing area and try to throw the ball to their captain. The captain and forwards are each assigned to respective spots and must always keep one foot on their assigned carpet square or marking spot. Guarding these four circle players are three guards.

The game is started by a jump at the centerline with two guards from opposing teams. The guards can rove in their half of the court but may not touch the opposing forwards. After a made basket, an opposing guard immediately puts the ball into play with an inbounds throw. Guards try to throw the ball to their forwards, who maneuver to be open. The forward then tries to throw it to the other forwards or into the captain. Three points are scored when three forwards handle the ball and it is passed to the captain. Two points are scored when the ball is passed to the captain but has not been handled by three forwards.

Stepping over the centerline is a foul. It is also a foul if a guard steps on a forward's spot or mat or makes personal contact with a player on a mat or spot. The penalty for a foul is a free throw. For a free throw, the ball is given to an unguarded forward, who has 5 seconds to get the ball successfully to the guarded captain. If the throw is successful, one point is scored. If it is not successful, the ball is in play. Rotate free throw shooting among all the forwards.

As in basketball, when the ball goes out of bounds, it is awarded to the team that did not cause it to go out. If a forward or a captain catches a ball without one a foot touching their mat or spot, the ball is taken out of bounds by the opposing guard. For violations such as traveling or kicking the ball, the ball is awarded to an opposing guard out of bounds. No score may be made from a ball that is thrown in directly from out of bounds.

An effective offensive formation places guards spaced along the centerline. By passing the ball back and forth among the guards, the forwards have more opportunity to be open, since the passing makes the guards shift position. The guards may dribble, but are restricted to three dribbles for the purpose of advancing the ball. The forwards and captain should shift back and forth to become open for passes. They must keep one foot on the mat or spot. Short and accurate passing uses both chest and bounce passes. Forwards and centers may jump for the ball but must come down with one foot on the mat or spot.
Variations:

1. Four guards can be used, but scoring is then more difficult.

2. A five-circle formation can be used, forming a five spot like that on a die. Nine players are needed on each team: four forwards, four guards, and one captain.

3. A platform 6 to 8 in. high and 20 in. square can elevate the captain to make reception of the ball easier.

Five Passes

Supplies: A basketball; colored shirts, markers, or pinnies

Skills: Passing, guarding

Two teams play. Divide the area into smaller areas so many teams can play simultaneously. The object of the game is to complete five consecutive passes, which scores a point. The game is started with a jump ball at the free-throw line. The teams observe regular basketball rules in ball handling and with regard to traveling and fouling. The team with the ball counts out loud as a pass is completed. The ball may not be passed back to the person from whom it was received. No dribbling is allowed. If for any reason the ball is fumbled and recovered or improperly passed, a new count is started. After a successful score, the ball is immediately turned over to the other team. A foul draws a free throw, which can score a point. Teams should be well marked to avoid confusion.

Around the Key
Supplies: A basketball
Skill: Shooting

Spots are arranged for shooting around the key. A player begins at the first spot and continues until a miss. When a miss occurs, the player can stop and wait for her next opportunity and begin from the point where the miss occurred, or she can "risk it" and try another shot immediately from the point where the first try was missed. If the shot is made, the player continues. If the shot is missed, the player must start over on the next turn. The winner is the player who completes the key first or who makes the most progress.

Dynamic Physical Education for Elementary School Children
Throwing Skills (2)
Level II – Week 19

Objectives:
To cooperatively participate in a simple tag game
To perform continuous fitness activity
To know the elements of proper throwing
To throw with maximum velocity

Equipment Required:
Beanbags for Introductory Activity
Tape for exercises
Many types of balls for throwing
Throwing targets; hoops, mats, bowling
    pins and/or cageball

Instructional Activities	Teaching Hints
Introductory Activity -- Locomotor and Manipulative Activity	
Each child is given a beanbag and moves around the area using various basic locomotor movements. Students toss and catch their beanbags while moving. On signal, they drop the beanbags and jump and/or hop over as many bags as possible.	Vary the challenge by specifying the number or color of beanbags to move over or around.

Fitness Development Activity -- Exercises to Music

Side Flex (switch sides)	30 seconds	Select music that has a strong rhythm and easy-to-hear beat. When the music is on students perform aerobic activities (for 25 seconds). When the music is not playing, students perform the strength development and flexibility exercises (30 seconds).
Jogging	25 seconds	
Abdominal Challenges	30 seconds	
Slide or Skip	25 seconds	
Triceps Push-Ups	30 seconds	
Jumping Jack Variations	25 seconds	
Curl-Up Challenges	30 seconds	
Gallop	25 seconds	
Push-Up Challenges	30 seconds	See chapter 12 of the textbook for descriptions of the exercises.
Aerobic Bouncing and Clapping	25 seconds	
Leg Extensions	30 seconds	
Walking to cool down	25 seconds	Use scatter formation.

Lesson Focus -- Throwing Skills (2)

Review and practice throwing for form
1. Review proper throwing form outlined in Lesson Plan 3.
    a. Throw yarn balls from a standing position 20 feet from the wall. Throw five balls, retrieve and repeat.
    b. Throw yarn balls or tennis balls using the proper grip. Throw at bowling pins or hoops leaning against the wall and encourage trying to knock down the hoops. Throw from a distance of 20 to 25 feet depending on skill level. Gradually increase the distance from the wall.

Review and practice throwing for velocity
1. Review throwing for velocity in Lesson Plan 3. Set up activities using large targets so students will throw forcefully.
    a. Throw at mats on the wall. Throw tennis balls hard from 16 to 20 feet. Retrieve only if the balls roll beyond the throwing line.
    b. Throw at hoops leaning against mats on the wall.
    c. Large target throw. Use a circle or square 4 feet in diameter placed on the wall. Students should throw from 20 to 35 feet.

Practice throwing at targets
1. Use targets to increase motivation. The targets should encourage throwing for velocity rather than accuracy. Some examples of targets are:
    a. Throw through hoops suspended from basketball goals.
    b. Use large boxes for targets and try to throw inside the box
    c. Cageball throw. Throwers try to move it into the corner by throwing at it.
    d. Many bowling pins set near the walls.
    e. Graduated-size targets. Use a large concentric circle (or square) with 4 feet, 3 feet and 2 feet diameter circles.

Throwing takes a great deal of practice to master. Two major issues to consider when teaching throwing are:
1. How can I arrange my class so students receive the most opportunity to throw?
2. How can I arrange my class so students get to throw with maximum velocity. A mature pattern of throwing cannot be learned if students are not allowed to throw with maximum force.

Proper form and velocity of throws are closely related. A reason for practicing form is to encourage students to think about technique.

Give each student 4 or 5 balls to throw. On signal, when all the balls have been thrown students go retrieve the same number of balls they have thrown.

Make throwing targets large so students throw with velocity rather than accuracy. Throwing for targets is exciting for youngsters. It can also increase the motivational level of the lesson.

In the Prison

Supplies: 15-20 throwing balls

Skill: Throwing

Two teams, one assigned to each half of the gym. Balls (15-20) are placed on the center line. On signal, each team throws the balls to the other side of the gym. The object of the game is to get all the balls into the other team's backcourt area (or prison) which extends 10 feet from the wall. The teacher stops play by blowing a whistle, then counting the number of balls in the "prison."

Snowball

Supplies: 36 yarn balls

Skill: Throwing

Two teams, one assigned to each half of the gym. Each student has a yarn ball. Players can be hit three times. Each time they are hit they call out the number (1, 2, 3) of times they have been hit. After the third hit they must go to the side of the area and count to 25 before they can reenter. Teams must stay in their half of the gym.

Center Target Throw

Supplies: 20 - 8" gray foam balls and 20 bowling pins

Skill: Throwing

The area is divided into quadrants. Two teams compete, and each team has its own set of targets (bowling pins) set on a centerline. Half of each team is placed in opposing quadrants with the pins in the middle. Team A, on the left half of the area, has players on both sides of the center line behind restraining lines 15 to 20 feet away from the center target line. Team B is positioned the same way on the right half of the area. Each team tries to knock down all of its bowling pins as quickly as possible.

Target Ball Throw

Supplies: 10 - 18" beachballs and 36 yarn balls

Skill: Throwing

Beachballs are placed on the center line of the gym. There are two teams and each must stay in its half of the gym. Players have yarn balls. The object of the game is to roll the beachballs into the other team's court by hitting them with the yarn balls. The team that has the least number of beachballs on its side when the teacher blows the whistle is the winner.

Dynamic Physical Education for Elementary School Children
Fundamental Skills Using Benches
Level II – Week 20

Objectives:
To be able to move continuously in moderately active activities
To learn the rules of recreational activities
To play in recreational activities independently without adult supervision

Equipment Required:
One yarnball for each student
Music for Exercises to Music
Six Benches and tumbling mats
Cageball, pinnies, and stopwatch for
    games

Instructional Activities	Teaching Hints

Introductory Activity -- Yarnball Fun

Each child has a yarnball. Allow students to kick, throw or move with the ball for a designated time. On signal, place the balls on the floor and perform movements around, between and over the balls.

Place the yarnballs around the perimeter of the area. When students enter, they can move to a yarnball and begin handling it.

Fitness Development Activity -- Exercises to Music

Side Flex (switch sides)	30 seconds
Jogging	25 seconds
Abdominal Challenges	30 seconds
Slide or Skip	25 seconds
Triceps Push-Ups	30 seconds
Jumping Jack Variations	25 seconds
Curl-Up Challenges	30 seconds
Gallop	25 seconds
Push-Up Challenges	30 seconds
Aerobic Bouncing and Clapping	25 seconds
Leg Extensions	30 seconds
Walking to cool down	25 seconds

Select music that has a strong rhythm and easy-to-hear beat. When the music is on students perform aerobic activities (for 25 seconds). When the music is not playing, students perform the strength development and flexibility exercises (30 seconds).

See chapter 12 of the textbook for descriptions of the exercises.

Use scatter formation.

Lesson Focus – Fundamental Skills Using Benches

Present activities from each of the categories so students receive a variety of skills to practice.

1. Animal movements on bench.
    a. Seal Crawl
    b. Cat Walk
    c. Lame Dog Walk
    d. Rabbit Jump
    e. Crab Walk
2. Locomotor movements.
    a. Skip on the bench.
    b. Gallop on the bench.
    c. Step on and off the bench.
    d. Jump on and off the bench.
    e. Hop on and off the bench.
    f. Jump or hop over the bench.
    g. Jump on and off the bench. (Jump down with legs in a straddle position.)
3. Pulls--pull body along the bench in various positions.
    a. Prone position--head first, feet first.
    b. Supine position--head first, feet first.
    c. Side position--head first, feet first.
4. Pushes--same as above activity except push with the arms in all positions.
5. Movements alongside the benches--proceed alongside the bench in the following positions.
    a. Prone position--hands on bench.

1. Mats should be placed at the ends of the benches to facilitate the dismount and various rolls and stunts executed after the dismount.

2. Four to five children is the maximum number that should be assigned to one bench

3. The child next in turn should begin when the performer ahead is about three-quarters of the way across the bench.

4. All activities on the benches should be broken down into three distinct parts: the approach to and mounting of the bench, the actual activity on the bench, and the dismount from the bench.

5. When students have completed their movement across the bench, perform a jump dismount to complete the activity.

b. Supine position--hands on bench.

c. Turn over--proceed along bench changing from prone to supine positions with hands on bench.

d. All of the above positions performed with the feet on the bench.

6. Scooter movements--sit on bench and proceed along bench without using hands.

    a. Regular scooter--feet leading.

    b. Reverse scooter--legs trailing.

    c. Seat walk--walk on the buttocks.

7. Crouch jumps.

    a. Straddle jump

    b. Regular jump

    c. One hand, two feet.

    d. One hand, one foot

6. All bench activities should end with a dismount. Some examples of dismounts are:

a. Single jump--forward or backward.

b. Jump with turns--1/2 or 3/4 or full.

c. Jackknife (Pike).

d. Jackknife split (straddle).

e. Jump, forward roll

f. Back jump, back roll

g. Side jump, side roll

h. Jump, Shoulder roll

i. Jump sideways, Cartwheel

Game Activity

Cageball Kick-Over

    Supplies: A cageball, 24- or 30-inch size

    Skill: Kicking

    Players are divided into two teams and sit facing each other, with legs outstretched and soles of the feet about 6 to 12 feet apart. While maintaining the sitting position, each player leans back and supports his weight on the hands, which are placed slightly to the rear. The cageball is rolled between the two teams. The object of the game is to kick the ball over the other team, thereby scoring a point. After a point is scored, restart the game by rolling the ball into play again. Rotate players by having a player on the left side of the line take a place on the right side after a point is scored, thus moving all the players one position to the left. When the ball is kicked out at either end, no score results, and the ball is rolled into play again.

Squad Tag

    Supplies: Pinnies or markers for one squad, stopwatch

    Skills: Running, dodging

    Delineate the running area with cones. An entire squad acts as taggers. The object is to see which squad can tag the remaining class members in the least amount of time. The tagging squad should be identified with pinnies. They stand in a football huddle formation in the center of the area with their heads down. The remainder of the class scatters as they wish throughout the area. On signal, the tagging squad scatters and tags the other class members. A class member who is tagged stops in place and remains there. Time is recorded when the last person is tagged. Each squad gets a turn at tagging.

Dynamic Physical Education for Elementary School Children
Hockey-Related Skills (1)
Level II – Week 21

Objectives:
To understand and translate into movement the concepts of level, direction and size
To demonstrate how the hockey stick should be handled for safety
To practice passing and fielding a hockey puck
To design drills for practicing hockey skills

Equipment Required:
Music and jump ropes for Continuity Drills
One puck (or whiffle ball) and hockey stick for each student
Marking spots for Lane Hockey
Tumbling mats for goals

Instructional Activities	Teaching Hints

Introductory Activity -- Movement Varieties

Move using a basic locomotor movement. Then add variety to the movement by asking students to respond to the following factors:
1. Level--low, high, in-between.
2. Direction--straight, zigzag, circular, curved, forward, backward, upward, downward.
3. Size--large, tiny, medium movements.

Help students understand the concepts of level, direction, and size by briefly discussing them.

Encourage creativity by reinforcing novel responses.

Fitness Development Activity -- Continuity Drills

Rope Jumping - Forward	30 seconds	
Double Crab Kick	45 seconds	
Rope Jumping - Backward	30 seconds	
Knee Touch Curl-Up	45 seconds	
Jump and Slowly Turn Body	30 seconds	
Push-Up Challenges	45 seconds	
Rocker Step	30 seconds	
Bend and Twist	45 seconds	
Swing-Step Forward	30 seconds	
Side Flex	45 seconds	
Free Jumping	30 seconds	
Sit and Stretch	45 seconds	

Other aerobic activities can be substituted for rope jumping.

Students alternate jump rope activity with exercises done in two-count fashion. Exercises can be done with the teacher saying "Ready;" and the class answering "One-two" while performing a repetition of exercise. In activities like Push-Ups and Curl-Ups, allow students to pick any challenge activity they feel capable of performing. Teachers or students can lead.

Allow students to adjust the workload to their level. This implies resting if the rope jumping is too strenuous.

Lesson Focus -- Hockey-Related Skills (1)

Skills
Practice the following skills:
1. Gripping and carrying the stick.
   The hockey stick should be held with both hands and carried as low to the ground as possible. The basic grip puts the left hand at the top of the stick and the right hand 6 to 12 inches below the left.

   To ensure accuracy as well as safety, the stick must not be swung above waist height.

2. Controlled Dribble.
   The controlled dribble consists of a series of short taps in the direction in which the player chooses to move. The hands should be spread 10 to 14 inches apart to gain greater control of the stick. As the player becomes more skilled, the hands can be moved closer together. The stick is turned so that the blade faces the ball. The grip should not be changed, but rather, the hands should be rotated until the back of the left hand and the palm of the right hand face the ball. The ball can then be tapped just far enough in front of the player to keep it away from the feet but not more than one full stride away from the stick.

   Dribbling instructional cues:
   1. Control the puck. It should always be within reach of the stick.
   2. Hold the stick firmly.
   3. Keep the elbows away from the body.

3. Front Field.
   For the front field, the student must keep an eye on the ball, move to a point in line with its path, and extend the flat side of the blade forward to meet the ball. The faster the ball approaches, the more she must learn to give with the stick to absorb the momentum of the ball. The player should field the ball in front of the body and not permit it to get too close.

   Front fielding instructional cues:
   1. Field with a "soft stick." This means holding the stick with relaxed hands.
   2. Allow the puck to hit the stick and then "give" to make a soft reception.
   3. Keep the hands apart on the stick.

4. Forehand Pass.

The forehand pass is a short pass that usually occurs from the dribble. It should be taught before driving, because the quick hit requires accuracy rather than distance. The player spreads the feet with toes pointed slightly forward when striking. Approach the ball with the stick held low and bring the stick straight back, in line with the intended direction of the hit. The hands should be the same distance apart as in the carrying position, and the stick should be lifted no higher than waist level. The player's right hand guides the stick down and through the ball. The head should be kept down with the eyes on the ball. A short follow-through occurs after contact.

Forehand passing instructional cues:
1. Approach the puck with the side facing the direction of the pass.
2. Keep the head down and eyes on the puck.
3. Keep the stick below waist level at all times.
4. Drive the stick through the puck.

Drills
Use the following drills to practice the skills above:
1. Dribbling
   a. Each student has a stick and ball. On signal, change directions while maintaining control of the ball.
   b. Dribble and dodge imaginary tacklers or dodge around a set of cones. Partners may act as tacklers.
   c. Students in pairs--20 feet apart. One partner dribbles toward the other, goes around him or her, and returns to starting point. The first student then drives the ball to the second, who completes the same sequence.
2. Forehand Passing and Front Fielding
   a. From 8 to 10 feet apart, partners forehand pass and front field the ball back and forth to each other both from moving and stationary positions.
   b. Partners 20 feet apart--players pass the ball back and forth with emphasis on *fielding* and *immediately* hitting the ball back.

Hockey is a rough game when children are not taught the proper methods of stick handling. They need to be reminded often to use caution and good judgment when handling hockey sticks.

Ample equipment increases individual practice time and facilitates skill development. A stick and a ball or puck for each child are desirable.

If hockey is played on a gym floor, a plastic puck or yarn ball should be used. If played on a carpeted area or outdoors, a whiffle ball is used. An 8-foot folding mat set on end makes a satisfactory goal.

Game Activity -- Hockey Lead-Up Games

Circle Keep-Away
Supplies: One stick per person, a puck or ball
Skills: Passing, fielding

Players are spaced evenly around the circle, with two or more players in the center. The object of the game is to keep the players in the center from touching the puck. The puck is passed back and forth, with emphasis on accurate passing and fielding. Center players see how many touches they can make during their turn. Change the center players after a time limit so all youngsters have an opportunity to be center players.

Star Wars Hockey
Supplies: One stick per player, four pucks or balls
Skill: Dribbling

Each team forms one side of a square formation. The game is similar to Star Wars, with the following exceptions:
1. Four pucks (or balls) are used. When a number is called, each player with that number goes to a puck and dribbles it out of the square through the opening they previously occupied, around the square counterclockwise, and back to the original spot. Circles 12 inches in diameter are drawn on the floor to provide a definite place where the puck must be returned. If the game is played outdoors, marking spots can be used to mark where the pucks must be returned.
2. No player is permitted to use anything other than the stick in making the circuit and returning the puck to the inside of the hoop. The penalty for infractions is disqualification.

Lane Hockey
Supplies: Hockey stick per player, puck, two goals
Skills: All hockey skills

The field is divided into eight lanes. A defensive and an offensive player are placed in each of the eight lanes. A goalkeeper for each team is also positioned in front of the goal area. Players may not leave their lane during play. A shot on goal may not be taken until a minimum of two passes has been completed. This rule encourages looking for teammates and passing to someone in a better position before taking a shot on goal. Encourage players to maintain their spacing during play. The purpose of the lanes is to force players to play a zone rather than swarming to the puck. Rules used for regulation hockey enforce situations not described here. A free hit (unguarded) is awarded a team if a foul occurs. Players should be rotated after a goal is scored or at regular time intervals.

Variation: Increase the number of lanes to five or six. This involves a larger number of players. On a large playing area, the lanes may be broken into thirds rather than halves. Increase the number of passes that should be made prior to a shot on goal.

Circle Hockey Straddleball

Supplies: Hockey sticks and pucks or yarnballs

Skills: Passing and fielding

Children are in circle formation, facing in. Each player stands in a wide straddle stance two or three feet apart. The object of the game is to pass one of the pucks between the legs of another. Each time a puck goes between the legs of an individual, a point is scored. The players having the fewest points scored against them are winners. Keep the circles small so students have more opportunities to handle the puck.

Dynamic Physical Education for Elementary School Children
Hockey-Related Skills (2)
Level II – Week 22

Objectives:
To practice passing and fielding a hockey puck
To design drills for practicing hockey skills
To understand and perform goaltending skills

Equipment Required:
Music and jump ropes for Continuity
    Drills
Hockey sticks and pucks or yarn balls
Marking spots and cones
Tumbling mats for goals

Instructional Activities	Teaching Hints

Introductory Activity -- Run, Stop and Pivot

The class should run, stop on signal and pivot. Vary the activity by having the class pivot on the left or right foot and increase the circumference of the pivot. Movement should be continuous. Students pivot and then continue running.	Relate the pivot to a sport such as basketball and explain how it involves rotating around one foot.

Fitness Development Activity -- Continuity Drills

Rope Jumping - Forward	30 seconds	Students alternate jump rope activity with
Double Crab Kick	45 seconds	exercises done in two-count fashion.
Rope Jumping - Backward	30 seconds	Exercises can be done with the teacher
Knee Touch Curl-Up	45 seconds	saying "Ready;" and the class answering
Jump and Slowly Turn Body	30 seconds	"One-two" while performing a repetition
Push-Up Challenges	45 seconds	of exercise. In activities like Push-Ups
Rocker Step	30 seconds	and Curl-Ups, allow students to pick any
Bend and Twist	45 seconds	challenge activity they feel capable of
Swing-Step Forward	30 seconds	performing. Teachers or students can
Side Flex	45 seconds	lead.
Free Jumping	30 seconds	
Sit and Stretch	45 seconds	

Other aerobic activities can be substituted for rope jumping.

Allow students to adjust the workload to their level. This implies resting if the rope jumping is too strenuous.

Lesson Focus -- Hockey-Related Skills (2)

Skills:
Review and practice skills introduced last week:
1. Gripping and carrying the stick
2. Controlled dribble
3. Front field
4. Forehand Pass

Introduce new skills:
1. Driving.
   Driving is used to hit the ball moderate to long distances and to shoot at the goal. It differs from other passes in that the hands are brought together more toward the end of the stick. This gives the leverage necessary to apply greater force to the ball and results in more speed and greater distance. The swing and hit are similar to the quick hit. Stick control should be stressed so that wild swinging does not occur.
2. Tackling
   The tackle is a means of taking the ball away from an opponent. The tackler moves toward the opponent with the stick held low. The tackle is timed so that the blade of the stick is placed against the ball when the ball is off the opponent's stick. The tackler then quickly dribbles or passes in the direction of the goal. Throwing the stick or striking carelessly at the ball should be discouraged. Players need to remember that a successful tackle is not always possible.
3. Goalkeeping
   The goalie may kick the ball, stop it with any part of the body, or allow it to rebound off the body or hand. He may not, however, hold the ball or throw it toward the other end of the playing area. The goalkeeper is positioned in front of the goal line and moves between the goal posts. When a ball is hit toward the goal, the goalie should attempt to move in front of the ball and to keep his feet together. This allows the body to block the ball should the stick miss it. After the block, the ball is passed immediately to a teammate.

Review the drills presented last week:
1. Dribbling
2. Forehand Passing and Front Fielding

Introduce new drills:

Passing and Fielding drills

1. The shuttle turn-back drill, in which two files of four or five players face each other, can be used. The first person in the file passes to the first person in the other file, who in turn fields the ball and returns the pass. Each player, when finished, goes to the end of the file.

2. The downfield drill for passing and fielding skills for on the move. Three files of players start at one end of the field. One player from each file proceeds downfield, passing to and fielding from the others until the other end of the field is reached. A goal shot can be made at this point. The players should remain close together for short passes until a high level of skill is reached.

3. Practice driving for distance and accuracy with a partner.

Dodging and Tackling Drills

1. Players spread out on the field, each with a ball. On command, they dribble left, right, forward, and backward. On the command "Dodge," the players dodge an imaginary tackler. Players should concentrate on ball control and dodging in all directions.

2. Players work in pairs. One partner dribbles toward the other, who attempts to make a tackle. If the tackle is successful, roles are reversed. This drill should be practiced at moderate speeds in the early stages of skill development.

Game Activity -- Hockey Lead-up Games

Modified Hockey

Supplies: One stick per person, a puck or ball

Skills: Dribbling, passing, dodging, tackling, face-off

The teams take any position on the field as long as they remain inside the boundaries. The object of the game is to hit the puck through the opponent's goal. No goalies are used. At the start of the game and after each score, play begins with a face-off. Each goal is worth one point. The distance between goal lines is flexible but should be on the long side. If making goals is too easy or too difficult, the width of the goals can be adjusted accordingly.

Lane Hockey

Supplies: Hockey stick per player, puck, two goals

Skills: All hockey skills

The field is divided into eight lanes. A defensive and an offensive player are placed in each of the eight lanes. A goalkeeper for each team is also positioned in front of the goal area. Players may not leave their lane during play. A shot on goal may not be taken until a minimum of two passes has been completed. This rule encourages looking for teammates and passing to someone in a better position before taking a shot on goal. Encourage players to maintain their spacing during play. The purpose of the lanes is to force players to play a zone rather than swarming to the puck. Rules used for regulation hockey enforce situations not described here. A free hit (unguarded) is awarded a team if a foul occurs. Players should be rotated after a goal is scored or at regular time intervals.

Variation: Increase the number of lanes to five or six. This involves a larger number of players. On a large playing area, the lanes may be broken into thirds rather than halves. Increase the number of passes that should be made prior to a shot on goal.

Dynamic Physical Education for Elementary School Children
Gymnastics Skills (3)
Level II – Week 23

Objectives:
To put together a combination of movements in a smooth and flowing manner
To support the body weight in a variety of settings
To work cooperatively with a partner

Equipment Required:
Music for introductory activity and
  Aerobic Fitness
Tumbling Mats
4-6 bowling pins for game

Introductory Activity -- Moving to Music

Use a different music to stimulate various locomotor and non-locomotor movements. Different dance steps such as polka, two-step and schottische could be practiced.

The primary purpose of this activity is to help students sense different rhythms and move to the rhythm.

Fitness Development Activity -- Aerobic Fitness

1. Rhythmic run with clap
2. Bounce turn and clap
3. Rhythmic 4-count curl-ups (knees, toes, knees, back)
4. Rhythmic Crab Kicks (slow time)
5. Jumping Jack combination
6. Double knee lifts
7. Lunges (right, left, forward) with single-arm circles (on the side lunges) and double-arms circles (on the forward lunge)
8. Rhythmic trunk twists
9. Directional run (forward, backward, side, turning)
10. Rock side to side with clap
11. Side leg raises (alternate legs)
12. Rhythmic 4-count push-ups (If these are too difficult for students, substitute single-arm circles in the push-up position.)

Use music to stimulate effort. Any combination of movements can be used.

Keep the steps simple and easy to perform. Some students will become frustrated if the learning curve is steep.

Signs that explain the aerobic activities will help students remember performance cues.

Don't stress or expect perfection. Allow students to perform the activities as best they can.

Alternate bouncing and running movements with flexibility and strength development movements.

Lesson Focus – Gymnastics Skills (3)

Animal Movements

Double-Lame Dog

    Support the body on one hand and one leg. Move forward in this position, maintaining balance. The distance should be short (5 to 10 feet), as this stunt is strenuous. Different leg-arm combinations should be employed such as cross-lateral movements (right arm with left leg and left arm with right leg).

Turtle

    Hold the body in a wide push-up position with the feet apart and the hands widely spread. From this position, move in various directions, keeping the plane of the body always about the same distance from the floor

Walrus Slap

    From the front-leaning rest position, push the body up in the air quickly by force of the arms, clap the hands together, and recover to position.

Tumbling and Inverted Balances

Forward Roll Combinations

    Review the Forward Roll (see Lesson Plan 7). Combinations such as the following can be introduced.

    a. Do a Forward Roll preceded by a short run.
    b. Do two Forward Rolls in succession.
    c. Do a Forward Roll to a vertical jump in the air, and repeat.

Five groups of activities in this lesson ensure that youngsters receive a variety of experiences. Pick a few activities from each group and teach them alternately. For example, teach one or two animal movements, then a tumbling and inverted balance, followed by a balance stunt, etc. Give equal time to each group of activities

Youngsters can do the animal walks around their mats. Many of the activities in this unit do not have to be performed on the mat.

Balance Stunts

Seat Balance

Sit on the floor, holding the ankles in front, with elbows inside the knees. The feet are flat on the floor, and the knees are bent at approximately a right angle. Raise the legs (toes pointed) so that the knees are straight, and balance on the seat for 5 seconds.

Face-to-Knee Touch

Begin in a standing position with feet together. Placing the hands on the hips, balance on one foot, with the other leg extended backward. Bend the trunk forward and touch the knee of the supporting leg with the forehead. Recover to original position.

Finger Touch

Put the right hand behind the back with the index finger straight and pointed down. Grasp the right wrist with the left hand. From an erect position with the feet about 6 inches apart, squat down and touch the floor with the index finger. Regain the erect position without losing balance.

Individual Stunts

Stoop and Stretch

Hold a beanbag with both hands. Stand with heels against a line and feet about shoulder width apart. Keeping the knees straight, reach between the legs with the beanbag and place it as far back as possible. Reach back and pick it up with both hands.

Tanglefoot

Stand with heels together and toes pointed out. Bend the trunk forward and extend both arms down between the knees and around behind the ankles. Bring the hands around the outside of the ankles from behind and touch the fingers to each other. Hold for a 5-second count. Balance for 5 seconds without releasing the handclasp.

Egg Roll

In a sitting position, assume the same clasped-hands position as for Tanglefoot. Roll sideways over one shoulder, then to the back, then to the other shoulder, and finally back up to the sitting position. The movements are repeated in turn to make a full circle back to place.

Toe Touch Nose

From a sitting position on the floor, touch the toes of either foot to the nose with the help of both hands. Do first one foot and then the other. More flexible youngsters will be able to place the foot on top of the head or even behind the neck. Although this is a flexibility exercise, caution should be used; the leg can be forced too far.

Toe Tug Walk

Bend over and grasp the toes with thumbs on top. Keep the knees bent slightly and the eyes forward. Walk forward without losing the grip on the toes. Walk backward and sideward to provide more challenge.

Partner and Group Stunts

Camel Lift and Walk

In the wheelbarrow position, the wheelbarrow raises the seat as high as possible, forming a camel. Camels can lower themselves or walk in the raised position.

Dump the Wheelbarrow

Get into the wheelbarrow position. Lift the legs and return to normal position.

Scatter tumbling mats throughout the area so that there is little standing in line waiting for a turn.

Children who have difficulty with forward rolls should not have to do them.

A major concern for safety is the neck and back region. Overweight children are at greater risk and might be allowed to avoid tumbling and inverted balances.

Limit the number of children per mat to 3 or 4.

All tumbling and inverted balances should be done on a tumbling mat.

Working in pairs can be helpful. One student critiques the other's performance to make sure that the key performance and safety areas are addressed.

After the activities are learned, place emphasis on correct performance emphasizing three phases:

1. Starting position
2. Execution
3. Finishing position

The secret to the egg roll is a vigorous sideward movement to secure initial momentum. If mats are used, two should be placed side by side to cover the extent of the roll. (Some children can do this stunt better from a crossed-ankle position.)

Dromedary Walk

One child (the support) gets down on the hands and knees. The other child sits on the support, facing the rear, and fixes the legs around the support's chest. The top child leans forward, to grasp the back of the support's ankles. The top child's arms are reasonably extended. The support takes the weight off the knees and walks forward with the top child's help.

Centipede

One child, the stronger and larger individual, gets down on the hands and knees. The other child faces the same direction, places the hands about 2 feet in front of the support's, then places the legs and body on top of the support. The knees should be spread apart and the heels locked together. The centipede walks with the top child using hands only and the supporting child using both hands and feet. The support should gather the legs well under while walking and not be on the knees.

Game Activity

Steal the Treasure

Supplies: A bowling pin

Skill: Dodging

A playing area about 20 feet square is outlined, with a small circle in the center. A bowling pin placed in the small circle (hula hoop) as the treasure. Two guards are selected to protect the treasure. The guards can move as far from the treasure as they like to tag a player. Anyone tagged must retire and wait for the next game. To successfully steal the treasure, a player must pick it up cleanly without getting tagged. The guards tag them when they come too near. If the treasure is knocked over by a player trying to steal it, that player must also wait out a turn. There is a delicate balance for the guards between being too far from the treasure and staying too near the treasure and never tagging anyone. If the guards tag all players, they are declared billionaires.

Trees

Supplies: None

Skills: Running, dodging

Two parallel lines are drawn at opposite ends of the playing area. All players, except two or three taggers, are on one side of the area. On the signal "Trees," the players run to the other side of the court. The taggers tries to tag as many as possible. Any player tagged becomes a tree, stopping where tagged and keeping both feet in place. A tree cannot move their feet but can tag any runners who come close enough. The taggers continue to chase the players as they cross on signal until a few are left. New players are selected to be taggers.

Dynamic Physical Education for Elementary School Children
Track and Field-Related Skills (1)
Level II – Week 24

Objectives:
To understand how to stretch prior to strenuous activity
To recognize the wide range of individual differences among peers

Equipment Required:
Stopwatches
Track and field equipment

Instructional Activities	Teaching Hints
Introductory and Fitness Development Activities -- Stretching and Jogging	

Combine the introductory and fitness activities during the track and field unit. This will help students understand how to stretch and warm up for demanding activity such as track and field.

Jog	1-2 minutes
Standing Hip Bend	30 seconds
Sitting Stretch	30 seconds
Partner Rowing	60 seconds
Bear Hug (stretch each leg)	40 seconds
Side Flex (stretch each leg)	40 seconds
Trunk Twister	30 seconds
Jog	3-4 minutes

Emphasis should be on jogging and stretching to prepare for strenuous activity.

Encourage smooth and controlled stretching. Hold each stretch for 6 to 10 seconds.

Lesson Focus -- Track and Field-Related Skills (1)

Skills

Standing Start

The standing start has a variety of uses in physical education activities. Many children find it more comfortable than the sprinter's start. When practical, however, children should use the sprinter's start for track work. In the standing start, the feet should be in a comfortable half-stride position. An extremely long stride is to be avoided. The body leans forward so that the center of gravity is forward. The weight is on the toes, and the knees are flexed slightly. The arms can be down or hanging slightly back.

The goal of track and field is self-improvement and developing proper techniques. Each student must accept responsibility for self-directed work and should be encouraged to try all activities.

Sprinter's Start

The "On your mark" position places the toe of the front foot from 4 to 12 inches behind the starting line. The thumb and first finger are just behind the line, with other fingers adding support. The knee of the rear leg is placed just opposite the front foot or ankle.

For the "Get set" position, the seat is raised so that it is nearly parallel to the ground. The knee of the rear leg is raised off the ground, and the shoulders are moved forward over the hands. The weight is evenly distributed over the hands and feet. The head is not raised, as the runner should be looking at a spot a few feet in front of the starting line.

On the "Go" signal, the runner pushes off sharply with both feet, with the front leg straightening as the back leg comes forward for a step. The body should rise gradually rather than pop up suddenly. The instructor should watch for a stumbling action on the first few steps. This results from too much weight resting on the hands in the "Get set" position.

The program should offer something for all---boys and girls, the highly skilled and the less skilled, and those with physical problems. Children with weight problems need particular attention. They must be stimulated and encouraged, since their participation will be minimal if little attention is paid to them. Special goals can be set for overweight children, and special events and goals can also be established for children with handicaps.

Sprinting

In proper sprinting form, the body leans forward, with the arms swinging in opposition to the legs. The arms are bent at the elbows and swing from the shoulders in a forward and backward plane, not across the body. Forceful arm action aids sprinting. The knees are lifted sharply forward and upward and are brought down with a vigorous motion, followed by a forceful push from the toes.

The goal of the program should be to allow students to develop at their own rate. The instructor needs to be perceptive enough to determine whether students are working too hard or too little. Special attention must be given to those who appear disinterested, dejected, emotionally upset, or withdrawn.

Distance Running

In distance running, as compared with sprinting, the body is more erect and the motion of the arms is less pronounced. Pace is an important consideration. Runners should try to concentrate on the qualities of lightness, ease, relaxation, and looseness. Relaxed striding action, a slight body lean, and good head position are also important. Encourage runners to strike the ground with the heel first and then push off with the toes.

Standing Long Jump

In the standing long jump, the jumper toes the line with feet flat on the ground and fairly close together. The arms are brought forward in a preliminary swing and are then swung down and back. The jump is made with both feet as the arms are swung forcibly forward to assist in lifting the body upward and forward. In the air, the knees should be brought upward and forward, with the arms held forward to sustain balance.

The long jump pit must be maintained properly. It should be filled with fresh sand of a coarse variety.

Long Jump

For the running long jump, a short run is needed. The run should be timed so that the toes of the jumping foot contact the board in a natural stride. The jumper takes off from one foot and strives for height. The landing is made on both feet after the knees have been brought forward. The landing should be in a forward direction, not sideward.

A fair jump takes off behind the scratch line. A foul (scratch) jump is called if the jumper steps beyond the scratch line or runs into or through the pit. Each contestant is given a certain number of trials (jumps). A scratch jump counts as a trial. Measurement is from the scratch line to the nearest point of touch.

If stopwatches and tape measures are used, it is important to make them highly visible. Tie bright colored cord to them or anchor to cones to assure that they are not misplaced.

High Jumping

The Scissors Jump is recommended for group instruction because of safety factors. The high-jump bar is approached from a slight angle. The takeoff is by the leg that is farther from the bar. The near leg is lifted and goes over, followed quickly in a looping movement by the rear leg. A good upward kick with the front leg, together with an upward thrust of the arms, is needed. The knees should be straightened at the highest point of the jump. The landing is made on the lead foot followed by the rear foot.

Make signs for each of the stations. The signs should include appropriate performance techniques, what is to be done at each station, and appropriate safety precautions.

The high jump bar should be at a height that offers challenge but allows concentration on technique rather than on height. Too much emphasis on competition for height quickly eliminates the poorer jumpers, who need the experience most. Safety is of utmost importance. Using a flexible elastic rope as a crossbar and avoiding any type of flop will prevent injury. The practice of keeping the entire class together on a single high-jump facility is poor methodology. This arrangement determines who are the best jumpers in class but does little else.

Hurdles

The hurdler should step so that the takeoff foot is planted 3 to 5 feet from the hurdle. The lead foot is extended straight forward over the hurdle; the rear (trailing) leg is bent, with the knee to the side. The lead foot reaches for the ground, quickly followed by the trailing leg. The hurdler should avoid floating over the hurdle. Body lean is necessary. A hurdler may lead with the same foot over consecutive hurdles or may alternate the leading foot. Some hurdlers like to thrust both arms forward instead of a single arm. A consistent step pattern should be developed.

Drills - Station (Small Group) Instruction

Divide the group into four groups and send an equal number of students to each station. Practice the skills at each station. Finish the lesson by running the relay activities listed in the game section below.

Station 1 – Starting, Sprinting, and Hurdling

Practice starting form. Work with a partner who gives the commands for starting. Sprint 40 to 60 yards and walk back to the starting line. Reverse roles.

Station 2 - Standing Long Jump and High Jump

The standing long jump can be done on a tumbling mat or the ground. A tape measure can be taped to the mat or placed on the ground so students can see how far they are jumping. Swing the arms forward on the takeoff.

Station 3 - Running Long Jump

Practice the running long jump by taking a short run, making contact with the takeoff board and jumping into the pit.

Station 4 - Distance Running for Pace

Outline a track with cones and have children run at a pace they can continue. If they need to stop frequently, they are running too fast. The running should be loose and relaxed. Work at this station is for learning a proper pace rather than racing.

Game Activity

Potato Shuttle Relay

A small box about a foot square is placed 5-ft in front of each lane. Four 12-in. circles are drawn at 5-ft intervals beyond the box. This makes the last circle 25-ft from the starting point. Four blocks or beanbags are needed for each team. To start, the blocks are placed in the box in front of each team. The first runner goes to the box, takes a single block, and puts it into one of the circles. She repeats this performance until there is a block in each circle; then she tags off the second runner. This runner brings the blocks back to the box, one at a time, and tags off the third runner, who returns the blocks to the circles, and so on. Paper plates or frisbees can be used instead of circles drawn on the floor.

Variation: The race can also be done with bowling pins. Instead of being placed in a box, they are in a large circle at the start.

Shuttle Relays

Since the runner is moving toward a stationary person, a difficulty in running shuttle relays is control of the exchange. In the excitement, the next runner may leave too early, and the tag or exchange is then made ahead of the restraining line. A high-jump standard or cone can be used to prevent early exchanges. The next runner awaits the tag with an arm around the standard or a hand on a cone.

One on One Contests

Allow students to find a friend and have a number of personal contests in track and field events such as sprints, hurdling, high jump, and standing long jump.

Dynamic Physical Education for Elementary School Children
Track and Field-Related Skills (2)
Level II – Week 25

Objectives:
To understand how to stretch prior to strenuous activity
To recognize the wide range of individual differences among peers

Equipment Required:
Stopwatches
Track and Field Equipment

Instructional Activities	Teaching Hints
Introductory and Fitness Development Activities -- Stretching and Jogging	

Combine the introductory and fitness activities during the track and field unit. This will help students understand how to stretch and warm up for demanding activity such as track and field.		Emphasis should be on jogging and stretching to prepare for strenuous activity.
Jog	1-2 minutes	
Standing Hip Bend	30 seconds	
Sitting Stretch	30 seconds	Encourage smooth and controlled
Partner Rowing	60 seconds	stretching. Hold each stretch for 6 to 10
Bear Hug (stretch each leg)	40 seconds	seconds
Side Flex (stretch each leg)	40 seconds	
Trunk Twister	30 seconds	
Jog	3-4 minutes	

Lesson Focus -- Track and Field-Related Skills (2)

Skills
Review the skills taught in the previous lesson. Introduce the following skills:
Baton Passing

The right hand to left hand method is used in longer distance relays and is the best choice for elementary school children as it is easy and offers a consistent method for passes. This pass allows the receiver to face the inside of the track while waiting to receive the baton in the left hand. The oncoming runner holds the baton in the right hand like a candle when passing it to a teammate. The receiver reaches back with the left hand, fingers pointing down, thumb to the inside, and begins to run as the runner advances to within 3 to 5 yards. The receiver grasps the baton and shifts it from the left to the right hand while moving. If the baton is dropped, it must be picked up, or the team is disqualified. An alternative way to receive the baton is to reach back with the hand facing up; however, the fingers-down method is considered more suitable for sprint relays.

Hop-Step-and-Jump

The hop-step-and-jump event requires a takeoff board and a jumping pit. The distance from the takeoff board to the pit should be one that even less skilled jumpers can make. The event begins with a run similar to that for the running long jump. The takeoff is with one foot, and the jumper must land on the same foot to complete the hop. He then takes a step followed by a jump. The event finishes like the long jump, with a landing on both feet. The pattern can be changed to begin with the left foot.

The jumper must not step over the takeoff board in the first hop, under penalty of fouling. Distance is measured from the front of the takeoff board to the closest place where the body touches. This is usually a mark made by one of the heels, but it could be a mark made by an arm or another part of the body if the jumper landed poorly and fell backward.

Drills - Station (Small Group) Instruction
Divide the group into four groups and send an equal number of students to each station. See Lesson 24 for a description of activities not listed here. Practice the skills at each station. Finish the lesson by running the relay activities listed in the game section below.

The goal of track and field is self-improvement and developing proper techniques. Each student must accept responsibility for self-directed work and should be encouraged to try all activities.

The program should offer something for all---boys and girls, the highly skilled and the less skilled, and those with physical problems. Children with weight problems need particular attention. They must be stimulated and encouraged, since their participation will be minimal if little attention is paid to them. Special goals can be set for overweight children, and special events and goals can also be established for children with handicaps.

Pits for the long jump and the hop-step-and-jump must be maintained properly. They should be filled with fresh sand of a coarse variety.

The goal of the program should be to allow students to develop at their own rate. The instructor needs to be perceptive enough to determine whether students are working too hard or too little. Special attention must be given to those who appear disinterested, dejected, emotionally upset, or withdrawn.

Station 1 – Starting, Sprinting, and Hurdling

Practice starting form. Work with a partner who gives the commands for starting. Sprint 40 to 60 yards and walk back to the starting line. Reverse roles.

Station 2 - Hop-Step-and-Jump and High Jump

Set up the hop-step-and-jump with instructions on proper form set on a cone.

Station 3 - Baton Passing

Practice the running long jump by taking a short run, making contact with the takeoff board and jumping into the pit.

Station 4 - Distance Running for Pace

Outline a track with cones and have children run at a pace they can continue. If they need to stop frequently, they are running too fast. The running should be loose and relaxed. Work at this station is for learning a proper pace rather than racing.

If stopwatches and tape measures are used, it is important to make them highly visible. Tie bright colored cord to them or anchor to cones to assure that they are not misplaced.

Make signs for each of the stations. The signs should include appropriate performance techniques, what is to be done at each station, and appropriate safety precautions.

Game Activity

Circular (Pursuit) Relays

Circular relays make use of the regular circular track. The baton exchange technique is important, and practice is needed. On a 220-yard or 200-meter track, relays can be organized in a number of ways, depending on how many runners are spaced for one lap. Four runners can do a lap, each running one-quarter of the way; two can do a lap, each running one half of the distance; or each runner can complete a whole lap. In these races, each member of the relay team runs the same distance. Relays can also be organized so team members run different distances.

Shuttle Relays

Since children are running toward each other, one great difficulty in running shuttle relays is control of the exchange. In the excitement, the next runner may leave too early, and the tag or exchange is then made ahead of the restraining line. A high-jump standard or cone can be used to prevent early exchanges. The next runner awaits the tag with an arm around the standard or a hand on a cone.

One on One Contests

Allow students to find a friend and have a number of personal contests in track and field events such as sprints, hurdling, high jump, and standing long jump.

Dynamic Physical Education for Elementary School Children
Manipulative Skills Using Beanbags
Level II – Week 26

Objectives:
To stop quickly and under control
To understand the differences in aerobic capacities among classmates
To toss and catch an object in a variety of situations

Equipment Required:
Music tape and Tom-tom for Walk, Trot, and Jog
One beanbag for each student

Instructional Activities	Teaching Hints

Introductory Activity – Move and Perform Task

Move around the area using any desired locomotor movement; on signal, stop and perform a task such as an exercise or stunt. Some suggested activities are: Heel Click, Push-Up, Stork Stand, Sit-up, or any desired stretch.

Allow students to demonstrate novel responses in order to increase the range of student response.

Fitness Development Activity -- Walk, Trot, and Jog

Move to the following signals:
1. One drumbeat - walk.
2. Two drumbeats - trot.
3. Three drumbeats - jog.
4. Whistle - freeze and perform exercises.

Perform strength and flexibility exercises between bouts of walk, trot and jog. Examples are:
1. Bend and Twist
2. Sitting Stretch
3. Push-Up Challenges
4. Abdominal Challenges
5. Trunk Twister
6. Body Circles
7. Crab Walk

Tape alternating segments of silence and music to signal duration of exercise. Music segments indicate walk, trot, or jog activity (30-45 seconds) while intervals of silence announce flexibility and strength development activities (30 seconds).

Assure that students run under control (not as fast as they can) and in the same direction.

Allow students to perform at a level they feel comfortable. Youngsters are genetically different and should not be expected to do the same amount of exercise repetitions.

Lesson Focus -- Beanbag Activities

In place, Tossing to self
1. Toss and catch with both hands - right hand, left hand
2. Toss and catch with the back of hands. This will encourage children to catch with "soft hands."
3. Toss the beanbag to increasingly high level, *emphasizing* a straight overhead toss. To encourage straight tossing, have the child sit down.

Give students two or three activities to practice so you have time to move and help youngsters. Alternate activities from each of the categories so students receive a variety of skills to practice.

In Place, Adding Stunts
1. Toss overhead and perform the following stunts and catch the bag.
   a. 1/4 and 1/2 turns, right and left
   b. Full turn
   c. Touch floor
   d. Clap hands
   e. Clap hands around different parts of body, behind back, under legs.
   f. Heel click
   g. Student choice

Stress a soft receipt of the beanbag by giving with the hands, arms, and legs. "Giving" involves the hands going out toward the incoming beanbag and bringing it in for a soft landing.

Remind students to keep their eyes on the beanbag when catching.

In place, kicking to self
1. Place beanbag on foot, kick up and catch--right foot, left foot.
2. Try above activity from sitting and lying positions.
3. Kick up and catch behind back.
4. Kick up overhead, make ½ turn and catch.
5. Put beanbag between feet, jump up and catch beanbag.
6. Toss beanbag with one foot and catch with the other foot.

When tossing and catching, toss slightly above eye level. Overly high tosses should be discouraged until catching is mastered.

Locomotor movements (Toss, Move and Catch)

1. Toss overhead, move to another spot and catch.
2. Toss, do a locomotor movement and catch.
3. Move from side to side.
4. Toss overhead behind self, move and catch.
5. Exploratory movements.

Beanbags should be at least 6 inches square. This size balances well and can be controlled on various parts of the body, thus offering greater challenge.

Balance the beanbag

1. Balance on the following body parts:
   a. Head
   b. Back of hand
   c. Shoulder
   d. Knee
   e. Foot
   f. Elbow
2. Balance and move as follows:
   a. Walk
   b. Run
   c. Skip
   d. Gallop
   e. Sit down
   f. Lie down
   g. Turn around
   h. Balance beanbag on body part and move on all fours.

Stress laterality and directionality when teaching manipulative skills. Children should be taught to throw, catch, and balance beanbags with both the left and right sides of their body. They should learn to catch and throw at different levels.

See who can balance the beanbag longest on various body parts while moving.

Emphasize quality not quantity. Motivation is often enhanced by practicing an activity for a short time and returning to it later.

Partner activities

1. Toss back and forth using the following throws:
   a. Two-handed throws--overhead, underhand, side and over shoulder.
   b. One-handed throws and catches.
   c. Throw at different levels and targets such as high, low, left, right.
   d. Throw under leg, around body, from behind back, center, as in football, etc.
   e. Sit down and play catch--try different throws and catches.
   f. Toss in various directions to make partner move and catch. Have one partner move around other in a circle while catching and throwing.
   g. Propel more than one beanbag back and forth. Toss both beanbags together, as well as at opposite times.

Children should toss at chest height to a partner, unless a different type of throw is specified. Teach all types of return: low, medium, high, left, and right.

In partner work, keep distances between partners reasonable, especially in introductory phases. Fifteen feet or so seems to be a reasonable starting distance. Throwing too hard or out of range, to cause the partner to miss, should be discussed.

Game Activity

Galloping Lizzie

Supplies: A beanbag or fleece ball
Skills: Throwing, dodging, running

Two or more players are it and have a beanbag or fleece ball. The other players are scattered around the playground. The players with the bag or ball run after the others and attempt to hit other players below the waist with the object. The person hit becomes it, and the game continues. The tagger must throw the bag or ball, not merely touch another person with it.

Crows and Cranes

Supplies: None
Skills: Running, dodging

Establish two goal lines on opposite sides of the area. The class is divided into two groups—the crows and the cranes. The groups face each other at the center of the area, about 5 feet apart. The leader calls out either "Crows" or "Cranes," using a cr-r-r-r-r sound at the start of either word to mask the result. If "Crows" is the call, the crows chase the cranes to the goal line. If "Cranes" is the call, the cranes chase. Any player caught goes over to the other side and becomes a member of that group. The team that has the most players when the game ends is the winner.

Dynamic Physical Education for Elementary School Children
Rhythmic Movement Skills (3)
Level II – Week 27

Objectives:
To be able to turn and jump a long rope.
To cooperatively perform parachute fitness activities
To perform locomotor movements to rhythm
To understand strategies in simple game activities

Equipment Required:
8-10 long jump ropes
Parachute for fitness
Music for rhythmic activities
Tinikling equipment
Clubs, balls, jump the shot rope, and
    beachballs for games

Instructional Activities	Teaching Hints

Introductory Activity – Long Jump Rope Routine

Have the squad form a loose column and hold a long jump rope in the right hand.

1. On the first signal: Run in a column with one child leading the way.
2. Second signal: Shift the rope overhead from right hand to left hand without stopping.
3. Third signal: Two inside children let go of rope, outside children begin turning the rope for the two who have released the rope. They continue jumping the rope until the next signal.
4. Fourth signal: The outside youngsters move to the inside positions and vice-versa. The sequence is then repeated.

Group youngsters into fours

Encourage students to think of other activities to perform with the rope on the second signal.

If desired, the groups can carry two ropes and practice Double Dutch on the third and fourth signals.

Fitness Development Activity -- Parachute Fitness

1. Jog in circle with chute held in left hand. Reverse directions and hold with right hand. (music)
2. Standing, raise the chute overhead, lower to waist, lower to toes, raise to waist, etc. (no music)
3. Slide to the right; return slide to the left. (music)
4. Sit and perform Abdominal Challenges. (no music)
5. Skip. (music)
6. Freeze; face the center, and stretch the chute tightly with bent arms. Hold for 8-12 seconds. Repeat five to six times. (no music)
7. Run in place, hold the chute at waist level and hit the chute with lifted knees. (music)
8. Sit with legs under the chute. Do a seat walk toward the center. Return to the perimeter. Repeat four to six times. (no music)
9. Place the chute on the ground. Jog away from the chute and return on signal. Repeat. (music)
10. On sides with legs under the chute, perform Side Flex and lift chute with legs. (no music)
11. Hop to the center of the chute and return. Repeat. (music)
12. Assume the push-up position with the legs aligned away from the center of the chute. Shake the chute with one arm while the other arm supports the body. (no music)
13. Lie on back with legs under the chute. Shake the chute with the feet. (music)
14. Sit with feet under the chute. Stretch by touching the toes with the chute. Relax with other stretches while sitting. (no music)

Tape alternating segments (25-30 seconds in length) of silence and music to signal duration of exercise. Music segments indicate aerobic activity with the parachute while intervals of silence announce using the chute to enhance flexibility and strength development.

Space youngsters evenly around the chute.

Use different hand grips (palms up, down, mixed).

All movements should be done under control. Some of the faster and stronger students will have to moderate their performance.

Lesson Focus -- Rhythmic Movement Skills (3)

Begin each lesson with a review of one or two dances youngsters know and enjoy. Review dances from Lesson Plans #13 and #16 as desired before teaching new ones.

Rhythms should be taught like other sport skills. Avoid striving for perfection so students know it is acceptable to make mistakes. Teach a variety of dances rather than one or two in depth in case some students find it difficult to master a specific dance. Make dances easy for students to learn by implementing some of the following techniques:
    1. Teach the dances without using partners.

2. Allow youngsters to move in any direction without left-right orientation.
3. Use scattered formation instead of circles.
4. Emphasize strong movements such as clapping and stamping to increase involvement.
5. Play the music at a slower speed when first learning the dance.

E-Z Mixer

Music Source: WWC-FFD or any music with a definite rhythm
Formation: Circle formation with couples in promenade position, inside hands joined, facing counterclockwise.
Directions:

Measures	Action
1--2	With partner B on the right, walk forward four steps. (Forward, 2, 3, 4) Back out to face center in a single circle. (Circle, 2, 3, 4)
3--4	Partners B walk to the center. (In, 2, 3, 4) Back out of the center. (Out, 2, 3, 4)
5--6	Partners A take four steps to the center, turning one half left face on the fourth step. (In, 2, 3, turn left face) They take four steps toward the corner. (Out, 2, 3, 4)
7--8	As swing the corner B twice around, opening up to face counterclockwise, back in starting position, to begin the dance again. (Swing, 2, 3, open)

Irish Washerwoman (Irish)

Music Source: WWCD-1043
Formation: Single circle, couples facing center, partner B to the right, hands joined
Directions: Dancers follow the call.

Call	Action
All join hands and go to the middle.	Beginning left, take four steps to the center. (Center, 2, 3, 4)
And with your big foot keep time to the fiddle.	Stamp four times in place (Stamp, 2, 3, 4)
And when you get back, remember my call.	Take four steps backward to place (Back, 2, 3, 4)
Swing your corner and promenade all.	Swing the corner and promenade in the line of direction. (Swing, 2, 3, promenade)

Dancers keep promenading until they hear the call again to repeat the pattern.

Gustaf's Skoal (Swedish)

Music Source: WWCD-1044; WWCD-FDN
Formation: The formation is similar to a square dance set of four couples, each facing center. Partner A is to the left of partner B. Couples join inside hands; the outside hand is on the hip. Two of the couples facing each other are designated the head couples. The other two couples, also facing each other, are the side couples.
Directions: The dance is in two parts. During Part I, the music is slow and stately. The dancers perform with great dignity. The music for Part II is light and represents fun.

Measures	Part I Action
1--2	The head couples, inside hands joined, walk forward three steps and bow to the opposite couple. (Forward, 2, 3, bow)
3--4	The head couples take three steps backward to place and bow to each other. (The side couples hold their places during this action.) (Back, 2, 3, bow)
5--8	The side couples repeat action of measures 1--4 while the head couples hold their places. (Forward, 2, 3, bow; Back, 2, 3, bow)
9--16	The dancers repeat measures 1--8.

Measures	Part II Action
17--22	The side couples raise joined hands to form an arch. Head couples skip forward four steps, release partners' hands, join inside hands with opposite person, and skip under the nearest arch with new partner. After going under the arch, they drop hands and head back home to their original partner. (Head couples: Skip, 2, 3, 4; Under, 2, 3, 4; Around, 2, 3, 4)
23--24	All couples join both hands with partners and swing once around with four skipping steps. (Swing, 2, 3, 4)
25--30	Head couples form arches while side couples repeat the action of measures 17--22. (Side couples: Skip, 2, 3, 4; Under, 2, 3, 4; Around, 2, 3, 4)
31--32	All couples then repeat the movements in measures 23--24. (Swing, 2, 3, 4)

Tinikling (Philippine Islands)

Music Source: WWCD-8095; WWC-9015
Formation: Sets of fours scattered around the room. Each set has two strikers and two dancers.
Directions: Two 8-foot bamboo poles and two crossbars on which the poles rest are needed for the dance. A striker kneels at each end of the poles; both strikers hold the end of a pole in each hand. The music is in waltz meter, 3/4 time, with an accent on the first beat. The strikers slide and strike the poles together on count 1. On the other two beats of the waltz measure, the poles

are opened about 15 inches apart, lifted an inch or so, and tapped twice on the crossbars in time to counts 2 and 3. The rhythm "close, tap, tap" is continued throughout the dance, each sequence constituting a measure.

Basically, the dance requires that a step be done outside the poles on the close (count 1) and that two steps be done inside the poles (counts 2 and 3) when the poles are tapped on the crossbars. Many step combinations have been devised. The basic tinikling step should be practiced until it is mastered. The step is done singly, although two dancers are performing. Each dancer takes a position at an opposite end and on the opposite side so that the dancer's right side is to the bamboo poles.

Count 1: Step slightly forward with the left foot.
Count 2: Step with the right foot between the poles.
Count 3: Step with the left foot between the poles.
Count 4: Step with the right outside to dancer's own right.
Count 5: Step with the left between the poles.
Count 6: Step with the right between the poles.
Count 7: Step with the left outside to the original position.

The initial step (count 1) is used only to get the dance under way. The last step (count 7) to original position is actually the beginning of a new series (7, 8, 9--10, 11, 12).

Tinikling steps also can be adjusted to 4/4 rhythm (close, close, tap, tap), which requires the poles to be closed on two counts and open on the other two. The basic foot pattern is two steps outside the poles and two inside. For the sake of conformity, we present all routines in the original 3/4 time (close, tap, tap). If other rhythms are used, adjust accordingly.

Dancers can go from side to side, or can return to the side from which they entered. The dance can be done singly, with the two dancers moving in opposite directions from side to side, or the dancers can enter from and leave toward the same side. Dancers can do the same step patterns or do different movements. They can dance as partners, moving side by side with inside hands joined, or facing each other with both hands joined.

Teaching suggestions:

Steps should be practiced first with stationary poles or with lines drawn on the floor. Jump ropes can be used as stationary objects over which to practice. Students handling the poles should concentrate on watching each other rather than the dancer to avoid becoming confused by the dancer's feet.

To gain a sense of the movement pattern for 3/4 time, slap both thighs with the hands on the "close," and clap the hands twice for movements inside the poles. For 4/4 time, slap the right thigh with the right hand, then the left thigh with the left hand, followed by two claps. This routine should be done to music, with the poles closing and opening as indicated. Getting the feel of the rhythm is important.

Polly Wolly Doodle (American)

Music Sources: WWCD-1041
Skills: Sliding, turning, walking
Formation: Double circle of dancers, partners facing with both hands joined, partner A with back to the center of the circle.
Directions:

Measures	Part I Action
1–4	All slide four steps—As to left, Bs to right, counterclockwise. (Slide, 2, 3, 4)
5–8	Drop hands and all turn solo circle, As to left, Bs to right, with five stamps in this rhythm: 1-2-1, 2, 3. (Stamp on the word "polly," stamp on the other foot on the word "doodle," and take three quick stamps on the word "day.") (Turn, 2, stamp, 2, 3)
9–16	Repeat measures 1–8, but in the opposite direction, As moving to right and Bs to left. (Slide, 2, 3, 4; Turn, 2, stamp 2, 3)

	Part II Action
1–4	Both bow to each other, As with hands on hips, Bs with hands at sides. (As bow; Bs bow)
5–8	With four walking steps (or skipping steps), both move backward, away from each other. (Back, 2, 3, 4)
9–12	Both move diagonally forward to own left to meet a new partner. (Diagonal, 2, 3, 4)
13–16	With the new partner, elbow swing in place using a skipping step. (Swing, 2, 3, 4) Repeat the dance from the beginning with the new partner.

Pop Goes the Weasel (American)

Music Source: WWCD-1043; WWCD-FDN
Skills: Walking, skipping, turning under
Formation: Double circle of sets of four; couples facing with partner B on partner A's right. Couples facing clockwise are number 1 couples; couples facing counterclockwise are number 2 couples.

Directions:

Measures Action

1–4　　　　Join hands in a circle of four and circle left, once around, with eight skipping or sliding steps. (Circle, 2, 3, 4, 5, 6, 7, 8)

5–6　　　　Take two steps forward, raising the joined hands, and two steps backward, lowering the hands. (Forward, 2; Back, 2)

7–8　　　　"Ones" pop the "Twos" under (i.e., couples number 1 raise their joined hands to form an arch and pass the number 2 couples under). All walk ahead to meet a new couple. (Forward, and pop through)

Repeat as desired.

Variations:

1. Dancers are in sets of three, all facing counterclockwise. Each forms a triangle with one child in front and the other two with joined hands forming the base. The front dancer reaches back and holds the outside hands of the other two dancers. The groups of three are in a large circle formation.

Measures Action

1–2　　　　Sets of three dancers skip forward four times. (Forward, 2, 3, 4)

3–4　　　　Sets of three skip backward four times. (Backward, 2, 3, 4)

5–6　　　　Sets of three skip forward four times. (Forward, 2, 3, 4)

7–8　　　　On "Pop goes the weasel," the two back dancers raise their joined hands, and the front dancer backs up underneath to the next set. This set, in the meantime, has "popped" its front dancer back to the set behind it. (Raise and pop under)

2. "Pop Goes the Weasel" is excellent for stimulating creative movement. The music actually consists of a verse and a chorus part. During the verse part, the children can slide, gallop, or skip until the "Pop" line, at which time they make a half or full turn in the air. During the chorus, they can do jerky nonlocomotor movements. Other options include ball routines, in which the children dribble in time to the music during the verse and pass the ball around various parts of the body during the chorus. Another variation involves ropes. The children carry a jump rope while skipping, sliding, or galloping. During the chorus, they jump in time to the music, and on the word "Pop," they try to do a double jump.

Game Activity

Jump the Shot

Supplies: A jump-the-shot rope

Skill: Rope jumping

The players stand in circle formation. One player with a long rope stands in the center. A soft object is tied to the free end of the rope to give it some weight. An old, deflated ball or beanbag makes a good weight (tie the rope to it and use duct tape to keep it from becoming untied). The center player turns the rope under the feet of the circle players, who must jump over it. A player who touches the rope with the feet must move up to the next group. Change the center player after one or two misses. The center player should be cautioned to keep the rope near the ground. The rope speed can be varied. An effective way to turn the rope is to sit cross-legged and turn it over the head. Different tasks can be performed such as hopping, jumping and turning, or jumping and clapping.

Beachball Bat Ball

Supplies: Four to six beachballs

Skills: Batting, tactile handling

Two games are played across the gymnasium area. The teams are scattered throughout the area without restriction as to where they may move. To begin the game, the balls are placed on the centerline dividing the court area. Four to eight beach balls are in play at the same time. A score occurs when the beach ball is batted over the end line. Once the ball moves across the end line it is dead. Players concentrate on the remaining balls in play. If a ball is on the floor, it is picked up and batted into play. At no time may a ball be carried. After all the balls are scored, the game ends. A new game is started after teams switch goals.

Club Guard

Supplies: A juggling club or bowling pin and foam rubber ball

Skill: Throwing

A circle about 15 feet in diameter is drawn. Inside the circle at the center, an 18-inch circle is drawn. The club is placed in the center of the small circle. Two or three youngsters guard the club. The other players stand outside the large circle, which is the restraining line for them. The circle players throw the ball at the club and try to knock it down. The guards try to block the throws with the legs and body but must stay out of the small inner circle. The outer circle players pass the ball around rapidly so that one of the players can get an opening to throw as the guards maneuver to protect the club. Rotate in new guards after a short period of time (15-20 seconds).

Dynamic Physical Education for Elementary School Children
Manipulative Skills Using Paddles and Balls
Level II – Week 28

Objectives:
To quickly assemble in a small group formation
To know the proper method of holding a paddle
To hit a ball in a predetermined proper direction with a paddle

Equipment Required:
Music and Parachute for fitness
One paddle and ball for each student
Bowling pins or clubs for game
Rubber marking spots

Instructional Activities	Teaching Hints

Introductory Activity – Squad Leader Movements

Organize class into small groups of 3-4 students. Each group moves around the area, following a leader. When a change is signaled, the last person goes to the head of the line and becomes the squad leader.

Encourage leaders to keep the group moving. The minimum activity is jogging in place.

Fitness Development Activity – Parachute Fitness

1. Jog in circle with chute held in left hand. Reverse directions and hold with right hand. (music)
2. Standing, raise the chute overhead, lower to waist, lower to toes, raise to waist, etc. (no music)
3. Slide to the right; return slide to the left. (music)
4. Sit and perform Abdominal Challenges. (no music)
5. Skip. (music)
6. Freeze; face the center, and stretch the chute tightly with bent arms. Hold for 8-12 seconds. Repeat five to six times. (no music)
7. Run in place, hold the chute at waist level and hit the chute with lifted knees. (music)
8. Sit with legs under the chute. Do a seat walk toward the center. Return to the perimeter. Repeat four to six times. (no music)
9. Place the chute on the ground. Jog away from the chute and return on signal. Repeat. (music)
10. On sides with legs under the chute, perform Side Flex and lift chute with legs. (no music)
11. Hop to the center of the chute and return. Repeat. (music)
12. Assume the push-up position with the legs aligned away from the center of the chute. Shake the chute with one arm while the other arm supports the body. (no music)
13. Lie on back with legs under the chute. Shake the chute with the feet. (music)
14. Sit with feet under the chute. Stretch by touching the toes with the chute. Relax with other stretches while sitting. (no music)

Tape alternating segments (25-30 seconds in length) of silence and music to signal duration of exercise. Music segments indicate aerobic activity with the parachute while intervals of silence announce using the chute to enhance flexibility and strength development.

Space youngsters evenly around the chute.

Use different hand grips (palms up, down, mixed).

All movements should be done under control. Some of the faster and stronger students will have to moderate their performance.

Lesson Focus -- Manipulative Skills Using Paddles and Balls

1. Introduce proper method of holding paddle: forehand and backhand grip.
2. Place ball on paddle and attempt to roll it around the edge of the paddle without allowing it to fall off the paddle. Flip the paddle over and roll ball.
3. Balance the ball on the paddle using both right and left hands, as well as both grips while trying the following challenges:
   a. Touch the floor with hand.
   b. Move to knees and back to feet.
   c. Sit down and get back on feet.
   d. Lie down and get back on feet.
   e. Skip, gallop or any other locomotor movement.
4. Bounce the ball in the air using the paddle.
   a. See how many times it can be bounced without touching the floor.
   b. Bounce it off the paddle into the air and catch it with the other hand.
   d. Kneel, sit down, other positions (student choice).
   e. Bounce ball off paddle, do a full turn and continue bouncing ball on paddle.
   f. Bounce ball in the air, switch paddle to the other hand.

The use of plastic or wooden paddles and appropriate balls can be used to establish a basis for future play in racquetball, table tennis, squash, and regular tennis. These activities, particularly paddle tennis, take considerable space, so emphasis must be placed on controlled stroking rather than wild swinging.

Proper grip must be emphasized, and seeing that children maintain this is a constant battle. The easiest method to teach the proper grip is to have the student hold the paddle perpendicular to the floor and shake hands with it.

5. Dribble ball with the paddle.
   a. From a kneeling position.
   b. From a sitting position.
   c. From a standing position.
   d. Move in different directions--forward, sideways, circle.
   e. Move using different locomotor movements.
6. Alternate bouncing the ball in the air and on the floor.
7. Bounce ball of the paddle into the air and "catch" it with the paddle.
   a. Increase the height of the bounce.
   b. Perform a heel click, full turn or similar activity and catch the ball.
8. Bounce the ball continuously off the paddle into the air.
   a. Bounce the ball on the side of the paddle.
   b. Alternate sides of the paddle.
9. Place ball on the floor.
   a. Scoop it up with the paddle.
   b. Roll the ball and scoop it up with the paddle.
   c. Start dribbling the ball without touching it with hands.
10. Partner Activities.
    a. Begin partner activities with controlled throwing (feeding) by one partner and the designated stroke return by the other.
    b. Bounce ball back and forth. How many times can you bounce it back and forth to your partner without missing it?
    c. Increase the distance between partners and the height of the ball.
    d. Catch the ball on your paddle after throw from your partner, then return throw.
    e. Perform stunts while ball is in the air, such as catch ball behind back, under leg, above head, clap hands, heel clicks, full turns, etc.
    f. Use two balls.
    g. Move and keep the balls going; try skipping, hopping, jumping, or sliding.

Young people tend to revert to the inefficient hammer grip, so named because it is similar to the grip used on a hammer.

Use the following instructional cues to improve paddle skills:

a. Hold the wrist reasonably stiff.

b. Use a smooth arm action.

c. Stroke through the ball and follow through.

d. Watch the ball strike the paddle.

All paddles should have leather wrist thongs. The hand goes through the leather loop before grasping the paddle. No play should be permitted without this safety precaution.

Early learning activities should be practiced with both the right and the left hand The dominant hand should be developed more as youngsters begin to use the skills in game activities.

Game Activity

Trades
Supplies: None
Skills: Imagery, running, dodging

Designate two lines at opposite ends of the area. The class is divided into two teams of equal number. One team, the chasers, stands on one of the lines. The other team, the runners, starts on the other line. The runners move toward the chasers while reciting the following dialogue:

Runners: *Here we come.*
Chasers: *Where from?*
Runners: *New Orleans.*
Chasers: *What's your trade?*
Runners: *Lemonade.*
Chasers: *Show us some.*

The runners move close to the other team's goal line and proceed to act out an occupation or a specific task that they have chosen previously. The opponents try to guess what the pantomime represents. When a correct guess is made, the chasers try to tag the running team before they reach the goal line. Any runner tagged must join the chasers. The game is repeated with roles reversed. The team ending with the greater number of players is the winner. If a team has trouble guessing the pantomime, the other team should provide hints.

Bounce Ball
Supplies: Volleyballs or rubber playground balls of about the same size
Skills: Throwing, ball rolling

The court is divided into halves. The class is divided into two teams and each team occupies one half of the court and is given a number of balls. Two players from each team should be assigned to retrieve balls that go behind their end lines. The object of the game is to bounce or roll the ball over the opponents' end line. A ball thrown across the line on a fly does not count. Two scorers are needed, one at each end line. Players can move wherever they wish in their own area but cannot cross the centerline. After the starting signal, the balls are thrown back and forth at will.

Dynamic Physical Education for Elementary School Children
Individual Rope Jumping Skills
Level II – Week 29

Objectives:
To be able to jump slow and fast time with a self-turned rope
To identify safety considerations for fast-moving games
To maintain continuous fitness activity

Equipment Required:
Tambourine or tom-tom
One beanbag per student
Exercises to Music tape
Jump rope for each student
Beanbags for games

Instructional Activities	Teaching Hints

Introductory Activity -- European Rhythmic Running with Equipment

Review European Rhythmic Running (Lesson Plan 7) and emphasize the following points:
1. Move to the rhythm.
2. Lift the knees and perform a trotting step.
3. Maintain proper spacing between each other.

After the review, give each child a beanbag. Every fourth step, they can toss up the bag. Other variations can be tried using different beats of the rhythm.

Fitness Development Activity -- Exercises to Music

Side Flex (switch sides)	30 seconds
Jogging	25 seconds
Abdominal Challenges	30 seconds
Slide or Skip	25 seconds
Triceps Push-Ups	30 seconds
Jumping Jack variations	25 seconds
Curl-Up Challenges	30 seconds
Gallop	25 seconds
Push-Up challenges	30 seconds
Aerobic Bouncing and Clapping	25 seconds
Leg Extensions	30 seconds
Walking to cool down	25 seconds

Select music that has a strong rhythm and easy-to-hear beat. When the music is on students perform aerobic activities (for 25 seconds). When the music is not playing, students perform the strength development and flexibility exercises (30 seconds).

See Chapter 12 of the textbook for descriptions of the exercises.

Use scatter formation.

Lesson Focus -- Individual Rope Jumping Skills

1. For students who are having trouble jumping the rope, try some of the following activities:
   a. Jump in place to a tom-tom beat without rope.
   b. Hold both ends of the jump rope in one hand (practice with right and left hands) and turn it to the side so a steady rhythm can be made through a consistent turn. Just before the rope hits the ground, the student should practice jumping.
   c. Start jumping the rope one turn at a time--gradually increase the number of turns.
2. Introduce the two basic jump rhythms:
   a. Slow-time rhythm. In slow time rhythm, the performer jumps the rope and then takes a second jump while the rope is overhead. The jump while the rope is overhead is usually a small, light rebound jump. In slow time, the rope makes one full turn for each two jumps.
   b. Fast time rhythm. In fast time rhythm, the student jumps the rope with every jump. The rope makes one full turn for every jump.
3. Introduce some of the basic step variations. The basic steps can be done in slow or fast time.
   a. Side Swing. Swing the rope, held with both hands to one side of the body. Switch and swing the rope on the other side of the body.
   b. Double Side Swing and Jump. Swing the rope once on each side of the body. Follow the second swing with a jump over the rope. The sequence should be swing, swing, jump.

The length of the rope is dependent on the height of the jumper. It should be long enough so that the ends reach to the armpits or slightly higher when the child stands on its center. Grades 3-4 students need mostly 8-foot ropes, with a few 7- and 9-foot lengths. Ropes or handles can be color-coded for length.

Two types of ropes are available; the beaded (plastic segment) and the plastic (licorice) rope. The beaded ropes are heavier and seem easier to turn for beginning jumpers. The drawback to the beaded ropes is that they hurt when they hit another student. Also, if the segments are made round, the rope will roll easily on the floor children may fall when they step on it. The plastic licorice ropes are lighter and give less wind resistance.

c. Alternate-Foot Basic Step. In the Alternate-Foot Basic Step, as the rope passes under the feet, the weight is shifted alternately from one foot to the other, raising the unweighted foot in a running position.

d. Bird Jumps. Jump with the toes pointed in (pigeon walk) and with the toes pointed out (duck walk). Alternate toes in and toes out.

e. Swing-Step Forward. The Swing-Step Forward is the same as the Alternate-Foot Basic Step, except that the free leg swings forward. The knee is kept loose and the foot swings naturally.

f. Rocker Step. In executing the Rocker Step, one leg is always forward in a walking-stride position. As the rope passes under the feet, the weight is shifted from the back foot to the forward foot. The rebound is taken on the forward foot while the rope is above the head. On the next turn of the rope, the weight is shifted from the forward foot to the back foot, repeating the rebound on the back foot.

4. Individual Rope Jumping with a Partner. One student turns and jumps the rope while her partner enters and jumps simultaneously. Entering is sometimes difficult for beginners, so it may be necessary to begin in position and then start turning the rope. The following are some challenges partners can try:

a. Run in and face partner, and both jump.

b. Run in and turn back to partner, and both jump.

c. Decide which steps are to be done; then run in and match steps.

d. Repeat with the rope turning backward.

Instructional cues to use for improving jumping technique are as follows:

a. Keep the arms at the side of the body while turning. (Many children lift the arms to shoulder level trying to move the rope overhead. This makes it impossible for the youngster to jump over the elevated rope.)

b. Turn the rope by making small circles with the wrists.

c. Jump on the balls of the feet.

d. Bend the knees slightly to absorb the force of the jump.

e. Don't jump too high. Make a small jump over the rope.

Game Activity

Wolfe's Beanbag Exchange

Supplies: One beanbag per child

Skills: Running, dodging, tossing, catching

Five or six children are identified as taggers. The remaining players start scattered throughout the area, each with a beanbag in hand. The taggers chase the players with beanbags. When a tag is made, the tagged player must freeze, keeping her feet still and beanbag in hand. To unfreeze a player, any player who is not frozen can exchange his beanbag for a beanbag held by a frozen player. If two frozen players are within tossing distance, they can thaw each other by exchanging their beanbags through the air using a toss and catch. Both tosses have to be caught or the beanbags are retrieved and tried again from their previous location.

Loose Caboose

Supplies: None

Skills: Running, dodging

Two or three players are designated as loose cabooses that try to hook onto a train. Trains are formed by three or four children standing in column formation with their hands placed on the shoulders of the person in front of them. The trains, by twisting and turning, endeavor to keep the caboose from hooking onto the back. When the caboose hooks on, the front child in the train becomes the new caboose. If a train is not able to stay together while evading the cabooses, the entire group must move to the side and count to 25 before returning.

Dynamic Physical Education for Elementary School Children
Volleyball-Related Skills (1)
Level II – Week 30

Objectives:	Equipment Required:
To perform overhand and underhand volleyball passing skills	Tambourine
To volley the ball a number of times against a wall	Music and signs for Circuit Training
To practice skills successfully with a partner	One beachball, 8" foam rubber, or
To learn the basic rules of volleyball	volleyball trainer for each student
	Volleyball net (6 ft height)

Instructional Activities	Teaching Hints
Introductory Activity -- Marking	
Each child has a partner who is somewhat equal in ability. Under control, one partner runs, dodges, and tries to lose the other, who tries to stay within 3 ft of the runner. On signal, both freeze. The chaser must be close enough to touch her partner to say that they have marked (scored a point) them. Partners then reverse roles.	1. Use different locomotor movements. 2. Allow a point to be scored only when they touch a specified body part (i.e., knee, elbow, left hand).

Fitness Development Activity -- Circuit Training

Students do the best they can at each station within the time limit. This implies that not all youngsters are required to do the same workload. Children differ and their ability to perform fitness workloads differs. Make fitness a personal challenge.

Rope Jumping
Triceps Push-Ups
Agility Run
Body Circles
Hula Hoop
Knee Touch Curl-Ups
Crab Walk
Tortoise and Hare
Bend and Twist

Conclude circuit training with 2-4 minutes of walking, jogging, rope jumping or other aerobic activity.

Tape alternating segments of silence and music to signal duration of exercise. Music segments (begin at 30 seconds) indicate activity at each station while intervals of silence (10 seconds) announce it is time to stop and move forward to the next station.

Use signals such as start, stop, and move up to ensure rapid movement to the next station.

Ask students to do the best they can. Expect workloads to differ.

Lesson Focus -- Volleyball-Related Skills (1)

Skills
Practice the following skills:
Overhand Pass

To execute an overhand pass, the player moves underneath the ball and controls it with the fingertips. The cup of the fingers is made so that the thumbs and forefingers are close together and the other fingers are spread. The hands are held forehead high, with elbows out and level with the floor. The player, when in receiving position, looks ready to shout upward through the hands. The player contacts the ball above eye level and propels it with the force of spread fingers, not with the palms. At the moment of contact, the legs are straightened and the hands and arms follow through.

Forearm Pass (Underhand Pass)

The hands are clasped together so that the forearms are parallel. The clasp should be relaxed, with the type of handclasp a matter of choice. The thumbs are kept parallel and together, and the fingers of one hand make a partially cupped fist, with the fingers of the other hand overlapping the fist. The wrists are turned downward and the elbow joints are reasonably locked. The forearms are held at the proper angle to rebound the ball, with contact made with the fists or forearms between the knees as the receiver crouches.

Using beach balls and trainer volleyballs will allow youngsters time to move into the path of the volleyball instead of reaching for the ball. Proper footwork is critical to the success of volleyball; using proper balls will help assure that youngsters learn correctly.

Instructional cues of passing include the following:
1. Move into the path of the ball; don't reach for it.
2. Bend the knees prior to making contact.
3. Contact the ball with the fingertips (overhand pass).
4. Extend the knees upon contact with the ball.
5. Follow through after striking the ball.

Individual Passing Drills

1. Practice wall rebounding: Stand 6 feet away from a wall. Pass the ball against the wall and catch it.
2. From a spot 6 feet from the wall, throw the ball against the wall and alternate an overhand pass with a forearm pass.
3. Throw the ball to one side (right or left) and move to the side to pass the ball to the wall. Catch the rebound.
4. Pass the ball directly overhead and catch it. Try making two passes before catching the ball. Later, alternate an overhand pass with a forearm pass and catch the ball. This is a basic drill and should be mastered before proceeding to others.

Partner Passing Drills

1. Players are about 10 feet apart. Play A tosses the ball (controlled toss) to player B, who passes the ball back to A, who catches the ball. Continue for several exchanges and then change throwers.
2. Two players are about 15 feet apart. Player a passes to himself or herself first and then makes a second pass to player B, who catches the ball and repeats. Follow with a return by B.
3. Players A and B try to keep the ball in the air continuously.
4. Players are about 15 feet apart. Player A remains stationary and passes in such a fashion that player B must move from side to side. An option is to have player B move forward and backward.
5. Players are about 10 feet apart. Both have hoops and attempt to keep one foot in the hoop while passing. Try keeping both feet in the hoop.
6. Player A passes to player B and does a complete turnaround. B passes back to A and also does a full turn. Other stunts can be used.

The usual basketball court should be divided into two volleyball courts on which players play crosswise. Nets should be lowered to 6 feet and raised 6 to 12 inches as children mature.

In the primary grades, children should have had ball-handling experiences related to volleyball skills. Rebounding and controlling balloons is an excellent related experience, particularly for younger children. Included in ball-handling experiences with beach balls or foam rubber training balls should be exploratory work in batting with the hands and other body parts.

Regulation volleyballs should not be used with third and fourth grade students. An 8-inch foam rubber training ball has much the same feel as a volleyball but does not cause pain. The foam balls should be used for skill practice. Another excellent ball is the volleyball trainer which closely resembles a volleyball but is larger in diameter and lighter in weight. Either ball helps keep children from developing a fear of the fast-moving object.

Game Activity -- Volleyball Lead-Up Games

Beachball Volleyball

Supplies: A beach ball 16 to 20 inches in diameter
Skills: Most passing skills, modified serving

The players of each team are in two lines on their respective sides of the net. The player on the right side of the back line serves, as in regulation volleyball. The distance is shortened, however, because serving a beach ball successfully from the normal volleyball serving distance is difficult. The player serves from the normal playing position on the court in the right back position. Scoring is similar to regulation volleyball. Play continues until the ball touches the floor. A team loses a point to the other team when it fails to return the ball over the net by the third volley or when it returns the ball over the net but the ball hits the floor out of bounds without being touched by the opposing team. The server continues serving as long as his team scores. Rotation is as in regulation volleyball. Position the server as close to the net as possible while still remaining in the right back position on the court.

Informal Volleyball

Supplies: A trainer volleyball
Skills: Passing

This game is similar to regulation volleyball, but there is no serving. Each play begins with a student on one side tossing the ball overhead and passing it over the net. Points are scored for every play, as there is no "side out." As soon as a point is scored, the nearest player takes the ball and immediately puts it into play. Otherwise, basic volleyball rules govern the game. Rotation occurs as soon as a team has scored 5 points, with the front and back lines changing place. Action is fast, and the game moves rapidly, as every play scores a point for one team or the other.

Dynamic Physical Education for Elementary School Children
Volleyball Related Skills (2)
Level II – Week 31

Objectives:
To perform overhand and underhand volleyball passing skills
To volley the ball a number of times against a wall
To hit an underhand serve over a 6' net
To learn the basic rules of volleyball

Equipment Required:
Marking spots for Home Base
Music & signs for Hexagon Hustle
One beachball, 8" foam rubber, or
    volleyball trainer for each student
Volleyball net (6 ft height)

Instructional Activities	Teaching Hints

Introductory Activity – Home Base

The class is divided in to teams of 5-6 players. One player in each group is designated the captain. Rubber spots are placed throughout the teaching area equal to the number of teams. Each spot serves as a home base for one of the squads. The teams begin in a straight line with the captain standing on a spot and the rest of the team lined up behind her. The teacher calls out a locomotor movement that the players use to move throughout the area. When the teacher calls "home base!" each team lines up in starting formation with the captain first in line. The first team to return to proper position is awarded wins that round.

This is an excellent game to teach youngsters how to get in small group formations quickly.

If desired, use the call "find your home" to assemble the class in pre-assigned squads. Some teachers use squads for station teaching and dividing the class into teams.

Fitness Development Activity -- Hexagon Hustle

Hustle	25 seconds	
Push-Up from Knees	30 seconds	
Hustle	25 seconds	
Bend and Twist (8 counts)	30 seconds	
Hustle	25 seconds	
Jumping Jacks (4 counts)	30 seconds	
Hustle	25 seconds	
Abdominal Challenges (2 counts)	30 seconds	
Hustle	25 seconds	
Double Leg Crab Kick	30 seconds	
Hustle	25 seconds	
Sit and Stretch (8 counts)	30 seconds	
Hustle	25 seconds	
Power Jumper	30 seconds	
Hustle	25 seconds	
Squat Thrust (4 counts)	30 seconds	

Outline a large hexagon with six cones. Place signs with directions on both sides of the cones. The signs identify the hustle activity students are to perform as they approach a cone. Tape alternating segments of silence and music to signal duration of exercise. Music segments indicate aerobic activity while intervals of silence announce flexibility and strength development activities.

Encourage students to do their best. Workloads should be personalized by each student by performing activities they feel able to do.

Lesson Focus -- Volleyball Related Skills (2)

Skills
Review skills taught in the previous week:
Overhand Pass
Forearm Pass (Underhand pass)

Introduce a new skill:
Underhand Serve

    Directions are for a right-handed serve. The player stands facing the net with the left foot slightly forward and the weight on the right (rear) foot. The ball is held in the left hand with the left arm across and a little in front of the body. On the serving motion, step forward with the left foot, transfer the weight to the front foot, and at the same time bring the right arm back in a preparatory motion. The right hand swings forward and contacts the ball just below center. The ball can be hit with an open hand or with the fist (facing forward or sideward).

The serve is used to start play. The underhand serve is easiest for elementary school children to learn even though the overhand (floater) serve is the most effective. Few youngsters will be capable of mastering the overhand serve.

The following instructional cues focus on correct performance of the serve:

1. Use opposition. Place the opposite foot of the serving hand forward.

2. Transfer the weight to the forward foot.

3. Keep the eyes on the ball.

Drills

Individual Passing Drills

1. Pass the ball 3 feet or so to one side, move under the ball, and pass it back to the original spot. The next pass should be to the other side.
2. Pass the ball directly overhead. On the return, jump as high as possible and make a second pass. Continue.
3. Stand with one foot in a hoop. Pass the ball overhead and attempt to continue passing while keeping one foot in the hoop. Try with both feet in the hoop.

Partner Passing Drills:

1. Players are about 15 feet apart. Player A remains stationary and passes in such a fashion that player B must move from side to side. An option is to have player B move forward and backward.
2. Players are about 10 feet apart. Both have hoops and attempt to keep one foot in the hoop while passing. Try keeping both feet in the hoop.
3. Player A passes to player B and does a complete turnaround. B passes back to A and also does a full turn. Other stunts can be used.

Partner Serving and Passing Drills

1. Partners are about 20 feet apart. Partner A serves to partner B, who catches the ball and returns the serve to partner A.
2. Partner A serves to partner B, who makes a pass back to partner A. Change responsibilities.
3. Service One-Step. Partners begin about 10 feet apart. Partner A serves to partner B, who returns the serve with partner A catching. If there is no error and if neither receiver moved the feet to catch, both players take one step back. This is repeated each time that no error or foot movement by the receivers occurs. If an error occurs or if appreciable foot movement is evident, the players revert to the original distance of 10 feet and start over.

4. Decide prior to the serve where it should be placed.

5. Follow through; don't punch at the ball.

Regulation volleyballs should not be used with third and fourth grade students. An 8-inch foam rubber training ball has much the same feel as a volleyball but does not cause pain. The foam balls should be used for skill practice. Another excellent ball is the volleyball trainer which closely resembles a volleyball but is larger in diameter and lighter in weight. Either ball helps keep children from developing a fear of the fast-moving object.

The use of the fist to hit balls on normal returns causes poor control and interrupts play. Except for dig passes, both hands should be used to return the ball. Teachers should rule hitting with the fist a loss of a point if the practice persists.

Game Activity - Volleyball Lead-Up Games

Continue playing the games listed in the Lesson Plan 30. The lead-up games for this age are:
> Beachball Volleyball
> Informal Volleyball

Introduce the following game:
Shower Service Ball
> Supplies: Four to six trainer volleyballs
> Skills: Serving, catching

A line parallel to the net is drawn through the middle of each court to define the serving area. Players are scattered in no particular formation. The game involves the skills of serving and catching. To start the game, two or three volleyballs are given to each team and are handled by players in the serving area. Balls may be served at any time and in any order by a server, who must be in the back half of the court. Any ball served across the net is to be caught by any player near the ball. The person catching or retrieving a ball moves quickly to the serving area and serves. A point is scored for a team whenever a served ball hits the floor in the other court or is dropped by a receiver. Two scorers are needed, one for each side. As youngsters improve, all serves should be made from behind the baseline.

Dynamic Physical Education for Elementary School Children
Rhythmic Movement Skills (4)
Level II – Week 32

Objectives:
To put together a combination of movements in a smooth and flowing manner
To evade or stay near a partner while traveling
To perform rhythmic activities while handling manipulative equipment

Equipment Required:
One jump rope for each student
Music for Continuity Drills
Two Lummi sticks for each student
One playground ball for each student

Instructional Activities	Teaching Hints

Introductory Activity -- Combination Movement Patterns

Explore some of the following movement combinations:
1. Run, leap and roll.
2. Run, collapse and roll.
3. Hop, turn around and shake.
4. Run, change direction and collapse.
5. Hop, make a shape in the air and balance.

Encourage a variety of responses

Try having students work in pairs and generate different combinations. They can mimic each other's ideas.

Fitness Development Activity – Continuity Drills

Rope Jumping - Forward	30 seconds
Double Crab Kick	45 seconds
Rope Jumping - Backward	30 seconds
Knee Touch Curl-Up	45 seconds
Jump and Slowly Turn Body	30 seconds
Push-Up Challenges	45 seconds
Rocker Step	30 seconds
Bend and Twist	45 seconds
Swing-Step Forward	30 seconds
Side Flex	45 seconds
Free Jumping	30 seconds
Sit and Stretch	45 seconds

Students alternate jump rope activity with exercises done in two-count fashion. Exercises can be done with a student leader saying "Ready;" and the class responding "One-two" and performing a repetition of exercise. In activities like Push-Ups and Curl-Ups, allow students to pick any challenge activity they feel capable of performing.

Allow students to adjust the workload to their level. This implies resting if the rope jumping is too strenuous.

Lesson Focus -- Rhythmic Movement Skills (4)

Rope Jumping Skills to Music
1. Perform the slow-time and fast-time rhythm with the rope held in one hand and turned.
2. Jump the rope and practice changing back and forth from slow to fast time.
3. Review basic steps student have learned in the earlier lesson plan on rope jumping (Lesson Plan 29).
4. Allow student time to put together a simple routine to music using some of the steps they have learned.

Music selected should have a steady and unchanging beat. It should be played loud so that it can easily be heard above the noise of jump ropes and/or balls.

Jumping rope is a demanding activity. Even though music will motivate youngsters to practice, it can't be done for long. Take a break and practice ball skills. If desired, come back to rope jumping after practicing ball skills.

Ball Skills to Music
Perform a number of ball skills to the rhythm of the music. See Lesson Plan 5 for a refresher of skills learned previously.
  a. Bounce and catch.
  b. Bounce, clap, catch; bounce, turn, catch--also use toss.
  c. Dribble continuously in place and while moving.
  d. Work with a partner or in groups, passing one or more balls to one another in rhythm.
  e. Create different movements using the ball such as swings, spins, and around the body
  f. Develop a routine utilizing some of the skills above.

Encourage students to bounce the ball on the beat of the rhythm. It may help to hit a tom-tom or tambourine to make the beat easy to feel.

Lummi Sticks

Music Source: WWCD-2015 or 2014; WWC-2000
Formation: Couples scattered throughout the area
Directions: Lummi sticks are smaller versions of wands; they are 12 to 15 inches long. Most Lummi stick activities are done by partners, although some can be done individually. Each child sits cross-legged, facing a partner at a distance of 18 to 20 inches. Children adjust this distance as the activities demand. The sticks are held in the thumb and fingers (not the fist) at about the bottom third of the stick. Routines are based on sets of six movements; each movement is completed in one count. Many different routines are possible. Only the basic ones are presented here. The following one-count movements are used to make up routines.

- a. Vertical tap: Tap both sticks upright on the floor.
- b. Partner tap: Tap partner's stick (right stick to right stick, or left to left).
- c. End tap: Tilt the sticks forward or sideward and tap the ends on the floor.
- d. Cross-tap: Cross hands and tap the upper ends to the floor.
- e. Side tap: Tap the upper ends to the side.
- f. Flip: Toss the stick in air, giving it a half turn, and catch other end.
- g. Tap together: Hold the sticks parallel and tap them together.
- h. Toss right (or left): Toss the right-hand stick to partner's right hand, at the same time receiving partner's right-hand stick.
- i. Pass: Lay the stick on the floor and pick up partner's stick.
- j. Toss right and left: Toss quickly right to right and left to left, all in the time of one count.

A number of routines, incorporating the movements described, are presented here in sequence of difficulty. Each routine is to be done four times to complete the 24 beats of the chant.

- a. Vertical tap, tap together, partner tap right, vertical tap, tap together, partner tap left.
- b. Vertical tap, tap together, pass right stick, vertical tap, tap together, pass left stick.
- c. Vertical tap, tap together, toss right stick, vertical tap, tap together, toss left stick.
- d. Repeat numbers 1, 2, and 3, but substitute an end tap and flip for the vertical tap and tap together. Perform the stated third movement (e.g., end tap, flip, partner tap right, end tap, flip, partner tap left).
- e. Vertical tap, tap together, toss right and left quickly, end tap, flip, toss right and left quickly.
- f. Cross-tap, cross-flip, vertical tap (uncross arms), cross-tap, cross-flip, vertical tap (uncross arms).

Popcorn (American)

Music Source: WWCD-RM7; WWC-RM7
Skills: Toe touches, knee lifts, jumps, ¼ turns
Formation: Single lines of students; no partners
Directions:

Counts	Measures
24	Wait 24 counts; gently bounce up and down by bending the knees during the introduction
1-4	Touch right toe in front and return; repeat. (Right, together, Right, together)
5-8	Touch left toe in front and return; repeat. (Left, together, left, together)
9-12	Touch right toe in back and return; repeat. (Back, together, back, together)
13-16	Touch left toe in front and return; repeat. (Back, together, back, together)
17-20	Lift right knee up in front of left knee and return; repeat. (Knee up, return, knee up, return)
21-24	Lift left knee up in front of right knee and return; repeat. (Knee up, return, knee up, return)
25-26	Lift right knee up in front of left knee and return. (Knee up, return)
27-28	Lift left knee up in front of right knee and return. (Knee up, return)
29-30	Clap both hands together once. (clap)
31-32	Jump and turn ¼ turn to the right. (jump and turn)

Repeat entire dance to the end of the music.

Red River Valley (American)

Music Source: WWCD-FDN
Skills: Walk, buzz swing
Formation: Triple circle with 3 dances side by side in sets of 6 dancers-2 trios facing each other. Half the trios face counterclockwise and half face clockwise
Directions:

Measures	Part I Action
4	Introduction
1-4	Middle person of each trio leads partners forward to right to meet oncoming trio using 8 walking steps. (Walk, 2, 3, … 8)

5-8	Join hands with oncoming trio and circle to the left (clockwise) 4 walking steps; then reverse direction and circle right using four walking steps. (Circle, left, 3, 4; circle, right, 3, 4)
9-12	Middle person swings around with person on left using 8 buzz (shuffling) steps. (Swing, 2, 3, ... 8)
13-16	Middle person swings around with person on right using 8 buzz (shuffling) steps. (Swing, 2, 3, ... 8)
	Part II Action
1-8	Repeat action of measures 1-8 in Part I. (Walk, 2, 3, ... 8)
9-12	The 4 outside youngsters form a right hand star in the center of the set and walk around once to starting point using 8 walking steps. (Star, 2, 3, ... 8)
13-16	The two middle youngsters "do-si-do" around each other, returning to own place using 8 walking steps. (Do-si-do, 2, 3, ... 8)
	Part III Action
1-8	Repeat action of measures 1-8 in Part I. (Walk, 2, 3, ... 8)
9-12	The two left-hand outside youngsters change places diagonally across using 8 walking steps. (Left, diagonal, 3, ... 8)
13-16	The two right-hand outside youngsters change places diagonally across using 8 walking steps. The middle person now has different partners. (Right, diagonal, 3, ... 8)

The entire dance is repeated 2 times.

Sicilian Circle (American)

Music Source: WWCD-FDN

Skills: Walking, two-hand swing (either walking or buzz turn), wheel turn

Formation: Double circle composed of groups of two couples facing each other with partners side by side. Couples are numbered 1 and 2 with #1 couples moving counterclockwise and #2 couples clockwise.

Directions:

Measures	Part I Action
4	Introduction
1-4	The sets of two couples join hands and walk 8 steps to the left ending where they started and drop hands. (Circle, left, 2, 3, 4, ... 8)
5-8	Partners join both hands and swing once around to the left using 8 walking or buzz steps (Swing, left, 2, 3, 4, ... 8)
9-12	Couples advance toward each other and pass right shoulders through to opposite's place using 4 walking steps. As soon as across, couples do a wheel-turn around with partner on the left walking backward 4 steps and moving into place on partner's left who turns in place using 4 steps. If desired, left partner can hold left hand with partner's left hand and right hand around back of partner's waist. Hands are dropped. (Pass, through, 3, 4; wheel, turn, 3,4)
13-16	Couples pass through again as described in measures 9-12. (Back, through, 3, 4; wheel, turn, 3,4)
17-20	Right hand partners advance toward each other, join right hands briefly, pass each other by right shoulders, drop hands, and join left hand with opposite left partner using 4 steps. The opposite left partner does a wheel turn as described in measures 9-12 using 4 steps. (Right partner, chain, 3, 4; wheel, turn, 3,4)
21-24	Right hand partner chain back again and turn as in measure 17-20 using 8 steps and end with left hands joined with partner. (Chain, back, 3, 4; wheel, turn, 3,4)
25-28	Partners join hands in promenade position and advance 4 steps toward opposite and 4 steps backward to place. (Forward, 2, 3, 4; Back, 2, 3, 4)
29-32	Each couple with hands in promenade position advance to the left of the opposite couple to the next couple using 8 steps. (New couple, 2, 3, ... 8)

Dance is repeated 3 times.

Savila Se Bela Loza (Serbian)

Music Source: WWCD-TCZ; WWC-572

Skills: Running step, crossover step, hop

Formation: Broken circle or line; joined hands held down

Directions: Explain Savila Se Bela Loza (pronounced SAH-vee-lah say BAY-lah LOH-zah) means a "grapevine entwined in itself."

Measures	Part I Action
	Introduction
1-20	Face slightly to right, move right starting with the right foot taking 18 small running steps forward. Do a step-hop on the 19th and 20th steps. (Run, 2, 3, ... 18, step, hop)
21-40	Face slightly left and repeat above action starting with the left foot. Finish with a step hop on the left foot. (Run, 2, 3, ... 18, step, hop)

Part II Action

41-44   Beginning with right, take one schottische step moving right. Translated this is a step to the right sideward on right foot, a step with the left foot behind the right followed by a step-hop on the right foot. (Right, left, right, hop)

45-48   Beginning with left, take one schottische step moving left. This is done with a step to the left sideward on left foot, a step with the right foot behind the left followed by a step-hop on the left foot. (Left, right left, hop)

49-64   Repeat the action of counts 41-48 two more times.

Repeat the dance. During the music for Part I, the leaders on the ends of the lines may lead the line anywhere, winding or coiling the line like a grapevine.

Ve David (Israeli)

Music Source: WWCD-RM3; WWC-RM3

Skills: Walking, pivoting, buzz-step turn

Formation: Double circle, couples facing counterclockwise, partner B on partner A's right. Inside hands joined, right foot free.

Directions:

Measures Part I Action

1-2   All walk forward and form a ring. Take four walking steps forward, starting with the right foot and progressing counterclockwise, then back out, taking four walking steps to form a single circle, facing center, with all hands joined. (Walk, 2, 3, 4; Single, circle, 3, 4)

3-4   All forward and back. Four steps forward to center and four steps backward, starting with the right foot. (Forward, 2, 3, 4; Back, 2, 3, 4)

Part II Action

1-2   Bs forward and back; As clap. Partners B, starting with the right foot, walk four steps forward to the center and four steps backward to place while Partners A clap. (Bs in, 2, 3, 4; Out 2, 3, 4)

Part III Action

1-2   Partners A forward, circle to the right, and progress to a new partner; all clap. As, clapping hands, walk four steps forward to the center, starting with the right foot. They turn right about on the last "and" count and walk forward four steps, passing their original partner and progressing ahead to the next. (As in, 2, 3, 4; Turn to new partner)

3-4   Swing the new partner. The A and the new partner B swing clockwise with right shoulders adjacent, right arms around each other across in front, and left arms raised—pivoting with right foot for an eight count "buzz-step" swing. (Swing, 2, 3, 4, 5, 6, 7, 8)

Repeat the entire dance.

Game Activity

Alaska Baseball

    Supplies: A volleyball or soccer ball

    Skills: Kicking, batting, running, ball handling

    Players are divided into two teams; one is at bat while the other is in the field. A straight line provides the only out-of-bounds line, and the team at bat is behind this line midway between the ends of the line. The other team is scattered around the fair territory. One player propels the ball, either batting a volleyball or kicking a stationary soccer ball. Her teammates are in a close file behind her. As soon as the batter sends the ball into the playing area, she starts to run around her own team. Each time the runner passes the head of the file, the team gives a loud count.

    There are no outs. The first fielder to get the ball stands still and starts to pass the ball back overhead to the nearest teammate, who moves directly behind to receive it. The remainder of the team in the field must run to the ball and form a file behind the fielder. The ball is passed back overhead, with each player handling the ball. When the last field player in line has a firm grip on it, she shouts "Stop." At this signal, a count is made of the number of times the batter ran around her team. To score more accurately, half rounds can be counted. Five batters or half of the team should bat; then the teams should change places. This is better than allowing an entire team to bat before changing to the field, because players in the field fatigue from many consecutive runs.

Addition Tag

    Supplies: None

    Skills: Running, dodging

    Two or more couples are it and each stands with inside hands joined. These are the taggers. The rest of the class runs individually. The couples move around the area, trying to tag with the free hands. The first person tagged joins the couple, making a trio. The three then chase until they catch a fourth. Once a fourth person is caught, the four divide and form two couples, adding another set of taggers to the game. This continues until the majority of the players are tagged. The game moves faster if started with two couples. A tag is legal only when the couple or group of three keeps their hands joined. The game can be used as an introductory activity, since all children are active.

Dynamic Physical Education for Elementary School Children
Manipulative Skills Using Frisbees
Level II – Week 33

Objectives:
To learn the unique throwing style required with frisbees
To learn the rules of frisbee golf
To perform continuous fitness activity

Equipment Required:
Tom-tom or tambourine
Signs and music for Aerobic Fitness
One Frisbee per student
Cones and hoops for Frisbee Golf

Instructional Activities	Teaching Hints

Introductory Activity -- European Rhythmic Running with Variations

Students clap to the beat of the tambourine and run in single-file formation. Practice some of the following variations:
1. Clap hands the first beat of a four beat rhythm.
2. Stamp foot and clap hands on the first beat.
3. On signal, make a complete turn, using four running steps.

Encourage students to originate different variations of rhythmic running.

After the rhythm is learned, stop striking the tambourine and let the class maintain the rhythm.

Fitness Development Activity -- Aerobic Fitness

1. Rhythmic run with clap
2. Bounce turn and clap
3. Rhythmic 4-count curl-ups (knees, toes, knees, back)
4. Rhythmic Crab Kicks (slow time)
5. Jumping Jack combination
6. Double knee lifts
7. Lunges (right, left, forward) with single-arm circles (on the side lunges) and double-arms circles (on the forward lunge)
8. Rhythmic trunk twists
9. Directional run (forward, backward, side, turning)
10. Rock side to side with clap
11. Side leg raises (alternate legs)
12. Rhythmic 4-count push-ups (If these are too difficult for students, substitute single-arm circles in the push-up position.)

Use music to stimulate effort. Any combination of movements can be used.

Keep the steps simple and easy to perform. Some students will become frustrated if the learning curve is steep.

Signs that explain the aerobic activities will help students remember performance cues.

Don't stress or expect perfection. Allow students to perform the activities as best they can.

Alternate bouncing and running movements with flexibility and strength development movements.

Lesson Focus -- Manipulative Skills Using Frisbees

Throwing the Disk
Backhand Throw
    The backhand grip is used most often. The thumb is on top of the disk, the index finger along the rim, and the other fingers underneath. To throw the Frisbee with the right hand, stand in a sideways position with the right foot toward the target. Step toward the target and throw the Frisbee in a sideways motion across the body, snapping the wrist and trying to keep the disk flat on release.
Underhand Throw
    The underhand throw uses the same grip as in the backhand throw, but the thrower faces the target and holds the disk at the side of the body. Step forward with the leg opposite the throwing arm while bringing the Frisbee forward. When the throwing arm is out in the front of the body, release the Frisbee. The trick to this throw is learning to release the disk so that it is parallel to the ground.

Catching the Disk
Thumb-Down Catch
    The thumb-down catch is used for catching when the disk is received at waist level or above. The thumb is pointing toward the ground.

Use the following instructional cues to improve skill performance:

a. Release the disk parallel to the ground. If it is tilted, a curved throw results.

b. Step toward the target and follow through on release of the disk.

c. Snap open the wrist and make the Frisbee spin.

If space is limited, all Frisbees should be thrown in the same direction. Students can line up on either side of the area and throw across to each other.

Thumb-Up Catch

The thumb-up catch is used when the Frisbee is received below waist level. The thumb points up, and the fingers are spread.

Throwing and Catching Activities:

a. Throw the Frisbee at different levels to partner.
b. Throw a curve--to the left, right and upward. Vary the speed of the curve.
c. Throw a bounce pass--try a low and a high pass.
d. Throw the disc like a boomerang. Must throw at a steep angle into the wind.
e. Throw the Frisbee into the air, run and catch. Increase the distance of the throw.
f. Throw the Frisbee through a hoop held by a partner.
g. Catch the Frisbee under your leg. Catch it behind your back.
h. Throw the Frisbees into hoops that are placed on the ground as targets. Different-colored hoops can be given different values. Throw through your partner's legs.
i. Frisbee bowling--One partner has a bowling pin which the other partner attempts to knock down by throwing the Frisbee.
j. Play catch while moving. Lead your partner so he doesn't have to break stride.
k. See how many successful throws and catches you can make in 30 seconds.
l. Frisbee Baseball Pitching--Attempt to throw the Frisbee into your partner's "Strike Zone."

Most activities are best when practiced by pairs of students using one disk.

Youngsters can develop both sides of the body by learning to throw and catch the disk with either hand. The teacher should design the activities so that youngsters get both right-hand and left-hand practice.

Since a Frisbee is somewhat different from the other implements that children usually throw, devote some time to teaching form and style in throwing and catching. Avoid drills that reward speed in throwing and catching.

Game Activity

Frisbee Keep Away

Supplies: Frisbees

Skills: Throwing and catching Frisbees

Students break into groups of three. Two of the players in the group try to keep the other player from touching the Frisbee while they are passing it back and forth. If the Frisbee is touched by a defensive player, the person who threw the Frisbee becomes the defensive player. Begin the game by asking students to remain stationary while throwing and catching. Later, challenge can be added by allowing all players in the group move.

Frisbee Golf

Supplies: One Frisbee per person, hoops for hole markers, cones

Skills: Frisbee throwing for accuracy

Frisbee Golf or disk golf is a favorite game of many students. Boundary cones with numbers can be used for tees, and holes can be boxes, hula-hoops, trees, tires, garbage cans, or any other available equipment on the school grounds. Draw a course on a map for students and start them at different holes to decrease the time spent waiting to tee off. Regulation golf rules apply. The students can jog between throws for increased activity.

Disk golf is played like regular golf. One stroke is counted for each time the disk is thrown and when a penalty is incurred. The object is to acquire the lowest score. The following rules dictate play:

Tee-throws: Tee-throws must be completed within or behind the designated tee area.

Lie: The lie is the spot on or directly underneath the spot where the previous throw landed.

Throwing order: The player whose disk is the farthest from the hole throws first. The player with the least number of throws on the previous hole tees off first.

Fairway throws: Fairway throws must be made with the foot closest to the hole on the lie. A run-up is allowed.

Dog leg: A dog leg is one or more designated trees or poles in the fairway that must be passed on the outside when approaching the hole. There is a two-stroke penalty for missing a dog leg.

Putt throw: A putt throw is any throw within 10 ft of the hole. A player may not move past the point of the lie in making the putt throw. Falling or jumping putts are not allowed.

Unplayable lies: Any disk that comes to rest 6 ft or more above the ground is unplayable. The next throw must be played from a new lie directly underneath the unplayable lie (one-stroke penalty).

Out-of-bounds: A throw that lands out-of-bounds must be played from the point where the disk went out (one-stroke penalty).

Course courtesy: Do not throw until the players ahead are out of range.

Completion of hole: A disk that comes to rest in the hole (box or hoop) or strikes the designated hole (tree or pole) constitutes successful completion of that hole.

Dynamic Physical Education for Elementary School Children
Fundamental Skills Using Balance Beams
Level II – Week 34

Objectives:
To design rhythmic activities for aerobic fitness
To maintain balance while doing a variety of beam challenges
To demonstrate controlled balance while manipulating equipment

Equipment Required:
Music and signs for Aerobic Fitness
6-balance beams and 6 tumbling mats
Desired equipment for balance beam
    challenges
8" foam balls for Hand Hockey

Instructional Activities	Teaching Hints

Introductory Activity -- Tortoise and Hare

When the leader calls out the word "tortoise," students run in place slowly. On the word "hare," they change to a rapid run. Students can work in small groups to allow for more leaders.

Try some different variations such as:
1. Moving throughout the area.
2. Performing various stretching activities.
3. Moving in different directions.

Fitness Development Activity -- Aerobic Fitness

1. Rhythmic run with clap
2. Bounce turn and clap
3. Rhythmic 4-count curl-ups (knees, toes, knees, back)
4. Rhythmic Crab Kicks (slow time)
5. Jumping Jack combination
6. Double knee lifts
7. Lunges (right, left, forward) with single-arm circles (on the side lunges) and double-arms circles (on the forward lunge)
8. Rhythmic trunk twists
9. Directional run (forward, backward, side, turning)
10. Rock side to side with clap
11. Side leg raises (alternate legs)
12. Rhythmic 4-count push-ups (If these are too difficult for students, substitute single-arm circles in the push-up position.)

Use music to stimulate effort. Any combination of movements can be used.

Keep the steps simple and easy to perform. Some students will become frustrated if the learning curve is steep.

Signs which explain the aerobic activities will help students remember performance cues.

Don't stress or expect perfection. Allow students to perform the activities as best they can.

Alternate bouncing and running movements with flexibility and strength development movements.

Lesson Focus -- Fundamental Skills Using Balance Beams

Perform balance beam activities using controlled walking movements. Speed of movement should always be avoided.

Dismounts
Complete all moves across the balance beam with a dismount. The following are examples of effective dismounts. Place a tumbling mat at the end of each beam so youngsters can dismount safely.
1. Single jump (forward or backward)
2. Jump with turns (half turn, three-quarter turn, or full turn).
3. Jackknife. Jump, kick the legs up, and touch the toes with the fingertips. Keep the feet together.
4. Jackknife Split. Same as the Jackknife, but spread the legs as far as possible.
5. Jump, land and do a Forward Roll.
6. Backward jump, land and do a Backward Roll.
7. Side jump to a Side Roll.

If balance beams are not available, use 2" X 4" boards placed on the floor. This will give students some elevation off the floor and offer balance challenges.

Place the beams parallel to each other and have a similar number of students lined up behind each one. Students progress down the beam.

After moving the length of the beam, have students do a locomotor movement (return activity) to the end of the teaching area and return. This offers students balance activities and the chance to practice locomotor movements.

Balance Beam Activities

1. Walk length of beam.
   a. Walk forward.
   b. Walk backward.
   c. Walk sideways--lead with both left and right sides of body.
2. Walk different directions and vary arm and body positions.
   a. Hands on hips.
   b. Hands on head.
   c. Hands folded across chest.
   d. Lean to one side or the other.
   e. Body bent forward or backward.
   f. Hands on knees or feet.
   g. Exploratory activity.
3. Balance objects such as beanbags, erasers or wands while walking across beam.
4. Move across the beam in various directions using the following movements:
   a. Slide
   b. Heel and toe
   c. Tiptoes
   d. Grapevine
   e. Dip step
5. Perform animal movements across the balance beam.
   a. Puppy dog walk
   b. Bear Walk
   c. Crab Walk
6. Use manipulative equipment while walking the beam.
   a. Play catch with beanbags. Try different throws and movements.
   b. Bounce a playground ball and catch it, dribble it, play catch with a partner.
   c. Step over a wand, go under a wand, change directions.
   d. Go through a hoop.

Return activities keep students engaged in activity for a longer period of time and reduce standing and waiting time. Specified movements can be placed on return activity signs.

If a student steps off the beam, have them get back on and progress. Sometimes, students stop walking the beam and receive little practice.

Move with controlled, deliberate movements across the beam. Speed is not a goal.

Game Activity

Hand Hockey

Supplies: 8-inch gray foam balls

Skills: Striking, volleying

Players are divided into two teams. Half of the players on each team are guards and are stationed on the goal line as defenders. The other half are active players and are scattered throughout the playing area in front of their goal line. The object of the game is to bat or push the ball with either hand so that it crosses the goal line the other team is defending. Players may move the ball as in hockey but may not throw, hoist, or kick it. The defensive goal line players are limited to one step into the playing field when playing the ball.

The ball is put into play by being rolled into the center of the field. After a goal has been scored or after a specified period, guards become active players, and vice versa. An out-of-bounds ball goes to the opposite team and is put into play by being rolled from the sidelines into the playing area. If the ball becomes entrapped among players, play is stopped, and a roll of the ball from the referee resumes play.Players must play the ball and not resort to rough tactics. A player who is called for unnecessary roughness or for illegally handling the ball must go to the sidelines (as in hockey) and remain in the penalty area until the players change positions. Players should scatter and attempt to pass to each other rather than bunch around the ball. Once youngsters learn the game, introduce more than one ball to increase the amount of activity.

Nonda's Car Lot

Supplies: None

Skills: Running, dodging

Two or three players are it and stand in the center of the area between two lines established at opposite ends of the playing area. The class selects four brands of cars (e.g., Honda, Corvette, Toyota, Cadillac). Each student then selects a car from the four but does not tell anyone what it is. One of the taggers calls out a car name. All students who selected that name attempt to run to the other line without getting tagged. The tagger calls out the cars until all students have run. When a child (car) gets tagged, he sits down at the spot of the tag. He cannot move but may tag other students who run nearby. When the one who is it calls out "Car lot," the entire class runs. Change taggers often.

Dynamic Physical Education for Elementary School Children
Softball Related Skills (1)
Level II – Week 35

Objectives:
To throw and catch a softball
To hit a softball
To be able to field softball grounders and fly balls

Equipment Required:
Parachute and exercise music
Whiffle balls
Plastic bats for whiffle balls
Batting tee and bases
Playground ball

Instructional Activities	Teaching Hints

Introductory Activity -- High Fives

Students move in different directions throughout the area. On signal, they are challenged to run toward a partner, jump, and give a "high five" (slap hands) while moving. Emphasis should be placed on timing so that the "high five" is given at the top of the jump.

Change the type of high fives, i.e., low, under leg, roundhouse.

High fives should be given gently. No hard slapping.

Fitness Development Activity -- Parachute Fitness

1. Jog in circle with chute held in left hand. Reverse directions and hold with right hand. (music)
2. Standing, raise the chute overhead, lower to waist, lower to toes, raise to waist, etc. (no music)
3. Slide to the right; return slide to the left. (music)
4. Sit and perform Abdominal Challenges. (no music)
5. Skip. (music)
6. Freeze; face the center, and stretch the chute tightly with bent arms. Hold for 8-12 seconds. Repeat five to six times. (no music)
7. Run in place, hold the chute at waist level and hit the chute with lifted knees. (music)
8. Sit with legs under the chute. Do a seat walk toward the center. Return to the perimeter. Repeat four to six times. (no music)
9. Place the chute on the ground. Jog away from the chute and return on signal. Repeat. (music)
10. On sides with legs under the chute, perform Side Flex and lift chute with legs. (no music)
11. Hop to the center of the chute and return. Repeat. (music)
12. Assume the push-up position with the legs aligned away from the center of the chute. Shake the chute with one arm while the other arm supports the body. (no music)
13. Lie on back with legs under the chute. Shake the chute with the feet. (music)
14. Sit with feet under the chute. Stretch by touching the toes with the chute. Relax with other stretches while sitting. (no music)

Tape alternating segments (25-30 seconds in length) of silence and music to signal duration of exercise. Music segments indicate aerobic activity with the parachute while intervals of silence announce using the chute to enhance flexibility and strength development.

Space youngsters evenly around the chute.

Use different hand grips (palms up, down, mixed).

All movements should be done under control. Some of the faster and stronger students will have to moderate their performance.

Lesson Focus -- Softball-Related Skills (1)

Skills
Practice the following skills:
1. Overhand Throw

For the overhand throw, the hand with the ball is then brought back over the head so that it is well behind the shoulder at about shoulder height. The left side of the body is turned in the direction of the throw, and the left arm is raised in front of the body. The weight is on the back (right) foot, with the left foot advanced and the toe touching the ground. The arm comes forward with the elbow leading, and the ball is thrown with a downward snap of the wrist. The body weight is brought forward into the throw, shifting to the front foot. There should be good follow-through so that the palm of the throwing hand faces the ground at completion of the throw. The eyes should be on the target throughout, and the arm should be kept free and loose during the throw.

Whiffle balls and plastic bats are a much safer alternative for children this age. It is easier for them to swing plastic bats and the fear of getting hit by a softball will not be an issue.

Instructional cues for **throwing** are:
1. Place the throwing arm side of the body away from the target.
2. Step toward the target with the foot opposite the throwing hand.

2. Pitching

Official rules call for the pitcher to have both feet in contact with the pitcher's rubber, but few elementary schools possess a rubber. Instead, the pitcher can stand with both feet about even, facing the batter, and holding the ball momentarily in front with both hands. The pitcher takes one hand from the ball, extends the right arm forward, and brings it back in a pendulum swing, positioning the ball well behind the body. A normal stride taken toward the batter with the left foot begins the throwing sequence for a right-handed pitcher. The arm is brought forward with an underhanded slingshot motion, and the weight is transferred to the leading foot. Only one step is permitted.

3. Fielding Grounders

To field a grounder, the fielder should move as quickly as possible into the path of the ball and then move forward and play the ball on a good hop. The eyes must be kept on the ball, following it into the hands or glove. The feet are spread, the seat is kept down, and the hands are carried low and in front. The weight is on the balls of the feet or on the toes, and the knees are bent to lower the body. As the ball is caught, the fielder straightens up, takes a step in the direction of the throw, and makes the throw.

4. Batting (Right-Handed)

The batter stands with the left side of the body toward the pitcher. The feet are spread and the weight is on both feet. The body should be facing the plate. The bat is held with the trademark up, and the left hand grasps the bat lower than the right. The bat is held over the right shoulder, pointing both back and up. The elbows are away from the body. The swing begins with a hip roll and a short step forward in the direction of the pitcher. The bat is then swung level with the ground at the height of the pitch. The eyes are kept on the ball until it is hit. After the hit, there must be good follow-through.

Station (Small Group) Instruction
Station 1 - Batting
Use a batting tee. For each station, two tees are needed, with a bat and at least two balls for each tee. Three to five children are assigned to each tee. There should be a batter, a catcher to handle incoming balls, and fielders. When only three children are in a unit, the catcher should be eliminated. Each batter is allowed a certain number of swings before rotating to the field. The catcher becomes the next batter, and a fielder moves up to catcher.

Station 2 - Throwing and Catching
Work with a partner and practice some of the following throwing drills:
    a. Throw back and forth, practicing various throws.
    b. gradually increase the distance of the throws.
    c. focus on accuracy; if the throws are not caught, reduce the distance between players

Station 3 - Pitching
Students find a partner and pitch and catch with each other. Set out a number of bases at each station so pitchers can pitch and catch using a base as a target (home plate).
    a. Pitch to another player over a plate.
    b. Call balls and strikes. One player is the pitcher, the second is the catcher, and the third is the umpire. A fourth player can be a stationary batter to provide a more realistic pitching target.

Station 4 - Fielding
Players find a partner and practice throwing grounders and fly balls to each other.
    a. One partner throws a grounder, the other partner fields the ball and throws it back to the other. Reverse roles.
    b. Do the same thing above except throw fly balls.

3. Bend and raise the arm at the elbow. Lead with the elbow.

Instructional cues for **pitching** are:
1. Face the plate.
2. Keep your eyes on the target.
3. Swing the pitching arm backward and step forward.

Instructional cues for **fielding** are:
1. Move into line with the path of the ball.
2. Give when catching the ball.
3. Use the glove to absorb the force of the ball.
4. For grounders, keep the head down and watch the ball move into the glove.

Instructional cues for **batting** are:
1. Keep the hands together.
2. Swing the bat horizontally.
3. Swing through the ball.
4. Hold the bat off the shoulder.
5. Watch the ball hit the bat.

Hitters should avoid the following: lifting the front foot high off the ground, stepping back with the rear foot, or bending forward.

Stand about 7 to 10 yards apart when practicing throwing.

For youngsters who are afraid of the ball, use a whiffle ball.

Face the batter, both feet on the rubber and the ball held in front with both hands. One step is allowed, and the ball must be delivered on that step. Ball must be pitched underhanded. No motion or fake toward the plate can be made without delivering the ball.

Show form for high and low catch.

Move into the path of the ball.

Throw It and Run

Supplies: A softball or similar ball

Skills: Throwing, catching, fielding, base running

Throw-It-and-Run Softball is played like regular softball with the following exception. With one team in the field at regular positions, the pitcher throws the ball to the batter, who, instead of batting the ball, catches it and immediately throws it into the field. The ball is then treated as a batted ball, and regular softball rules prevail. No stealing is permitted, however, and runners must hold bases until the batter throws the ball. A foul ball is an out.

Variations:

1. Under-Leg Throw. Instead of throwing directly, the batter can turn to the right, lift the left leg, and throw the ball under the leg into the playing field.

2. Beat-Ball Throw. The fielders, instead of playing regular softball rules, throw the ball directly home to the catcher. The batter, in the meantime, runs around the bases. A point is scored for each base that she touches before the catcher receives the ball. A ball caught on the fly would mean no score. Similarly, a foul ball would not score points but would count as a turn at bat.

Two-Pitch Softball

Supplies: A softball, a bat

Skills: Most softball skills, except regular pitching

Two-Pitch Softball is played like regular softball with the following changes.

1. A member of the team at bat pitches. A system of rotation should be set up so that every child takes a turn as pitcher.

2. The batter gets only two pitches to make a hit and must hit a fair ball on one of these pitches or is out. The batter can foul the first ball, but if the second is fouled, the batter is out. There is no need to call balls or strikes.

3. The pitcher does not field the ball. A member of the team in the field acts as the fielding pitcher.

4. If the batter hits the ball, regular softball rules are followed. No stealing is permitted, however.

Since the pitcher is responsible for pitching a ball that can be hit, the pitching distance can be shortened to give the batter ample opportunity to hit the ball. The instructor can act as the pitcher.

Hit and Run

Supplies: A volleyball or soccer ball or playground ball, home plate, base markers

Skills: Catching, throwing, running, dodging

One team is at bat, and the other is scattered in the field. Boundaries must be established, but the area does not have to be shaped like a baseball diamond. The batter stands at home plate with the ball. In front of the batter, 12 ft away, is a short line over which the ball must be hit to be in play. In the center of the field, about 40 ft away, is the base marker. The distance the batter runs around the base marker may have to be shortened or lengthened, depending on the ability of the players.

The batter bats the ball with the hands or fists so that it crosses the short line and lands inside the area. She then attempts to run down the field, around the base marker, and back to home plate without being hit by the ball. The members of the other team field the ball and throw it at the runner. The fielder may not run or walk with the ball but may throw to a teammate who is closer to the runner. A run is scored each time a batter runs around the marker and back to home plate without getting hit by the ball. A run also is scored if a foul is called on the fielding team for walking or running with the ball.

The batter is out in any of the following circumstances.

1. A fly ball is caught.

2. He is hit below the shoulders with the ball.

3. The ball is not hit beyond the short line.

4. The team touches home plate with the ball before the runner returns. (This out is used only when the runner stops in the field and does not continue.)

The game can be played in innings of three outs each, or a change of team positions can be made after all members of one team have batted.

Teaching suggestion:

Dynamic Physical Education for Elementary School Children
Softball Related Skills (2)
Level II – Week 36

Objectives:
To throw and catch a softball size ball
To hit a softball
To be able to field softball grounders and fly balls

Equipment Required:
Music for Teacher Leader Exercises
Whiffle balls
Plastic bats for whiffle balls
Batting tee and bases
Soccer ball

Instructional Activities	Teaching Hints

Introductory Activity – Tag Games

Teach a tag game or two selected by students. Examples of previous tag games learned are Addition Tag, Fastest Tag in the West, and Group Tag.

Select tag games that keep all students involved in activity.

Fitness Development Activity -- Teacher Leader Exercises

Arm Circles	30 seconds
Sitting Stretch	30 seconds
Treadmill	30 seconds
Abdominal Challenges	30 seconds
Single-Leg Crab Kick	30 seconds
Knee to Chest Curl	30 seconds
Power Jumper	30 seconds
Trunk Twister	30 seconds

Conclude the routine with 2 to 4 minutes of jogging, rope jumping or other continuous activity.

Tape alternating segments of silence (10 seconds) to signal a change of exercise and music to signal the duration of exercise (30 seconds).

Increase the duration of exercises by 10 to 20% over the previous week.

Allow students to adjust the workload to their ability and fitness level. This means that some students will perform more repetitions than others.

Lesson Focus -- Softball-Related Activities (2)

Skills
Review skills learned last week:
1. Overhand Throw
2. Pitching
3. Fielding Grounders
4. Batting

Whiffle balls and plastic bats are a much safer alternative for children this age. It is easier for them to swing plastic bats and the fear of getting hit by a softball will not be an issue.

Station (Small Group) Instruction
Station 1 - Play Pepper (Hitting and Fielding)
A line of three or four players is about 10 yards in front of and facing a batter. The players toss the ball to the batter, who attempts to hit controlled grounders back to them. The batter stays at bat for a period of time and then rotates to the field.

If youngsters are not able to hit the ball, they can catch and throw it to the fielders.

Station 2 - Pitching and Umpiring
Students find a partner and pitch and catch with each other. Set out a number of bases at each station so pitchers can pitch and catch using a base as a target (home plate).
    a. Pitch to another player over a plate.
    b. Call balls and strikes. One player is the pitcher, the second is the catcher, and
       the third is the umpire. A fourth player can be a stationary batter to provide a
       more realistic pitching target.

When umpiring, strikes are called by raising the right hand and balls require raising the left hand.

Station 3 - Infield Practice
1. Throw around the bases clockwise and counterclockwise.
2. Roll ball to infielders and make the play at first. After each play, throw around the infield.
3. If enough skill, bat the ball to the infielders in turn.

While having infield practice, one person at the station can run the bases and try to complete a circuit around the bases before the ball does.

Station 4 - Batting Practice

Each batter takes six swings and then rotates to the field. Catcher becomes batter and pitcher moves up to catcher.

Have more than one ball at the stations so the pitching can continue when a ball is hit or not caught.

Game Activity

Kick Softball

Supplies: A soccer ball or another ball to be kicked

Skills: Kicking a rolling ball, throwing, catching, running bases

The batter stands in the kicking area, a 3-ft-square home plate. The batter kicks the ball rolled on the ground by the pitcher. The ball should be rolled at moderate speed. An umpire calls balls and strikes. A strike is a ball that rolls over the 3-ft square. A ball rolls outside this area. Strikeouts and walks are called the same as in regular softball. The number of foul balls allowed should be limited. No base stealing is permitted. Otherwise, the game is played like softball.

Variations:

1. The batter kicks a stationary ball. This saves time, since there is no pitching.

2. Punch Ball. The batter can hit a volleyball as in a volleyball serve or punch a ball pitched by the pitcher.

In a Pickle

Supplies: A softball, two bases 45 to 55 ft apart

Skills: Throwing, catching, running down a base runner, tagging

When a base runner gets caught between two bases and is in danger of being run down and tagged, she is "in a pickle." To begin, both fielders are on bases, one with a ball. The runner is positioned in the base path 10 to 15 ft away from the fielder with the ball. The two fielders throw the ball back and forth in an attempt to run down the runner between the bases and tag her. If the runner escapes and secures a base, she gets to try again. Otherwise, a system of rotation is established, including any sideline (waiting) players. No sliding is permitted.

Beat Ball

Supplies: Soft softball, bat, batting tee (optional)

Skills: All softball skills

One team is at bat and the other team in the field. The object of the game is to hit the ball and run around the bases before the fielding team can catch the ball, throw it to first base, and then throw it to the catcher at home plate. If the ball beats the hitter home or a fly ball is caught, it is an out. If the hitter beats the ball to home plate, a run is scored. All players on a team bat once before switching positions with the fielding team. The ball must be hit into fair territory before the hitter can run. Only three pitches are allowed each hitter.

Variations:

1. Depending on the maturity of the players, a batting tee may be used. The hitter can be allowed the option of using the batting tee or hitting a pitched ball.

2. The pitcher can be selected from the batting team. This assures that an attempt will be made to make pitches that can be hit.

3. The distance can be varied so that hitters have a fair opportunity to score. If hitters score too easily, another base can be added.

Dynamic Physical Education for Elementary School Children
Fundamental Skills Using Climbing Ropes
Level II – Alternate Lesson Plan

Objectives:
To be able to recite safety rules for rope climbing
To be able to hang on a climbing rope for 5 seconds
To be able to hang and swing on a climbing rope

Equipment Required:
Climbing Ropes
Tumbling mats placed under ropes
Benches or Jumping Boxes

Instructional Activities	Teaching Hints

Introductory Activity

Substitute from a selected Lesson Plan

Fitness Development Activity

Substitute from a selected Lesson Plan

Lesson Focus – Fundamental Skills Using Climbing Ropes

Supported Pull-Ups

In supported Pull-Up activities, a part of the body remains in contact with the floor. The Pull-Up is hand-over-hand and the return is hand-under-hand.
1. Kneel directly under the rope. Pull up to the tiptoes and return to kneeling position.
2. Start in a sitting position under the rope. Pull up; the legs are supported on the heels. Return to sitting position.
3. Start in a standing position. Grasp the rope, rock back on the heels, and lower the body to the floor. Keep a straight body. Return to standing position.

1. Mats should be placed under all ropes.

2. The hand-over-hand method should be used for climbing and the hand-under-hand method for descending.

Hangs

In a hang, the body is pulled up in one motion and held up for a length of time (5, 10, or 20 seconds). Progression is important.
1. From a seated position, reach up as high as possible and pull the body from the floor, except for the heels. Hold.
2. Same as the previous stunt but pull the body completely free of the floor. Hold.
3. From a standing position, jump up, grasp the rope, and hang. This should be a Bent-Arm Hang with the hands about even with the mouth. Hold.
4. Repeat the previous stunt, but add leg movements---one or both knees up, bicycling movement, Half Lever (one or both legs up, parallel to the floor), Full Lever (feet up to the face).

3. Caution the children not to slide; sliding can cause rope burns on the hands and legs.

4. A climber who becomes tired should stop and rest. Proper rest stops should be taught as part of the climbing procedure.

Pull-Ups

In the Pull-Up, the body is raised and lowered repeatedly. The initial challenge should be to accomplish one Pull-Up in the defined position. The number of repetitions should be increased with care. All of the activities described for hangs are adaptable to Pull-Ups. The chin should touch the hands on each Pull-Up.

5. Children also should be taught to leave enough margin for a safe descent. No children should go higher than their strength allows.

Swinging and Jumping

For swinging and jumping, a bench, box, or stool can serve as a takeoff point. To take off, the child reaches high and jumps to a bent-arm position. Landing should be with bent knees.
1. Swing and jump. Add half turns and full turns.
2. Swing and return to the perch. Add single- and double-knee bends.
3. Jump for distance, over a high-jump bar or through a hoop.
4. Swing and pick up a bowling pin and return to the perch.
5. Carry objects (e.g., beanbags, balls, deck tennis rings). A partner, standing to the side away from the takeoff bench, can put articles to be carried back on the takeoff perch by placing each article between the knees or feet.
6. Not using a takeoff device, run toward a swinging rope, grasp it, and gain momentum for swinging.

6. Spotters should be used initially for activities in which the body is inverted.

Climbing the Rope

1. *Scissors Grip.* For the Scissors Grip, approach the rope and reach as high as possible, standing with the right leg forward of the left. Raise the back leg, bend at the knee, and place the rope inside the knee and outside the foot. Cross the forward leg over the back leg, and straighten the legs with the toes pointed down. This should give a secure hold. To climb using the Scissors Grip, raise the knees up close to the chest, the rope sliding between them, while supporting the body with the hand grip. Lock the rope between the legs and climb up, using the hand-over-hand method and stretching as high as the hands can reach. Bring the knees up to the chest and repeat the process.

2. *Leg-Around Rest.* Wrap the left leg completely around the rope, keeping the rope between the thighs. The bottom of the rope then crosses over the instep of the left foot from the outside. The right foot stands on the rope as it crosses over the instep, providing pressure to prevent slippage. To provide additional pressure, release the hands and wrap the arms around the rope, leaning away from the rope at the same time. To climb using the Leg-Around Rest, proceed as in climbing with the Scissors Grip, but loosen the grip each time and re-grip higher.

Descending the Rope

There are four methods to descend the rope. The only differences are in the use of the leg locks, as the hand-under-hand is used for all descents.

1. *Scissors Grip.* From an extended scissors grip position, lock the legs and lower the body with the hands until the knees are against the chest. Hold with the hands, and lower the legs to a new position.

2. *Leg-Around Rest.* From the leg-around rest position, lower the body until the knees are against the chest. Lift the top foot, and let the feet slide to a lower position. Secure with the top foot and repeat.

3. *Instep Squeeze.* Squeeze the rope between the insteps by keeping the heels together. Lower the body while the rope slides against the instep.

4. *Stirrup Descent.* Place the rope on the outside of the right foot and carry it over the instep of the left. Pressure from the left foot holds the position. To get into position, let the rope trail along the right leg, reach under, and hook it with the left instep. When the pressure from the left leg is reduced, the rope slides smoothly while the descent is made with the hands.

Stunts Using Two Ropes

Two ropes hanging close together are needed for the following activities.

Straight-Arm Hang. To do the Straight-Arm Hang, jump up, grasp one rope with each hand, and hang with the arms straight.

Bent-Arm Hang. Perform as for the Straight-Arm Hang, but bend the arms at the elbows.

Arm Hangs with Different Leg Positions

    a. Do single- and double-knee lifts.

    b. Do a Half Lever. Bring the legs up parallel to the floor and point the toes.

    c. Do a Full Lever. Bring the feet up to the face and keep the knees straight.

    d. Do a Bicycle. Pedal as on a bicycle.

Pull-Ups. The Pull-Up is the same as on a single rope, except that each hand grasps a rope.

Inverted Hangs.

    a. Hang with the feet wrapped around the ropes.

    b. Hang with the feet against the inside of the ropes.

    c. Hang with the toes pointed and the feet not touching the ropes

Skin the Cat. From a bent-arm position, kick the feet overhead and continue the roll until the feet touch the mat. Return to the starting position.

7. Rosin in powdered form and magnesium chalk aid in gripping. It is particularly important that they be used when the rope becomes slippery.

8. Children swinging on the ropes should be instructed to make sure that other children are out of the way.

9. Marks to limit the climb can be put on the rope with adhesive tape. A height of 8 to 10 feet above the floor is reasonable until a child demonstrates proficiency.

10. If the ceiling is higher than 15 or 16 feet, a bright piece of tape should be wrapped around the rope to limit climbing height.

Game Activity

Substitute from a selected Lesson Plan

DYNAMIC PHYSICAL EDUCATION LESSON PLANS
Developmental Level III

WEEK	INTRODUCTORY ACTIVITY	FITNESS DEVELOPMENT ACTIVITY	LESSON FOCUS ACTIVITY	GAME ACTIVITY	PAGE
1	Move and Freeze on Signal	Teacher Leader Exercises	Orientation	Toe to Toe Whistle Mixer	197
2	European Running	Teacher-Leader Exercises	Manipulative Skills with Wands & Hoops	Galactic Empire & Rebels Jolly Ball Circle Touch	199
3	Move and Freeze	Teacher-Leader Exercises	Long Rope Jumping Skills	Cageball Target Throw Sunday Wolfe's Beanbag Exchange	202
4	Move and Manipulate	Hexagon Hustle	Football Skills (1)	Football End Ball Five Passes Speed Football Kick-Over	204
5	Fastest Tag in the West	Hexagon Hustle	Football Skills (2)	Speed Football Fourth Down Flag Football	207
6	Following Activities	Circuit Training	Relay Activities	Relaxation Activities	210
7	Medic Tag	Circuit Training	Gymnastics Skills (1)	Team Handball Octopus Knockout	213
8	Hospital Tag	Astronaut Exercises	Soccer Skills (1)	Dribblerama Sideline Soccer Line Soccer Mini-Soccer	217
9	Agility Run	Astronaut Exercises	Soccer Skills (2)	Bull's Eye Line Soccer Mini-Soccer Regulation Soccer	220
10	Beanbag Touch & Go	Aerobic Fitness	Soccer Skills (3)	Line Soccer Mini-Soccer Regulation Soccer	223

WEEK	INTRODUCTORY ACTIVITY	FITNESS DEVELOPMENT ACTIVITY	LESSON FOCUS ACTIVITY	GAME ACTIVITY	PAGE
11	Jog & Stretch	Aerobic Fitness	Recreational Activities	Recreational Activities	225
12	Vanishing Beanbags	Astronaut Exercises	Walking and Jogging Skills	Recreational Activities	226
13	Hospital Tag	Challenge Course	Rhythmic Movement Skills (1)	Triplet Stoop Pacman	228
14	Stretching	Stretching	Cross Country Running & Walking Skills	Recreational Activities	231
15	Marking	Challenge Course	Juggling Skills & Pyramids	Fast Pass One-Base Tagball	232
16	European Running with Variations	Challenge Course	Rhythmic Movement Skills (2)	Cageball Target Throw Chain Tag	235
17	Dribble and Pivot	Partner Aerobic Fitness & Resistance Exercises	Basketball Skills(1)	Flag Dribble Captain Basketball Sideline Basketball	239
18	Barker's Hoopla	Partner Aerobic Fitness & Resistance Exercises	Basketball Skills(2)	Twenty-One Lane Basketball One Goal Basketball Basketball Snatch Ball	242
19	Run, Stop, & Pivot	Exercises to Music	Basketball Skills (3)	Regulation Basketball Three-on-Three	245
20	Agility Run	Exercises to Music	Gymnastics Skills (2)	Pin Knockout Over the Wall	246
21	Rubber Band	Continuity Drills	Hockey Skills (1)	Lane Hockey Goalkeeper Hockey Sideline Hockey	250
22	Move & Exercise on Signal	Continuity Drills	Hockey Skills (2)	Sideline Hockey Regulation Hockey	253
23	Pyramid Power	Aerobic Fitness	Gymnastics Skills (3)	Star Wars Flag Chase Jolly Ball	255

WEEK	INTRODUCTORY ACTIVITY	FITNESS DEVELOPMENT ACTIVITY	LESSON FOCUS ACTIVITY	GAME ACTIVITY	PAGE
35	Personal Choice	Squad Leader Exercises with Task Cards	Softball Skills(1)	Batter Ball Tee Ball Scrub	286
36	Personal Choice	Squad Leader Exercises with Task Cards	Softball Skills(2)	Slow-Pitch Softball Babe Ruth Ball Three-Team Softball	289
This alternate lesson focus can be substituted for any of the lesson above			Fundamental Skills Using Climbing Ropes		291

Dynamic Physical Education for Elementary School Children
Orientation and Class Management Activities
Level III – Week 1

Objectives:
To learn and follow basic management activities necessary for participation in
  physical education classes

Equipment Required:
Tom-tom
Tape player and music for fitness
  challenges

Instructional Activities	Teaching Hints

Orientation Instructional Procedures

The first week of school should be used to teach students the system you are going to use throughout the year. The following are reminders you might find useful in establishing your expectations and routines.

1. Establish rules and expectations. Discuss your expectations with the class to assure students understand reasons for your guidelines. Explain what the consequences are when rules are not followed. Show where time-out boxes are located and how they will be used.

2. Explain to the class the method you will use to learn names. It might be helpful to ask classroom teachers to have students put their name on a piece of masking tape (nametag). Tell students that you will ask them their name on a regular basis until it is learned.

3. Develop entry and exit behaviors for students coming and leaving physical education classes. Students should know how to enter the instructional area and to leave equipment alone until told to use it. If squads are used for instruction, place students into squads and practice moving into formation on signal.

4. Decide how excuses for non-participation will be handled. If possible, set up a routine where the school nurse determines which students are excused for health reasons.

5. Safety is important. Children should receive safety rules to be followed on apparatus and playground equipment. Safety procedures to be followed in physical education classes should be discussed.

6. Illustrate how you will stop and start the class. In general, a whistle (or similar loud signal) and a raised hand is effective for stopping the class. A voice command should be used to start the class. Telling the class when before what (Chapter 5 will assure they do not begin before instructions are finished.

7. Discuss the issue, distribution, and care of equipment. Make students responsible for acquiring a piece of equipment and returning it at the end of the lesson. Place equipment around the perimeter of the teaching area to reduce the chance of students fighting over a piece of equipment.

8. Explain to the class that the format of the daily lesson will include an introductory activity, fitness development, lesson focus, and finish with a game activity.

9. Practice various teaching formations such as open-squad formation and closed-squad formation. Practice moving into a circle while moving (fall-in). Transitions between formations should be done while moving, i.e., jogging from scatter formation into a circular formation.

10. Refer to Chapter 3, 4, and 5 in the text for detailed information about planning, developing an effective learning environment, and class management strategies.

Introductory Activity -- Move and Freeze on Signal

Have students move throughout the area using a variety of locomotor movements. On signal (whistle), they quickly freeze. Try to reduce the response latency by reinforcing students who stop quickly on signal.

The primary objective is to teach students the importance of moving under control (without bumping others or falling down) and quickly freezing.

Fitness Development Activity -- Teacher Leader Exercises

Arm Circles	30 seconds	Tape alternating segments (30 seconds) of silence and music. The music signals aerobic activity. During the silent segments the exercises are performed
Bend and Twist	30 seconds	
Treadmill	30 seconds	
Abdominal Challenges	30 seconds	
Single-Leg Crab Kick	30 seconds	
Knee to Chest Curl	30 seconds	Allow students to adjust the workload to their personal ability and fitness level. This means that some students may perform more repetitions than others.
Run in Place	30 seconds	
Trunk Twister	30 seconds	

Follow each exercise with 30 seconds of aerobic activity.

Move and help students with the exercises.

Lesson Focus -- Orientation

Since much time during the first week is used for orientation procedures and management, no lesson focus activity is scheduled.

Game Activity -- Management Games

Play one or two management games to teach students how to move into partner and small group formation

Toe to Toe

Supplies: None
Skills: Fundamental locomotor movements

Youngsters perform a locomotor movement around the area. On signal, each child must find a partner and stand toe to toe (one foot only) with that person. An important skill is to take the nearest person for a partner without searching for a friend. Youngsters who can't find a partner within their immediate area must run quickly to the center of the area (use a marking spot or cone) to find a partner. The goal is to find a nearby partner as quickly as possible and avoid being the last pair formed. If the number of youngsters playing is uneven, the teacher can join in and play. Change locomotor movements often.

Whistle Mixer

Supplies: None
Skills: All basic locomotor movements

Children are scattered throughout the area. To begin, they walk around in any direction they wish. A whistle is blown a number of times in succession with short, sharp blasts. Children then form small groups with the number in each group equal to the number of whistle blasts. If there are four blasts, children form groups of four—no more, no less. When players have the correct number, they sit down immediately to signal that no one may leave the group and no one may enter the group. The goal is not to be left out or caught in a circle with the incorrect number of students. Encourage players to move toward the center of the area and raise their hands to facilitate finding others without a group. After the circles are formed, the teacher calls "Walk," and the game continues. In walking, children should move in different directions.

Dynamic Physical Education for Elementary School Children
Manipulative Skills Using Wands and Hoops
Level III – Week 2

Objectives:
To run rhythmically to the beat of a tambourine
To demonstrate activities designed to improve cardiovascular fitness
To develop manipulative skills using hoops and wands in a variety of challenges

Equipment Required:
Tambourine
One wand and one hoop for each student
Cageball
12 yarnballs

Instructional Activities	Teaching Hints

Introductory Activity – European Running

Students move around the area to the beat of a tambourine. The step is a trot with the knees lifted. Emphasize proper spacing and moving rhythmically. Stop on a double beat of the tambourine.

Have the leader move in different shapes and designs. Have class freeze and see if they can identify the shape or formation.

Fitness Development Activity -- Teacher Leader Exercises

Arm Circles	30 seconds
Bend and Twist	30 seconds
Treadmill	30 seconds
Abdominal Challenges	30 seconds
Single-Leg Crab Kick	30 seconds
Knee to Chest Curl	30 seconds
Run in Place	30 seconds
Trunk Twister	30 seconds

Follow each exercise with 30 seconds of aerobic activity.

Tape alternating segments (30 seconds) of silence and music. The music signals aerobic activity. During the silent segments the exercises are performed

Allow students to adjust the workload to their personal ability and fitness level. This means that some students may perform more repetitions than others.

Move and help students with the exercises.

Lesson Focus – Manipulative Skills Using Wands and Hoops

Select activities from the each of the exercises and challenges groups.

Strength Exercises with Wands
1. Pull the Wand Apart. Place the hands 6 inches apart near the center of the wand. With a tight grip to prevent slippage and with arms extended, pull the hands apart. Change grip and position.
2. Push the Wand Together. Hold the wand as previously, except push the hands together.
3. Wand Twist. Hold the wand with both hands about 6 inches apart. Twist the hands in opposite directions.
4. Bicycle. Holding the wand horizontally throughout and using an overhand grip, extend the wand outward and downward. Bring it upward near the body, completing a circular movement. On the downward movement, push the wand together, and on the upward movement, pull the wand apart.
5. Arm Spreader. Hold the wand overhead with hands spread wide. Attempt to compress the stick. Reverse force, and attempt to pull the stick apart.
6. Dead Lift. Partially squat and place the wand under the thighs. Place the hands between the legs and try to lift. Try also with hands on the outside of the legs.
7. Abdominal Tightener. From a standing position, place the wand behind the buttocks. With hands on the ends of the wand, pull forward and resist with the abdominal muscles.

Stretching Exercises with Wands
1. Side Bender. Grip the wand and extend the arms overhead with feet apart. Bend sideways as far as possible, maintaining straight arms and legs. Recover, and bend to the other side.

Wands can be made from ¾ inch maple dowels or from a variety of broom and mop handles. They should be cut to a length of 36 inches. Wands are noisy when they hit the floor. Putting rubber crutch tips on the ends of a wand alleviates most of the noise and makes them easier to pick up.

The isometric exercises with wands presented can be performed with a variety of grips. With the wand horizontal, use either the overhand or underhand grip. With the wand in vertical position, grip with the thumbs pointed up, down, or toward each other.

Repeat each exercise with a different grip. Exercises can also be repeated with the wand in different positions: in front of the body (either horizontal or vertical), overhead, or behind the back. Hold each exercise for 8 to 12 seconds.

2. Body Twist. Place the wand behind the neck, with arms draped over the wand from behind. Rotate the upper body first to the right as far as possible and then to the left. The feet and hips should remain in position. The twist is at the waist.
3. Body Twist to Knee. Assume body twist position. Bend the trunk forward and twist so that the right end of the wand touches the left knee. Recover, and touch the left end to the right knee.
4. Shoulder Stretcher. Grip the wand at the ends in a regular grip. Extend the arms overhead and rotate the wand, arms, and shoulders backward until the stick touches the back of the legs. The arms should be kept straight. Those who find the stretch too easy should move their hands closer to the center of the wand.
5. Toe Touch. Grip the wand with the hands about shoulder width apart. Bend forward, reaching down as far as possible without bending the knees. The movement should be slow and controlled. Try the same activity from a sitting position.
6. Over the Toes. Sit down, flex the knees, place the wand over the toes, and rest it against the middle of the arch. Grip the stick with the fingers at the outside edge of the feet. Slowly extend the legs forward, pushing against the stick and trying for a full extension of the legs.

Be gentle when stretching. Reach and stretch the muscles, hold the stretch for a few seconds and relax. Repeat a number of times.

Wand Challenges
1. Can you reach down and pick up your wand without bending your knees?
2. Try to balance your wand on different body parts. Watch the top of the wand to get cues on how to retain the balance.
3. Can you hold your stick against the wall and move over it? Gradually raise the height of the wand.
4. Let's see whether you can hold the stick at both ends and move through the gap.
5. Put one end of the wand on the floor and hold the other end. How many times can you run around your wand without getting dizzy?
6. Place one end of the wand against a wall. Holding the other end and keeping the wand against the wall, duck underneath. Place the wand lower and lower on the wall and go under.
7. Toss the wand from one hand to the other.
8. Hold the wand vertically near the middle. Can you release your grip and catch the wand before it falls to the floor?
9. Have a partner hold a wand horizontally above the floor. Jump, leap, and hop over the wand. Gradually raise the height of the wand.
10. Balance the wand vertically on the floor. Release the wand and try to complete different stunts--clapping the hands, doing a heel click, touching different body parts--before the wand falls to the floor.

Because wands are noisy when dropped, youngsters should hold their wands with both hands or put them on the floor during instruction.

An adequate amount of space is needed for each individual, because wand stunts demand room.

Children may easily be injured using wands improperly. Teach children proper use of wands. Emphasize the need to use care when handling wands to avoid injury to self and others. Do not allow any improper use of wands.

Hoop Activities
1. Hula-hoop using various body parts such as waist, neck, knees, arms and fingers.
   a. While hula-hooping on the arms, try to change the hoop from one arm to the other.
   b. Change hoop from one partner to another while hula-hooping.
   c. Try leg-skippers--hula-hoop with one leg and jump the hoop with the other leg.
2. Jump-rope with the hoop--forward, sideways, and backward. Begin with a back-and-forth swing.
3. Roll hoop and run alongside it. Run in front of it.
4. Roll hoop with a reverse spin to make it return to the thrower.
5. Roll with a reverse spin and see how many times a partner can go through it.
6. Roll the hoop with a reverse spin, jump over it, and catch it as it returns. Roll the hoop with a reverse spin, and as it returns, hoist it with the foot and catch it. Roll the hoop with a reverse spin, kick it up with the toe, and go through the hoop. Roll the hoop with a reverse spin, run around it, and catch it. Roll the hoop with a reverse spin, pick it up, and begin hooping on the arm---all in one motion.
7. Balance the hoop on your head, try to walk through it ("thread the needle") forward, backward and sideways.

Hoops produce noisy activity. You may find it helpful to have the children lay their hoops on the floor when they are to listen.

The key to the reverse spin is to pull down (toward the floor) on the hoop as it is released When teaching the reverse spin with hoops, have the students throw the hoop up, in place, rather than forward along the floor. After they learn the upward throw, they can progress to the forward throw for distance.

8. Try partner activities:
   a. Play catch with hoop.
   b. Hula-hoop on one arm, toss to partner who catches it on one arm.
   c. Use two hoops for catching.
   d. Hoop with one hoop and play catch with other.
   e. Move through a hoop held by a partner.

Game Activity

Galactic Empire and Rebels

Supplies: None

Skills: Chasing, fleeing, dodging

This game can be played indoors or outdoors in a square that is approximately 100 feet on each side. Each team's spaceport is behind the end line, where the single space fighters are stationed, waiting to issue against the enemy. To begin, one or more space fighters from either team move from their spaceport to entice enemy fliers for possible capture. A flyer leaving the spaceport may capture only opposing flyers who previously have left their respective spaceport. **This is the basic rule of the game.** A flyer may go back to her spaceport and be eligible immediately to issue again to capture an opponent who was already in general space. The technique of the game is to entice enemy flyers close to the spaceport so fellow flyers can issue and capture (tag) an opposing flyer.

An illustration of how the game proceeds: Rebel flyer 1 moves into general space to entice Empire flyer 1 so that he can be captured. Rebel flyer 1 turns back and heads for her spaceport, chased by Empire flyer 1. Rebel flyer 2 now leaves her spaceport and tags Empire flyer 1 before the Empire flyer can tag Rebel flyer 1. The Empire flyer is now a prisoner.

A player captured by an opposing flyer is taken to the tagger's prison—both captor and captive are given free passage to the prison. In prison, the captives form a chain gang, holding hands and extending the prisoners' line toward their own spaceport. The last captive is always at the end of the prisoners' line with one foot in the prison. Captives can be released if a teammate can get to them without being tagged. The released prisoner (only the end one) is escorted back to her own spaceport, and both players are given free passage. The game becomes one of capturing opposing flyers and securing the release of captured teammates. Flyers stepping over the sideline automatically become prisoners. One or two players in the spaceport should be assigned to guard the prison.

Set a time limit of 10 minutes, and declare the team with the most prisoners the winner.

Jolly Ball

Supplies: A cageball 24 in. or larger (or a 36- to 48 inch pushball)

Skill: Kicking

Four teams are organized, each of which forms one side of a square. Children sit down, facing in, with hands braced behind them. The members of each team are numbered consecutively. Players wait until their number is called. Four active players (one from each team) move in crab position and try to kick the cageball over any one of the three opposing teams. The sideline players can also kick the ball. Ordinarily, the hands are not used, but can be allowed in the learning stages of the game.

A point is scored against a team that allows the ball to go over its line. A ball that goes out at the corner between teams is dead and replayed. After a short bout of time (10 to 20 seconds), the active children retire to their teams and another number is called. The team with the fewest points wins the game. This game is strenuous for the active players, so rotate them often. Two children from each team can be active at once.

Circle Touch

Supplies: Yarnballs

Skills: Dodging, body management

One child plays against three others, who form a small circle with joined hands. The object of the game is for the lone child to touch a designated child (on the shoulders) in the circle with a yarnball. The other two children in the circle, by dodging and maneuvering, attempt to keep the tagger away from the third member of the circle. The circle players may maneuver and circle in any direction but may not release their hand grips. The tagger, in attempting to touch the protected circle player, must go around the outside of the circle. He is not permitted to go underneath or through the joined hands of the circle players. To avoid roughness, the game should be played in short, 20-second bouts with a new tagger for each bout.

Dynamic Physical Education for Elementary School Children
Long Rope Jumping Skills
Level III – Week 3

Objectives:
To jump a rope turned by others
To know the difference in long-rope jumping between entering front and back doors
To understand how to enter and exit in Double Dutch rope jumping

Equipment Required:
Music for exercises and rope jumping
6-12 long jump ropes (16 ft long)
Cageball and 12-15 throwing balls for game

Instructional Activities	Teaching Hints
Introductory Activity -- Move and Freeze	

1. Review the run, walk, hop, jump, leap, slide, gallop and skip with proper stopping.	Add variety by asking students to respond to the some of the following
2. Practice moving and stopping correctly—emphasize basics of proper movement.	movement factors such as high, low, zigzag, large, small, square, triangles, circles.

Fitness Development Activity -- Teacher Leader Exercises

Arm Circles	35 seconds	Tape alternating segments (35 seconds)
Bend and Twist	35 seconds	of silence and music. The music signals
Treadmill	35 seconds	aerobic activity. During the silent
Abdominal Challenges	35 seconds	segments the exercises are performed
Single-Leg Crab Kick	35 seconds	
Knee to Chest Curl	35 seconds	Allow students to adjust the workload to
Run in Place	35 seconds	their personal ability and fitness level.
Trunk Twister	35 seconds	This means that some students may
		perform more repetitions than others.

Follow each exercise with 35 seconds of aerobic activity.

Move and help students with the exercises.

Lesson Focus - Long Rope Jumping Skills

Single Long-Rope Activities
1. Review previously learned jumping skills. Teach the difference between entering front and back doors. Front door means entering from the side where the rope is turning forward and toward the jumper after it reaches its peak. Back door means entering from the side where the rope is turning backward and away from the jumper. To enter front door, the jumper follows the rope in and jumps when it completes the turn. To enter back door, the jumper waits until the rope reaches its peak and moves in as the rope moves downward. Learning to enter at an angle is usually easier, but any path that is comfortable is acceptable.
2. Have more than one youngster jump at a time. Students can enter in pairs or triplets.
3. Jump while holding a beanbag or playground ball between the knees.
4. While turning rope, rotate under the rope and jump. Continue jumping and rotate back to the turning position.
5. Play catch with a playground ball while jumping.
6. Do the Egg Beater: Two or more long ropes are turned simultaneously. The ropes are aligned perpendicular to each other; the jumper jumps the rope where they cross.
7. Try combinations of three or four ropes turning. The ropes are aligned parallel to each other and students jump and move through to the next rope.

Four children is an appropriate group size for practicing long-rope skills. Two members of the group turn the rope while the others practice jumping. A plan for rotating turners is important so that all children receive similar amounts of practice jumping.

Long ropes should be 16 feet in length.

Instructional cues to teach long-rope jumping skills are:
a. Turn the rope with the forearm.
b. Lock the wrist and keep the thumb up while turning.
c. Stand perpendicular to the rope.
d. Barely touch the floor with the turning rope.
e. Don't cross the midline of the body with the forearm while turning the rope.
f. Jump on the balls of the feet.

Double Dutch (two ropes) Activities

1. Teach entering and exiting. Basic jump on both feet. Land on the balls of the feet, keeping ankles and knees together with hands across the stomach.
   Entering: When entering, stand beside a turner and run into the ropes when the back rope (farther from the jumper) touches the floor. Turners should be taught to say "Go" each time the back rope touches the floor.
   Exiting: Exit the ropes by facing and jumping toward one turner and exiting immediately after jumping. The exit should be made as close to the turner's shoulder as possible.
2. Jogging Step. Run in place with a jogging step. Increase the challenge by circling while jogging.
3. Scissors Jump. Jump to a stride position with the left foot forward and the right foot back about 8 inches apart. Each jump requires reversing the position of the feet.
4. Straddle Jump. Jump to the straddle position and return to closed position. Try a Straddle Cross Jump by crossing the legs on return to the closed position. The straddle jumps should be performed facing away from the turners.
5. Turnaround. Circle left or right using the basic jump. Begin circling slowly at first and then increase speed. To increase the challenge, try the turnaround on one foot.
6. Hot Peppers. Use the Jogging Step and gradually increase the speed of the ropes.
7. Half Turn. Perform a half turn with each jump. Remember to lead the turn with the head and shoulders.
8. Ball Tossing. Toss and catch a playground ball while jumping.
9. Individual Rope Jumping. Enter Double Dutch with an individual rope and jump. Face the turner and decrease the length of the individual jump rope.

Arm positions and turning motions are similar to turning a single long rope. In short, keep the upper arm stationary, rotate at the elbow with locked wrist, and keep the thumb up. Avoid crossing the midline of the body, and establish an even cadence. Rotate the hands inward toward the midline of the body (right forearm counterclockwise and left forearm clockwise).

Double Dutch turning takes considerable practice. Take time to teach it as a skill that is necessary for successful jumping experiences.

Students should concentrate on the sound of the ropes hitting the floor so that they make an even and rhythmic beat.

Concentrate on jumping in the center of the ropes facing a turner. Use white shoe polish to mark a jumping target.

Game Activity

Cageball Target Throw

Supplies: A cageball (18- to 30-in.), 12 to 15 smaller balls of various sizes
Skill: Throwing

An area about 20 feet wide is marked across the center of the playing area, with a cageball in the center. The object of the game is to throw the smaller balls against the cageball, thus forcing it across the goalline in front of the other team. Players may come up to the line to throw, but they may not throw while inside the cageball area. A player may enter the area, however, to recover a ball. No one is to touch the cageball at any time, nor may a ball in the hands of a player push the cageball. If the cageball seems to roll too easily, it should be deflated slightly. The throwing balls can be of almost any size—soccer balls, volleyballs, playground balls, for example.

Sunday

Supplies: None
Skills: Running, dodging

Two parallel lines are delineated at each end of the playing area. Three or more players are it and stand in the center of the area between the two lines. The rest of the class is placed on one of the designated lines. The object is to cross to the other line without being tagged or making a false start. All line players stand with their front foot on the line. The line players must run across the line immediately when one of the taggers calls "Sunday." Anyone who does not run immediately is considered caught. The tagger can call other days of the week to confuse the runners. No player can move if another day of the week is called. "Making a start" must be defined clearly. To begin, it can be defined as a player moving either foot. Later, when children get better at the game, any movement of the body constitutes a start.

Wolfe's Beanbag Exchange

Supplies: One beanbag per child
Skills: Running, dodging, tossing, catching

Five or six children are identified as taggers. The remaining players start scattered throughout the area, each with a beanbag in hand. The taggers chase the players with beanbags. When a tag is made, the tagged player must freeze, keeping her feet still and beanbag in hand. To unfreeze a player, a non-frozen player can exchange his beanbag for a beanbag held by a frozen player. If two frozen players are within tossing distance, they can thaw each other by exchanging their beanbags through the air using a toss and catch. Both tosses have to be caught or the beanbags are retrieved and tried again from their previous location. After students have learned the game, taggers can interfere with the tossing of beanbags between two frozen players by batting them to the floor. The toss is tried again and the players remain frozen until both players make successful catches.

Dynamic Physical Education for Elementary School Children
Football Skills (1)
Level III – Week 4

Objectives:
To participate in a balanced fitness routine
To learn the basic rules of football
To perform the basic skills of football
To enjoy participating in football lead-up activities

Equipment Required:
Signs, cones, and music for Hexagon Hustle
10-15 foam rubber junior size footballs
4 soccer balls or 8" foam rubber balls
12 cones for boundaries
Pinnies and flags for lead-up games

Instructional Activities	Teaching Hints

Introductory Activity -- Move and Manipulate

Each student is given a piece of equipment and moves around the area using locomotor movements. Students toss and catch the equipment while moving. On signal, the equipment is dropped, and students move over and around equipment.

Use any type of equipment available. The goal is to move and be able to manipulate an object.

Fitness Development Activity -- Hexagon Hustle

Tape alternating segments of silence and music to signal duration of exercise. Music segments (25 seconds) indicate moving around the hexagon while intervals of silence (30 seconds) announce flexibility and strength development activities.

Hustle	25 seconds
Push-Up from Knees	30 seconds
Hustle	25 seconds
Bend and Twist (8 counts)	30 seconds
Hustle	25 seconds
Jumping Jacks (4 counts)	30 seconds
Hustle	25 seconds
Curl-Ups (2 counts)	30 seconds
Hustle	25 seconds
Crab Kick (2 counts)	30 seconds
Hustle	25 seconds
Sit and Stretch (8 counts)	30 seconds
Hustle	25 seconds
Power Jumper	30 seconds
Hustle	25 seconds
Squat Thrust (4 counts)	30 seconds

Conclude the Hexagon Hustle with a slow jog or walk.

Outline a large hexagon with six cones. Place signs with locomotor movements on both sides of the cones. Locomotor movements to use are: Jogging, skipping, galloping, hopping, jumping, sliding, leaping, and animal movements. Sport movements such as defensive sliding, running backwards, and running and shooting jump shots can also be used. The signs identify the hustle activity students are to perform as they approach a cone.

During the hustle, faster moving students should pass on the outside of the hexagon.

Change directions at times to keep students spaced out properly.

Lesson Focus – Football Skills (1)

Skills
Practice the following skills:
1. Forward Passing
   The ball should be gripped lightly behind the middle with the fingers on the lace. The thumbs and fingers should be relaxed. In throwing, the opposing foot should point in the direction of the pass, with the body turned sideways. In preparation for the pass, the ball is raised up and held over the shoulders. The ball is delivered directly forward with an overhand movement of the arm and with the index finger pointing toward the line of flight.
2. Catching
   When making a catch, the receiver should keep both eyes on the ball and catch it in the hands with a slight give. As soon as the ball is caught, it should be tucked into the carrying position. The little fingers are together for most catches.
3. Centering
   Centering involves transferring the ball, on a signal, to the quarterback. In elementary school, the shotgun formation is most often used. This requires snapping the ball a few yards backward to the quarterback. A direct snap involves placing the

Use instructional cues for throwing:
1. Turn the non-throwing side toward the direction of the throw.
2. Throw the ball with an overhand motion.
3. Step toward the pass receiver.

Instructional cues help improve catching technique:
1. Thumbs together for a high pass (above shoulder level).
2. Thumbs apart for a low pass (below shoulder level).
3. Reach for the ball, give, and bring the ball to the body.

hands under the buttocks of the center. The ball is then lifted, rotated a quarter turn, and snapped into the hands of the quarterback.

The centering player takes a position with the feet well spread and toes pointed straight ahead. Knees are bent and close enough to the ball to reach it with a slight stretch. The right hand takes about the same grip as is used in passing. The other hand is on the side near the back of the ball and merely acts as a guide. On signal from the quarterback, the center extends the arms backward through the legs and centers the ball to the quarterback.

Instructional cues for centering include the following:
1. Reach forward for the ball.
2. Snap the ball with the dominant hand.
3. Guide the ball with the non-dominant hand.

4. Punting

The kicker stands with the kicking foot slightly forward. The fingers are extended in the direction of the center. The eyes should be on the ball from the time it is centered until it is kicked, and the kicker should actually see the foot kick the ball. After receiving the ball, the kicker takes a short step with the kicking foot and then a second step with the other foot. The kicking leg is swung forward and, at impact, the leg is straightened to provide maximum force. The toes are pointed, and the long axis of the ball makes contact on the top of the instep. The leg should follow through well after the kick. Emphasis should be placed on dropping the ball properly. Beginners have a tendency to throw it in the air, making the punt more difficult.

Instructional cues for punting are:
1. Drop the football; don't toss it upward.
2. Keep the eyes focused on the ball.
3. Kick upward and through the ball.
4. Contact the ball on the outer side of the instep.

Signs which describe key points for each skill should be placed on cones at each station. Instructional cues should also be placed on the signs so students can analyze their form and performance.

Drills

Set up stations for skill practice. Rotate students to each station.

Station 1 - Stance Practice

Students work with a partner and practice getting into the proper stance position. When stance form is mastered, partners can practice getting into position and racing to cones five yards away. Offensive players should use a 3-point stance with toes pointed forward and head up. Defensive players usually use a 4-point stance with more weight on hands. Blockers should avoid falling and should stay on their toes and in front of defensive player.

Junior size footballs are best for this age group. Regulation size footballs are unacceptable because youngster's hands are too small and the balls are too heavy.

Station 2 - Centering and Carrying the Ball

Students work in pairs and practice centering to each other. The player receiving the ball tucks the ball in and runs 5 to 10 yards.

Station 3 - Passing and Receiving with a Partner

Students work in pairs and practice passing and receiving the ball. Place emphasis on proper throwing and catching technique. Begin practice with short passes to a stationary receiver. After success, practice throwing to moving receivers, placing emphasis on leading the receiver with the pass.

The ball should be carried with the arm on the outside and the end of the ball tucked into the notch formed by the elbow and arm. The fingers add support for the carry.

Station 4 - Punting

Concentrate on technique rather than distance when teaching punting. Emphasize keeping the head down with the eyes on the ball. Drop the football rather than tossing it upward prior to the kick. Work in groups of three. One player is the punter, one the receiver, and one receives the pass from the punt receiver.

For beginning punters, using a round foam rubber ball will be easier than kicking a football. Foam rubber footballs are the next step before using junior size footballs.

Game Activity - Football Lead-Up Games

Football End Ball

Supplies: Foam rubber junior footballs

Skills: Passing, catching

The court is divided in half by a centerline. End zones are marked 3 ft wide, completely across the court at each end. Players on each team are divided into three groups: forwards, guards, and ends. The object is for a forward to throw successfully to one of the end-zone players. End-zone players take positions in one of the end zones. Their forwards and guards then occupy the half of the court farthest from this end zone. The forwards are near the centerline, and the guards are back near the end zone of their half of the court. The ball is put into play with a center jump between the two tallest opposing forwards. When a team gets the ball, the forwards try to throw over the heads of the opposing team to an end-zone player. To score, the ball must be caught by an end-zone player with both feet inside the zone. No moving with the ball is permitted by any player. After each score, play is resumed by a jump ball at the centerline.

A penalty results in loss of the ball to the other team. Penalties are assessed for the following.

1. Holding a ball for more than 5 seconds

2. Stepping over the end line or stepping over the centerline into the opponent's territory

3. Pushing or holding another player

In case of an out-of-bounds ball, the ball belongs to the team that did not cause it to go out. The nearest player retrieves the ball at the sideline and returns it to a player of the proper team. Encourage fast, accurate passing. Players in the end zones need to jump high to catch the ball while still landing with both feet inside the end-zone area. A system of rotation is desirable. Each time a score is made, players on that team can rotate one person.

To outline the end zones, some instructors use folding mats (4 by 7 ft or 4 by 8 ft). Three or four mats forming each end zone make a definite area and eliminate the problem of defensive players (guards) stepping into the end zone.

Five Passes

Supplies: Foam rubber junior footballs and pinnies

Skills: Passing, catching

Players scatter on the field. The object of the game is for one team to make five consecutive passes to five different players without losing control of the ball. This scores 1 point. The defense may play the ball only and may not make personal contact with opposing players. No player can take more than three steps when in possession of the ball. More than three steps is called traveling, and the ball is awarded to the other team.

The ball is given to the opponents at the nearest out-of-bounds line for traveling, minor contact fouls, after a point has been scored, and for causing the ball to go out-of-bounds. No penalty is assigned when the ball hits the ground. It remains in play, but the five-pass sequence is interrupted and must start again. Jump balls are called when the ball is tied up or when there is a pileup. The official should call out the pass sequence.

Speed Football

Supplies: Foam rubber junior footballs, flag for each player

Skills: Passing, catching, running with ball

The ball can be kicked off or started at the 20-yd line. The object is to move the ball across the opponent's goal by running or passing. If the ball drops to the ground or a player's flag is pulled when carrying the ball, it is a turnover and the ball is set into play at that spot. Interceptions are turnovers and the intercepting team moves on offense. Teams must make at least four complete passes before they are eligible to move across the opponent's goal line. No blocking is allowed.

Playing more than one game at a time on smaller fields will allow more students to be actively involved in the game. This is also an enjoyable game when played with Frisbees.

Kick-Over

Playing area: Football field with a 10-yd end zone

Players: Six to ten on each team

Supplies: Foam rubber junior footballs

Skills: Kicking, catching

Teams are scattered on opposite ends of the field. The object is to punt the ball over the other team's goal line. If the ball is caught in the end zone, no score results. A ball kicked into the end zone and not caught scores a goal. If the ball is kicked beyond the end zone on the fly, a score is made regardless of whether the ball is caught. One team starts play with a punt from a point 20 to 30 ft in front of its own goal line. On a punt, if the ball is not caught, the team must kick from the spot of recovery. If the ball is caught, three long strides are allowed to advance the ball for a kick.

The player kicking next should move quickly to the area from which the ball is to be kicked. Players should be numbered and should kick in rotation. If the players do not kick in rotation, one or two aggressive players will dominate the game.

Dynamic Physical Education for Elementary School Children
Football Skills (2)
Level III – Week 5

Objectives:
To critique football throwing techniques of peers
To learn the basic rules of football
To perform the basic skills of football
To enjoy participating in football lead-up activities

Equipment Required:
Signs, cones, and music for Hexagon Hustle
8 junior or foam rubber footballs
12 cones for boundaries
One flag belt and one pinnie for each student

Instructional Activities	Teaching Hints
Introductory Activity – Fastest Tag in the West	
All students are it. On signal, they try to tag each other. If they are tagged, they must freeze, but they are eligible to tag other students who pass near them. If two or more players tag each other simultaneously, they are both/all "frozen."	The idea of the game is to get all students involved in activity. Restart the game often rather than waiting for all students to be tagged.

Fitness Development Activity -- Hexagon Hustle

Tape alternating segments of silence and music to signal duration of exercise. Music segments indicate moving around the hexagon while intervals of silence announce flexibility and strength development activities.

Hustle	25 seconds
Push-Up from Knees	30 seconds
Hustle	25 seconds
Bend and Twist (8 counts)	30 seconds
Hustle	25 seconds
Jumping Jacks (4 counts)	30 seconds
Hustle	25 seconds
Curl-Ups (2 counts)	30 seconds
Hustle	25 seconds
Crab Kick (2 counts)	30 seconds
Hustle	25 seconds
Sit and Stretch (8 counts)	30 seconds
Hustle	25 seconds
Power Jumper	30 seconds
Hustle	25 seconds
Squat Thrust (4 counts)	30 seconds

Conclude the Hexagon Hustle with a slow jog or walk.

Teaching Hints:
Outline a large hexagon with six cones. Place signs with locomotor movements on both sides of the cones. Locomotor movements to use are: Jogging, skipping, galloping, hopping, jumping, sliding, leaping, and animal movements. Sport movements such as defensive sliding, running backwards, and running and shooting jump shots can also be used. The signs identify the hustle activity students are to perform as they approach a cone.

During the hustle, faster moving students should pass on the outside of the hexagon.

Change directions at times to keep students spaced out properly.

Lesson Focus – Football Skills (2)

Since this is the second week of football, emphasis should be placed on playing some of the lead-up football games. Review last week's skills and introduce the new skills. Devote the rest of the time to playing the games.

Skills
Practice the following skills:
Review the skills taught last week:
1. Forward Passing
2. Catching
3. Centering
4. Punting
Introduce new skills:
1. Lateral Passing
    Lateral passing is a simple underhand toss of the ball to a teammate. The ball must be tossed sideward or backward to qualify as a lateral. It should be tossed with an easy motion, and no attempt should be made to make it spiral like a forward pass.

Teaching Hints:
Students can work with a partner and practice the skills they learned last week. A ball for each two players will assure the most practice time.

The lateral pass is used when a ball carrier wants to get rid of the ball before being stopped.

2. Blocking

In blocking for Flag Football, the blocker must maintain balance and not fall to the knees. The elbows are out and the hands are held near the chest. The block should be more of an obstruction than a takeout and should be set with the shoulder against the opponent's shoulder or upper body. Making contact from the rear in any direction not only is a penalty but also could cause serious injury.

Instructional cues for blocking technique are the following:
1. Keep feet spread and knees bent.
2. Keep head up.
3. Stay in front of the defensive player.
4. Move your feet; stay on the balls of the feet.

Game Activity

Speed Football
See the Week 4 Lesson Plan, Football Skills for a complete game description.

Fourth Down
Supplies: Foam rubber junior football
Skills: Most football skills, except kicking and blocking

Every play is a fourth down, which means that the play must score or the team loses the ball. No kicking is permitted, but players may pass at any time from any spot and in any direction. There can be a series of passes on any play, either from behind or beyond the line of scrimmage.

The teams line up in an offensive football formation. To start the game, the ball is placed into the center of the field, and the team that wins the coin toss has the chance to put the ball into play. The ball is put into play by centering. The back receiving the ball runs or passes to any of his teammates. The one receiving ball has the same privilege. No blocking is permitted. After each touchdown, the ball is brought to the center of the field, and the team against which the score was made puts the ball into play.

To down a runner or pass receiver, a two-handed touch above the waist is made. The back first receiving the ball from the center has immunity from tagging, provided that he does not try to run. All defensive players must stay 10 ft away unless he runs. The referee should wait for a reasonable length of time for the back to pass or run. If the ball is still held beyond that time, the referee should call out, "Ten seconds." The back must then throw or run within 10 seconds or be rushed by the defense.

The defensive players scatter to cover the receivers. They can use a one-on-one defense, with each player covering an offensive player, or a zone defense. Since the team with the ball loses possession after each play, the following rules are used to determine where the ball should be placed when the other team takes possession.

1. If a ball carrier is tagged with two hands above the waist, the ball goes to the other team at that spot.

2. If an incomplete pass is made from behind the line of scrimmage, the ball is given to the other team at the spot where the ball was put into play.

3. When an incomplete pass is made by a player beyond the line of scrimmage, the ball is brought to the spot from which it was thrown.

The team in possession should be encouraged to pass as soon as is practical, because children tire from running around to become free for a pass. The defensive team can score by intercepting a pass. Since passes can be made at any time, on interception the player should look down the field for a pass to a teammate.

Variation: The game can be called Third Down, with the offensive team having two chances to score.

Flag Football
Supplies: Foam rubber junior football, two flags per player (about 3 in. wide and 24 in. long)
Skills: All football skills

The field is divided into three zones by lines marked off at 20-yd intervals. There also should be two end zones, from 5 to 10 yd in width, defining the area behind the goal in which passes may be caught. Flag Football is played with two flags on each player. The flag is a length of cloth that is hung from the side at the waist of each player. To down (stop) a player with the ball, one of the flags must be pulled.

Flag Football should rarely, if ever, be played with 11 players on a side. This results in a crowded field and leaves little room to maneuver. If six or seven are on a team, four players are required to be on the line of scrimmage. For eight or nine players, five offensive players must be on the line.

The game consists of two halves. A total of 25 plays makes up each half. All plays count in the 25, except the try for the point after a touchdown and a kickoff out-of-bounds.

The game is started with a kickoff. The team winning the coin toss has the option of selecting the goal it wishes to defend or choosing to kick or receive. The loser of the toss takes the option not exercised by the first team. The kickoff is from the goal line, and all players on the kicking team must be onside. The kick must cross the first zone line or it does not count as a play. A kick that is kicked out-of-bounds (and is not touched by the receiving team) must be kicked again. A second consecutive kick out-of-bounds gives the ball to the receiving team in the center of the field. The kicking team may not recover the kickoff unless it is caught and then fumbled by the receivers.

A team has four downs to move the ball into the next zone or they lose the ball. If the ball is legally advanced into the last zone, then the team has four downs to score. A ball on the line between zones is considered in the more forward zone.

Time-outs are permitted only for injuries or when called by the officials. Unlimited substitutions are permitted. Each must report to the official.

The team in possession of the ball usually huddles to make up the play. After any play, the team has 30 seconds to put the ball into play after the referee gives the signal.

Blocking is done with the arms close to the body. Blocking must be done from the front or side, and blockers must stay on their feet.

A player is down if one of her flags has been pulled. The ball carrier must make an attempt to avoid the defensive player and is not permitted to run over or through the defensive player. The tackler must play the flags and not the ball carrier. Good officiating is needed, because defensive players may attempt to hold or grasp the ball carrier until they are able to remove one of her flags.

All forward passes must be thrown from behind the line of scrimmage. All players on the field are eligible to receive and intercept passes.

All fumbles are dead at the spot of the fumble. The first player who touches the ball on the ground is ruled to have recovered the fumble. When the ball is centered to a back, she must gain definite possession of it before a fumble can be called. She is allowed to pick up a bad pass from the center when she does not have possession of the ball.

All punts must be announced. Neither team can cross the line of scrimmage until the ball is kicked. Kick receivers may run or use a lateral pass. They cannot make a forward pass after receiving a kick.

A pass caught in an end zone scores a touchdown. The player must have control of the ball in the end zone. A ball caught beyond the end zone is out-of-bounds and is considered an incomplete pass.

A touchdown scores 6 points, a completed pass or run after touchdown scores 1 point, and a safety scores 2 points. A point after touchdown is made from a distance of 3 ft from the goal line. One play (pass or run) is allowed for the extra point. Any ball kicked over the goal line is ruled a touchback and is brought out to the 20-yd line to be put into play by the receiving team. A pass intercepted behind the goal line can be a touchback if the player does not run it out, even if she is tagged behind her own goal line.

A penalty of 5 yd is assessed for the following:
1. Being offside
2. Delay of game (too long in huddle)
3. Failure of substitute to report
4. Passing from a spot not behind line of scrimmage (This also results in loss of down.)
5. Stiff-arming by the ball carrier, or not avoiding a defensive player
6. Failure to announce intention to punt
7. Shortening the flag in the belt, or playing without flags in proper position
8. Faking the ball by the center, who must center the pass on the first motion

The following infractions are assessed a 15-yd loss:
1. Holding, illegal tackling
2. Illegal blocking
3. Unsportsmanlike conduct (This also can result in disqualification.)

Teaching suggestions: Specifying 25 plays per half eliminates the need for timing and lessens arguments about a team's taking too much time in the huddle. Using the zone system makes the first-down yardage point definite and eliminates the need for a chain to mark off the 10 yd needed for a first down.

Dynamic Physical Education for Elementary School Children
Relay Activities
Level III – Week 6

Objectives:
To follow rules when participating in relays
To accept winning gracefully
To understand the importance of cooperation when competing

Equipment Required:
Cones, signs, and tape for Circuit Training
Cageball and 15 playground balls
Cones and equipment for relays

Instructional Activities	Teaching Hints

Introductory Activity – Following Activities

One partner leads and performs various kinds of movements. The other partner follows and performs the same movements. This can also be done with small groups, with the group following a leader.

Encourage students to challenge their partner. Change partners once or twice to maintain interest in the activity.

Fitness Development Activity – Circuit Training

Students do the best they can at each station within the time limit. This implies that not all youngsters are required to do the same workload. Children differ and their ability to perform fitness workloads differs. Make fitness a personal challenge.
Rope Jumping
Triceps Push-Ups
Agility Run
Body Circles
Hula Hoops
Reverse Curls
Crab Walk
Tortoise and Hare
Bend and Twist

Conclude circuit training with 2-4 minutes of walking, jogging, rope jumping or other self-paced aerobic activity

Tape alternating segments of silence and music to signal duration of exercise. Music segments (begin at 30 seconds) indicate activity at each station while intervals of silence (10 seconds) announce it is time to stop and move forward to the next station.

Use signals such as start, stop, and move up to ensure rapid movement to the next station.

Ask students to do their personal best they can. Expect workloads to differ.

Lesson Focus – Relay Activities
Instructional Procedures for Relays

1. Teams should be restricted to four or five players. Too many on a team increase the amount of time spent waiting for a turn.
2. If teams have uneven numbers, some players on the smaller teams can run twice. All children on teams with fewer members must take a turn running twice; otherwise, the more skilled runners may always run and create an unfair advantage.
3. Teams should be changed regularly so that all youngsters have a chance to be on a winning team. Teachers should reserve the right to change team makeup as well as the order in which the students are placed on individual teams.
4. Placing less skilled players in the first or last position of the relay team will force these students to perform in front of the class and reveal to others that they are inferior. To avoid this situation, place less skilled students in the middle of the team. Discretion can be used when moving players to avoid labeling them as unskilled performers.
5. Infractions of the rules should be discussed. Relays are a social learning experience. Children are in a situation where they must conform to rules if the experience is going to be enjoyable for all students. This is an effective time to discuss how cooperation precedes competition; it is impossible to compete if players choose not to cooperate.
6. The finishing order must be determined properly. In giving instructions, teachers should be definite about the start, the turning point, and the finishing act.
7. A marker to prevent running into a wall should delineate a deceleration area. Cones, bowling pins, jump standards, or beanbags can mark this turn-around and end area. With cones and bowling pins, knocking over the marker is a disqualification unless the runner resets it before proceeding.
8. Too much emphasis on winning makes the skilled resent losing and intimidates those of lesser ability. The idea of winning at any cost must be discussed and discouraged.
9. A trial run should always be made so that each team understands the procedures. If a new relay does not seem to have been started properly, stop the activity and review the instructions. Practice the relay first before embarking on a serious competitive run.

10. Make traffic rules clear. In most cases, the way to the right governs. When runners go around the turning point, they do it from the right (counterclockwise), returning past the finish line on the right side. Some procedures to ensure a fair tagging off of the next runner should be instituted. Runners should not leave the restraining line before being tagged. Exchanging a baton or a beanbag can help ensure fair play.

Relays

Introduce a variety of relays. The following are listed in sequence from easy to difficult. None of the relays require specialized sport skills (throwing, catching, etc.). This helps assure all students have the opportunity to contribute to their team's cooperative effort.

1. Carry-and-Fetch Relay

Players are in closed squad formation, with a hoop or circle positioned up to 30 feet in front of each team. The first runner on each team has a beanbag. On the command "Go," this player carries the beanbag forward and puts it inside the hoop, then returns and tags off the next runner. The second runner goes forward, picks up the beanbag, and hands it off to the third runner. One runner carries the beanbag forward and the next runner fetches it back. Different locomotor movements can be specified.

2. Attention Relay

The players on each team are facing forward in lane formation with team members about arms' distance apart. The distance between the teams should be about 10 feet. Two turning points are established for each team---one 10 feet in front of the team and the other 10 feet behind. Players are numbered consecutively from front to rear. The teacher calls, "Attention." All come to the attention position. The teacher calls out a number. The player on each team holding that number steps to the right, runs around the front and the back markers, and returns to place. The rest of the team runs in place. The first team to have all members at attention, including the returned runner, wins a point.

3. Pass and Squat Relay

One player (number 1) with a ball stands behind a line 10 feet in front of his teammates, who are in lane formation. Number 1 passes the ball to number 2, who returns the ball to number 1. As soon as he has returned the ball to number 1, number 2 squats down so that the throw can be made to number 3, and so on, down the file. When the last person in line receives the ball, she does not return it but carries it forward, straddling the members of her team, including number 1, who has taken a place at the head of the file. The player carrying the ball forward then acts as the passer. The race is over when the original number 1 player receives the ball in the back position and straddles the players to return to his original position.

4. Rescue Relay

Lane formation is used, with the first runner behind a line about 30 feet in front of the team. The first runner runs back to the team, takes the first player in line by the hand, and "rescues" him by leading him back to the 30-foot line. The player who has just been rescued then runs back to the team and gets the next player, and so on, until the last player has been conducted to the line. Some care must be taken that the front player in the file is behind the team line as the passing starts. After the straddling, repositioning the file is necessary. Each player should form a compact ball during the straddling activity.

5. Potato Relay

A small box about a foot square is placed 5 feet in front of each lane. Four 12-inch circles are drawn at 5-foot intervals beyond the box. This makes the last circle 25 feet from the starting point. Four blocks or beanbags are needed for each team. To start, the blocks are placed in the box in front of each team. The first runner goes to the box, takes a single block, and puts it into one of the circles. She repeats this performance until there is a block in each circle; then she tags off the second runner. This runner brings the blocks back to the box, one at a time, and tags off the third runner, who returns the blocks to the circles, and so on. Using a box to receive the blocks makes a definite target. When the blocks are taken to the circles, some rules must be made regarding placement. The blocks should be considered placed only when they are inside or touching a line. Blocks outside need to be replaced before the runner can continue. Paper plates or pie plates can be used instead of circles drawn on the floor.

6. Iceberg Relay

Teams are in lane formation, with each team having two rubber marking spots. The marks represent icebergs, and the task is to use the spots as stepping-stones. Players race two at a time. One player is the stepper, and one moves the marking spots. The stepper may not touch the floor (fall in the ocean). The handler moves the marking spots to the turning point and then exchanges places with the stepper for the return trip. An alternative is to have the handler convey the stepper back to the starting point, give the marking spots to the next player at the head of the line, and then become the new stepper.

7. Jack Rabbit Relay (Jump Stick Relay)

The relay starts with the first player in line running forward around the turning point and back to the head of the line. In the meantime, the next person in line is holding a 36-in. wand. The runner returns and grabs one end of the wand from the player in line. These two runners then pass the stick under the other team members in line, who jump over it. When the stick has passed under all players, the first runner hands the stick to the next person in line while the first stick holder runs. The second runner runs around the turning point and returns, and helps the next player in line with the stick who becomes the next runner.

Relaxation Activities

Relays are spirited. It might be useful to spend a few minutes relaxing.

1. In a supine position, practice some deep breathing with the eyes gently closed. Daydream while deep breathing about a favorite place.

2. Tense a muscle group, take a deep breath and hold it for 6 counts. Slowly exhale and relax the muscle group. Do the same with other muscle groups.

Dynamic Physical Education for Elementary School Children
Gymnastics Skills (1)
Level III – Week 7

Objectives:
To exercise independently in the circuit training activity
To understand the principles of stability and balance
To control the body weight in a variety of tumbling and stunt activities
To participate in "one on one" competition and accept the outcome

Equipment Required:
Circuit training music, signs, and cones
10-12 tumbling mats
Flags for "Grab the Flag"
8 to 12 bowling pins
10 to 15 8" foam rubber balls
Pinnies for Team Handball

Instructional Activities	Teaching Hints

Introductory Activity -- Medic Tag

Three or four students are designated as "taggers." They try to tag the others; when tagged, a student kneels down as if injured. Another student (not one of the taggers) can "rehabilitate" the injured player, enabling her to reenter play.

Different types of rehabilitation can be used. The easiest is to touch a body part or run a full circle around the person.

Fitness Development Activity -- Circuit Training

Students do the best they can at each station within the time limit. This implies that not all youngsters are required to do the same workload. Children differ and their ability to perform fitness workloads differs. Make fitness a personal challenge.
Rope Jumping
Triceps Push-Ups
Agility Run
Body Circles
Hula Hoops
Reverse Curls
Crab Walk
Tortoise and Hare
Bend and Twist

Conclude circuit training with 2-4 minutes of walking, jogging, rope jumping or other self-paced aerobic activity

Tape alternating segments of silence and music to signal duration of exercise. Music segments (begin at 30 seconds) indicate activity at each station while intervals of silence (10 seconds) announce it is time to stop and move forward to the next station.

Use signals such as start, stop, and move up to ensure rapid movement to the next station.

Ask students to do their personal best they can. Expect workloads to differ.

Lesson Focus – Gymnastics Skills (1)

Tumbling and Inverted Balances
Review the Forward Roll
　　Stand facing forward, with the feet apart. Squat and place the hands on the mat, shoulder width apart, with elbows against the insides of the thighs. Tuck the chin to the chest and make a rounded back. A push-off with the hands and feet provides the force for the roll. Carry the weight on the hands, with the elbows bearing the weight of the thighs. If the elbows are kept against the thighs and the weight is assumed there, the force of the roll is transferred easily to the rounded back. Try to roll forward to the feet. Later, try with the knees together and no weight on the elbows.

Review the Backward Roll (Handclasp Position)
　　Clasp the fingers behind the neck, with elbows held out to the sides. From a crouched position, sit down rapidly, bringing the knees to the chest for a tuck to secure momentum. Roll completely over backward, taking much of the weight on the forearms. With this method, the neck is protected.

Forward and Backward Roll Combinations
　　Begin with a Forward Roll, coming to a standing position with feet crossed. Pivot the body to uncross the feet and to bring the back in the line of direction for a Backward Roll.
　　Hold the toes, heels, ankles, or a wand while rolling. Use different arm positions, such as out to the sides or folded across the chest. Use a wide straddle position for both the Forward Roll and the Backward Roll.

Five groups of activities in this lesson ensure that youngsters receive a variety of experiences. Pick a few activities from each group and teach them alternately. For example, teach one or two balance stunts, then a tumbling and inverted balance, followed by a combative, etc. Give equal time to each group of activities.

Scatter tumbling mats throughout the area so that there is little standing in line waiting for a turn.

Do not perform many repetitions of tumbling and inverted balances. For most children, limiting the number of forward or backward roll repetitions to four or five will prevent fatigue and injury.

Balance Stunts
V-Up
Lie on the back, with arms overhead and extended. Keeping the knees straight and the feet pointed, bring the legs and the upper body up at the same time to form a V shape. The entire weight is balanced on the seat. Hold the position for 5 seconds.

Push-Up Variations
Begin the development of Push-Up variations by reviewing proper Push-Up techniques. The only movement is in the arms. The body should come close to, but not touch, the floor. Explore the following variations.

    a. Monkey Push-Up. Point the fingers toward each other. Next, bring the hands close enough for the fingertips to touch.

    b. Circle-O Push-Up. Form a circle with each thumb and forefinger.

    c. Fingertip Push-Up. Get up high on the fingertips.

    d. One-Legged Push-Up. Lift one leg from the floor.

Flip-Flop
From a push-up position, propel the body upward with the hands and feet, doing a Turn-Over. Flip back. The stunt should be done on a mat.

Individual Stunts
Wall Walk-Up
From a push-up position with feet against a wall, walk up the wall backward to a handstand position. Walk down again.

Skier's Sit
Assume a sitting position against a wall with the thighs parallel to the floor and the knee joints at right angles. (The position is the same as if sitting in a chair, but, of course, there is no chair.) The hands are placed on the thighs with the feet flat on the floor and the lower legs straight up and down. Try to sit for 30 seconds, 45 seconds, and 1 minute.

Rocking Horse
Lie facedown on a mat with arms extended overhead, palms down. With back arched, rock back and forth.

Heel Click (Side)
Balance on one foot, with the other out to the side. Hop on the supporting foot, click the heels, and return to balance. Try with the other foot.

Partner and Group Stunts
Double Scooter
Two children about the same size face each other, sitting on each other's feet. With arms joined, scoot forward or backward with cooperative movements. When one child moves the seat, the other child should help by lifting with the feet. Progress is made by alternately flexing and extending the knees and hips.

Tandem Bicycle
One child forms a bicycle position, with back against a wall and knees bent, as if sitting. The feet should be placed under the body. The second child backs up and sits down lightly on the first child's knees. Other children may be added in the same fashion, their hands around the waist of the player immediately in front for support. Moving the feet on the same side together makes forward progress.

Circle High Jump
Stand in circles of three, each circle having children of somewhat equal height. Join hands. One child tries to jump over the opposite pair of joined hands. To be completely successful, each circle must have each child jump forward in turn over the opposite pair of joined hands. (Jumping backward is not recommended.) To reach good height, an upward lift is necessary. Try two small preliminary jumps before exploding into the jump over the joined hands.

No youngster should be expected to roll if they are fearful or think it is too difficult. In stunts and tumbling, it is important that the student decide if they are capable and confident enough to try the activity.

Youngsters can do many of the activities around their mats. Many of the activities in this unit do not have to be performed on the mat.

A major concern for safety is the neck and back region. Overweight children are at greater risk and might be allowed to avoid tumbling and inverted balances.

When doing partner stunts and combatives, consider the following instructional procedures:

1. Safety factors must be emphasized. Youngsters should be matched for size; a common method is to ask students to pair up with someone who is similar in height. The length of bouts should be short--- usually 5--10 seconds of contesting is adequate. Children should freeze immediately when the whistle is blown. In tug-of-war contests, no one should let go suddenly to avoid sending other children sprawling backward.

2. Instructions for combatives should be as explicit as necessary. Starting positions should be defined so that both contestants begin in an equal and neutral position. What constitutes a win and the number of trials permitted should be defined.

3. Fair play should be stressed. Children should be encouraged to find strategies and maneuvers to gain success, but always within the framework of the rules.

Combatives

Hand Wrestle

Starting Position: Contestants place right foot against right foot and grasp right hands in a handshake grip. The left foot is planted firmly to the rear for support.

Action: Try to force the other, by hand and arm pressure, to move either foot. Any movement by either foot means a loss.

Finger Fencing

Starting Position: Contestants stand on the right foot and hold the left foot with the left hand.

Action: Hook index fingers of the right hands and try to push the opponent off balance. Change feet and hands. Any movement of the supporting foot means a loss.

Touch Knees

Starting Position: Contestants stand on both feet and face each other.

Action: Touch one of the opponent's knees without letting the opponent touch yours. Five touches determine the victor.

Grab the Flag

Starting Position: Opponents are on their knees, facing each other on a tumbling mat. Each has a flag tucked in the belt near the middle of the back.

Action: Remain on the knees at all times. Try to grab the flag from the other.

Rooster Fight

Starting Position: Players stoop down and clasp hands behind the knees.

Action: Try to upset the other player or cause the handhold to be released.

4. The teacher can start contests on signal, or children can be allowed to start contests on their own. If children are not self-disciplined, it is best for the instructor to start and stop all contests.

5. To add variety, contests should be done with the right side (arm or leg), the left side, and both sides. Body position can be varied. Children can stand, crouch, sit, or lie for the same contest.

6. Develop a system of rotation, so youngsters have more than one opponent. Rotating assures that one child will not continually dominate another.

Game Activity

Team Handball

Supplies: Team handball, foam rubber ball, or volleyball; cones; pinnies

Skills: Running, dribbling, passing, throwing, catching

The court is marked with a 6-meter goal area, a 7-meter penalty line, and a 9-meter free-throw line. The goal is 2 by 3 meters. The goal area inside the 6-meter line is only for the goalie; other players are not allowed in this area. The 7-meter line is used for a major penalty shot and the 9-meter line is used for a minor penalty shot. A regulation court is 20 by 40 meters. Boundary cones, tape on the wall, rope through a chain-link fence, soccer goals, or field hockey goals can be substituted for actual team handball goals. For indoor play, a basketball court can be modified for team handball by running a line from the corners of the court to top of the key.

The object of the game is to move a small soccer ball down the field by passing and dribbling and then to throw the ball into a goal area that is 3 meters wide and 2 meters high. In regulation play, each team has six court players and one goalie. The six court players cover the entire court. A player is allowed three steps before and after dribbling the ball. There is no limit on the number of dribbles. Dribbling is, however, discouraged because passing is more effective. A double dribble is a violation. A player can hold the ball for 3 seconds only before passing, dribbling, or shooting. Players cannot kick the ball in any way, except the goalie.

One point is awarded for a goal. Violations and penalties are similar to basketball. A free throw is taken from the point of the violation, and defense must remain 3 meters away while protecting the goal. A penalty throw is awarded from the 7-meter line for a major violation. A major violation occurs when an offensive player who is inside the 9-meter line in an advantageous shooting position is fouled. During a penalty throw, all players must be behind the 9-meter line.

The offensive team starts the game with a throw-on from the centerline. A throw-on also initiates play after each goal. All six offensive players line up at the centerline, and a teammate throws the ball to a teammate. The defense is in position, using either a zone or person-to-person defense. Offensive strategy is similar to basketball with picks, screens, rolls, and movement to open up shots on the goal. With a zone defense, short, quick passes are made in an overloaded portion of the zone.

The defensive strategy is similar to basketball, with person-to-person and zone defense being popular. Beginning players should start with the person-to-person defense and learn how to stay with an offensive player. The back players in the zone are back against the goal line, while the front players are just inside the 9-meter line. The zone rotates with the ball as passes are made around the court.

Octopus

Supplies: None

Skills: Maneuvering, problem solving

Octopus is a game that gets its name from the many hands joined together in the activity. Children stand shoulder to shoulder in a tight circle. Everyone thrusts their hands forward and reaches through the group of hands to grasp other hands across the circle. Players may not hold both hands of the same player. Players also may not hold the hand of an adjacent player. The object is to untangle the mess created by the joined hands by going under, over, or through fellow players. No one is permitted to release a handgrip during the unraveling. What is the end result? Perhaps one large circle or two smaller connected circles. If, after a period of time, the knotted hands do not seem to unravel, call a pause. The teacher and group can decide where the difficulty is and allow a change in position of those hands until the knot is dissolved. This is a good example of a cooperative game that requires close teamwork.

Pin Knockout

Supplies: 8 to 12 bowling pins per team, 10 to 12 foam rubber balls

Skill: Throwing

Two teams of equal number play the game. Each team is given many playground balls and six bowling pins. A court with a centerline is needed. The size of the court depends on the number of children in the game. The object of the game is to knock down all of the opponents' bowling pins. The balls are used for rolling at the opposing team's pins. Each team stays in its half of the court.

A player is eliminated if any of the following occurs:

1. He is touched by any ball at any time, regardless of the situation (other than picking up a ball).

2. She steps over the centerline to roll or retrieve a ball. (Any opposing team member hit as a result of such a roll is not eliminated.)

3. He attempts to block a rolling ball with a ball in his hands and the rolling ball touches him in any manner.

A foul is called when a player holds a ball longer than 10 seconds without rolling at the opposing team. The ball must be immediately given to the opposing team. The bowling pins are placed anywhere in the team's area. Players may guard the pins, but must not touch them. When a pin is down, even if a member of the defending team knocked it over unintentionally, it is removed immediately from the game. The game is over when all pins on one side have been knocked down.

Dynamic Physical Education for Elementary School Children
Soccer Skills (1)
Level III – Week 8

Objectives:
To participate in tag games in a cooperative fashion
To strike a ball with a variety of body parts
To dribble a ball with the feet
To trap a with a variety of body parts
To play a soccer lead-up activity and understand the joy of participation

Equipment Required:
Cones and music for Astronaut Exercises
8" foam rubber or junior soccerball for each student
Pinnies (optional)
Cones for marking the drill areas and goals

Instructional Activities	Teaching Hints

Introductory Activity -- Hospital Tag

All students are it. When tagged, they must cover that area of their body with one hand. Students may be tagged twice, but they must be able to hold both tagged spots and keep moving. When a student is tagged three times, he must freeze.

Restart the game when the majority of students have been frozen. It is counterproductive to wait until the last student is frozen.

Fitness Development Activity -- Astronaut Exercises

Walk, do Arm Circles	35 seconds	Tape alternating segments of silence (30 seconds) and music (35 seconds) to signal the duration of exercise. Music segments indicate aerobic activity while intervals of silence announce flexibility and strength development activities.
Crab Full-Leg Extension	30 seconds	
Skip sideways	35 seconds	
Body Twist	30 seconds	
Slide; change lead leg	35 seconds	
Jumping Jack variations	30 seconds	
Crab Walk	35 seconds	
Curl-Ups with Twist	30 seconds	See Chapter 12 for a description of how to perform the exercises.
Hop to center and back	35 seconds	
Four Count Push-Ups	30 seconds	
Gallop Backwards	35 seconds	Allow students to adjust the workload to an intensity that is consistent with their ability level.
Bear Hugs	30 seconds	
Grapevine Step (Carioca)	35 seconds	
Trunk Twisters	30 seconds	
Power Jumper	35 seconds	

Cool down with stretching and walking.

Use scatter formation; ask students to change directions from time to time in order to keep spacing.

Lesson Focus -- Soccer Skills (1)

Skills

Practice the following skills:

1. Dribbling

Dribbling is moving the ball with a series of taps or pushes to cover ground and still retain control. It allows a player to change direction quickly and to avoid opponents. The best contact point is the inside of the foot, but the outside of the foot will be used at faster running speeds. The ball should be kept close to the player to maintain control.

2. Inside-of-the-Foot Pass (Push Pass)

The inside-of-the-foot pass is used for accurate passing over distances of up to 15 yards. Because of the technique used, this pass is sometimes referred to as the push pass. The nonkicking foot is placed well up, alongside the ball. As the kicking foot is drawn back, the toe is turned out. During the kick, the toe remains turned out so that the inside of the foot is perpendicular to the line of flight. The sole is kept parallel to the ground. At contact, the knee of the kicking leg should be well forward, over the ball, and both knees should be slightly bent.

Contact the ball with the inside, outside, or instep of the foot.

Keep the ball near the body so it can be controlled. (Don't kick it too far in front of the body.) Dribble the ball with a controlled tap.

Place the nonkicking foot alongside the ball. Keep the head down and eyes focused on the ball during contact.

3. Inside-of-the-Foot Trap

This is the most common method of control, and is used when the ball is either rolling along the ground or bouncing up to knee height. The full surface of the foot, from heel to toe, should be presented perpendicular to the ball.

4. Goalkeeping

Goalkeeping involves stopping shots by catching, stopping, or otherwise deflecting the ball. Goalkeepers should become adept at catching low rolling balls, diving on rolling balls, catching airborne balls at waist level and below, and catching airborne balls at waist height and above.

When trapping, move in line with the path of the ball and reach with the foot to meet the ball. Give when ball contact is made to absorb force.

Goalkeepers should practice catching low rolling balls by getting down on one knee, with their body behind the ball to act as a backstop, and catching the ball with both hands, fingers pointing toward the ground.

Drills Using Four or More Players

Use the following partner drills to practice the skills above. Drills for four or more players should be organized so that a rotation gives all players an equal opportunity to practice skills.

1. Dribbling. Two teams of four players are lined up and facing each other about 10 yards apart. Each player at the front of the team has a ball. Both front players dribble to the center, where they exchange balls and continue dribbling to the other side. The next players perform similarly.

A variation is to have the two players meet at the center, exchange balls, and dribble back to their starting point. Action should be continuous.

2. Shooting, goalkeeping, and defense. A shooting drill against defense can be run with four players and a 15-foot goal set off with cones or other markers. One player has the ball. He advances and attempts to maneuver around a second player so that he can shoot past the goalkeeper guarding a goal. A fourth player acts as the retriever. Rotate positions.

Use foam rubber balls for goalkeeping drills to avoid hurting someone with the ball.

3. Dribbling. Four or five players, each with a ball, form a line. A "coach" stands about 15 yards in front of the line. Each player, in turn, dribbles up to the coach, who indicates with a thumb in which direction the player should dribble past. The coach should give the direction at the last possible moment.

Make sure all students get a chance to be the "coach."

4. Passing, controlling, and defense. Four players stand in the four corners of a square, 10 yards on a side. Two defensive players are inside the square. The corner players stay in place within the square and attempt to pass the ball among themselves, while the two defenders attempt to recover the ball. After a period of time, another two players take over as defenders.

This is a traditional game of keepaway using soccer balls. Encourage students to avoid body contact.

Play the soccer lead-up games after sufficient time has been allotted for skills and drills.

Game Activity – Soccer Lead-Up Games

Dribblerama

Supplies: One soccer ball for each player

Skills: Dribbling, protecting the ball

The playing area is a large circle or square, clearly outlined. All players dribble within the area. The game is played on two levels.

Level 1: Each player dribbles throughout the area, controlling the ball so it does not touch another ball. If a touch occurs, both players go outside the area and dribble around the area. Once youngsters have completed dribbling one lap, they may reenter the game.

Level 2: Two equal playing areas are delineated. All players start in one of the areas. While dribbling and controlling the ball, each player attempts to kick any other ball out of the area. When a ball is kicked out, the player owning that ball takes it to the other area and dribbles. As more players move to the second area, a second game ensues. Players in this area move back to the opposite side. This keeps all players actively involved in the games.

Sideline Soccer

Supplies: A soccer ball, four cones, pinnies (optional)

Skills: Most soccer skills, competitive play

Teams line up on the sidelines of the rectangle. Three or four active players from each team are called from the end of the team line. These players remain active until a point is scored; then they rotate to the other end of the line. The object is to kick the ball between cones (goals) that define the scoring area. The active players on each team compete against each other, aided by their teammates on the sidelines.

To start play, the ball can be given to one team or dropped between two opposing players at the center of the field. To score, the ball must be kicked last by an active player and must go through the goal at or below shoulder height. A goal counts one point. Sideline players can pass to other sideline players or an active teammate, but a sideline kick cannot score a goal.

Regular soccer rules generally prevail, with special attention to the restrictions of no pushing, holding, tripping, or other rough play. Rough play is a foul and causes a point to be awarded to the other team. For an out-of-bounds ball, the team on the side of the field where the ball went out-of-bounds is awarded a free kick near that spot. No score can result from a free kick. Violation of the touch rule also results in a free kick.

Rotate in a new set of players after 30 to 45 seconds. More active players can be added when the class is large. A number of passes to sideline players can be mandated before a shot on goal can be taken. After some expertise is acquired, the cones should be moved in to narrow the goal area. If the ball goes over the end line but not through the goal area, the ball is put into play by a defender with a kick.

Line Soccer

Supplies: A soccer ball, four cones, pinnies
Skills: Most soccer skills, competitive play

Two goal lines are drawn 80 to 120 feet apart. A restraining line is drawn 15 feet in front of and parallel to each goal line. Field width can vary from 50 to 80 feet. Each team stands on one goal line, which it defends. The referee stands in the center of the field and holds a ball. At the whistle, three players (more if the teams are large) run from the right side of each line to the center of the field and become active players. The referee drops the ball to the ground, and the players try to kick it through the other team defending the goal line. The players in the field may advance by kicking only.

A score is made when an active player kicks the ball through the opposing team and over the end line (provided that the kick was made from outside the restraining line). Cones should be put on field corners to define the goal line. One point is scored when the ball is kicked over the opponent's goal line below shoulder level. One point is also scored in case of a personal foul involving pushing, kicking, tripping, and the like.

Line players act as goalies and are permitted to catch the ball. Once caught, however, the ball must be laid down immediately and either rolled or kicked. It cannot be punted or drop-kicked.

For illegal touching by the active players, a direct free kick from a point 12 yards in front of the penalized team's goal line is given. All active players on the defending team must stand to one side until the ball is kicked. Only goalies defend. An out-of-bounds ball is awarded to the opponents of the team last touching it. The regular soccer throw-in from out of bounds should be used. If the ball goes over the shoulders of the defenders at the end line, any end-line player may retrieve the ball and put it into play with a throw or kick.

A time limit of 1 minute is set for any group of active players. After time is up, play is halted and the players are changed. Use a system of player rotation so all participants get to play.

Mini-Soccer

Supplies: A soccer ball, pinnies or colors to mark teams, four cones for the corners
Skills: All soccer skills

Each end of the field has a 21-foot-wide goal marked by jumping standards. A 12-yard semicircle on each end outlines the penalty area. The center of the semicircle is at the center of the goal.
The game follows the general rules of soccer, with one goalie for each side. One new feature, the corner kick is incorporated in this game. This kick is used when the ball, last touched by the defense, goes over the end line but not through the goal. The ball is taken to the nearest corner for a direct free kick, and a goal can be scored from the kick. In a similar situation, if the attacking team last touched the ball, the goalkeeper kick is awarded. The goalie puts the ball down and placekicks it forward.

The players are designated as center forward, outside right, outside left, right halfback, left halfback, fullback, and goalie. Players should rotate positions. The forwards play in the front half of the field, and the guards in the back half. Neither position, however, is restricted to these areas entirely, and all may cross the centerline without penalty.

A foul by the defense within its penalty area (semicircle) results in a penalty kick, taken from a point 12 yards distant, directly in front of the goal. Only the goalie is allowed to defend. The ball is in play, with others waiting outside the penalty area.

Position play should be emphasized. The lines of three should be encouraged to spread out and stay in their area. The number of players can vary, with some games using as few as three on a side in a more restricted area.

Dynamic Physical Education for Elementary School Children
Soccer Skills (2)
Level III – Week 9

Objectives:
To strike a soccer ball with a variety of body parts
To dribble a ball with the feet
To trap a ball with a variety of body parts
To play a soccer lead-up activity and understand the joy of participation

Equipment Required:
Cones and tape for Astronaut Exercises
One 8" foam rubber ball or junior soccer ball per student
Pinnies for lead-up games
Cones for marking the drill areas and goals

Instructional Activities	Teaching Hints

Introductory Activity -- PACER Run

Pick two lines or markers 20 meters apart. Students run (or use other locomotor movements) back and forth between the lines in a specified time (i.e., 10 seconds). Students can add a personal challenge by seeing how many times they can move back and forth within the given time limit.

Students can try this with a partner they pick. They can race each other to the lines and back.

Students can walk when necessary.

Fitness Development Activity -- Astronaut Exercises

Walk, do Arm Circles	35 seconds
Crab Full-Leg Extension	35 seconds
Skip sideways	35 seconds
Body Twist	35 seconds
Slide; change lead leg	35 seconds
Jumping Jack variations	35 seconds
Crab Walk	35 seconds
Curl-Ups with Twist	35 seconds
Hop to center and back`	35 seconds
Four Count Push-Ups	35 seconds
Gallop Backwards	35 seconds
Bear Hugs	35 seconds
Grapevine Step (Carioca)	35 seconds
Trunk Twisters	35 seconds
Power Jumper	35 seconds

Cool down with stretching and walking.

Tape alternating segments of silence (35 seconds) and music (35 seconds) to signal the duration of exercise. Music segments indicate aerobic activity while intervals of silence announce flexibility and strength development activities.

See Chapter 12 for a description of how to perform the exercises.

Allow students to adjust the workload to an intensity that is consistent with their ability level.

Use scatter formation; ask students to change directions from time to time in order to keep spacing.

Lesson Focus -- Soccer Skills (2)

Skills

Divide the skills into four stations and place necessary equipment at each station. Students should practice skills they learned in last week's lesson.
1. Review and practice the long pass. Set up a station with plenty of room and students with a partner. They long pass back and forth to each other.
2. Review the inside-of-the foot pass and trapping: Work with a partner and practice passing and trapping.
3. Practice dribbling skills: Give each student a ball and have them practice dribbling. Move the ball with a series of taps. Start slowly and keep the ball in front of the body.
4. Goalkeeping and shooting: Students work with a partner. One dribbles the ball a short distance and then takes shot at goal. The other partner tries to prevent the score.

Make signs that tell students the skills they are to practice at each station. Set the signs on cones in the areas where students are to practice. Ask students to read the signs before they begin.

The foam training balls are best for teaching introductory soccer skills. They don't hurt students when kicked or when they are struck by a ball.

Drills Using Four or More Players

Use the following partner drills to practice the skills above. Drills for four or more players should be organized so that a rotation gives all players an equal opportunity to practice skills.

1. Shooting. For two-way goal practice, two to six players are divided, half on each side of the goal. The width of the goal can vary, depending on the skill of the players. Two types of shooting should be practiced: (a) kicking a stationary ball from 10 to 20 yards out and (b) preceding a kick with a dribble. In the second type, a restraining line 12 to 15 yards out is needed. Use spots or cones to mark this line. Use at least four balls for this two-way drill. After a period of kicking, the groups should change sides. Ball chasers are the players at the end of each line.

2. Shooting and goalkeeping. Scoring can also be practiced with a goalkeeper. Practice should be done with a stationary ball from 12 yards out (penalty distance) and with kicks preceded by a dribble. The goalie and the chaser should remain for one complete round and then rotate. Having a second ball to play with saves time because play can continue while the chaser is recovering the previous ball.

3. Kicking and trapping. This is an excellent squad drill. Approximately eight players form a circle 15 yards in diameter. Two balls are passed back and forth independently. Passes should be kept low, using primarily the side-of-the-foot kick. Using three balls can be tried also.

4. Passing and shooting. The drill can be done with four to six players. Two balls are needed. A passer is stationed about 15 yards from the goal, and a retriever is behind the goal. The shooters are in line, 20 yards from the goal and to the right. The first shooter passes to the passer, and then runs forward. The passer returns the ball to the shooter. The shooter tries to time her run forward so that she successfully shoots the pass through the goal. Both the passer and the retriever should stay in position for several rounds of shooting and then rotate to become shooters. The first pass can be from a stationary ball. Later, however, the kicker can be allowed to dribble forward a short distance before making the first pass. Reverse the field and practice from the left, shooting with the nondominant leg.

Using cones or chalk, a grid system of 10-yard squares can be marked on a playing field. The grid can be useful when organizing drills, activities, and small-sized games. The number of squares needed depends on the size of the class, but at least one square for every three students is recommended. The drills can also be set up as individual stations where students rotate after a specified time.

In soccer drills, two approaches should be recognized. The first is the practice of technique with no opposition from any defense. The second is the skill approach, which involves both offensive and defensive players and perhaps a target. In drills using the skill approach, the goal is to outmaneuver the opponent. Some drills begin with the technique approach and then move to the skill approach.

Game Activity - Soccer Lead-Up Games

Bull's-Eye

Supplies: One soccer ball per player

Skills: Dribbling, protecting the ball

The playing area is a large outlined area--circle, square, or rectangle. One player holds a ball in her hands, which serves as the bull's-eye. The other players dribble within the area. The player with the bull's-eye attempts to throw her ball (basketball push shot) at any other ball. The ball that is hit now becomes the new bull's-eye. The old bull's-eye becomes one of the dribblers. A new bull's-eye cannot hit back immediately at the old bull's-eye. If the group is large, have two bull's-eyes. No score is kept and no one is eliminated.

Line Soccer

See the Lesson Plan, Week 8 for a complete game description.

Mini-Soccer

See the Lesson Plan, Week 8 for a complete game description.

Regulation Soccer

Supplies: A soccer ball, pinnies

Skills: All soccer skills

A team usually consists of three forwards, three midfield players, four backline defenders, and one goalkeeper. Forwards are the main line of attack. They need to develop good control, dribbling, and shooting skills, and they must have a strong desire to score. They should be encouraged to shoot frequently. Midfield players tend to be the powerhouse of the team. They need good passing and tackling skills as well as a high level of cardiovascular fitness. Defenders should work well together and know when to tackle. They should play safely by clearing the ball away from their own penalty area, and not risk dribbling or passing toward their own goal unless it is absolutely safe to do so. Goalkeepers must be quick and agile, be good decision makers, and have ball-handling skills.

On the toss of the coin, the winning team gets its choice of kicking off or selecting which goal to defend. The loser exercises the option not selected by the winner.

On the kickoff, the ball must travel forward about 1 yd, and the kicker cannot touch it again until another player has kicked it. The defensive team must be 10 yd away from the kicker. After each score, the team not winning the point gets to kick off. Both teams must be onside at the kickoff. The defensive team must stay onside and out of the center circle until the ball is kicked. Regular soccer rules call for scoring by counting the number of goals made.

Elementary school children usually play 6-minute quarters. There should be a rest period of 1 minute between quarters and 10 minutes between halves.

When the ball goes out-of-bounds on the sideline, it is put into play with a throw-in from the spot where it crossed the line. No goal may be scored, nor may the thrower play the ball a second time until it has been touched by another player. All opponents are to be 10 yd back at the time of the throw.

If the ball is caused to go out-of-bounds on the end line by the attacking team, a goal kick is awarded. The ball is placed in the goal area and kicked beyond the penalty area by a defending player, who may not touch the ball twice in succession. If the ball is touched by a player before it goes out of the penalty area, it is not yet in play and should be kicked again.

If the defensive team causes the ball to go out-of-bounds over the end line, a corner kick is awarded. The ball is placed 1 yd from the corner of the field and kicked into the field of play by an attacking player. The 10-yd restriction also applies to defensive players.

If the ball is touched by two opponents at the same time and caused to go out-of-bounds, a drop ball is called. The referee drops the ball between two opposing players, who cannot kick it until it touches the ground. A drop ball also is called when the ball is trapped among downed players.

If a player is closer to the opponent's goal line than to the ball at a time when the ball is played in a forward direction, it is an offside infraction. Exceptions exist, and a player is not offside when she is in her half of the playing field, when two opponents are nearer their goal line than the attacking player at the moment when the ball is played, or when the ball is received directly from a corner kick, a throw-in, or a goal kick.

Personal fouls involving unnecessary roughness are penalized. Tripping, striking, charging, holding, pushing, and jumping an opponent intentionally are forbidden.

It is a foul for any player, except the goalkeeper, to handle the ball with the hands or arms. The goalkeeper is allowed only four steps and must then get rid of the ball. After the ball has left her possession, the goalkeeper may not pick it up again until another player has touched it. Players are not allowed to screen or obstruct opponents, unless they are in control of the ball.

Penalties are as follows:

1. A direct kick is awarded for all personal fouls and handballs. A goal can be scored from a direct free kick. Examples of infringements are pushing, tripping, kicking a player, and holding.

2. A penalty kick is awarded if direct free-kick infringements are committed by a defender in his own penalty area.

3. An indirect free kick is awarded for offsides, obstruction, dangerous play such as high kicking, a goalkeeper's taking more than four steps or repossessing the ball before another player has touched it, and playing the ball twice after a dead-ball situation. The ball must be touched by a second player before a goal can be scored. The referee should signal if the kick is indirect by pointing one arm upward vertically.

Teaching suggestions: Players should be encouraged to use the space on the field to the best advantage. When a team is in possession of the ball, players should attempt to find a position from which they can pass either behind the player with the ball to give support, or toward the goal to be in a better position to shoot. When a team is forced into defense, the defenders should get "goalside" of attackers (between the attackers and their own goal) to prevent them from gaining an advantage.

From an early stage, players should be taught to give information to each other during the game, especially when they have possession of the ball. Valuable help can be given by shouting instructions such as "Man on," "You have time," or "Player behind," and also by calling for the ball when in a good position to receive a pass.

Dynamic Physical Education for Elementary School Children
Soccer Skills (3)
Level III – Week 10

Objectives:
To strike a soccer ball with a variety of body parts
To dribble a ball with the feet
To trap a ball with a variety of body parts
To play a soccer lead-up activity and understand the joy of participation

Equipment Required:
One beanbag for each student
Music tape and signs for fitness
One 8" foam rubber ball or junior soccer ball per student
Cones for marking playing areas
Pinnies for lead-up games

Instructional Activities	Teaching Hints
Introductory Activity – Beanbag Touch and Go	
Spread beanbags throughout the area. On signal, students move and touch as many beanbags as possible. Different body parts can be specified for touching (i.e., "Touch five yellow beanbags with your right knee.")	Stipulate students touch different colors of beanbags Challenge to move over and around beanbags
Fitness Development Activity -- Aerobic Fitness	
The following aerobic movements are suggestions only. When youngsters begin to fatigue, stop the aerobic fitness movements and do some of the flexibility and strength development activities learned in previous lessons. This will allow students time to recover aerobically.	Use music to stimulate effort. Any combination of movements can be used.
1. Rhythmic run with clap	Keep the steps simple and easy to perform. Some students will become frustrated if the learning curve is steep.
2. Bounce turn and clap	
3. Rhythmic 4-count curl-ups (knees, toes, knees, back)	
4. Rhythmic Crab Kicks (slow time)	Signs that explain the aerobic activities will help students remember performance cues.
5. Jumping Jack combination	
6. Double knee lifts	
7. Lunges (right, left, forward) with single-arm circles (on the side lunges) and double-arms circles (on the forward lunge)	Don't stress or expect perfection. Allow students to perform the activities as best they can.
8. Rhythmic trunk twists	
9. Directional run (forward, backward, side, turning)	
10. Rock side to side with clap	
11. Side leg raises (alternate legs)	Alternate bouncing and running movements with flexibility and strength development movements.
12. Rhythmic 4-count push-ups (If these are too difficult for students, substitute single-arm circles in the push-up position.)	

Lesson Focus -- Soccer Skills (3)

Since this is the third week of soccer, emphasis should be placed on playing regulation soccer. Introduce the following skills and devote the rest of the time to the game of soccer

Skills

1. Punting
Used by the goalkeeper only, the punt can be stationary or can be done on the run. The ball is held in both hands at waist height in front of the body and directly over the kicking leg. For the stationary punt, the kicking foot is forward. A short step is taken with the kicking foot, followed by a full step on the other foot. With the knee bent and the toe extended, the kicking foot swings forward and upward. As contact is made with the ball at the instep, the knee straightens, and additional power is secured from the other leg through a coordinated rising on the toes or a hop.

2. Throw-Ins
The throw-in is the only time the ball can be handled by field players with their hands. The throw-in is guided by rules that must be followed closely or the result is a turnover to the other team. The rules are as follows:
a. Both hands must be on the ball.
b. The ball must be released from over the thrower's head.
c. The thrower must face the field.
d. The thrower may not step onto the field until the throw is released.
e. Both feet must remain in contact with the ground until the ball is released.

f. The thrower cannot play the ball until another player on the field has touched it.

The throw-in from out of bounds may be executed from a standing or running position. Beginning players should learn the throw without a running start. The feet often are placed one behind the other, with the rear toe trailing along the ground. Delivery of the ball should be from behind the head, using both arms equally. Release should be from in front of the forehead with arms outstretched. Instructional cues to help students perform correctly are "drag your back foot" and "follow through with both hands pointing toward the target."

Game Activity - Soccer Lead-Up Games

Use the Soccer-Lead-Up games described in Lesson Plans, Weeks 8 and 9.

Dynamic Physical Education for Elementary School Children
Recreational Activities
Level III – Week 11

Objectives:
To be able to move continuously in moderately active activities
To learn the rules of recreational activities
To play in recreational activities independently without adult supervision

Equipment Required:
Music and signs for Aerobic Fitness
Equipment for recreational activities

Instructional Activities	Teaching Hints

Introductory Activity -- Jog and Stretch

The class jogs around the area. On signal, they stop and stretch a body part. Students work independently and are responsible for stretching as many body parts as possible.

Use students to demonstrate a variety of stretches.

Fitness Development Activity -- Aerobic Fitness

The following aerobic movements are suggestions only. When youngsters begin to fatigue, stop the aerobic fitness movements and do some of the flexibility and strength development activities learned in previous lessons. This will allow students time to recover aerobically.
1. Rhythmic run with clap
2. Bounce turn and clap
3. Rhythmic 4-count curl-ups (knees, toes, knees, back)
4. Rhythmic Crab Kicks (slow time)
5. Jumping Jack combination
6. Double knee lifts
7. Lunges (right, left, forward) with single-arm circles (on the side lunges) and double-arms circles (on the forward lunge)
8. Rhythmic trunk twists
9. Directional run (forward, backward, side, turning)
10. Rock side to side with clap
11. Side leg raises (alternate legs)
12. Rhythmic 4-count push-ups (If these are too difficult for students, substitute single-arm circles in the push-up position.)

Use music to stimulate effort. Any combination of movements can be used.

Keep the steps simple and easy to perform. Some students will become frustrated if the learning curve is steep.

Signs that explain the aerobic activities will help students remember performance cues.

Don't stress or expect perfection. Allow students to perform the activities as best they can.

Alternate bouncing and running movements with flexibility and strength development movements.

Lesson Focus and Game Activity -- Recreational Activities

The purpose of this unit is to teach children activities that they can play during the time when school is not in session.
1. Shuffleboard
2. Four Square
3. Double Dutch rope jumping
4. Team Handball
5. Around the Key Basketball
6. Beachball Volleyball (2 on 2)
7. Jacks
8. Marbles
9. Sidewalk Tennis
10. Horseshoes
11. Rope Quoits
12. Tetherball
13. Tennis Volleyball

Teach students the rules of recreational activities so they are able to participate effectively during free time.

Teach games that are traditional in your area. Older youngsters may be a good source of advice for often-played games.

If desired, set up a number of stations and have youngsters rotate to different stations during the lesson.

Dynamic Physical Education for Elementary School Children
Walking and Jogging Skills
Level III – Week 12

Objectives:
To develop a personalized warm-up routine
To participate in vigorous activity for an extended period of time
To demonstrate activities which stretch specified body parts

Equipment Required:
One beanbag per student
Music for Astronaut Exercises

Instructional Activities	Teaching Hints

Introductory Activity -- Vanishing Beanbags

Beanbags (one per student) are spread throughout the area. Students move throughout the area. On signal, they find a beanbag and sit on it. On the next signal or command, the students move again, with a few beanbags being removed during the interval. On signal, they once again sit on a beanbag. The object is to try not to be left without a beanbag move than five times.

There are no ties when finding a beanbag to sit on. If students feel it is a tie, both must leave that bag and find another.

Specify placing different body parts on the beanbag.

Fitness Development Activity -- Astronaut Exercises

Walk, do Arm Circles	40 seconds
Crab Full-Leg Extension	35 seconds
Skip sideways	40 seconds
Body Twist	35 seconds
Slide; change lead leg	40 seconds
Jumping Jack variations	35 seconds
Crab Walk	40 seconds
Curl-Ups with Twist	35 seconds
Hop to center and back	40 seconds
Four Count Push-Ups	35 seconds
Gallop Backwards	40 seconds
Bear Hugs	35 seconds
Grapevine Step (Carioca)	40 seconds
Trunk Twisters	35 seconds
Power Jumper	40 seconds

Cool down with stretching and walking.

Tape alternating segments of silence (35 seconds) and music (40 seconds) to signal the duration of exercise. Music segments indicate aerobic activity while intervals of silence announce flexibility and strength development activities.

See Chapter 12 for a description of how to perform the exercises.

Allow students to adjust the workload to an intensity that is consistent with their ability level.

Use scatter formation; ask students to change directions from time to time in order to keep spacing.

Lesson Focus -- Walking and Jogging Skills

The walking and jogging lesson should be a relaxed lesson with emphasis on developing activity patterns that can be used outside of the school environment. An educational approach to this lesson can teach students that walking and jogging is done without equipment and offers excellent health benefits. It is an activity that can literally be done for a lifetime. The following are suggestions for implementing this unit of instruction:

1. Youngsters should be allowed to find a friend with whom they want to jog or walk. The result is usually a friend of similar ability level. A way to judge correct pace is to be able to talk with a friend without undue stress. If students are too winded to talk, they are probably running too fast. A selected friend will encourage talking and help assure that the experience is positive and within the student's aerobic capacity. *Pace, not race* is an excellent motto.

2. Jogging and walking should be done in any direction so people are unable to keep track of the distance covered. Doing laps on a track is one of the surest ways to discourage less able youngsters. They always finish last and are open to chiding by the rest of the class.

3. Jogging and walking should be done for a specified time rather than a specified distance. All youngsters should not have to run the same distance. This goes against the philosophy of accompanying individual differences and varying aerobic capacities. Running or walking for a set amount of time will allow the less able child to move without fear of ridicule.

4. Teachers should not be concerned about foot action, since the child selects naturally the means that is most comfortable. Arm movement should be easy and natural, with elbows bent. The head and upper body should be held up and back. The eyes look ahead. The general body position in walking and jogging should be erect but relaxed. Jogging on the toes should be avoided.

5. Jogging and walking should not be a competitive, timed activity. Each youngster should move at a self-determined pace. Racing belongs in the track program. Another reason to avoid speed is that racing keeps youngsters from learning to run at an even pace. For developing endurance and gaining health benefits, it is more important to move longer at a slow speed than to run at top speed for a short distance.

6. It can be motivating for youngsters if they run with a piece of equipment, i.e., beanbag or jump rope. They can play catch with a beanbag or roll a hoop while walking or jogging.

Game Activity - Individual or Recreational Activities

When youngsters are finished walking and jogging, allow them the opportunity to participate in a choice of individual or recreational activities.

Dynamic Physical Education for Elementary School Children
Rhythmic Movement Skills (1)
Level III – Week 13

Objectives:
To perform a number of physical challenges with body control
To move rhythmically in a variety of situations
To participate cooperatively in a game setting

Equipment Required:
Equipment for Challenge Course
Music for Challenge Course
Music for rhythmic activities
Markers for Pacman game

Instructional Activities	Teaching Hints

Introductory Activity -- Hospital Tag

All students are it. When tagged, they must cover that area of their body with one hand. Students may be tagged twice, but they must be able to hold both tagged spots and keep moving. When a student is tagged three times, he must freeze.

Restart the game when the majority of students have been frozen. It is counterproductive to wait until the last student is frozen.

Fitness Development Activity – Challenge Course

Design a course around the perimeter of the area using some of the following ideas:
1. Step on jumping box, dismount to tumbling mat, and do a forward roll.
2. Run and weave through four wands held upright by cones.
3. Handwalk across a horizontal ladder or do a flexed-arm hang from a climbing rope for 5 seconds.
4. Step on and off three jumping boxes (small-large-small)
5. Agility run through hoops.
6. Perform jump turns
7. Leap over a magic rope held taut with two chairs or jumping boxes.
8. Hop on one foot.
9. Do a log roll across a tumbling mat.
10. Alternate going over and under six obstacles (cones and wands or hoops)
11. Crouch jump or scooter movements the length of a balance-beam bench.
12. Slide through a parallel tumbling mat maze (mats stood on their sides)

Use taped intervals of music and silence. When the music is playing students travel through the challenge course. When the music stops, youngsters do some stretching and strength development exercises. This gives them a chance to recover aerobically.

Distribute students throughout the course rather than lining them up at a starting point. Faster moving students can pass on the outside.

Change directions periodically to prevent a build-up of students at one station.

Lesson Focus -- Rhythmic Movement Skills (1)

Make dances easy for students to learn by implementing some of the following techniques:
Rhythms should be taught like other sport skills. Avoid striving for perfection so students know it is acceptable to make mistakes. Teach a variety of dances rather than one or two in depth in case some students find it difficult to master a specific dance.
1. Teach the dances without using partners.
2. Allow youngsters to move in any direction without left-right orientation.
3. Use scattered formation instead of circles.
4. Emphasize strong movements such as clapping and stamping to increase involvement.
5. Play the music at a slower speed when first learning the dance.

Jessie Polka (American)

Music Source: WWCD-RM8
Formation: Circle, couples facing counterclockwise with inside arms around each other's waist
Directions:

Measures	Part I Action
1	Beginning left, touch the heel in front, then step left in place. (Left heel, together)
2	Touch the right toe behind. Then touch the right toe in place, or swing it forward, keeping the weight on the left foot. (Right toe, touch)
3	Touch the right heel in front, then step right in place. (Right heel, together)
4	Touch the left heel to the left side, sweep the left foot across in front of the right. Keep the weight on the right. (Left heel, crossover)

Measures	Part II Action
5--8	Take four two-steps or polka steps forward in the line of direction. (Step, close, step; Step, close, step; Step, close, step; Step, close, step)

Inside-Out Mixer

Music Source: Any music with a pronounced beat suitable for walking at a moderate speed

Formation: Triple circle (three children standing side by side), facing counterclockwise, with inside hands joined. A pinnie can be worn by the center person for identification.

Directions:

Measures	Action
1--4	Take eight walking steps forward. (Forward, 2, 3, 4, 5, 6, 7, 8)
5--8	Form a small circle and circle left in eight steps back to place. (Circle, 2, 3, 4, 5, 6, 7, 8)
9--12	The center person walks forward under the raised arms opposite, pulling the other two under to turn the circle inside out. (Inside-out, 2, 3, 4, 5, 6, 7, 8)
13--16	The trio circles left in eight steps, returning to place. When almost back to place, drop hands. The center person walks forward counterclockwise, and the other two walk clockwise (the way they are facing) to the nearest trio for a change of partners. (Circle, 2, 3, 4, mix, 6, 7, 8)

Cotton-Eyed Joe (American)

Music Source: WWCD-FDN

Formation: Double circle of couples with partner B on the right, holding inside hands and facing counterclockwise. Varsouvienne position can also be used.

Directions:

Measures	Action
1--2	Starting with the left foot, cross the left foot in front of the right foot, kick the left foot forward. (Cross, kick)
3--4	Take one two-step backward. (Left, close, left)
5--6	Cross the right foot in front of the left foot; kick the right foot forward. (Cross, kick)
7--8	Do one two-step backward. (Right, close, right)
9--16	Repeat measures 1--8.
17--32	Perform eight two-steps counterclockwise beginning with the left foot. (Step, close, step; Repeat eight times)

Alley Cat (American)

Music Source: WWCD-4903

Skills: Grapevine step, touch step, knee lifts

Formation: None, although all should face the same direction during instruction.

Directions:

Measures	Action
1–2	Do a grapevine left and kick: Step sideward left, step right behind left, step left again, and kick. Repeat to the right. (Left, behind, left, kick; Right, behind, right, kick)
3–4	Touch the left toe backward, bring the left foot to the right, touch the left toe backward again, bring the left foot to the right, taking the weight. Repeat, beginning with the right toe. (Left and, left and; Right and, right and)
5–6	Raise the left knee up in front of the right knee and repeat. Raise the right knee up twice, similarly. (Left and, left and; Right and, right and)
7–8	Raise the left knee and then the right knee. Clap the hands once and make a jump quarter turn to the left. (Left and, right and, clap and, jump)

After the routine is repeated three times, the dancer should be facing in the original direction.

Big Sombrero Circle Mixer (American)

Music Source: WWC-FFD

Skills: Circling, do-si-do, star, swing

Formation: Sicilian Circle. Couples facing couples clockwise and counterclockwise around the circle.

Directions:

Measures	Action
2	Introduction (8 counts total)
1-2	Join hands with the facing couple and circle left using 8 walking steps (circle, 2, 3, ... 8)
3-4	Keep hands joined circle right using 8 walking steps. (circle right, 2, 3, ... 8)
5-6	Face partner and do-si-do using 8 walking steps. (Do-si-do, 2, 3,... 8)
7-8	Face opposite and do-si-do using 8 walking steps. (Opposite, 2, 3, ... 8)
9-10	All four circle while doing a right hand star using 8 walking steps. (Star, 2, 3, ... 8)
11-12	All four circle while doing a left hand star using 8 walking steps. (Star, 2, 3, ... 8)
13-14	Swing partner by linking right elbows and swinging once or twice. (Swing, 2, 3, ... 8)
15-16	Pass through the opposite couple passing right shoulders and walk to the next couple using 8 steps. (Pass, through, 3, 4, ... 8)

Repeat the dance to the end of the music. Youngsters should always return back to their starting position after every 8 count movement.

Circle Virginia Reel (American)

Music Source: WWCD-57; WWC-57

Skills: Star, swing, do-si-do, swing, promenade

Formation: Couples facing in a double circle with dancers about 4 feet apart

Directions:

Measures	Action
1-4	Partners walk forward 4 and backward 4 steps; repeat. (Forward, 2, 3, 4; back, 2, 3, 4; Forward, 2, 3, 4; back, 2, 3, 4)
5-8	Partners make a start by joining right hands (with bent elbows) and circling around once clockwise in 8 steps. Reverse direction and star with left hands back to place in 8 steps. (Right star, 2, 3, … 8; Left star, 2, 3, … 8)
9-10	Partners join hands with bent elbows held chest high and circle clockwise back to place in 8 steps. (Circle, 2, 3, … 8)
11-12	Partners walk forward and do-si-do passing right shoulders and stepping to the right when passing back to back. After passing, each partner moves diagonally (veers) to the right to end in front of a new partner. (Do-si-do, 2, 3, 4, veer, 2, 3, 4)
13-16	Facing a new partner and joining hands, inside circle partner begins with left foot and outside circle begins with right foot doing a 2 heel-toe steps and 4 slide steps counterclockwise. Repeat to the other side sliding clockwise. (Heel, toe, heel toe, slide, slide, slide, slide; heel, toe, heel, toe, slide, slide, slide, slide)
17-20	Partners do a right elbow swing in place for 12 counts using a walking step and use 4 counts to end in promenade position. (Swing, 2, 3, …12, promenade position 15, 16)
21-24	In promenade position, partners walk forward counterclockwise 16 steps and end facing each other. (Promenade, 2, 3, … 16)

Game Activity

Triplet Stoop

Supplies: Music

Skill: Moving rhythmically

Break the class into groups of three. The groups march abreast around the area. On signal, the outside person of the three continues marching in the same direction. The middle person stops and marches in place. The inside player reverses direction and marches in the opposite direction. When the music stops, the groups of three reunite at the spot where the middle player stopped. The last three to join hands and stoop move to the center to wait out one turn. The game can also be played with two or three students designated as extras. They can march wherever they desire. When the music stops, they can join any middle player. Any excluded person becomes an extra.

Pacman

Supplies: Markers in the shape of Pacman

Skills: Fleeing, reaction time

Three students are it and carry the Pacman marker. The remainder of the class is scattered throughout the area, standing on a floor line. Movement can only be made on a line. Begin the game by placing the three taggers at the corners of the perimeter lines. Play is continuous; a player who is tagged takes the marker and becomes a new tagger. If a player leaves a line to escape being tagged, that player must secure a marker and become an additional tagger.

Dynamic Physical Education for Elementary School Children
Cross-Country Running and Walking Skills
Level III – Week 14

Objectives:
To participate in cross-country activities as a participating team member
To show respect for peers regardless of individual differences in ability
To develop a personalized warm-up routine that enhances flexibility

Equipment Required:
Finish markers and team score cards
8-12 cones for cross-country "funnel"
Recreational and individual equipment as needed

Instructional Activities	Teaching Hints

Introductory Activity and Fitness Development Activity - Stretching

Combine the introductory and fitness activities during the track and field unit. This workout helps students learn to stretch and warm up for cross-country running.

Standing Hip Bend	30 seconds
Sitting Stretch	30 seconds
Partner Rowing	60 seconds
Bear Hug (do each leg)	40 seconds
Side Flex (do each leg)	40 seconds
Trunk Twister	30 seconds

Keep stretching activities smooth and sustained. Stretches can be held for 6 to 10 seconds.

Allow students to lead each other in their warm-up routine. A goal should be for students to develop a personal warm-up routine they can use when they are away from school.

Youngsters should work independently during their warm-up. If they desire, they can work with a friend.

Lesson Focus -- Cross-Country Running/Walking

Cross-country courses can be marked with a chalk line and cones so that runners follow the course as outlined. Checkpoints every 220 yards offer runners a convenient reference point so that they can gauge accurately how far they have run. Three courses of differing lengths and difficulty can be laid out. The beginning course can be 1 mile in length, the intermediate 1.25 miles, and the advanced 1.5 miles. Including sandy or hilly areas in the course increases the challenge. When students run cross-country, they can select the course that challenges them appropriately. **It is entirely appropriate to select a fast-paced walk if students judge themselves unable to run the entire distance.**

1. Discuss the sport of cross-country running and how it is scored.
   a. Seven members to a team.
   b. Lowest score wins.
   c. Total points for each team based on places finished in race.

2. Divide the class into equal teams by recording times for all members of the class regardless of whether they walked or ran. Create teams of equal ability by dividing students to that the total elapsed time (for all team members) is equal.

3. Depending on the age of youngsters, as well as their ability, teams can run different length courses. The following lengths are suggested:
   a. Beginning—1 mile
   b. Intermediate—1.25 miles
   c. Advanced—1.5 miles

4. Explain how to "warm down" after each course run.

The attractiveness of cross-country competition lies in the fact that it is a team activity and all members of the team are crucial to its success. Youngsters should learn how to score a meet. Probably the easiest way to keep team scores is to assign seven (depending on class size) members to each team. Points are assigned to finishers based on their placement in the race. For example, the first-place runner receives 1 point, the tenth-place runner 10 points, and so on. The points for all team members are totaled, and the team with the lowest score is declared the winner.

A funnel made of cones at the finish line prevents tying times. As runners go through the funnel, the meet judges and helpers can hand each one a marker with the place of finish on it. This simplifies scoring at the end of the meet. Each team captain can total the scores and report the result.

Game Activity - Individual or Recreational Activities

When youngsters are finished with cross-country running, allow them the opportunity to participate in a choice of individual or recreational activities.

Dynamic Physical Education for Elementary School Children
Juggling Skills & Pyramids
Level III – Week 15

Objectives:
To be able to juggle three scarves
To be able to juggle two balls
To participate in low organized games and contribute to the team outcome

Equipment Required:
Music and equipment for Challenge
  Course
Juggling scarves (3 for each student)
Different types of balls for juggling
Base and balls for game activities

Instructional Activities	Teaching Hints

Introductory Activity -- Marking

Each child has a partner who is somewhat equal in ability. Under control, one partner runs, dodges, and tries to lose the other, who must stay within 3 feet of the runner. On signal, both stop. Chasers must be able to touch their partners to say that they have marked them. Partners then change roles.

Allow a point to be scored only when they touch a specified body part (i.e., knee, elbow, left hand).

Fitness Development Activity – Challenge Course

Design a course around the perimeter of the area using some of the following ideas:
1. Step on jumping box, dismount to tumbling mat, and do a forward roll.
2. Run and weave through four wands held upright by cones.
3. Handwalk across a horizontal ladder or do a flexed-arm hang from a climbing rope for 5 seconds.
4. Step on and off three jumping boxes (small-large-small)
5. Agility run through hoops.
6. Perform jump turns
7. Leap over a magic rope held taut with two chairs or jumping boxes.
8. Hop on one foot.
9. Do a log roll across a tumbling mat.
10. Alternate going over and under six obstacles (cones and wands or hoops)
11. Crouch jump or scooter movements the length of a balance-beam bench.
12. Slide through a parallel tumbling mat maze (mats stood on their sides)

Use taped intervals of music and silence. When the music is playing students travel through the challenge course. When the music stops, youngsters do some stretching and strength development exercises. This gives them a chance to recover aerobically.

Distribute students though out the course rather than lining them up at a starting point. Faster moving students can pass on the outside.

Change directions periodically to prevent a build-up of students at one station.

Lesson Focus -- Juggling Skills
Juggling with Scarves

Scarves are held near the center by the fingertips. To throw the scarf, it should be lifted and pulled into the air above eye level. Scarves are caught by clawing, a downward motion of the hand, and grabbing the scarf from above as it is falling.

Cascading—Cascading is the easiest pattern for juggling three objects. The following sequence can be used to learn this basic technique.
a. One scarf. Hold the scarf in the center. Quickly move the arm across the chest and toss the scarf with the palm out. Reach out with the other hand and catch the scarf in a straight-down motion (clawing). Toss the scarf with this hand using the motion and claw it with the opposite hand. Continue the tossing and clawing sequence over and over.
b. Two scarves and one hand. Hold the scarves with the fingertips in one hand. Toss the first scarf upward. As the first scarf reaches its zenith, toss the second scarf and catch the first one. Continue.
c. Two scarves and two hands. Hold a scarf with the fingertips of each hand. Toss the first one across the body as described above. Toss the second scarf across the body in the opposite direction.
d. Three-scarf cascading. A scarf is held in each hand by the fingertips as described above. The third scarf is held with the ring and little fingers against the palm of the hand. The first scarf to be thrown will be from the hand that is holding two scarves.

Reverse Cascading—Reverse cascading involves tossing the scarves from the waist level to the outside of the body and allowing the scarves to drop down the midline of the body.
a. One scarf.
b. Two scarves.
c. Three scarves.

Column Juggling—Column juggling is so named because the scarves move straight up and down as though they were inside a large pipe or column and do not cross the body.

Showering—Start with two scarves in the right hand and one in the other. Begin by throwing the first two scarves from the right hand. Toss the scarves in a large circle away from the midline of the body and overhead as high as possible. As soon as the second scarf is released, toss the scarf from the left to the right hand and throw it in the same path with the right hand. All scarves are caught with the left hand and passed to the right hand.

Juggling Challenges

a. While cascading, toss a scarf under one leg.
b. While cascading, toss a scarf from behind the back.
c. Instead of catching one of the scarves, blow it upward with a strong breath of air.
d. Begin cascading by tossing the first scarf into the air with a foot. Lay the scarf across the foot and kick it into the air.
e. Try juggling three scarves with one hand. Do not worry about establishing a pattern, just catch the lowest scarf each time. Try both regular and reverse cascading, as well as column juggling.
f. While doing column juggling, toss up one scarf, hold the other two and make a full turn. Resume juggling.
g. Try juggling more than three scarves (up to six) while facing a partner.
h. Juggle three scarves while standing beside a partner with inside arms around each other. This is easy to do since it is regular three-scarf cascading.

Juggling with Balls

Instructional Procedures

1. Juggling requires accurate, consistent tossing, and this should be the first emphasis. The tosses should be thrown to the same height on both sides of the body, about 2 to 2 feet upward and across the body, since the ball is tossed from one hand to the other. Practice tossing the ball parallel to the body; the most common problem in juggling is that the balls are tossed forward and the juggler has to move forward to catch them.
2. The fingers, not the palms, should be used in tossing and catching. Stress relaxed wrist action.
3. The student should look upward to watch the balls at the peak of their flight, rather than watching the hands. Focus on where the ball peaks, not the hands.
4. The balls should be caught about waist height and released a little above this level.
5. Two balls must be carried in the starting hand, and the art of releasing only one must be mastered.
6. Progression should be working successively with first one ball, then two balls, and finally three balls.

Recommended Progression for Cascading

1. Using one ball and one hand only, toss the ball upward (2 to 2 feet), and catch it with the same hand. Begin with the dominant hand, and later practice with the other. Toss quickly, with wrist action. Then handle the ball alternately with right and left hands, tossing from one hand to the other.
2. Now, with one ball in each hand, alternate tossing a ball upward and catching it in the same hand so that one ball is always in the air. Begin again with a ball in each hand. Toss across the body to the other hand. To keep the balls from colliding, toss under the incoming ball. After some expertise has been acquired, alternate the two kinds of tosses by doing a set number (four to six) of each before shifting to the other.
3. Hold two balls in the starting hand and one in the other. Toss one of the balls in the starting hand, toss the ball from the other hand, and then toss the third ball.

Pyramids

Emphasis is on making small pyramid groups. Stunts using two performers should be practiced as preliminary to pyramid building with three students. Groups larger than three are not recommended since it is difficult to supervise safely. Place a number of signs or pictures around the area to encourage different types of pyramids.

Game Activity

Fast Pass

Supplies: One 8-inch foam rubber ball, pinnies
Skills: Passing, catching, moving to an open area

One team begins with the ball. The object is to complete five consecutive passes without the ball touching the floor. The team without the ball attempts to intercept the ball or recover an incomplete pass. Each time a pass is completed, the team shouts the number of consecutive passes completed it represents. Each time a ball touches the floor or is intercepted, the count starts over. Players may not contact each other. Emphasis should be placed on spreading out and using the entire court area. If players do not spread out, the area can be broken into quadrants and players restricted to one quadrant.

One-Base Tagball

Supplies: A base (or standard), a volleyball (8-inch foamball for younger children)
Skills: Running, dodging, throwing

A home line is drawn at one end of the playing space. A base or standard is placed about 50 feet in front of the home line. Two teams are formed. One team is scattered around the fielding area, the boundaries of which are determined by the number of children. The other team is lined up in single file behind the home line.

The object of the game is for the fielding team to tag the runners with the ball. Two runners at a time try to round the base and head back for the home line without being tagged. The game is continuous, meaning that as soon as a running team player is tagged or crosses the home line, another player starts immediately. The fielding team may run with the ball and pass it from player to player, trying to tag one of the runners. The running team scores a point for each player who runs successfully around the base and back to the home line.

At the start of the game, the running team has two players ready at the right side of the home line. The others on the team are in line, waiting for a turn. The teacher throws the ball anywhere in the field, and the first two runners start toward the base. They must run around the base from the right side. After all of the players have run, the teams exchange places. The team scoring the most points wins.

To facilitate tagging a runner, players on the fielding team should make passes to a person close to the runner. They must be alert, because two children at a time are running. The next player on the running team must watch carefully in order to start the instant one of the two preceding runners is back safely behind the line or has been hit.

Dynamic Physical Education for Elementary School Children
Rhythmic Movement Skills (2)
Level III – Week 16

Objectives:
To run rhythmically to the beat of a tambourine
To perform sustained fitness activity
To be able to perform a variety of folk dances
To understand the social significance of folk dances

Equipment Required:
Equipment and music for Challenge Course
Music for rhythmic activities
Cageball and 15 foam balls (8")
Pinnies

Instructional Activities	Teaching Hints

Introductory Activity -- European Running with Variations

Students move around the area to the beat of a tambourine. The step is a trot with the knees lifted. Emphasize proper spacing and moving rhythmically. Stop on a double beat of the tambourine. Try some of the following variations:
1. Clap hands on every fourth beat.
2. Stamp foot on every second beat.
3. On signal, make a complete turn using four running steps.
4. On signal, stop, pivot and move in the opposite direction.
5. Let a student lead the class through various formations.

Have the leader move in different shapes and designs. Have class freeze and see if they can identify the shape or formation.

At times, stop the drumbeat and have the class continue running. Challenge them to maintain the rhythm with their feet. Avoid the tendency to speed the rhythm.

Fitness Development Activity – Challenge Course

Design a course around the perimeter of the area using some of the following ideas:
1. Step on jumping box, dismount to tumbling mat, and do a forward roll.
2. Run and weave through four wands held upright by cones.
3. Handwalk across a horizontal ladder or do a flexed-arm hang from a climbing rope for 5 seconds.
4. Step on and off three jumping boxes (small-large-small)
5. Agility run through hoops.
6. Perform jump turns
7. Leap over a magic rope held taut with two chairs or jumping boxes.
8. Hop on one foot.
9. Do a log roll across a tumbling mat.
10. Alternate going over and under six obstacles (cones and wands or hoops)
11. Crouch jump or scooter movements the length of a balance-beam bench.
12. Slide through a parallel tumbling mat maze (mats stood on their sides)

Use taped intervals of music and silence. When the music is playing students travel through the challenge course. When the music stops, youngsters do some stretching and strength development exercises. This gives them a chance to recover aerobically.

Distribute students throughout the course rather than lining them up at a starting point. Faster moving students can pass on the outside.

Change directions periodically to prevent a build-up of students at one station.

Lesson Focus -- Rhythmic Movement Skills (2)

Make dances easy for students to learn by implementing some of the following techniques:
Rhythms should be taught like other sport skills. Avoid striving for perfection so students know it is acceptable to make mistakes. Teach a variety of dances rather than one or two in depth in case some students find it difficult to master a specific dance.
1. Teach the dances without using partners.
2. Allow youngsters to move in any direction without left-right orientation.
3. Use scattered formation instead of circles.
4. Emphasize strong movements such as clapping and stamping to increase involvement.
5. Play the music at a slower speed when first learning the dance.

Hora (Hava Nagila) (Israeli)

Music Source: WWCD-3528; WWC-3528
Formation: Single circle, facing center, hands joined. The circle can be partial.
Note: The hora is regarded as the national dance of Israel. It is a simple dance that expresses joy. The traditional hora is done in circle formation, with the arms extended sideward and the hands on the neighbors' shoulders. It is easiest to introduce the dance step individually. Once the step is learned, youngsters can join hands and practice the circle formation counterclockwise or clockwise. The clockwise version is presented here.

Directions:

Measures Action

1--3   Step left on the left foot. Cross the right foot in back of the left, with the weight on the right. Step left on the left foot and hop on it, swinging the right foot forward. Step-hop on the right foot and swing the left foot forward. The same step is repeated over and over. (Side, behind, side, swing; Side, swing)

The circle may move to the right also, in which case the same step is used, but the dancers begin with the right foot.

Limbo Rock

Music Source: WWCD-4903

Formation: Single circle or scattered

Directions:

Measures Part I Action

1--2   Touch left foot in. Touch left foot out. Three steps in place. (In, out, left, right, left)

3--4   Repeat measures 1 and 2 beginning with opposite foot. (In, out, right, left, right)

5--8   Repeat measures 1--4.

Measures Part II Action

9--10   Swivel toes right, swivel heels right. Repeat and straighten feet. (Swivel, 2, 3, straighten)

11--12   Repeat beats 1 and 2 beginning with swivel toes left.

13--14   Jump in, clap; jump out, clap. (Jump, clap, jump, clap)

15--16   Repeat measures 13 and 14. Variation:

Teton Mountain Stomp (American)

Music Source: WWCD-FDN

Formation: Single circle of partners in closed dance position, partners A facing counterclockwise, partners B facing clockwise

Directions:

Measures Action

1--4   Step to the left toward the center of the circle on the left foot, close right foot to the left, step again to the left on the left foot, stomp right foot beside the left but leave the weight on the left foot. Repeat this action, but start on the right foot and move away from the center. (Side, close; Side, stomp; Side, close; Side, stomp)

5--8   Step to the left toward the center on the left foot; stomp the right foot beside the left. Step to the right away from the center on the right foot, and stomp the left foot beside the right. In "banjo" position (modified closed position with right hips adjacent), partner A takes four walking steps forward while partner B takes four steps backward, starting on the right foot. (Side, stomp, side, stomp; Walk, 2, 3, 4)

9--12   Partners change to sidecar position (modified closed position with left hips adjacent) by each making a one half turn to the right in place, A remaining on the inside and B on the outside. A walks backward while B walks four steps forward. Partners change back to banjo position with right hips adjacent by each making a left-face one half turn; then they immediately release from each other. A walks forward four steps to meet the second B approaching, while B walks forward four steps to meet the second A approaching. (Change, 2, 3, 4; New partner, 2, 3, 4)

13--16   New partners join inside hands and do four two-steps forward, beginning with A's right foot and B's left. (Step, close, step; Repeat four times)

D'Hammerschmiedsgselln (Bavarian)

Music Source: WWCD-TC1; WWC-TC1

Skills: Clapping routine, step-hops

Formation: Circle of four

Directions: Translated, the title of the dance means "The Journey Blacksmith."

Measures Action

1–16   First opposites do a clapping pattern beginning on the first count of measure 1, while the other pair does a clapping pattern beginning on the first count of measure 2. The six-count pattern is performed as follows: With both hands, slap own thighs (count 1), slap own chest (count 2), clap own hands (count 3), clap right hands (count 4), clap left hands (count 5), and clap opposite's hands (count 6). (Thighs, chest, together, right, left, both) Repeat the six-count pattern seven additional times.

Part I

17–24   Join hands and circle left with eight step-hops. (Step-hop, 2-hop, ... 8-hop)

25–32   Circle right in the same manner. (Step-hop, 2-hop, ... 8-hop)

33–48   Repeat the chorus action.

Part II—Star

49–56   Right-hand star with eight step-hops. (Step-hop, 2-hop, ... 8-hop)

57–64   Left-hand star in the same manner. (Step-hop, 2-hop, ... 8-hop)

65–80   Repeat the chorus action.

Part III—Big Circle

81–88   Circles of four open to form one large circle, and circle left with eight step-hops. (Step-hop, 2-hop, ... 8-hop)

89–96   Reverse direction, continuing with eight step-hops. (Step-hop, 2-hop, ... 8-hop)

Variation: As a mixer, try the following sequence.

Measures Action

1–16   Use the chorus clapping pattern described.

17–24   As in Part I or II, circle left, or do a right-hand star with step-hops (or simple walking steps).

25–32   Do eight step-hops with the corner in general space or in any comfortable position, progressing anywhere.

Repeat the entire sequence with a new foursome.

Doudlebska Polka (Czechoslovakian)

Music Source: WWCD-572; WWC-572

Skills: Polka step, walking, clapping pattern

Formation: Make either one large circle or several smaller circles scattered around the floor. The following description is for one large circle.

Directions:

Measures Part I Action

1–16   Partners assume the Varsouvienne position and do 16 polka steps around the circle, one couple following another. (Polka, 2, 3, ... 16)

Part II Action

17–32   Partner A puts the right arm around partner B's waist as they stand side by side, while B puts the left hand on A's right shoulder. A puts the left hand on the shoulder of the A in front. This closes the circle. Partners A move sideward to the center to catch up with the A ahead. In this position, all march forward counterclockwise and sing loudly, "La, la, la," and so forth. This takes 32 walking steps. (Walk, 2, 3, ... 32)

Part III Action

33–48   Partners A face the center, and partners B drop behind their partner. Bs turn to face the other way, clockwise, and polka around the circle (around the As) with their hands on hips. At the same time, As, who face center, clap a rhythm as follows: Clap hands twice, then extend both hands, palms outward, toward the neighbor on each side, and clap hands once with the neighbor. Repeat this pattern over and over. For variation, As may slap a thigh occasionally, or duck down, or cross their arms when clapping the neighbor's hand. (As: Clap, clap, out; Repeat 16 times) (Bs: Polka, 2, 3, ... 16)

At the end of Part III, partners A turn around, take whichever partner B is behind them, and resume the dance from the beginning. If some children are without a partner, they move to the center and thus find a partner.

Extra children can enter the dance during the clapping part for partners A, and some can join the ring to polka around the outside. Those left without a partner wait for the next turn. When the group is large, several circles can be made, and it is perfectly proper for unpartnered children to steal into another circle. The polka in this case is done anywhere around the room. During the march, make circles of any number of people.

Kalvelis (Little Blacksmith) (Lithuanian)

Music Source: WWCD-WOF3

Skills: Polka step, swing, clapping pattern, grand right and left

Formation: Single circle of couples facing center, partner B on partner A's right, all hands joined in a single circle with the right foot free.

Directions:

Measures Part I Action

1–8   Circle right with seven polka steps, ending with three stamps. (Circle and, 2 and, 3 and, 4 and, 5 and, 6 and, 7 and, stamp, stamp, stamp)

9–16   Circle left with seven polka steps, ending with three stamps. (Circle and, 2 and, 3 and, 4 and, 5 and, 6 and, 7 and, stamp, stamp, stamp)

Chorus

1–2   Clap own hands four times, alternating, left hand onto own right, then right hand onto own left. (Clap, 2, 3, 4)

3–4   Right elbow swing with four skips. (Swing, 2, 3, 4)

5–6   Repeat the clapping pattern of measures 1 and 2. (Clap, 2, 3, 4)

7–8   Left elbow swing with four skips. (Swing, 2, 3, 4)

9–16   Repeat the pattern of measures 1–8.

Part II Action

1–8   Partners B dance three polka steps forward toward the center, ending with three stamps. They then turn to face their partner and return to place with three polka steps forward, ending with three stamps, facing center again. (Step-close-step-hop; Step-close-step-hop; Step-close-step-hop; Stamp, stamp, stamp)

9–16   Partners A repeat the pattern of measures 1–8, but dance more vigorously, stamping on the first beat of each measure. (Step-close-step-hop; Step-close-step-hop; Step-close-step-hop; Stamp, stamp, stamp)

Chorus

1–16   As described above.

Part III Action

1–16   Grand right and left around the circle with 16 polka steps, meeting a new partner on the last measure. (Step-close-step-hop; Repeat 16 times)

Chorus

1–16   As described, but with a new partner.

Game Activity

Cageball Target Throw

Supplies: A cageball or large beachball (18- to 30-in.), 15 foam balls (8")

Skill: Throwing

An area about 20 ft wide is marked across the center of the playing area, with a cageball in the center. The object of the game is to throw the foam balls against the cageball, thus forcing it across the line in front of the other team. Players may come up to the line to throw, but they may not throw while inside the cageball area. A player may enter the area, however, to recover a ball. No one is to touch the cageball at any time, nor may the cageball be pushed with a ball in the hands of a player. If the cageball seems to roll too easily, it should be deflated slightly.

Chain Tag

Supplies: None

Skills: Running, dodging

Two parallel lines are established at opposite ends of the playing area. Two groups of three players form a chain with joined hands and occupy the center. The players with free hands on either end of the chain do the tagging. All other players line up on one of the parallel lines. The players in the center call "Come on over," and children cross from one line to the other. The chains try to tag the runners. Anyone caught joins the chain. When the chain grows to six players, it divides into two groups of three players.

Dynamic Physical Education for Elementary School Children
Basketball Skills (1)
Level III – Week 17

Objectives:
To learn the basic rules of basketball
To participate in a self-directed manner in basketball drills
To work with teammates in basketball lead-up games

Equipment Required:
One junior basketball or 8" foam ball for
   each student
Cones, signs and tape for Partner Aerobic
   and Resistance Exercises
Flags and Pinnies for lead-up games
Hoops or individual mats for lead-up
   games

Instructional Activities	Teaching Hints

Introductory Activity -- Dribble and Pivot

Students acquire a basketball or playground ball and begin dribbling around the area. On signal, they stop and pivot. On the command "go," they begin dribbling again.

Alternate right and left hands while dribbling.

Change the pivot foot every other time.

Fitness Development Activity -- Partner Aerobic Fitness and Resistance Exercises

Students find a partner and lead each other in aerobic activities. Partners switch leader and follower roles after each partner resistance exercise. This routine assumes that students have previous aerobic fitness experience. If not, the aerobic activities will have to be led by the teacher.

Bounce and Clap	25 seconds
Arm Curl-Up	45 seconds
Jumping Jack variations	25 seconds
Camelback	45 seconds
Lunge variations	25 seconds
Fist Pull apart	45 seconds
Directional Runs	25 seconds
Scissors	45 seconds
Rhythmic Running	25 seconds
Butterfly	45 seconds
Bounce with Body Twist	25 seconds
Resistance Push-Up	45 seconds

Walk, stretch and relax for a minute or two.

Tape alternating segments of silence and music to signal duration of exercise. Music segments indicate aerobic activity (25 seconds) while intervals of silence announce partner resistance exercises (45 seconds).

Teach the exercises first; See Chapter 12 for complete descriptions. A sign with aerobic activities on one side and partner resistance exercises on the other help students remember the activities. The signs can be held upright by cones and shared by 2-4 students.

Take 6-10 seconds to complete a resistance exercise.

Lesson Focus -- Basketball Skills, Drills, and Lead-Up Games (1)

Skills

Practice the following skills:

1. Chest (or Two-Hand) Pass

   For the chest, or two-hand, pass, one foot is ahead of the other, with the knees flexed slightly. The ball is released at chest level, with the fingers spread on each side of the ball. The elbows remain close to the body, and the ball is released by extending the arms and snapping the wrists as one foot moves toward the receiver.

2. Catching

   Receiving the ball is a most important fundamental skill. Many turnovers involve failure to handle a pass properly. The receiver should move toward the pass with the fingers spread and relaxed, reaching for the ball with elbows bent and wrists relaxed. The hands should give as the ball comes in.

3. Dribbling

   Dribbling is used to advance the ball, break for a basket, or maneuver out of a difficult situation. The dribbler's knees and trunk should be slightly flexed, with hands and eyes forward. The fingertips propel the ball with the hand cupped and relaxed. There is little arm motion. Students tend to slap at the ball rather than push it. The dribbling hand should be alternated.

Instructional cues help students focus on proper performance of passing.
1. Fingers spread with thumbs behind the ball.
2. Step forward, extend arms, and rotate hands slightly inward.
3. Throw at chest level to the receiver.
4. For bounce passes, bounce the ball past the halfway point nearer the receiver.

Instructional cues for catching include the following:
1. Move into the path of the ball.
2. Spread the fingers and catch with the fingertips.
3. Reach and give with the ball (absorb the force of the ball by reaching and bringing the ball to the chest).

4. Shooting - One-Hand (set) Push Shot

The one-hand push shot is used as a set shot for young children. The ball is held at shoulder-eye level in the supporting hand with the shooting hand slightly below center and behind the ball. As the shot begins, the supporting (nonshooting) hand remains in contact as long as possible. The shooting hand then takes over with fingertip control, and the ball rolls off the center three fingers. The hand and wrist follow through, finishing in a flexed position. Vision is focused on the hoop during the shot. Proper technique should be emphasized rather than accuracy.

Drills

Passing and Catching Drills

1. Slide Circle Drill

In the slide circle drill, a circle of four to six players slides around a person in the center. The center person passes to and receives from the sliding players. After the ball has gone around the circle twice, another player takes the center position.

2. Circle-Star Drill

With only five players, a circle-star drill is particularly effective. Players pass to every other player, and the path of the ball forms a star. The star drill works well as a relay. Any odd number of players will cause the ball to go to all participants, assuring that all receive equal practice.

Dribbling Drills

3. Random Dribbling

Each child has a ball. Dribbling is done in place, varied by using left and right hands. Develop a sequence of body positions (i.e., standing, kneeling, lying on the side, on two feet and one hand). Dribble with each hand.

4. One-Hand Control Drill

Begin with the right hand holding the ball. Make a half circle around the right leg to the back. Bounce the ball between the legs (back to front) and catch it with the right hand and move it around the body again. Change hands.

5. Obstacle, or Figure-Eight, Dribbling

For obstacle, or figure-eight, dribbling, three or more obstacles are positioned about 5 feet apart. The first player at the head of each file dribbles in and around each obstacle, changing hands so that the hand opposite the obstacle is the one always used.

Dribbling and Pivoting Drills

6. File Drill

For the file drill, each player in turn dribbles forward to a designated line, stops, pivots, faces the file, passes back to the next player, and runs to a place at the end of the line. The next player repeats the pattern.

7. Dribble-and-Pivot Drill

For the dribble-and-pivot drill, players are scattered by pairs around the floor. One ball is required for each pair. On the first whistle, the front player of the pair dribbles in any direction and fashion on the court. On the second whistle, she stops and pivots back and forth. On the third whistle, she dribbles back and passes to the partner, who immediately dribbles forward, repeating the routine.

Shooting Drills

8. Basic Shooting Drill

In one simple shooting drill, players form files of no more than four people, and take turns shooting a long and a short shot or some other prescribed series of shots.

9. Set-Shot Drill

In the set-shot drill, players are scattered around a basket in a semicircle, with a leader in charge. Players should be close enough to the basket so that they can shoot accurately. The leader passes to each in turn to take a shot. The leader chases the ball after the shot.

Instructional cues for dribbling include the following:
1. Push the ball to the floor. Don't slap it.
2. Push the ball forward when moving.
3. Eyes forward and head up.

Shooting instructional cues focus on proper form:
1. Keep the shooting elbow near the body.
2. Bend the knees and use the legs.
3. Release the ball off the fingertips.

Baskets should be lowered to 8 or 9 feet, depending on the size of the youngsters.

Lowered baskets help students shoot with proper form. Shooting is not a throw. If students have to throw the ball at the basket, it is too high.

Practice the skills in an individual manner as much as possible. The best alternative is a ball for every student to shoot and dribble. Reduce taking turns as much as possible when practicing skills.

Use junior basketballs or smaller for third and fourth grade students. It is difficult for students to learn skills with regulations size balls. They are too heavy and to large in diameter for youngsters.

Flag Dribble

Supplies: A junior basketball and a flag for each player

Skill: Dribbling

The object is to eliminate other players and avoid being eliminated. Players are eliminated if they lose control of the ball, if their flag is pulled, or if they go out of bounds. Keeping control of the ball by dribbling is interpreted to mean continuous dribbling without missing a bounce. A double dribble (both hands) is regarded as a loss of control.

Start the game with players scattered around the area near the sidelines. Each has a ball, and all have flags tucked in the back of their belts. On signal, all players begin to dribble in the area. While keeping control of the dribble and staying in bounds, they attempt to pull a flag from any other player's back. When players lose control, they move to the perimeter of the area and practice their dribbling skills. As soon as the game is down to a few players, start the game over. Sometimes two players lose control of their basketball at about the same time. In this case, both are eliminated.

Variations:

1. If using flags is impractical, the game can be played without this feature. The objective then becomes to knock aside or deflect the other basketballs while retaining control of one's own ball.

2. Flag Dribble can be played with teams or squads. In this case, each squad or team is clearly marked.

Captain Basketball

Supplies: A junior basketball, pinnies

Skills: All basketball skills except shooting

A captain's area is laid out by drawing a line (or placing a tumbling mat) between the two foul restraining lines 4 feet out from the end line. The captain must keep one foot in this area. Captain Basketball is more like regulation basketball than Captain Ball. Captain Ball limits the movements of the forwards. Captain Basketball brings in more natural passing and guarding situations without the movement restrictions on the forwards.

A team typically is composed of three forwards, one captain, and four guards. The captain must keep one foot in her area under the basket. The game is started with a jump ball, after which the players advance the ball as in basketball. No player may cross the centerline, however. The guards must bring the ball up to the centerline and throw it to one of their forwards. The forwards maneuver and attempt to pass successfully to the captain. A throw by one of the forwards to the captain scores 2 points; a free throw scores 1 point.

Fouls are the same as in basketball. In addition, stepping over the centerline or a guard stepping into the captain's area draws a foul. In the case of a foul, the ball is given to a forward at the free-throw line. She is unguarded and has 5 seconds to pass successfully to the captain, who is guarded by one player. The ball is in play if the free throw is unsuccessful.

Use a folding tumbling mat to designate the captain's area at each end of the court to discourage intrusion by guards. Even though players are required to remain in their own half of the court, they should be taught to move freely within that area. Short, quick passes should be stressed, because long passes are often ineffective. Captain Basketball offers the chance for practicing proper guarding techniques.

Sideline Basketball

Supplies: A junior basketball, pinnies

Skills: All basketball skills

Divide the class into two teams, each lined up along one side of the court, facing the other. Three or four active players from each team enter the floor to play regulation basketball. The remainder of the players, who stand on the sideline, can catch and pass the ball to the active players. Sideline players may not shoot, nor may they enter the playing floor. They must keep one foot completely out of bounds at all times.

The active players play regulation basketball, with the addition that they must pass and receive the ball three times from sideline players before they can attempt a goal. Sideline players may pass to each other but must pass back to an active player after three sideline passes. The game starts with active players occupying their half of the court. The ball is taken out of bounds under its own basket by the team that was scored on. Play continues until a period of time (1 minute) elapses. The active players then go to the end of their line and three new active players come out from the right. All other players move down and adjust to fill the space left by the new players.

No official out of bounds on the sides is called. The players on that side of the floor simply recover the ball and put it into play with a pass to an active player without delay. Out of bounds on the ends is the same as in regular basketball. If one of the sideline players enters the court and touches the ball, it is a violation, and the ball is awarded out of bounds on the other side to a sideline player of the other team. Free throws are awarded when a player is fouled.

Dynamic Physical Education for Elementary School Children
Basketball Skills (2)
Level III – Week 18

Objectives:
To learn the basic rules of basketball
To participate in a self-directed manner in basketball drills
To work with teammates in basketball lead-up games

Equipment Required:
Five hoops and 30 beanbags for Barker's Hoopla
Cones, signs, and tape for Partner Aerobics and Resistance Exercises
One junior basketball or 8" foam ball for each student
Pinnies for lead-up games

Instructional Activities	Teaching Hints

Introductory Activity -- Barker's Hoopla

Place one hoop in each of four corners and in the middle of a square playing area. A distance between hoops of 25-30 feet is challenging. Five or six beanbags are placed in each hoop. There are five teams, one beside each hoop (home base). The object is to take beanbags from other hoops and return them to the home base hoop.

Beanbags must be taken *out* of home base hoop and placed in other hoops. It is not acceptable to pass or throw beanbags. No more than one beanbag may moved at one time.

Fitness Development Activity -- Partner Aerobic Fitness and Resistance Exercises

Students find a partner and lead each other in aerobic activities. Partners switch leader and follower roles after each partner resistance exercise. This routine assumes that students have previous aerobic fitness experience. If not, the aerobic activities will have to be led by the teacher.

Bounce and Clap	25 seconds
Arm Curl-Up	45 seconds
Jumping Jack variations	25 seconds
Camelback	45 seconds
Lunge variations	25 seconds
Fist Pull apart	45 seconds
Directional Runs	25 seconds
Scissors	45 seconds
Rhythmic Running	25 seconds
Butterfly	45 seconds
Bounce with Body Twist	25 seconds
Resistance Push-Up	45 seconds

Walk, stretch and relax for a minute or two.

Tape alternating segments of silence and music to signal duration of exercise. Music segments indicate aerobic activity (25 seconds) while intervals of silence announce partner resistance exercises (45 seconds).

Teach the exercises first; See Chapter 12 for complete descriptions. A sign with aerobic activities on one side and partner resistance exercises on the other help students remember the activities. The signs can be held upright by cones and shared by 2-4 students.

Take 6-10 seconds to complete a resistance exercise.

Lesson Focus -- Basketball Skills, Drills, and Lead-Up Games (2)

Skills
Review previously learned skills (lesson #17) including: Chest and bounce passes, catching, dribbling and pivoting, and the one-hand set shot.

Introduce new skills:
1. Defending
   Defending involves bending the knees slightly, spreading the feet, and facing the opponent at a distance of about 3 feet. The weight should be distributed evenly on both feet to allow for movement in any direction. Sideward movement is done with a sliding motion. The defender should wave one hand to distract the opponent and to block passes and shots.
2. Lay-Up Shot
   The lay-up is a short shot taken when going in toward the basket either after receiving a pass or at the end of a dribble. In a shot from the right side, the takeoff is with the left foot, and vice versa. The ball is carried with both hands early in the shot and then shifted to one hand for the final push. The ball, guided by the fingertips, should be laid against the backboard with a minimum of spin.

Instructional cues for proper defending are:
1. Keep the knees bent.
2. Keep the hands up.
3. Don't cross the feet when moving.

Instructional cues for the lay-up shot are:
1. Take off on the foot opposite the shooting hand
2. Lay the ball on the backboard above the basketball.

3. Jump Shot

The jump should be straight up, rather than at a forward or backward angle. The ball should be released at the height of the jump. Since the legs cannot be used to increase the force applied to the ball, the jump shot is difficult for the majority of elementary school youngsters. It may be best to avoid teaching the shot to youngsters who lack enough strength to shoot the ball correctly and resort to throwing it. If the jump shot is presented, the basket should be at the lowest level available and a junior-sized basketball used to develop proper shooting habits.

3. Jump upward and slightly forward on the takeoff.

4. Two-Hand Overhead Pass

The two-hand overhead pass is effective against a shorter opponent. The passer is in a short stride position, with the ball held overhead. The momentum of the pass comes from a forceful wrist and finger snap. The pass should take a slightly downward path.

Another way to practice proper form with the jump shot is to use gray foam balls. They are light and can be shot easily by children. Concentrate on proper form rather than making baskets. Reinforce students who use good technique.

Drills

Review and introduce drills from last week's lesson (#17). Introduce the following new drills:

Jump-Shot Drill

The jump-shot drill is similar to the lay-up drill, except that the incoming shooter receives the ball, stops, and takes a jump shot. The line of shooters should move back so that there is room for forward movement to the shooting spot. As soon as the passer releases the ball to the shooter, he moves to the end of the shooter's line. The shooter goes to the passer's line after shooting

The jump shot drill may be inappropriate for less strong players. They can choose to shoot the lay-up shot in lieu of the jump shot.

Three Lane Rush Drill

This is a lead-up to the three-player weave, which is difficult for elementary school youngsters to learn. Youngsters are in three lines across one end of the area. The first three players move parallel down the court while passing the ball back and forth to each other. A lay-up shot can be taken as players near the basket.

1. Use chest and/or bounce passes.
2. "Lead" the receiver with the pass.
3. Follow your pass, going behind the receiver; then cut for basket, awaiting receipt of a pass.

Game Activity - Basketball Lead-Up Games

Captain Basketball

See the Lesson Plan, Basketball Skills (Week 17) for a complete game description.

Sideline Basketball

See the Lesson Plan, Basketball Skills (Week 17) for a complete game description.

Twenty-One

Supplies: A junior basketball

Skills: Shooting

Players are in file formation by teams. Each player is permitted a long shot (from a specified distance) and a follow-up shot. The long shot, if made, counts 2 points and the short shot counts 1 point. The follow-up shot must be made from the spot where the ball was recovered from the first shot. The normal one-two-step rhythm is permitted on the short shot from the place where the ball was recovered. The first player scoring a total of 21 points is the winner. If the ball misses the backboard and basket altogether on the first shot, the second shot must be taken from the corner.

Variations:

1. Start with a simpler game that allows dribbling before the second shot.
2. Allow players to shoot as long as every shot is made. This means that if both the long and the short shot are made, the player goes back to the original position for a third shot. All shots made count and the shooter can continue until a miss.
3. Play with team competition, with each player contributing to the team score.
4. Use various combinations and types of shots.

Lane Basketball

Supplies: Junior basketball, pinnies, cones to mark zones

Skills: All basketball skills

The court is divided into six lanes. Players must stay in their lane and cannot cross the midcourt line. Regular basketball rules prevail, with the exception that players cannot dribble more than three times. Play is started with a jump ball. At regular intervals, youngsters rotate to the next lane to assure they get to play offense and defense. A number of rule changes can be implemented to change the focus of the game. For example, three passes may be required before shooting may occur. Also, to increase the amount of activity, youngsters can move the entire length of the floor within their lane.

One-Goal Basketball

Supplies: A junior basketball, pinnies (optional)

Skills: All basketball skills

This is an excellent class activity if four or more baskets are available. The game is played by two teams according to the rules of basketball but with the following exceptions.

1. When a defensive player recovers the ball, either from the backboard or on an interception, the ball must be taken out beyond the foul-line circle before offensive play is started and an attempt at a goal is made.

2. After a basket is made, the ball is taken in the same fashion away from the basket to the center of the floor, where the other team starts offensive play.

3. Regular free throw shooting can be observed after a foul, or some use can be made of the rule whereby the offended team takes the ball out-of-bounds.

4. An offensive player who is tied up in a jump ball loses the ball to the other team.

5. Individuals are responsible for calling fouls on themselves.

Basketball Snatch Ball

Supplies: Two junior basketballs, two hoops

Skills: Passing, dribbling, shooting

Each of two teams occupies one side of a basketball floor. The players on each team are numbered consecutively from the right hand end of the line. Two balls are placed inside two hoops, one hoop on each side of the centerline. When the teacher calls three or more numbers, players from each team whose numbers were called run to the ball assigned them. These players pass and dribble to the basket on their right and try to make a basket. Three passes must be made and all players must handle the ball before a basket can be shot. As soon as a basket is made, the players pass and dribble back and place the ball in the hoop. The first team to return the ball after making a basket scores a point for that team. Use a system to keep track of the numbers so that all children have a turn. Numbers are called in any order.

Dynamic Physical Education for Elementary School Children
Basketball Skills (3)
Level III – Week 19

Objectives:
To run, stop, and pivot under control without falling
To learn the basic rules of basketball
To participate in a self-directed manner in basketball drills
To work with teammates in basketball lead-up games

Equipment Required:
Exercise to music tape
One junior basketball or 8" foam ball for
  each student
Pinnies for lead-up games

Instructional Activities	Teaching Hints

Introductory Activity -- Run, Stop and Pivot

The class runs, stops on signal and pivots. Vary the activity by pivoting on the left foot or the right foot, increasing the circumference, and performing pivots in quick succession. Teach both the stride stop (one foot in front of the other) and the jump stop (with both feet parallel to each other) prior to the pivot.

Emphasize bending the knees and lowering the center of gravity.

Students should continue running after the pivot.

Fitness Development Activity -- Exercises to Music

Forward Lunges	30 seconds	
Alternate Crab Kicks	25 seconds	
Windmills	30 seconds	
Walk and do Arm Circles	25 seconds	
Abdominal Crunchers	30 seconds	
Side Flex	25 seconds	
Triceps Push-Ups	30 seconds	
Two-Step or Gallop	25 seconds	
Jumping Jack variations	30 seconds	
Aerobic Jumping	25 seconds	
Leg Extensions	30 seconds	
Push-Ups	25 seconds	
Walking to cool down	30 seconds	

Select music that has a strong rhythm and easy-to-hear beat. When the music is on students perform aerobic activities (for 30 seconds). When the music is not playing, students perform the strength development and flexibility exercises (25 seconds).

See Chapter 12 of the textbook for descriptions of the exercises.

Use scatter formation.

Lesson Focus and Game Activity -- Basketball Skills and Lead-Up Games (3)

Since this is the third week of basketball, emphasis should be placed on playing basketball lead-up games. If necessary, review any skills and drills from the past two weeks of basketball instruction.

Sideline Basketball
See the Lesson Plan, Basketball Skills (Week 17) for a complete game description.

Flag Dribble
See the Lesson Plan, Basketball Skills (Week 17) for a complete game description.

One-Goal Basketball
See the Lesson Plan, Basketball Skills (Week 18) for a complete game description.

Basketball Snatch Ball
See the Lesson Plan, Basketball Skills (Week 18) for a complete game description.

Three-on-Three
Supplies: A junior basketball
Skills: All basketball skills

Three teams of three are assigned to a basket. The offensive team stands at the top of the key facing the basket. The defensive team starts at the free throw line. The remaining team waits for their turn beyond the end line. Regular basketball rules are used. The offensive team tries to score. The offensive team plays until they score or the ball is stolen by the defense. In either case, the defensive team moves to the center of the floor and becomes the offensive unit. The waiting team moves onto the floor and plays defense. The previous offensive team goes to the rear of the line of waiting players. Each team keeps its own score. A team wins when they score three points. Winning teams can be rotated to games at other baskets.

Dynamic Physical Education for Elementary School Children
Gymnastics Skills (2)
Level III – Week 20

Objectives:
To understand the principles of stability and balance
To control the body weight in a variety of tumbling and stunt activities
To participate in "one on one" competition and accept the outcome

Equipment Required:
Exercise to music tape
Beanbags, jump ropes, and playground balls
Tumbling mats
12 bowling pins

Instructional Activities	Teaching Hints
Introductory Activity -- Agility Run	
Pick two lines or markers 5 to 10 yards apart. Students run (or use other locomotor movements) back and forth between the lines for a specified time (10, 15, or 20 seconds). Students can add a personal challenge by seeing how many times they can move back and forth within the given time limit.	Students can try this with a partner they pick. They can race each other to the lines and back.
	Students can walk when necessary.

Fitness Development Activity -- Exercises to Music

Forward Lunges	30 seconds	Select music that has a strong rhythm and easy-to-hear beat. When the music is on students perform aerobic activities (for 30 seconds). When the music is not playing, students perform the strength development and flexibility exercises (25 seconds).
Alternate Crab Kicks	25 seconds	
Windmills	30 seconds	
Walk, do Arm Circles	25 seconds	
Abdominal Crunchers	30 seconds	
Side Flex	25 seconds	
Triceps Push-Ups	30 seconds	
Two-Step or Gallop	25 seconds	
Jumping Jack variations	30 seconds	See Chapter 12 of the textbook for descriptions of the exercises.
Aerobic Jumping	25 seconds	
Leg Extensions	30 seconds	
Push-Ups	25 seconds	Use scatter formation.
Walking to cool down	30 seconds	

Lesson Focus – Gymnastics Skills(2)

Tumbling and Inverted Balances
Judo Roll

For a left Judo Roll, stand facing the mat with the feet well apart and the left arm extended at shoulder height. Bring the arm down and throw the left shoulder toward the mat in a rolling motion, with the roll made on the shoulder and the upper part of the back. Reverse for a right Judo Roll. Both right and left Judo Rolls should be practiced. Later, a short run and a double-foot takeoff should precede the roll. The Judo Roll is essentially a Forward Roll with the head turned to one side. The point of impact is the back of one shoulder and the finish is a return to the standing position.
Cartwheel

Start with the body in an erect position, arms outspread and legs shoulder width apart. Bend the body to the right and place the right hand on the floor. Follow this, in sequence, by the left hand, the left foot, and the right foot. Perform with a steady rhythm. Each body part should touch the floor at evenly spaced intervals. The body should be straight and extended when in the inverted position. The entire body must be in the same plane throughout the stunt, and the feet must pass directly overhead.
Cartwheel and Round-Off

Practice the Cartwheel, adding a light run with a skip for a takeoff. To change to a Round-Off, place the hands somewhat closer together during the early Cartwheel action. Bring the feet together and make a quarter turn to land on both feet, with the body facing the starting point. A Backward Roll can follow the Round-Off.

Five groups of activities in this lesson ensure that youngsters receive a variety of experiences. Pick a few activities from each group and teach them alternately. For example, teach an individual stunt or two, then a tumbling skill or inverted balance, followed by a balance stunt, etc. Give equal time to each group of activities

Children who have difficulty with the Cartwheel should be instructed to concentrate on taking the weight of the body on the hands in succession. They need to get the feel of the weight support and later can concentrate on getting the body into proper position. After the class has had some practice in doing Cartwheels, a running approach with a skip can be added before takeoff.

Scatter tumbling mats throughout the area so that there is little standing in line waiting for a turn.

Advanced Forward and Backward Roll Combinations

Put together different combinations of Forward Rolls and Backward Rolls. The emphasis should be on choice, exploration, and self-discovery. Variations can involve different approaches, execution acts, and finishes.

Try the following variations of the Forward Roll.

1. Roll while holding the toes, heels, ankles, or a wand.
2. As above, but cross the hands.
3. Roll with hands on the knees or with a ball between the knees.

Try the following suggestions with the Backward Roll.

1. Begin with a Stiff-Legged Sitdown and go into the roll.
2. Roll to a finish on one foot only.
3. Roll with a ball between the knees.

Balance Stunts

Long Reach

Place a beanbag about 3 feet in front of a line. Keeping the toes behind the line, lean forward on one hand and reach out with the other hand to touch the beanbag. Recover in one clean, quick movement to the original position, lifting the supporting hand off the floor. Increase the distance of the bag from the line.

Toe Jump

Hold the left toes with the right hand. Jump the right foot through without losing the grip on the toes. Try with the other foot. (Teachers should not be discouraged if only a few can do this stunt; it is quite difficult.)

Front Seat Support

Sit on the floor, with the legs together and forward. Place the hands flat on the floor, somewhat between the hips and the knees, with fingers pointed forward. Push down so the hips come off the floor, with the weight supported on the hands and heels. Next, lift the heels and support the entire weight of the body on the hands for 3 to 5 seconds. (Someone can help the performer get into position by giving slight support under the heels.)

Individual Stunts

Walk-Through

From a front-leaning rest position, walk the feet through the hands, using tiny steps, until the body is fully extended with the back to the floor. Reverse the body to original position. The hands stay in contact with the floor throughout.

Jump-Through

Starting in a front-leaning rest position, jump the feet through the arms in one motion. Reverse with another jump and return to original position. The hands must push off sharply from the floor, so the body is high enough off the floor to allow the legs to jump under. (Some children may find it easier to swing a little to the side with one leg, going under the lifted hand)

Circular Rope Jump

Crouch down in a three-quarter knee bend, holding a folded jump rope in one hand. Swing the rope under the feet in a circular fashion, jumping it each time. Reverse the direction of the rope. Work from both right and left sides with either a counterclockwise or clockwise turn of the rope.

Bouncer

Start in a push-up position. Bounce up and down with the hands and feet leaving the ground at the same time. Try clapping while doing this. Move in various directions. Turn around.

Partner and Group Stunts

Two-Way Wheelbarrow

One child holds two wheelbarrows, but with one in front and one behind. The child secures the front wheelbarrow first in a normal wheelbarrow position. The back wheelbarrow assumes position by placing the ankles over the already established hand position of the holder.

Do not perform many repetitions of tumbling and inverted balances. For most children, limiting the number of forward or backward roll repetitions to four or five will prevent fatigue and injury.

No youngster should be expected to roll over if they fear getting hurt. In stunts and tumbling, it is important that the student decide if they are capable and confident enough to try the activity.

Youngsters can do many of the activities around their mats. Many of the activities in this unit do not have to be performed on the mat.

A major concern for safety is the neck and back region. Overweight children are at greater risk and might be allowed to avoid tumbling and inverted balances.

Circular Rope Jump Variations:

1. Perform the rope jump with a partner.
2. Jump using different foot patterns (e.g., one foot or alternate feet) and using slow and fast time.
3. Establish standards for declaring a class champion in different areas. Some categories could be maximum number of turns in 30 seconds, most unique routine, and most jumps without a miss.

Partner Rising Sun

Partners lie facedown on the floor, with heads together and feet in opposite directions. They hold a volleyball or a basketball (or a ball of similar size) between their heads. Working together, they stand up and return to position while retaining control of the ball. Do not touch the ball with the hands.

Triple Roll

Three children get down on their hands and knees on a mat, with heads all in the same direction to one of the sides. The performers are about 4 feet apart. Each is numbered---1, 2, or 3---with the number 1 child in the center. Number 2 is on the right and number 3 is on the left. Number 1 starts rolling toward and under number 2, who projects upward and over number 2. Number 2 is then in the center and rolls toward number 3, who projects upward and over number 2. Number 3, in the center, rolls toward and under number 1, who, after clearing number 3, is back in the center. Each performer in the center thus rolls toward and under the outside performer.

Combatives

Palm Push

Starting Position: Contestants face each other, standing 12 inches apart. They place the palms of their hands together and must keep them together throughout the contest.

Action: Try to push the opponent off balance.

Bulldozer

Starting Position: Opponents are on their hands and feet (not knees), facing each other, with right shoulders touching.

Action: Try to push (not bump) each other backward. Pushing across the mat or across a restraining line determines the winner. Change shoulders and repeat.

Breakdown

Starting Position: Opponents are in a front-leaning rest (push-up) position, facing each other.

Action: Using one hand, try to break down the other's position by pushing or dislodging his support while maintaining your own position.

Elbow Wrestle

Starting Position: Contestants lie on the floor or sit at a table and face each other. Their right hands are clasped, with right elbows bent and resting on the surface, and right forearms pressed against each other.

Action: Force the other's arm down while keeping the elbows together. Raising the elbow from the original position is a loss.

Partner Rising Sun: A slightly deflated ball works best. Some caution is necessary to prevent bumping heads if the ball is suddenly squeezed out.

Triple Roll: Children should be taught that as soon as they roll to the outside, they must get ready to go over the oncoming child from the center. There is no time for delay. The upward projection of the body to allow the rolling child to go under is important.

When doing combatives, consider the following instructional procedures:

Safety factors must be emphasized. Youngsters should be matched for size; a common method is to ask students to pair up with someone who is similar in height. The length of bouts should be short--- usually 5--7 seconds of contesting is adequate. Children should freeze immediately when the whistle is blown.

Instructions for the contest should be as explicit as necessary. Starting positions should be defined so that both contestants begin in an equal and neutral position. What constitutes a win and the number of trials permitted should be defined.

Develop a system of rotation, so that youngsters have more than one opponent. Rotating assures that one child will not continually dominate another.

Game Activity

Pin Knockout

Supplies: Many playground balls, 12 bowling pins

Skills: Rolling, dodging

Two teams of equal number play the game. Each team is given many playground balls and six bowling pins. A court with a centerline is needed. The size of the court depends on the number of children in the game. The object of the game is to knock down all of the opponents' bowling pins. The balls are used for rolling at the opposing team's pins. Each team stays in its half of the court.

A player is eliminated if any of the following occurs:

1. He is touched by any ball at any time, regardless of the situation (other than picking up a ball).

2. She steps over the centerline to roll or retrieve a ball. (Any opposing team member hit as a result of such a roll is not eliminated.)

3. He attempts to block a rolling ball with a ball in his hands and the rolling ball touches him in any manner.

A foul is called when a player holds a ball longer than 10 seconds without rolling at the opposing team. The ball must be immediately given to the opposing team. The bowling pins are placed anywhere in the team's area. Players may guard the pins, but must not touch them. When a pin is down, even if a member of the defending team knocked it over unintentionally, it is removed immediately from the game. The game is over when all pins on one side have been knocked down.

Over the Wall

Supplies: None

Skills: Running, dodging

Two parallel goal lines are drawn about 60 feet apart. Two additional parallel lines about 3 feet apart are laid out parallel to the goal lines in the middle of the game area. This is the wall. Two or 3 players are it and stand on the wall. All of the other players are behind one of the goal lines. The tagger calls "Over the wall." All of the players must then run across the wall to the other goal line. The taggers try to tag any crossing player. Anyone caught helps catch the others. Players also are considered caught when they step on the wall. They must clear it with a leap or a jump and cannot step on it anywhere, including on the lines. After crossing over to the other side safely, players wait for the next call. The game can be made more difficult by increasing the width of the wall. Taggers can step on or run through the wall at will.

Dynamic Physical Education for Elementary School Children
Hockey Skills (1)
Level III – Week 21

Objectives:
To lead other students through warm-up activities
To learn hockey skills and apply them in lead-up games
Accept decisions made by game officials in hockey lead-up activities
To play group games and cooperate with teammates

Equipment Required:
Music for Continuity Drills
One individual jump rope for each
    student
Hockey stick and puck (fleeceball) for
    each student
Cones or tumbling mats for goals

Instructional Activities	Teaching Hints

Introductory Activity -- Rubber Band

Students begin from a central point with the teacher. On signal, students move away from the teacher with a designated movement such as run, hop sideways, skip backward, double-lame dog, or Carioca. On signal, they sprint back to the central point.

An alternative way of doing rubber band is to give students 5 seconds to see how far they can move. On signal, they return and see if they reach the original point in 5 seconds.

Fitness Development Activity -- Continuity Drills

Rope jumping—forward	25 seconds	
Double Crab Kick	30 seconds	
Rope jumping—backward	25 seconds	
Knee Touch Curl-Up	30 seconds	
Jump and turn body	25 seconds	
Push-Ups	30 seconds	
Rocker Step	25 seconds	
Bend and Twist	30 seconds	
Swing -Step forward	25 seconds	
Side Flex	30 seconds	
Free jumping	25 seconds	

Relax and stretch for a short time.

Make a tape with music segments (25 seconds) alternated with silence segments (30 seconds). When the music is playing, students jump rope; when silence occurs, students do a flexibility and strength development exercise.

Exercises can be done in two-count fashion. Exercises are done when the leader says "Ready." The class answers "One-two" and performs a repetition.

Allow students to adjust the workload to their level. This implies resting if the rope jumping is too strenuous.

Lesson Focus -- Hockey Skills (1)

Skills
Practice the following skills:

1. Gripping and carrying the stick.
   The hockey stick should be held with both hands and carried as low to the ground as possible. The basic grip puts the left hand at the top of the stick and the right hand 6 to 12 inches below the left.

2. Controlled Dribble.
   The controlled dribble consists of a series of short taps in the direction in which the player chooses to move. The hands should be spread 10 to 14 inches apart to gain greater control of the stick. As the player becomes more skilled, the hands can be moved closer together. The stick is turned so that the blade faces the ball. The grip should not be changed, but rather, the hands should be rotated until the back of the left hand and the palm of the right hand face the ball. The ball can then be tapped just far enough in front of the player to keep it away from the feet but not more than one full stride away from the stick.

3. Front Field.
   For the front field, the student must keep an eye on the ball, move to a point in line with its path, and extend the flat side of the blade forward to meet the ball. The faster the ball approaches, the more she must learn to give with the stick to absorb the momentum of the ball. The player should field the ball in front of the body and not permit it to get too close.

To ensure accuracy as well as safety, the stick must not be swung above waist height.

Dribbling instructional cues:
1. Control the puck. It should always be within reach of the stick.
2. Hold the stick firmly.
3. Keep the elbows away from the body.

Front fielding instructional cues:
1. Field with a "soft stick." This means holding the stick with relaxed hands.
2. Allow the puck to hit the stick and then "give" to make a soft reception.
3. Keep the hands apart on the stick.

4. Forehand Pass.

The forehand pass is a short pass that usually occurs from the dribble. It should be taught before driving, because the quick hit requires accuracy rather than distance. The player spreads the feet with toes pointed slightly forward when striking. Approach the ball with the stick held low and bring the stick straight back, in line with the intended direction of the hit. The hands should be the same distance apart as in the carrying position, and the stick should be lifted no higher than waist level. The player's right hand guides the stick down and through the ball. The head should be kept down with the eyes on the ball. A short follow-through occurs after contact.

5. Face-Off

The face-off is used at the start of the game, after a goal, or when the ball is stopped from further play by opposing players. Two players take the face-off, each facing a sideline, with their right sides facing the goal that their team is defending. Each player hits the ground on her side of the ball and the opponent's stick over the ball, alternately, three times. After the third hit the ball is played, and each player attempts to control the ball or to pass it to a teammate. The right hand can be moved down the stick to facilitate a quick, powerful movement. An alternate means of starting action is for a referee to drop the ball between the players' sticks.

6. Goalkeeping

The goalie may kick the ball, stop it with any part of the body, or allow it to rebound off the body or hand. He may not, however, hold the ball or throw it toward the other end of the playing area. The goalkeeper is positioned in front of the goal line and moves between the goal posts. When a ball is hit toward the goal, the goalie should attempt to move in front of the ball and to keep his feet together. This allows the body to block the ball should the stick miss it. After the block, the ball is passed immediately to a teammate.

Drills
The following drills can be used to practice the skills above:

1. Dribbling
    a. Each student has a stick and ball. On signal, change directions while maintaining control of the ball.
    b. Dribble and dodge imaginary tacklers or dodge around a set of cones. Partners may act as tacklers.
    c. Students in pairs--20 feet apart. One partner dribbles toward the other, goes around him or her, and returns to starting point. The first student then drives the ball to the second, who completes the same sequence.

2. Forehand Passing and Front Fielding
    a. From 8 to 10 feet apart, partners forehand pass and front field the ball back and forth to each other both from moving and stationary positions.
    b. Partners 20 feet apart--players pass the ball back and forth with emphasis on fielding and immediately hitting the ball back.
    c. The shuttle turn-back formation, in which two files of four or five players face each other, can be used. The first person in the file passes to the first person in the other file, who in turn fields the ball and returns the pass. Each player, when finished, goes to the end of the file.
    d. The downfield drill is useful for polishing passing and fielding skills while moving. Three files of players start at one end of the field. One player from each file proceeds downfield, passing to and fielding from the others until the other end of the field is reached. A goal shot can be made at this point. The players should remain close together for short passes until a high level of skill is reached.

3. Dodging and Tackling Drills
    a. Players are spread out on the field, each with a ball. On command, they dribble left, right, forward, and backward. On the command "Dodge," the players dodge an imaginary tackler. Players should concentrate on ball control and dodging in all directions.

Forehand passing instructional cues:
1. Approach the puck with the side facing the direction of the pass.

2. Keep the head down and eyes on the puck.
3. Keep the stick below waist level at all times.
4. Drive the stick through the puck.

Hockey is a rough game when children are not taught the proper methods of stick handling. They need to be reminded often to use caution and good judgment when handling hockey sticks.

Ample equipment increases individual practice time and facilitates skill development. A stick and a ball (puck) for each child are desirable.

If hockey is played on a gym floor, a plastic puck or yarn ball should be used. If played on a carpeted area or outdoors, a whiffle ball is used. An 8-foot folding mat set on end makes a satisfactory goal.

Hockey is a team game that is more enjoyable for all when the players pass to open teammates. Excessive control of the ball by one person should be discouraged.

An individual who is restricted to limited activity can be designated as a goalie. This is an opportunity for children with disabilities to participate and receive reinforcement from peers. An asthmatic child, for example, might serve as a goalkeeper.

b. Players work in pairs. One partner dribbles toward the other, who attempts to make a tackle. If the tackle is successful, roles are reversed. This drill should be practiced at moderate speeds in the early stages of skill development.

c. A three-on-three drill affords practice in many skill areas. Three players are on offense and three are on defense. The offense can concentrate on passing, dribbling, and dodging, while the defense concentrates on tackling. A point is given to the offense when they reach the opposite side of the field. The defensive team becomes the offensive team after a score.

If fatigue becomes a problem, use0 rotation and rest periods.

Game Activity – Hockey Lead-Up Games

Lane Hockey

Supplies: Hockey stick per player, puck, two goals
Skills: All hockey skills

The field is divided into eight lanes (see Chapter 25 for a diagram). A defensive and an offensive player are placed in each of the eight sections. A goalkeeper for each team is also positioned in front of the goal area. Players may not leave their lane during play. A shot on goal may not be taken until a minimum of two passes has been completed. This rule encourages looking for teammates and passing to someone in a better position before taking a shot on goal.

Encourage players to maintain their spacing during play. The purpose of the lanes is to force players to play a zone rather than swarming to the puck. Rules used for regulation hockey enforce situations not described here. A free hit (unguarded) is awarded a team if a foul occurs. Players should be rotated after a goal is scored or at regular time intervals.

Variation: Increase the number of lanes to 10 or 12. This involves a larger number of players. On a large playing area, the lanes may be broken into thirds rather than halves. Increase the number of passes that should be made prior to a shot on goal.

Goalkeeper Hockey

Supplies: One stick per player, a puck or ball
Skills: Passing, fielding, goalkeeping

Each team occupies two adjacent sides of the square (see Chapter 25 for a diagram). The puck or ball is placed in the center of the square. Team members are numbered consecutively from left to right. The instructor calls two or three numbers. These players enter the playing area and attempt to capture the ball and to pass it through the opposing team. A point is scored when the ball goes through the opponent's side. Sideline players are goalies and have the opportunity to practice goalkeeping skills. When a score is made, the active players return to their positions, and new players are called.

Keep track of the numbers called so all players have an equal opportunity to play. Different combinations of numbers can be called.

Sideline Hockey

Supplies: One hockey stick per player, a puck or ball, two 4-by-8-ft folding tumbling mats
Skills: Most hockey skills, except goaltending

Each team is divided into two groups. Three to six players from each team move onto the court; these are the active players. The others will actively participate on the sidelines. No goalkeeper is used. A face-off at the center starts the game and puts the ball into play after each score. Each team on the field, aided by the sideline players, attempts to score a goal. The sideline players help keep the ball in bounds and can pass it onto the court to the active players. Sideline players may pass to an active player or to each other.

Any out-of-bounds play on a sideline belongs to the team guarding that sideline and is immediately put into play with a pass. An out-of-bounds shot over the end line that does not score a goal is put into play by the team defending the goal. The group of players on the field changes places with the sideline players on their team as soon as a goal is scored or after a specified time period.

Illegal touching, sideline violations, and other minor fouls result in loss of the ball to the opposition. Roughing fouls and illegal striking should result in banishment to the sideline for the remainder of the competitive period. Try to encourage team play and passing strategies rather than having all players charge and swarm the puck. An effective rule is to require active players to make three passes to their teammates before taking a shot on goal. This makes all players an important part of the game.

Dynamic Physical Education for Elementary School Children
Hockey Skills (2)
Level III – Week 22

Objectives:
To keep away an object (puck) from opponents in three on three game
To strike a hockey puck so it travels in the desired direction
To understand the basic rules of hockey

Equipment Required:
Music for Continuity Drills
Hockey stick and puck for each student
Cones or tumbling mats for goals

Instructional Activities	Teaching Hints

Introductory Activity – Move and Exercise on Signal

Students do a locomotor movement, stop on signal and perform an exercise such as the following suggested activities: Push-Ups, Curl-Ups, Crab Kick, V-Ups, and Treadmills.

Use any locomotor movement. Students should get up and move as soon as they have completed the exercise.

Fitness Development Activity -- Continuity Drills

Rope jumping—forward	30 seconds	
Double Crab Kick	35 seconds	
Rope jumping—backward	30 seconds	
Knee Touch Curl-Up	35 seconds	
Jump and turn body	30 seconds	
Push-Ups	35 seconds	
Rocker Step	30 seconds	
Bend and Twist	35 seconds	
Swing -Step forward	30 seconds	
Side Flex	35 seconds	
Free jumping	30 seconds	

Relax and stretch for a short time.

Make a tape with music segments (25 seconds) alternated with silence segments (30 seconds). When the music is playing, students jump rope; when silence occurs, students do a flexibility and strength development exercise.

Exercises can be done in two-count fashion. Exercises are done when the leader says "Ready." The class answers "One-two" and performs a repetition.

Allow students to adjust the workload to their level. This implies resting if the rope jumping is too strenuous.

Lesson Focus -- Hockey Skills and Drills (2)

Since this is the final lesson of hockey, devote more time to playing hockey lead-up activities. For specific teaching hints, see the previous Lesson Plan, Week 21.

Skills

Review skills taught in previous lesson:
1. Gripping and carrying the stick.
2. Controlled dribble
3. Front Field
4. Forehand Pass
5. Face-off
6. Goalkeeping

Introduce new skills:

1. Tackling

The tackle is a means of taking the ball away from an opponent. The tackler moves toward the opponent with the stick held low. The tackle is timed so that the blade of the stick is placed against the ball when the ball is off the opponent's stick. The tackler then quickly dribbles or passes in the direction of the goal. Throwing the stick or striking carelessly at the ball should be discouraged. Players need to remember that a successful tackle is not always possible.

2. Dodging

Dodging is a means of evading a tackler and maintaining control of the ball. The player dribbles the ball directly at the opponent. At the last instant, the ball is pushed to one side of the tackler, depending on the direction the player is planning to dodge. If the ball is pushed to the left, the player should move around the right side of the opponent to regain control of the ball, and vice versa. Selecting the proper instant to push the ball is the key to successful dodging. Dodging should not be attempted if a pass would be more effective.

Introduce the following drills:
1. Three-on-Three Drill. Set up many goals and allow six students to work in small groups of three offensive and three defensive players.

2. Shooting Drill. Mats are set up as goals (three or four on each end of the floor). Half of class on each half of the floor. Each team attempts to hit pucks into opponents' goals without crossing centerline of gym. Use a large number of pucks.

3. Dodging and Tackling Drill. Players work in pairs. One partner dribbles toward the other, who attempts to make a tackle. If the tackle is successful, roles are reversed. This drill should be practiced at moderate speeds in the early stages of skill development.

Game Activity – Hockey Lead-Up Games

Sideline Hockey

See the Lesson Plan, Hockey Skills (Week 21) for a complete game description.

Regulation Elementary Hockey

Supplies: One stick per player, a puck or ball

Skills: All hockey skills

In a small gymnasium, the walls can serve as the boundaries. In a large gymnasium or on an outdoor field, the playing area should be delineated with traffic cones. The area should be divided in half, with a 12-ft restraining circle centered on the midline. This is where play begins at the start of the periods, after goals, or after foul shots. The official goal is 2 ft high by 6 ft wide, with a restraining area 4 ft by 8 ft around the goal to protect the goalie. Each team has a goalkeeper, who stops shots with her hands, feet, or stick; a center, who is the only player allowed to move full court and who leads offensive play (the center has her stick striped with black tape); two guards, who cannot go beyond the centerline into the offensive area and who are responsible for keeping the puck out of their defensive half of the field; and two forwards, who work with the center on offensive play and who cannot go back over the centerline into the defensive area.

A game consists of three periods of 8 minutes each, with a 3-minute rest between periods. Play is started with a face-off by the centers at midcourt. Other players cannot enter the restraining circle until the ball has been hit by the centers. The clock starts when the puck is put into play and runs continuously until a goal is scored or a foul is called. Substitutions can be made only when the clock is stopped. If the ball goes out-of-bounds, it is put back into play by the team that did not hit it last.

Whenever the ball passes through the goal on the ground, 1 point is scored. If, however, the ball crosses the goal line while in the air, it must strike against the mat or back wall to count for a score. Under no circumstances can a goal be scored on a foul. The puck can deflect off a player or equipment to score, but it cannot be kicked into the goal.

The goalkeeper may use her hands to clear the puck away from the goal, but she may not hold or throw it toward the other end of the playing area. She is charged with a foul for holding the puck. The goalkeeper may be pulled from the goal area but cannot go beyond the centerline. No other player may enter the restraining area without being charged with a foul.

The following are fouls and are penalized by loss of the puck at the spot of the foul.

1. Illegally touching the puck with the hands
2. Swinging the stick above waist height (called sticking)
3. Guards or forwards moving across the centerline
4. Player other than the goalie entering the restraining area
5. Goalie throwing the puck
6. Holding, stepping on, or lying on the puck

Defenders must be 5 yd back when the puck is put into play after a foul. If the spot where the foul occurred is closer than 5 yd to the goal, only the goalkeeper may defend. The puck is then put into play 5 yd directly out from the goal.

Personal fouls include any action or rough play that endangers other players. A player committing a personal foul must retire to the sidelines for 2 minutes. The following are personal fouls.

1. Hacking or striking with a stick
2. Tripping with either the foot or the stick
3. Pushing, blocking

Dynamic Physical Education for Elementary School Children
Gymnastics Skills (3)
Level III – Week 23

Objectives:

To understand the principles of stability and balance

To control the body weight in a variety of tumbling and stunt activities

To participate in "one on one" competition and accept the outcome

To play group games and cooperate with teammates

Equipment Required:

Aerobic fitness tape

Beanbags and wands

Tumbling mats

Cageball, four bowling pins and flags for game activities

Instructional Activities	Teaching Hints

Introductory Activity – Pyramid Power

Pyramid Power

Students move throughout the area. On signal, they find a partner and build a simple partner support stunt or pyramid (i.e., double bear, table, hip-shoulder stand, statue). On the next signal, pyramids are quickly and safely dismantled and students move again.

Select a partner of similar size.

Remind students to stand on the proper points of body support.

Fitness Development Activity -- Aerobic Fitness

The following aerobic movements are suggestions only. When youngsters begin to fatigue, stop the aerobic fitness movements and do some of the flexibility and strength development activities learned in previous lessons. This will allow students time to recover aerobically.

1. Rhythmic run with clap
2. Bounce turn and clap
3. Rhythmic 4-count curl-ups (knees, toes, knees, back)
4. Rhythmic Crab Kicks (slow time)
5. Jumping Jack combination
6. Double knee lifts
7. Lunges (right, left, forward) with single-arm circles (on the side lunges) and double-arms circles (on the forward lunge)
8. Rhythmic trunk twists
9. Directional run (forward, backward, side, turning)
10. Rock side to side with clap
11. Side leg raises (alternate legs)
12. Rhythmic 4-count push-ups (If these are too difficult for students, substitute single-arm circles in the push-up position.)

Use music to stimulate effort. Any combination of movements can be used.

Keep the steps simple and easy to perform. Some students will become frustrated if the learning curve is steep.

Signs that explain the aerobic activities will help students remember performance cues.

Don't stress or expect perfection. Allow students to perform the activities as best they can.

Alternate bouncing and running movements with flexibility and strength development movements.

Lesson Focus – Gymnastics Skills (3)

The following five groups of activities in this lesson ensure that youngsters receive a variety of experiences. Pick a few activities from each group and teach them alternately.

Tumbling and Inverted Balances

Headstand

Begin on a mat in a kneeling position, with hands placed about shoulder width apart and the fingers spread and pointed forward. Place the head forward of the hands, so that the head and hands form a triangle on the mat. Walk the body weight forward so that most of it rests on the hands and head. Go directly into a Headstand, using a kick-up to achieve the inverted position. Maintain the triangle position of the hands and the head. In the final inverted position, the feet should be together, with legs straight and toes pointed. The weight is evenly distributed among the three points---the two hands and the forward part of the head. The body should be aligned as straight as possible.

The safest way to come down from the inverted position is to return to the mat in the direction that was used in going up. Bending at both the waist and the knees helps recovery. The child should be instructed, in the case of overbalancing, to tuck the head under and go into a Forward Roll. Both methods of recovery from the inverted position should be included in the instructional sequences early in the presentation.

Spotting the Headstand: The spotter is stationed directly in front of the performer and steadies as needed. The spotter can first apply support to the hips and then transfer to the ankles as the climb-up position is lengthened into a Headstand. If unable to control the performer, the spotter must be alert to moving out of the way when the performer goes into a Forward Roll to come out of the inverted position.

Backward Roll Combinations

Review the Backward Roll. Continue emphasis on the Push-Off with the hands. Try some of the following combinations:

1. Do a Backward Roll to a standing position. A strong push by the hands is necessary to provide enough momentum to land on the feet.
2. Do two Backward Rolls in succession.
3. Do a Crab Walk into a Backward Roll.
4. Add a jump in the air at the completion of a Backward Roll.

Balance Stunts
Long Reach

Place a beanbag about 3 feet in front of a line. Keeping the toes behind the line, lean forward on one hand and reach out with the other hand to touch the beanbag. Recover in one clean, quick movement to the original position, lifting the supporting hand off the floor. Increase the distance of the bag from the line.

Toe Jump

Hold the left toes with the right hand. Jump the right foot through without losing the grip on the toes. Try with the other foot. (Teachers should not be discouraged if only a few can do this stunt; it is quite difficult.)

Individual Stunts
Pretzel

Touch the back of the head with the toes by raising the head and trunk and bringing the feet to the back of the head. Try first to bring the toes close enough to the head so the head-to-toe distance can be measured by another child with a handspan (the distance between the thumb and little finger when spread). If this distance is met, then try touching one or both feet to the back of the head.

Jackknife

Stand erect with hands out level to the front and a little to the side. Jump up and bring the feet up quickly to touch the hands. Vary by starting with a short run. Be sure the feet come up to the hands, rather than the hands moving down to the feet. Do several Jackknives in succession. The takeoff must be with both feet, and good height must be achieved.

Heel-and-Toe Spring

Place the heels against a line. Jump backward over the line while bent over and grasping the toes. (Lean forward slightly to allow for impetus and then jump backward over the line.) Try jumping forward to original position. To be successful, the child should retain the grasp on the toes. The teacher can introduce the stunt by first having children grasp their ankles when making the jumps. This is less difficult.

Single-Leg Circle (Pinwheel)

Assume a squatting position, with both hands on the floor, left knee between the arms and right leg extended to the side. Swing the right leg forward and under the lifted right arm, under the left leg and arm, and back to starting position. Several circles should be made in succession. Reverse position and try with the left leg.

Partner and Group Stunts
Quintuplet Roll

Five children can make up a roll series. They are numbered 1 through 5. Numbers 3 and 5 begin by going over numbers 2 and 4, respectively, who roll under. Number 1 goes over number 3 as soon as possible. Each then continues to go alternately over and under.

Dead Person Lift

One child lies on her back, with body stiff and arms at the sides. Two helpers stand, one on each side of the "dead" person, with hands at the back of the neck and fingers touching. Working together, they lift the child, who remains rigid, to a standing position. From this position, the child is released and falls forward in a Dead Body Fall.

Injured Person Carry

The "injured" child lies on the back. Six children, three on each side, kneel down to do the carry. The lifters work their hands, palms upward, under the person to form a human stretcher, and then lift up. (The "injured" child must maintain a stiff position.) They walk a short distance and set the person down carefully.

Merry-Go-Round

From 8 to 12 children are needed. Half of the children form a circle with joined hands, using a wrist grip. The remaining children drape themselves (each over a pair of joined hands) to become riders. The riders stretch out their bodies, faces up, toward the center of the circle, with the weight on the heels. Each rider then leans back on a pair of joined hands and connects hands, behind the circle of standing children, with the riders on either side. There are two sets of joined hands---the first circle, or merry-go-round, and the riders. The movement of the Merry-Go-Round is counterclockwise. The circle children, who provide the support, use sidesteps. The riders keep pace, taking small steps with their heels.

Combatives

Catch-and-Pull Tug-of-War

Starting Position: Two teams face each other across a line.

Action: Try to catch hold of and pull any opponent across the line. A player pulled across the line waits in back of the opposing team until time is called. The team capturing the most players wins.

Stick Twist

Starting Position: Contestants face each other with their feet approximately 12 inches apart. They hold a wand above their heads with both hands, the arms completely extended.

Action: On signal, try to bring the wand down slowly without changing the grip. The object is to maintain the original grip and not to let the wand twist in the hands. The wand does not have to be forced down, but rather should be moved down by mutual agreement. It can be moved down completely only if one player allows it to slip.

Toe Touch

Starting Position: Contestants form a large circle.

Action: On signal, try to step lightly on the opponent's toes (those on the left and right side) while not allowing the opponent to step on your toes. Keep score by counting the number of touches made.

Crab Contest

Starting Position: Both contestants are in crab position with seats held high.

Action: On signal, try, by jostling and pushing, to force the other's seat to touch the mat.

Game Activity

Star Wars

Supplies: Four bowling pins

Skill: Running

Four teams, each of which occupies one side, facing in, form a hollow square, about 10 yards on each side. Members of each team are numbered consecutively from right to left. This results in one person from each team having the same assigned number. When a number is called, four children with that number run to the right, around the square, and through their own vacated space to the center of the square. At the center four bowling pins are placed an equal distance from each team. The first child to lay a bowling pin down on the floor is the winner. The pins should be placed apart so collisions in the center can be avoided.

Scoring is kept by letters in the words Star Wars. The player who puts the pin down first gets receives two letters while the second player gets one letter. The first team to spell Star Wars is the winner and a new game begins. Since numbers are not called in order, keep a tally to make sure every number is called.

Flag Chase

Supplies: Flags, stopwatch

Skills: Running, dodging

The class is divided into two teams. One team wears flags positioned in the back of the belt. The flag team scatters throughout the area. On signal, the object is for the chasing team to capture as many flags as possible in a designated amount of time. The flags are placed in a box. Players cannot use their hands to ward off a chaser. Roles are reversed. The team pulling the most flags is declared the winner.

Jolly Ball

Supplies: A cageball 24 inches or larger (or a 36- to 48-inch pushball)

Skill: Kicking

Four teams are organized, each of which forms one side of a square. Children sit down, facing in, with hands braced behind them. The members of each team are numbered consecutively. Players wait until their number is called. Four active players (one from each team) move in crab position and try to kick the cageball over any one of the three opposing teams. The sideline players can also kick the ball. Ordinarily, the hands are not used, but can be allowed in the learning stages of the game.

A point is scored against a team that allows the ball to go over its line. A ball that goes out at the corner between teams is dead and replayed. After a short bout of time (10 to 20 seconds), the active children retire to their teams and another number is called. The team with the fewest points wins the game. This game is strenuous for the active players, so rotate them often. Two children from each team can be active at once.

Dynamic Physical Education for Elementary School Children
Track and Field Skills (1)
Level III – Week 24

Objectives:
To demonstrate activities designed to improve flexibility
To demonstrate proper starting techniques
To perform the scissors high jump properly

Equipment Required:
High jump equipment
Batons, stopwatches, and tape measures
Hurdles

Instructional Activities	Teaching Hints

Introductory and Fitness Development Activities—Stretching Activities

Combine the introductory and fitness activities during the track and field unit. This will help students understand how to stretch and warm up for demanding activity such as track and field.

Jog	1-2 minutes
Standing Hip Bend	30 seconds
Sitting Stretch	30 seconds
Partner Rowing	60 seconds
Bear Hug (20 seconds each leg)	40 seconds
Side Flex (20 seconds each leg)	40 seconds
Trunk Twister	30 seconds

Emphasis should be on jogging and stretching to prepare for strenuous activity.

See the textbook, chapter 12, for a description of exercises

Encourage smooth and controlled stretching. Hold each stretch for 6 to 10 seconds.

Lesson Focus -- Track and Field Skills (1)

Skills

Teach the following skills if students haven't learned them in earlier grades.

Standing Start

The standing start should be practiced, for this type of start has a variety of uses in physical education activities. Many children find it more comfortable than the sprinter's start. When practical, however, children should use the sprinter's start for track work. In the standing start, the feet should be in a comfortable half-stride position. An extremely long stride is to be avoided. The body leans forward so that the center of gravity is forward. The weight is on the toes, and the knees are flexed slightly. The arms can be down or hanging slightly back.

Sprinter's Start

"On your mark" position places the toe of the front foot from 4 to 12 inches behind the starting line. The thumb and first finger are just behind the line, with other fingers adding support. The knee of the rear leg is placed just opposite the front foot or ankle.

For the "Get set" position, the seat is raised so that it is nearly parallel to the ground. The knee of the rear leg is raised off the ground, and the shoulders are moved forward over the hands. The weight is evenly distributed over the hands and feet. The head is not raised, as the runner should be looking at a spot a few feet in front of the starting line.

On the "Go" signal, the runner pushes off sharply with both feet, with the front leg straightening as the back leg comes forward for a step. The body should rise gradually rather than pop up suddenly. The instructor should watch for a stumbling action on the first few steps. This results from too much weight resting on the hands in the "Get set" position.

Sprinting

In proper sprinting form, the body leans forward, with the arms swinging in opposition to the legs. The arms are bent at the elbows and swing from the shoulders in a forward and backward plane, not across the body. Forceful arm action aids sprinting. The knees are lifted sharply forward and upward and are brought down with a vigorous motion, followed by a forceful push from the toes.

The goal of track and field is self-improvement and developing proper techniques. Each student must accept responsibility for self-directed work and should be encouraged to try all activities.

The program should offer something for all---boys and girls, the highly skilled and the less skilled, and those with physical problems. Children with weight problems need particular attention. They must be stimulated and encouraged, since their participation will be minimal if little attention is paid to them. Special goals can be set for overweight children, and special events and goals can also be established for children with handicaps.

The long jump must be maintained properly. It should be filled with fresh sand of a coarse variety.

Baton Passing

The right hand to left hand method is the best choice for elementary school children as it is easy and offers a consistent method for passes. This pass allows the receiver to face the inside of the track while waiting to receive the baton in the left hand. The oncoming runner holds the baton in the right hand like a candle when passing it to a teammate. The receiver reaches back with the left hand, fingers pointing down and thumb to the inside, and begins to run as the runner advances to within 3 to 5 yards. The receiver grasps the baton and shifts it from the left to the right hand while moving. If the baton is dropped, it must be picked up, or the team is disqualified. An alternative way to receive the baton is to reach back with the hand facing up; however, the fingers-down method is considered more suitable for sprint relays.

Receivers can look over their shoulders to see the oncoming runner or can look forward in the direction of the run. Looking backward is called a visual pass and is slower than passing while looking forward (called a blind pass). However, there is a greater chance for error when the receiver is not looking backward and at the baton during the pass. The visual pass is recommended for elementary school children.

Distance Running

In distance running, as compared with sprinting, the body is more erect and the motion of the arms is less pronounced. Pace is an important consideration. Runners should try to concentrate on the qualities of lightness, ease, relaxation, and looseness. Good striding action, a slight body lean, and good head position are also important. Runners should be encouraged to strike the ground with the heel first and then push off with the toes.

If stop watches and tape measures are used, it is important to make them highly visible. Tie bright colored cord to them or anchor to cones to assure that they are not misplaced.

High Jumping - Scissors Jump

The scissors jump is by far the safest high jump and should be used for elementary school children when direct supervision is not available. For the scissors jump, the high-jump bar is approached from a slight angle. The takeoff is by the leg that is farther from the bar. The near leg is lifted and goes over, followed quickly in a looping movement by the rear leg. A good upward kick with the front leg, together with an upward thrust of the arms, is needed. The knees should be straightened at the highest point of the jump. The landing is made on the lead foot followed by the rear foot.

High-jump techniques are developed by practice. The bar should be at a height that offers challenge but allows concentration on technique rather than on height. Too much emphasis on competition for height quickly eliminates the poorer jumpers, who need the experience most.

Long Jump

For the running long jump, a short run is needed. The run should be timed so that the toes of the jumping foot contact the board in a natural stride. The jumper takes off from one foot and strives for height. The landing is made on both feet after the knees have been brought forward. The landing should be in a forward direction, not sideward.

A fair long jump takes off behind the scratch line. A foul (scratch) jump is called if the jumper steps beyond the scratch line or runs into or through the pit. Each contestant is given a certain number of trials (jumps). A scratch jump counts as a trial. Measurement is from the scratch line to the nearest point of touch.

Hop-Step-and-Jump

The hop-step-and-jump event is increasing in popularity, particularly because it is now included in Olympic competition. A takeoff board and a jumping pit are needed. The distance from the takeoff board to the pit should be one that even less skilled jumpers can make. The event begins with a run similar to that for the running long jump. The takeoff is with one foot, and the jumper must land on the same foot to complete the hop. He then takes a step followed by a jump. The event finishes like the long jump, with a landing on both feet. The pattern can be changed to begin with the left foot. A checkpoint should be used, as for the running long jump.

The jumper must not step over the takeoff board in the first hop, under penalty of fouling. Distance is measured from the front of the takeoff board to the closest place where the body touches. This is usually a mark made by one of the heels, but it could be a mark made by an arm or another part of the body if the jumper landed poorly and fell backward.

Hurdles

The hurdler should step so that the takeoff foot is planted 3 to 5 feet from the hurdle. The lead foot is extended straight forward over the hurdle; the rear (trailing) leg is bent, with the knee to the side. The lead foot reaches for the ground, quickly followed by the trailing leg. The hurdler should avoid floating over the hurdle. Body lean is necessary. A hurdler may lead with the same foot over consecutive hurdles or may alternate the leading foot. Some hurdlers like to thrust both arms forward instead of a single arm. A consistent step pattern should be developed.

Station (Small Group) Instruction

The teacher should instruct at a different station each day. Start at the station that demands the most instruction. Set up a system of rotation that assures all stations will be covered during the unit.

Make signs for each of the stations. The signs should include appropriate performance techniques, what is to be done at each station, and appropriate safety precautions.

Station 1
Starting and Sprinting
1. Front foot 4-12" behind line.
2. Thumb and first finger behind line, other fingers support.
3. Knee of other leg placed just opposite front foot.
4. On "get set," seat is raised, the down knee comes up a little, and the shoulders move forward over the hands.
5. On "go," push off sharply and take short, driving steps.

Hop-Step-and-Jump (Triple Jump)
1. Important to get the sequence and rhythm first, then later try for distance.
2. Sprinting.

Station 2
Running High Jump
1. Keep stretch rope low enough so all can practice.
2. Approach at 45°.
3. Good kick-up and arm action.

Baton Passing
1. Decide on method of passing.
2. Incoming runner passes with left hand to right hand of receiver.
3. After receiving, change to the left hand.
4. Estimate how fast to take off with respect to the incoming runner.

Station 3
Running Long Jump
1. Decide on jumping foot.
2. Establish checkpoint.
3. Control last four steps.
4. Seek height.

Standing Long Jump or Shuttle Relays

Station 4
Hurdling
1. At beginning, use one or two hurdles.
2. Leading foot is directly forward.

Practice Striding for Distance Running
1. Work on pace.
2. Easy, relaxed strides.

The goal of the program should be to allow students to develop at their own rate. The instructor needs to be perceptive enough to determine whether students are working too hard or too little. Special attention must be given to those who appear disinterested, dejected, emotionally upset, or withdrawn.

The high jump bar should be at a height that offers challenge but allows concentration on technique rather than on height. Too much emphasis on competition for height quickly eliminates the poorer jumpers, who need the experience most. Safety is of utmost importance. Using a flexible elastic rope as a crossbar and avoiding any type of flop will prevent injury. The practice of keeping the entire class together on a single high-jump facility is poor methodology. This arrangement determines who are the best jumpers in class but does little else.

Game Activity

Circular (Pursuit) Relays
Circular relays make use of the regular circular track. The baton exchange technique requires practice. On a 220-yard or 200-meter track, relays can be organized in a number of ways, depending on how many runners are spaced for one lap. Four runners can do a lap, each running one-quarter of the way; two can do a lap, each running one half of the distance; or each runner can complete a whole lap. In these races, each member of the relay team runs the same distance. Relays can also be organized so members run different distances.

Shuttle Relays
Because children are running toward each other, one great difficulty in running shuttle relays is control of the exchange. In the excitement, the next runner may leave too early, and the tag or exchange is then made ahead of the restraining line. A high-jump standard or cone can be used to prevent early exchanges. The next runner awaits the tag with an arm around the standard or a hand on a cone.

One on One Contests
Allow students to find a friend and have a number of personal contests in track and field events such as sprints, hurdling, high jump, and standing long jump.

Dynamic Physical Education for Elementary School Children
Track and Field Skills (2)
Level III – Week 25

Objectives:
To understand how to stretch prior to strenuous activity
To recognize the wide range of individual differences among peers
To enjoy one-on-one competition in track and field activities

Equipment Required:
High jump equipment
Batons, stopwatches, and tape measures
Hurdles

Instructional Activities	Teaching Hints
Introductory and Fitness Development Activities—Stretching Activities	
Combine the introductory and fitness activities during the track and field unit. This will help students understand how to stretch and warm up for demanding activity such as track and field.	Emphasis should be on jogging and stretching to prepare for strenuous activity.
Jog 1-2 minutes	
Standing Hip Bend 30 seconds	See the textbook, Chapter 12, for a
Sitting Stretch 30 seconds	description of exercises
Partner Rowing 60 seconds	
Bear Hug (20 seconds each leg) 40 seconds	Encourage smooth and controlled
Side Flex (20 seconds each leg) 40 seconds	stretching. Hold each stretch for 6 to 10
Trunk Twister 30 seconds	seconds.

Lesson Focus -- Track and Field Skills (2)

Skills
Introduce the following skills before proceeding to small group instruction.
Striding

In distance running, as compared with sprinting, the body is more erect and the motion of the arms is less pronounced. Pace is an important consideration. Runners should try to concentrate on the qualities of lightness, ease, relaxation, and looseness. Good striding action, a slight body lean, and good head position are also important. Runners should be encouraged to strike the ground with the heel first and then push off with the toes

Hurdling

Several key points govern good hurdling technique. The runner should adjust his stepping pattern so that the takeoff foot is planted 3 to 5 feet from the hurdle. The lead foot is extended straight forward over the hurdle; the rear (trailing) leg is bent, with the knee to the side. The lead foot reaches for the ground, quickly followed by the trailing leg. The hurdler should avoid floating over the hurdle. Body lean is necessary. A hurdler may lead with the same foot over consecutive hurdles or may alternate the leading foot. Some hurdlers like to thrust both arms forward instead of a single arm. A consistent step pattern should be developed.

Wands supported on blocks or cones can also be used as hurdles. Hurdles should begin at about 12 inches in height and increase to 18 inches. They should be placed about 25 feet apart.

Station (Small Group) Instruction
Review skills that were taught last week, if necessary. The teacher should instruct at a different station each day. Start at the station that demands the most instruction. Set up a system of rotation that assures all stations will be covered during the unit. Allow youngsters to work with a partner of somewhat equal ability. At each station, set out signs that tell students what they are to practice and list key performance points.

Station 1
Sprinting - Partners time each other over different distances.
1. 60 yard distance
2. 75 yard distance
3. Record best performance

Hop-Step-and-Jump - Partners take turns practicing the hop, step, and jump.
1. Three trials
2. Record best performance

Station 2
High Jump - Partners practice the scissors jump
1. Each jump begins at a height they desire. If the jump is made, they can dictate how much to raise the height.
2. Three trials.
3. Record best performance
Baton Passing - Practice passing the baton with partner while waiting for high jump turn.

Station 3
Running Long Jump - Partners take turns performing the running long jump.
1. Three trials.
2. Record best performance
Shuttle Relays - Partners practice with another set of partners, about 20 yards apart and facing each other. See below for a description of shuttle relays.

Station 4
Hurdling - Partners time each other over a three hurdle course.
1. Set up 60-yard hurdle course.
2. Two trials.
3. Record best performance.
Striding Practice - Striding practice can be done while waiting for turns on the hurdles.

Game Activity

Circular (Pursuit) Relays

Circular relays make use of the regular circular track. The baton exchange technique is important, and practice is needed. On a 220-yd or 200-m track, relays can be organized in a number of ways, depending on how many runners are spaced for one lap. Four runners can do a lap, each running one-quarter of the way; two can do a lap, each running one half of the distance; or each runner can complete a whole lap. In these races, each member of the relay team runs the same distance. Relays can also be organized so team members run different distances.

Shuttle Relays

Since children are running toward each other, one great difficulty in running shuttle relays is control of the exchange. In the excitement, the next runner may leave too early, and the tag or exchange is then made ahead of the restraining line. A high-jump standard or cone can be used to prevent early exchanges. The next runner awaits the tag with an arm around the standard or a hand on a cone.

One on One Contests

Allow students to find a friend and have a number of personal contests in track and field events such as sprints, hurdling, high jump, and standing long jump.

Dynamic Physical Education for Elementary School Children
Track & Field Skills (3)
Level III – Week 26

Objectives:
To understand how to stretch prior to strenuous activity
To recognize the wide range of individual differences among peers
To enjoy one-on-one competition in track and field activities

Equipment Required:
High jump equipment
Batons, stopwatches, and tape measures
Hurdles

Instructional Activities	Teaching Hints
Introductory and Fitness Development Activities—Stretching Activities	

Instructional Activities		Teaching Hints
Combine the introductory and fitness activities during the track and field unit. This will help students understand how to stretch and warm up for demanding activity such as track and field.		Emphasis should be on jogging and stretching to prepare for strenuous activity.
Jog	1-2 minutes	
Standing Hip Bend	30 seconds	See the textbook, Chapter 12, for a
Sitting Stretch	30 seconds	description of exercises
Partner Rowing	60 seconds	
Bear Hug (20 seconds each leg)	40 seconds	Encourage smooth and controlled
Side Flex (20 seconds each leg)	40 seconds	stretching. Hold each stretch for 6 to 10
Trunk Twister	30 seconds	seconds.

Lesson Focus -- Track and Field Skills (3)

Track and Field Skills
1. Utilize the last week of this unit to conduct a track and field meet. The same rotation plan and groups of students started the previous two weeks can be continued for the meet.
2. Utilize the same stations, events, number of trials and scoring procedures outlined in last week's track and field lesson.

Game Activity

Circular (Pursuit) Relays
  Circular relays make use of the regular circular track. The baton exchange technique is important, and practice is needed. On a 220-yd or 200-m track, relays can be organized in a number of ways, depending on how many runners are spaced for one lap. Four runners can do a lap, each running one-quarter of the way; two can do a lap, each running one half of the distance; or each runner can complete a whole lap. In these races, each member of the relay team runs the same distance. Relays can also be organized so team members run different distances.

Shuttle Relays
  Since children are running toward each other, one great difficulty in running shuttle relays is control of the exchange. In the excitement, the next runner may leave too early, and the tag or exchange is then made ahead of the restraining line. A high-jump standard or cone can be used to prevent early exchanges. The next runner awaits the tag with an arm around the standard or a hand on a cone.

One on One Contests
  Allow students to find a friend and have a number of personal contests in track and field events such as sprints, hurdling, high jump, and standing long jump.

Dynamic Physical Education for Elementary School Children
Rhythmic Movement Skills (3)
Level III – Week 27

Objectives:
To work cooperatively with peers in parachute fitness activities
To perform locomotor movements to rhythm
To understand strategies in simple game activities
To hear changes in musical accompaniment and move accordingly

Equipment Required:
Parachute and music tape for fitness
Tinikling equipment
Music for rhythmic activities
Pinnies
6 playground balls or coated foam balls
Jump the shot rope

Instructional Activities	Teaching Hints

Introductory Activity -- Following Activity

One partner leads and performs various kinds of movements. The other partner follows and performs the same movements. This can also be done with small groups, with the group following a leader.

Encourage students to challenge their partner. Change partners once or twice to maintain interest in the activity.

Fitness Development Activity -- Parachute Fitness

1. Jog in circle with chute held in left hand. Reverse directions and hold with right hand.
2. Standing, raise the chute overhead, lower to waist, lower to toes, raise to waist, etc.
3. Slide to the right; return slide to the left.
4. Sit and perform curl-ups with a twist.
5. Skip.
6. Freeze, face the center, and stretch the chute tightly with bent arms. Hold for 8-12 seconds. Repeat.
7. Run in place, hold the chute at waist level, and hit the chute with lifted knees.
8. Sit with legs under the chute. Do a seat walk toward the center. Return to the perimeter. Repeat four to six times.
9. Place the chute on the ground. Jog away from the chute and return on signal. Repeat.
10. On sides with legs under the chute. Perform Side Flex and lift chute with legs.
11. Lie on back with legs under the chute. Shake the chute with the feet.
12. Hop to the center of the chute and return. Repeat.
13. Assume the push-up position with the legs aligned away from the center of the chute. Shake the chute with one arm while the other arm supports the body.
14. Sit with feet under the chute. Stretch by touching the toes with the chute. Relax with other stretches while sitting.

Tape alternating segments (25-30 seconds in length) of silence and music to signal duration of exercise. Music segments indicate aerobic activity with the parachute while intervals of silence announce using the chute to enhance flexibility and strength development.

Space youngsters evenly around the chute.

Use different hand grips (palms up, down, mixed).

All movements should be done under control. Some of the faster and stronger students will have to moderate their performance.

Lesson Focus -- Rhythmic Movement Skills (3)

Make dances easy for students to learn by implementing some of the following techniques:
Rhythms should be taught like other sport skills. Avoid striving for perfection so students know it is acceptable to make mistakes. Teach a variety of dances rather than one or two in depth in case some students find it difficult to master a specific dance.
1. Teach the dances without using partners.
2. Allow youngsters to move in any direction without left-right orientation.
3. Use scattered formation instead of circles.
4. Emphasize strong movements such as clapping and stamping to increase involvement.
5. Play the music at a slower speed when first learning the dance.

Jugglehead Mixer (American)

Music Source: Any music with a definite and steady beat
Formation: Double circle facing counterclockwise in promenade position
Directions: Actions described are for the inside partner; directions are opposite for the partner on the outside of the circle.

Measures	Action
1--4	Do a two-step left and two-step right and take four walking steps forward.
5--8	Repeat measures 1--4.
9--10	Inside partner takes the outside partner's right hand and walks around to face the person behind.
11--12	Inside partner turns the person behind with the left hand.
13--14	Inside partner turns partner with the right hand going all the way around.
15--16	Inside partner steps up one place to the outside person ahead, who becomes the new partner.

Ten Pretty Girls (American)

Music Source: WWCD-1042
Formation: Circle of groups of any number, with arms linked or hands joined, all facing counterclockwise
Directions:

Measures	Action
1--2	Starting with the weight on the right foot, touch the left foot in front, swing the left foot to the left and touch, swing the left foot behind the right foot and put the weight on the left foot, step to the right, close the left foot to the right. (Front, side, back-side, together)
3--4	Repeat, starting with the weight on the left foot and moving to the right. (Front, side, back-side, together)
5--6	Take four walking or strutting steps forward, starting on the left foot. (Walk, 2, 3, 4)
7--8	Swing the left foot forward with a kicking motion; swing the left foot backward with a kicking motion; stamp left, right, left, in place. (Swing, swing, stamp, stamp, stamp)

Repeat the entire dance 11 times, starting each time with the alternate foot. The dance can be used as a mixer when performed in a circle by groups of three. On measures 7--8, have the middle person move forward to the next group during the three stamps.

Klumpakojis (Swedish)

Music Source: WWCD-1042
Formation: Couples in a circle, side by side, all facing counterclockwise, with partner B to the right
Directions:

Measures	Part I Action
1--4	With inside hands joined, free hand on hip, all walk briskly around the circle for eight steps counterclockwise. (Walk, 2, 3, 4, 5, 6, 7, turn)
5--8	Turn individually to the left, reverse direction, change hands, and walk eight steps clockwise. (Walk, 2, 3, 4, 5, 6, 7, turn)

Measures	Part II Action
9--12	Face partner and make a star by joining right hands (making certain that the right elbow is bent). The left hand is on the hip. With partner, walk around clockwise for eight walking steps. Change hands and repeat the eight steps, reversing direction. (Star, 2, 3, 4, 5, 6, 7, 8; Reverse, 2, 3, 4, 5, 6, 7, 8)

Measures	Part III Action
13--16	Listen to the musical phrase, then stamp three times on the last two counts. Listen to the phrase again, then clap own hands three times. (Listen, listen, stamp, 2, 3; Listen, listen, clap, 2, 3)
17--20	Shake the right finger in a scolding motion at partner. (Scold, 2, 3) Shake the left finger. (Scold, 2, 3)
21--24	Turn solo to the left, clapping partner's right hand once during the turn. Use two walking steps to make the turn, and finish facing partner. (Turn, 2, stamp, 2, 3)
25--32	Repeat the action of measures 13--24.

Measures	Part IV Action
33--40	With inside hands joined, do 16 polka steps (or two-steps) forward, moving counterclockwise. (Later, as the dance is learned, change to the promenade position.) On polka steps 15 and 16, partner A moves forward to take a new partner B while handing the original partner B to the A in back. New couple joins inside hands. (Step, close, step, hop; Step, close, step, hop; Repeat for a total of 16 polka steps)

Tinikling (Philippine Islands)

Music Source: WWCD-8095; WWC-9015
Formation: Sets of fours scattered around the room. Each set has two strikers and two dancers.
Directions: Two 8-foot bamboo poles and two crossbars on which the poles rest are needed for the dance. A striker kneels at each end of the poles; both strikers hold the end of a pole in each hand. The music is in waltz meter, 3/4 time, with an accent on the first beat.

The strikers slide and strike the poles together on count 1. On the other two beats of the waltz measure, the poles are opened about 15 inches apart, lifted an inch or so, and tapped twice on the crossbars in time to counts 2 and 3. The rhythm "close, tap, tap" is continued throughout the dance. Basically, the dance requires that a step be done outside the poles on the close (count 1) and that two steps be done inside the poles (counts 2 and 3) when the poles are tapped on the crossbars. Many step combinations have been devised. The basic tinikling step should be practiced until it is mastered. The step is done singly, although two dancers are performing. Each dancer takes a position at an opposite end and on the opposite side so that the dancer's right side is to the bamboo poles.

    Count 1: Step slightly forward with the left foot.
    Count 2: Step with the right foot between the poles.
    Count 3: Step with the left foot between the poles.
    Count 4: Step with the right outside to dancer's own right.
    Count 5: Step with the left between the poles.
    Count 6: Step with the right between the poles.
    Count 7: Step with the left outside to the original position.

The initial step (count 1) is used only to get the dance under way. The last step (count 7) to original position is actually the beginning of a new series (7, 8, 9--10, 11, 12).

    Tinikling steps also can be adjusted to 4/4 rhythm (close, close, tap, tap), which requires the poles to be closed on two counts and open on the other two. The basic foot pattern is two steps outside the poles and two inside. For the sake of conformity, we present all routines in the original 3/4 time (close, tap, tap). If other rhythms are used, adjust accordingly.

    Dancers can go from side to side, or can return to the side from which they entered. The dance can be done singly, with the two dancers moving in opposite directions from side to side, or the dancers can enter from and leave toward the same side. Dancers can do the same step patterns or do different movements. They can dance as partners, moving side by side with inside hands joined, or facing each other with both hands joined.

Teaching suggestions:

    Steps should be practiced first with stationary poles or with lines drawn on the floor. Jump ropes can be used as stationary objects over which to practice. Students handling the poles should concentrate on watching each other rather than the dancer to avoid becoming confused by the dancer's feet.

    To gain a sense of the movement pattern for 3/4 time, slap both thighs with the hands on the "close," and clap the hands twice for movements inside the poles. For 4/4 time, slap the right thigh with the right hand, then the left thigh with the left hand, followed by two claps. This routine should be done to music, with the poles closing and opening as indicated. Getting the feel of the rhythm is important.

Old Dan Tucker (American)

Music Source: WWCD-57; WWC-57
Skills: Slide, grand right and left, swing, promenade
Formation: Couples in a single circle with hands joined facing the center. One person is in the center as "Dan Tucker" and will take someone's partner.
Directions:

Counts	Part I Action
1-8	All take 4 walking steps forward and 4 steps backward. (Forward, 2, 3, 4; back, 2, 3, 4)
9-16	Partners face, join both hands, and take 4 slides in and 4 slides out. (Slide in, 2, 3, 4; slide out, 2, 3, 4)
17-24	Repeat walking steps as described in counts 1-8. (Forward, 2, 3, 4; back, 2, 3, 4)
25-32	Repeat slide steps as described in counts 9-16 (Slide in, 2, 3, 4; slide out, 2, 3, 4)
	Part II Action
1-16	Partners face and do a grand right and left for 16 walking steps and passing 7 partners before taking the 8th and preparing to swing. (Right, 2, left, 4, right, 6...right, 14, left, new partner)
	Part III Action
17-24	On the call, "swing," each person takes the nearest partner (they should have passed 7 partners and be swinging the 8th) and swings 4 times. The person in the middle of the ring ("Dan Tucker") takes a partner anywhere in the ring.
	Part IV Action
1-16	On the call, "promenade," couples promenade 16 steps around the circle counterclockwise and end facing the center. (Promenade, 2, 3, ... 15, face center)

Repeat the dance until the end of the music.

Shindig in the Barn (American)

Music Source: WWC-FFD
Skills: Walking, do-si-do, swinging, sliding
Formation: Contra Style (two lines with partners facing each other). Seven couples will fit the music
Directions:

3-4	All pass through to the other side by walking forward 4 steps toward partner, do a half turn while passing right shoulder of partner, and walk 4 steps backward. (Walk, 2, 3, 4, turn, 6, 7, 8)
5-6	Everybody forward and back – repeat measures 1-2 above. (Forward, 2, 3, 4; back, 2, 3, 4)
7-8	Everybody pass through to the other side with 8 steps – repeat measures 3-4 above. (Walk, 2, 3, 4, turn, 6, 7, 8)
9-10	All couples do-so-do by passing right shoulders and back. (Do-si-do, 2, 3, … 8)
11-12	All couples do a two-hand swing one time around to the left using 8 steps. After the swing, all couples except the head couple go back to their original position. The head couples remain in the middle with their hands joined facing each other. (Swing, 2, 3, … 8)
13-14	The head couple takes 8 sliding (sashay) or skipping steps to the foot of the line. All the other couples clap to the beat and watch. (Slide, 2, 3, … 8)
15-16	Head couple does a right elbow swing at the foot of the line for 8 counts and remains at the foot of the line creating a new head couple. (Swing, 2, 3, … 8)

Repeat dance to the end of the music.

Game Activity

Whistle Ball

Supplies: A ball for each group of six to eight players

Skills: Passing, catching

Eight or fewer children move into circle formation. A ball is passed rapidly back and forth among them in any order. The object is to stay in the game as long as possible. A player sits down in place after making any of the following errors:

1. A player has the ball or the ball is on the way when the signal occurs. (Time intervals can be signaled with music on—music off taped segments of 5 to 15 seconds.

2. A poor throw is made or a catch is not made after a catchable throw.

3. A pass is made back to the person from whom it was received.

Another way to control the time periods is to appoint a child as timer and to give her a list of the time periods, a whistle, and a stopwatch. The timer should be cautioned not to give any advance indication of when the stop signal will be blown. Start the game over when there are four or five players left so players sit out for a short time.

Jump the Shot Variations

Supplies: A jump-the-shot rope

Skill: Rope jumping

Before the following variations are tried, the jump-the-shot routines and variations taught previously should be reviewed.

1. Two or more squads are in file formation facing the rope turner. Each player runs clockwise (against the turn of the rope), jumping the rope as often as necessary to return to the squad.

2. Each player runs counterclockwise and tries to run around the circle before the rope can catch up with him. If this happens, he must jump to allow the rope to go under him. The best time for a player to start his run is just after the rope has passed.

3. Players can try some of the stunts in which the hands and feet are on the ground, to see whether they can have the rope pass under them. The Rabbit Jump, push-up position, Lame Dog, and others are possibilities.

Dynamic Physical Education for Elementary School Children
Racquet Sport Skills
Level III – Week 28

Objectives:
To exercise independently in the circuit training activity
To understand the difference in racquet strokes between sports
To compete in the game of volley tennis

Equipment Required:
Parachute
Music for parachute fitness routine
One racquet and ball for each student
Volleyballs for volley tennis

Instructional Activities	Teaching Hints

Introductory Activity -- High Fives

Students move in different directions throughout the area. On signal, they are challenged to run toward a partner, jump, and give a "high five" (slap hands) while moving. Emphasis should be placed on timing so that the "high five" is given at the top of the jump.

Combinations of changing the level of the high five and changing the speed of the locomotor movement can be developed.

Fitness Development Activity -- Parachute Fitness

1. Jog in circle with chute held in left hand. Reverse directions and hold with right hand.
2. Standing, raise the chute overhead, lower to waist, lower to toes, raise to waist, etc.
3. Slide to the right; return slide to the left.
4. Sit and perform curl-ups with a twist.
5. Skip.
6. Freeze, face the center, and stretch the chute tightly with bent arms. Hold for 8-12 seconds. Repeat.
7. Run in place, hold the chute at waist level, and hit the chute with lifted knees.
8. Sit with legs under the chute. Do a seat walk toward the center. Return to the perimeter. Repeat four to six times.
9. Place the chute on the ground. Jog away from the chute and return on signal. Repeat.
10. On sides with legs under the chute. Perform Side Flex and lift chute with legs.
11. Lie on back with legs under the chute. Shake the chute with the feet.
12. Hop to the center of the chute and return. Repeat.
13. Assume the push-up position with the legs aligned away from the center of the chute. Shake the chute with one arm while the other arm supports the body.
14. Sit with feet under the chute. Stretch by touching the toes with the chute. Relax with other stretches while sitting.

Tape alternating segments (25-30 seconds in length) of silence and music to signal duration of exercise. Music segments indicate aerobic activity with the parachute while intervals of silence announce using the chute to enhance flexibility and strength development.

Space youngsters evenly around the chute.

Use different hand grips (palms up, down, mixed).

All movements should be done under control. Some of the faster and stronger students will have to moderate their performance.

Lesson Focus -- Racquet Sport Skills

1. Discuss the proper method of holding the racquet using the forehand and backhand grips.
2. Air dribble the ball and try the following challenges:
   a. How many bounces without touching the floor?
   b. Bounce it as high as possible. Perform a heel click (or other stunt) while the ball is in the air.
   c. Kneel, sit and lie down while air dribbling.
3. Dribble the ball on the floor with the racquet:
   a. Move in different directions—forward, backward, sideways.
   b. Move using different steps, such as skip, grapevine, gallop.
   c. Move to a kneeling, sitting and supine position while continuing the dribble. Return to a standing position.
4. Bounce the ball off the racquet and "catch" it with the racquet.
5. Place the ball on the floor:
   a. Scoop it up with the racquet.
   b. Roll the ball and scoop it up with the racquet.
   c. Start dribbling the ball without touching it with the hands.

The focus of this unit should be to give youngsters an introduction to tennis, badminton and racquetball. Give students two or three activities to practice so you have time to move and help youngsters. Alternate activities from each of the categories so students receive a variety of skills to practice.

Use instructional cues to improve technique:
a. Hold the wrist reasonably stiff.
b. Use a smooth arm action.
c. Stroke through the ball and follow through.
d. Watch the ball strike the paddle.

6. Self-toss and hit to a fence, net or tumbling mat. This drill should be used to practice the forehand and backhand. The ball should be dropped so it bounces to waist level.
7. Partner activities:
   a. One partner feeds the ball to the other, who returns the ball with a forehand or backhand stroke.
   b. Stroke the ball back and forth to each other with one or more bounces between contact.
   c. Self-toss and hit. Drop the ball and stroke it to a partner 20-30 feet away. Partner does the same thing to return the ball.
   d. Partner throw and hit. One partner throws the ball to the other, who returns the ball by stroking it with the racquet.
   e. Wall volley: If a wall is available, partners can volley against it.
8. Serving:
   a. Teach tennis serve without a racquet. Use a yarn ball and practice hitting it with the open hand. The serve is similar to the overhand throwing motion. The toss is a skill that will need to be mastered prior to learning the striking motion.
   b. Teach the racquetball serve in similar fashion. The hard, driving serve is done using a side-underhand throwing motion. The striking hand should be raised on the backswing. A small foam (Nerf) ball that bounces should be dropped to the floor and struck on the rebound.
   c. For a racquetball lob serve, the ball is bounced and hit with an underhand motion. The ball is hit high on the wall and bounces to the back wall.
   d. The foam ball can be used for the badminton serve also. For this serve, the ball is dropped and hit with an underhand motion before it hits the floor.
   e. Depending on facilities, racquets can be used after the basic motion has been learned.

Proper grip must be emphasized, and seeing that children maintain this is a constant battle. The easiest method to teach the proper grip is to have the student hold the paddle perpendicular to the floor and shake hands with it. Practice in racquet work should move from individual to partner work as quickly as is feasible, because partner work is basic to racquet sports.

For the forehand stroke, the body is turned sideways; for a right-handed player, the left side points in the direction of the hit.

For the backhand stroke, the thumb is placed against the handle of the racquet for added support and force, and the body is turned sideways so the shoulder on the side of the racquet hand points in the direction of the stroke.

During either type of stroke, a step is made with the foot that is forward with respect to the direction of the stroke.

Game Activity

Volley Tennis

Supplies: A volleyball

Skills: Most volleyball and tennis skills

The game can be played as a combination of volleyball and tennis. The net is put on the ground, as in tennis, and the ball is put into play with a serve. It may bounce once or can be passed directly to a teammate. The ball must be hit three times before going over the net. Spiking is common because of the low net. A point is scored when it cannot be returned over the net to the opposing team.

One-Wall Handball and Racquetball

Supplies: Racquetballs (or tennis balls) and racquets

Skills: Racquet skills

Two players find a wall and volley the ball back and forth off the wall. If desired, let players develop rules for the style of serve and out of bounds rules. The basic rule is that the ball can only bounce once on its return from the wall. When a player returns the ball to the wall, it cannot touch the floor before it hits the wall. Any of these rules can be modified by agreement of the players.

Dynamic Physical Education for Elementary School Children
Individual Rope Jumping Skills
Level III – Week 29

Objectives:
To perform exercises to rhythmic accompaniment
To understand the aerobic benefits of rope jumping
To recognize that learning any skill take repetition and refinement

Equipment Required:
One individual jump rope for each
 student
Exercise to music tape
Base and volleyball for game

Instructional Activities	Teaching Hints

Introductory Activity -- Partner Over and Around

Students pair up with one person on the floor and the other standing ready to move. On signal, the standing students move over and around the person on the floor. On signal, reverse positions. Students on the floor can also alternate between positions such as curl, stretch and bridge.

Students should see how many different ways they can accomplish the challenge.

Avoid touching each other when moving.

Fitness Development Activity -- Exercises to Music

Forward Lunges	30 seconds
Alternate Crab Kicks	25 seconds
Windmills	30 seconds
Walk and do Arm Circles	25 seconds
Abdominal Crunchers	30 seconds
Side Flex	25 seconds
Triceps Push-Ups	30 seconds
Two-Step or Gallop	25 seconds
Jumping Jack variations	30 seconds
Aerobic Jumping	25 seconds
Leg Extensions	30 seconds
Push-Ups	25 seconds
Walking to cool down	30 seconds

Select music that has a strong rhythm and easy-to-hear beat. When the music is on students perform aerobic activities (for 30 seconds). When the music is not playing, students perform the strength development and flexibility exercises (25 seconds).

See Chapter 12 of the textbook for descriptions of the exercises.

Use scatter formation.

Lesson Focus -- Individual Rope-Jumping Skills

1. Introduce the two basic jump rhythms:
    a. Slow-time rhythm. In slow time rhythm, the performer jumps the rope and then takes a second jump while the rope is overhead. The jump while the rope is overhead is usually a small, light rebound jump. In slow time, the rope makes one full turn for each two jumps.
    b. Fast time rhythm. In fast time rhythm, the student jumps the rope with every jump. The rope makes one full turn for every jump.
2. Introduce some of the basic step variations. The basic steps can be done in slow or fast time.
    a. Side Swing. Swing the rope, held with both hands to one side of the body. Switch and swing the rope on the other side of the body.
    b. Double Side Swing and Jump. Swing the rope once on each side of the body. Follow the second swing with a jump over the rope. The sequence should be swing, swing, jump.
    c. Alternate-Foot Basic Step. In the Alternate-Foot Basic Step, as the rope passes under the feet, the weight is shifted alternately from one foot to the other, raising the non-support foot in a running position.
    d. Spread Legs Forward and Backward. For Spread Legs Forward and Backward, start in a stride position (as in the Rocker) with weight equally distributed on both feet. As the rope passes under the feet, jump into the air and reverse the position of the feet.
    e. Straddle Jump. Alternate a regular jump with a straddle jump. The straddle jump is performed with the feet spread to shoulder width.

1. The length of the rope is dependent on the height of the jumper. It should be long enough so that the ends reach to the armpits or slightly higher when the child stands on its center. Grades 5 and 6 need a mixture of 7-, 8-, and 9-foot ropes. Ropes or handles can be color-coded for length.

Two types of ropes are available; the beaded (plastic segment) and the plastic (licorice) rope. The beaded ropes are heavier and seem easier to turn for beginning jumpers. The drawback to the beaded ropes is that they hurt when they hit another student. Also, if the segments are made round, the rope will roll easily on the floor and cause children to fall when they step on it. The plastic licorice ropes are lighter and give less wind resistance. For experienced jumpers more speed and control can be gained with this type of rope. An ideal situation would be to have a set of each type.

f. Cross Legs Sideward. In Cross Legs Sideward, as the rope passes under the feet, spread the legs in a straddle position (sideward) to take the rebound. As the rope passes under the feet on the next turn, jump into the air and cross the feet with the right foot forward. Then repeat with the left foot forward and continue this alternation.

g. Toe-Touch Forward. To do the Toe-Touch Forward, swing the right foot forward as the rope passes under the feet and touch the right toes on the next count. Then alternate, landing on the right foot and touching the left toes forward.

h. Toe-Touch Backward. The Toe-Touch Backward is similar to the Swing-Step Sideward, except that the toes of the free foot touch to the back at the end of the swing.

i. Shuffle Step. The Shuffle Step involves pushing off with the right foot and sidestepping to the left as the rope passes under the feet. Land with the weight on the left foot and touch the right toes beside the left heel. Repeat the step in the opposite direction.

3. Teach the Crossing Arms Step

Once the basic steps are mastered, crossing the arms while turning the rope provides an interesting variation. Crossing the arms during forward turning is easier than crossing behind the back during backward turning. During crossing, the hands exchange places. This means that for forward crossing, the elbows are close to each other. This is not possible during backward crossing. Crossing and uncrossing can be done at predetermined points after a stipulated number of turns. Crossing can be accomplished during any of the routines.

4. Teach Double Turning

The double turn of the rope is also interesting. The jumper does a few basic steps in preparation for the double turn. As the rope approaches the feet, the child gives an extremely hard flip of the rope from the wrists, jumps from 6 to 8 inches in height, and allows the rope to pass under the feet twice before landing. The jumper must bend forward at the waist somewhat, which increases the speed of the turn. A substantial challenge for advanced rope jumpers is to see how many consecutive double-turn jumps they can do.

5. Teach shifting from forward to backward jumping

To switch from forward to backward jumping without stopping the rope, any of the following techniques can be used.

a. As the rope starts downward in forward jumping, rather than allowing it to pass under the feet, the performer swings both arms to the left (or right) and makes a half turn of the body in that direction (i.e., facing the rope). On the next downward swing, the jumper spreads the arms and starts turning in the opposite direction. This method also works for shifting from backward to forward jumping.

b. When the rope is directly above the head, the performer extends both arms, causing the rope to hesitate momentarily, at the same time making a half-turn in either direction and continuing to skip with the rope turning in the opposite direction.

c. From a crossed-arm position, as the rope is going above the performer's head, the jumper may uncross the arms and turn simultaneously. This starts the rope turning and the performer jumping in the opposite direction.

6. Teach Jumping with a Partner. One student turns and jumps the rope while her partner enters and jumps simultaneously. The following are some challenges partners can try:

a. Run in and face partner, and both jump.

b. Run in and turn back to partner, and both jump.

c. Decide which steps are to be done; then run in and match steps.

d. Repeat with the rope turning backward.

Posture is an important consideration in rope jumping. The body should be in good alignment, with the head up and the eyes looking straight ahead. The jump is made with the body in an erect position. A slight straightening of the knees provides the lift for the jump, which should be of minimal height (about 1 inch). The wrists supply the force to turn the rope, with the elbows kept close to the body and extended at a 90-degree angle. A pumping action and lifting of the arms is unnecessary. The landing should be made on the balls of the feet, with the knees bent slightly to cushion the shock. Usually, the feet, ankles, and legs are kept together, except when a specific step calls for a different position.

The rope should be held by the index finger and thumb on each side with the hands making a small circle. The elbows should be held near the sides to avoid making large arm circles with the rope.

Music can be added when jumpers have learned the first stages of jumping. Music provides a challenge for continued jumping.

To collect ropes at the completion of a rope-jumping activity, have two or three children act as monitors. They put both arms out to the front or to the side at shoulder level. The other children then drape the ropes over their arms. The monitors return the ropes to the correct storage area.

Instructional cues to use for improving jumping technique are:

a. Keep the arms at the side of the body while turning. (Many children lift the arms to shoulder level trying to move the rope overhead. This makes it impossible for the youngster to jump over the elevated rope.)

b. Turn the rope by making small circles with the wrists.

c. Jump on the balls of the feet.

d. Bend the knees slightly to absorb the force of the jump.

e. Make a small jump over the rope.

7. Teach side-by-side jumping. Partners clasp inside hands and turn the rope with outside hands.
   a. Face the same direction and turn the rope.
   b. Face opposite directions, clasp left hands, and turn the rope.
   c. Face opposite directions, clasp right hands, and turn the rope.
   d. Repeat routines with inside knees raised.
   e. Repeat routines with elbows locked. Try other arm positions.

Partner jumping may require a slightly longer rope and partners of similar height.

Game Activity

Right Face, Left Face (Maze Tag)

Supplies: None

Skills: Running, dodging

Children stand in rows that are aligned both front to rear and side to side. Two runners and two chasers are chosen. Players all face the same way and join hands with the players on each side. The chasers try to tag the runners, who run between the rows with the restriction that they cannot break through or go under the arms. The teacher helps the runners by calling "Right face" or "Left face" at the proper time. On command, the children drop hands, face the new direction, and grasp hands with those who are then on each side, thus making new passages available. When the runner is caught or when children become tired, a new runner and chaser are chosen.

Variations:

1. Directions (north, south, east, west) can be used instead of the facing commands.

2. Streets and Alleys. The teacher calls, "Streets," and the children face in one direction. The call "Alleys" causes them to face at right angles.

3. The command "Air raid" can be given, and children drop to their knees and make themselves into small balls, tucking their heads and seats down. This allows unlimited movement by the taggers and runners.

One Base Tagball

Supplies: A base (or standard), a volleyball (8-in. foam ball for younger children)

Skills: Running, dodging, throwing

A home line is drawn at one end of the playing space. A base or standard is placed about 50 feet in front of the home line. Two teams are formed. One team is scattered around the fielding area, the boundaries of which are determined by the number of children. The other team is lined up in single file behind the home line. The object of the game is for the fielding team to tag the runners with the ball. Two runners at a time try to round the base and head back for the home line without being tagged. The game is continuous, meaning that as soon as a running team player is tagged or crosses the home line, another player starts immediately. The fielding team may run with the ball and pass it from player to player, trying to tag one of the runners. The running team scores a point each time a player runs successfully around the base and back to the home line.

At the start of the game, the running team has two players ready at the right side of the home line. The others on the team are in line, waiting for a turn. The teacher throws the ball anywhere in the field, and the first two runners start toward the base. They must run around the base from the right side. After all of the players have run, the teams exchange places. The team scoring the most points wins.

Dynamic Physical Education for Elementary School Children
Volleyball Skills (1)
Level III – Week 30

Objectives:
To lead other students through warm-up activities
To serve a volleyball in a predetermined direction
To understand basic principles of training

Equipment Required:
Signs and music for Circuit Training
One beachball, volleyball trainer or foam
  training ball for each student
Volleyball net or magic stretch ropes

Instructional Activities	Teaching Hints

Introductory Activity -- New Leader

Divide class into small groups and appoint one member in each group to lead. Groups move around the area following any movement the leader does. On signal, another person in the group becomes the leader. The leader can use various types of locomotor movements and/or exercises.

Assign each group a specific area if desired. Each area could include a piece of equipment to aid in the activity (beanbag, fleece ball, etc.).

Fitness Development Activity -- Circuit Training

Students do the best they can at each station within the time limit. This implies that not all youngsters are required to do the same workload. Children differ and their ability to perform fitness workloads differs. Make fitness a personal challenge.
Rope Jumping
Push-Ups
Agility Run
Lower Leg Stretch
Juggling Scarves
Curl-Ups with Twist
Alternate Leg Extension
Tortoise and Hare
Bear Hug

Conclude circuit training with 2-4 minutes of walking, jogging, rope jumping or other self-paced aerobic activity

Tape alternating segments of silence and music to signal duration of exercise. Music segments (begin at 35 seconds) indicate activity at each station while intervals of silence (10 seconds) announce it is time to stop and move forward to the next station.

Use signals such as start, stop, and move up to ensure rapid movement to the next station.

Ask students to do their personal best they can. Expect workloads to differ.

Lesson Focus -- Volleyball Skills, Drills, and Lead-Up Games (1)

Skills
Practice the following skills:
Overhand Pass

To execute an overhand pass, the player moves underneath the ball and controls it with the fingertips. The cup of the fingers is made so that the thumbs and forefingers are close together and the other fingers are spread. The hands are held forehead high, with elbows out and level with the floor. The player, when in receiving position, looks ready to shout upward through the hands. The player contacts the ball above eye level and propels it with the force of spread fingers, not with the palms. At the moment of contact, the legs are straightened and the hands and arms follow through.

Forearm Pass (Underhand Pass)

The hands are clasped together so that the forearms are parallel. The clasp should be relaxed, with the type of handclasp a matter of choice. The thumbs are kept parallel and together, and the fingers of one hand make a partially cupped fist, with the fingers of the other hand overlapping the fist. The wrists are turned downward and the elbow joints are reasonably locked. The forearms are held at the proper angle to rebound the ball, with contact made with the fists or forearms between the knees as the receiver crouches.

Using beachballs or trainer volleyballs will allow youngsters time to move into the path of the volleyball instead of reaching for the ball. Proper footwork is critical to the success of volleyball; using proper balls will help assure that youngsters learn correctly.

Instructional cues for passing include the following:
1. Move into the path of the ball; don't reach for it.
2. Bend the knees prior to making contact.
3. Contact the ball with the fingertips (overhand pass).
4. Extend the knees upon contact with the ball.
5. Follow through after striking the ball.

Underhand Serve

Directions are for a right-handed serve. The player stands facing the net with the left foot slightly forward and the weight on the right (rear) foot. The ball is held in the left hand with the left arm across and a little in front of the body. On the serving motion, the server steps forward with the left foot, transfers the weight to the front foot, and at the same time brings the right arm back in a preparatory motion. The right hand now swings forward and contacts the ball just below center. The ball can be hit with an open hand or with the fist (facing forward or sideward). Children should explore the best way to strike the ball, with the flat of the hand or the fist. Each player can select the method that is personally most effective.

Setup

The term setup applies to a pass that sets the ball for a possible spike. The object is to raise the ball with a soft, easy pass to a position 1 or 2 feet above the net and about 1 foot away from it. The setup is generally the second pass in a series of three. An overhand pass is used for the setup. It is important for the back line player, who has to tap to the setter, to make an accurate and easily handled pass.

Individual Passing Drills

1. Practice wall rebounding: Stand 6 feet away from a wall. Pass the ball against the wall and catch it.
2. From a spot 6 feet from the wall, throw the ball against the wall and alternate an overhand pass with a forearm pass.
3. Throw the ball to one side (right or left) and move to the side to pass the ball to the wall. Catch the rebound.
4. Pass the ball directly overhead and catch it. Try making two passes before catching the ball. Later, alternate an overhand pass with a forearm pass and catch the ball. This is a basic drill and should be mastered before proceeding to others.

Partner Passing Drills

1. Players are about 10 feet apart. Play A tosses the ball (controlled toss) to player B, who passes the ball back to A, who catches the ball. Continue for several exchanges and then change throwers.
2. Two players are about 15 feet apart. Player A passes to themselves first and then makes a second pass to player B, who catches the ball and repeats. Follow with a return by B.
3. Players A and B try to keep the ball in the air continuously.
4. Players are about 15 feet apart. Player A remains stationary and passes in such a fashion that player B must move from side to side. An option is to have player B move forward and backward.
5. Players are about 10 feet apart. Both have hoops and attempt to keep one foot in the hoop while passing. Try keeping both feet in the hoop.
6. Player A passes to player B and does a complete turnaround. B passes back to A and also does a full turn. Other stunts can be used.

Partner Work (Serving and Passing)

1. Partners are about 20 feet apart. Partner A serves to partner B, who catches the ball and returns the serve to partner A.
2. Partner A serves to partner B, who makes a pass back to partner A. Change responsibilities.
3. Service One-Step. Partners begin about 10 feet apart. Partner A serves to partner B, who returns the serve with partner A catching. If there is no error and if neither receiver moved the feet to catch, both players take one step back. This is repeated each time no error or foot movement by the receivers occur. If an error occurs or if appreciable foot movement is evident, the players revert to the original distance of 10 feet and start over.
4. A player stands at the top of the key on a basketball court. The object is to serve the ball into the basket. Scoring can be as in other basket-making drills: 3 points for a basket, 2 points for hitting the rim, and 1 point for hitting the backboard but not the rim. Partner retrieves the ball.

Instructional cues for the serve:
1. Use opposition. Place the opposite foot of the serving hand forward.
2. Transfer the weight to the forward foot.
3. Keep the eyes on the ball.
4. Decide prior to the serve where it should be placed.
5. Follow through; don't punch at the ball.

The usual basketball court should be divided into two volleyball courts on which players play crosswise. Nets should be lowered to 6 feet and raised 6 to 12 inches as children mature.

Pass and Dig

Supplies: A trainer volleyball for each team

Skills: Overhand, forearm, and dig passes

Each team forms a small circle of not more than eight players. The object of the game is to see which team can make the greater number of volleys in a specified time or which team can keep the ball in the air for the greater number of consecutive volleys without error.

On the signal "Go," the game is started with a volley by one of the players. The following rules are in force.

1. Balls are volleyed back and forth with no specific order of turns, except that the ball cannot be returned to the player from whom it came.

2. A player may not volley a ball twice in succession.

3. Any ball touching the ground does not count and ends the count.

Teaching suggestions: Players should be responsible for calling illegal returns on themselves and thus interrupting the consecutive volley count. The balls used should be of equal quality, so that one team cannot claim a disadvantage. Groups should be taught to count the volleys out loud, so that their progress is known.

Mini-Volleyball

Supplies: A volleyball or trainer volleyball

Skills: Most volleyball skills

Mini-Volleyball is a modified activity designed to offer opportunities for successful volleyball experiences to children between the ages of 9 and 12. The playing area is 15 ft wide and 40 ft long. The spiking line is 10 ft from the centerline. Many gymnasiums are marked for badminton courts that are 20 by 44 ft with a spiking line 6.5 ft from the center. This is an acceptable substitute court.

The modified rules used in Mini-Volleyball are as follows.

1. A team consists of three players. Two substitutions may be made per game.

2. Players are positioned for the serve so that there are two front-line players and one back-line player. After the ball is served, the back-line player may not spike the ball from the attack area or hit the ball into the attack area unless the ball is below the height of the net.

3. The height of the net is 6 ft, 10 in.

4. Players rotate positions when they receive the ball for serving. The right front-line player becomes the back-line player, and the left front-line player becomes the right front-line player.

5. A team wins a game when it scores 15 points and has a 2-point advantage over the opponent. A team wins the match when it wins two out of three games.

The back-line player cannot spike and thus serves a useful function by allowing the front players to receive the serves while he moves to the net to set up for the spikers.

Modify the game to suit the needs of participants. Sponge training balls work well in the learning stages of Mini-Volleyball.

Regulation Volleyball

Supplies: A volleyball

Skills: All volleyball skills

Regulation volleyball should be played with one possible rule change: In early experiences, it is suggested that the server be allowed a second chance if she fails to get the first attempt over the net and into play. This should apply only to the initial serve. Some instructors like to shorten the serving distance during the introductory phases of the game. It is important for the serving to be done well enough to keep the game moving.

A referee should supervise the game. There are generally three calls.

1. "Side out." The serving team fails to serve the ball successfully to the other court, fails to make a good return of a volley, or makes a rule violation.

2. "Point." The receiving team fails to make a legal return or is guilty of a rule violation.

3. "Double foul." Fouls are made by both teams on the same play, in which case the point is replayed. No score or side out results.

Backcourt players should be encouraged to pass to frontcourt players rather than merely batting the ball back and forth across the net.

Dynamic Physical Education for Elementary School Children
Volleyball Skills (2)
Level III – Week 31

Objectives:
To handle a ball in a variety of situations
To show respect for peers with different skill levels
To accept decisions made by officials
To enjoy a variety of volleyball games

Equipment Required:
Cones, signs, and tape for Hexagon
    Hustle
One beachball, volleyball trainer or foam
    training ball for each student
Volleyball net or magic stretch ropes

Instructional Activities	Teaching Hints

Introductory Activity – Ball Activities

Each student has a ball and dribbles around the area. On signal, stop and perform a number of activities with the ball. Examples are passing the ball behind the back, under a leg, and overhead. Try variations such as tossing the ball into the air instead of dribbling while moving or play catch with a friend while moving.

Focus on ball control and quality movement.

Place the balls around the perimeter of the area for quick acquisition and immediate activity.

Fitness Development Activity -- Hexagon Hustle

Tape alternating segments of silence and music to signal duration of exercise. Music segments indicate aerobic activity while intervals of silence announce flexibility and strength development activities.

Hustle	25 seconds
Push-Up from Knees	30 seconds
Hustle	25 seconds
Bend and Twist (8 counts)	30 seconds
Hustle	25 seconds
Jumping Jacks (4 counts)	30 seconds
Hustle	25 seconds
Curl-Ups (2 counts)	30 seconds
Hustle	25 seconds
Crab Kick (2 counts)	30 seconds
Hustle	25 seconds
Sit and Stretch (8 counts)	30 seconds
Hustle	25 seconds
Power Jumper	30 seconds
Hustle	25 seconds
Squat Thrust (4 counts)	30 seconds

Conclude the Hexagon Hustle with a slow jog or walk.

Outline a large hexagon with six cones. Place signs with locomotor movements on both sides of the cones. Locomotor movements to use are:
Jogging, skipping, galloping, hopping, jumping, sliding, leaping, and animal movements. Sport movements such as defensive sliding, running backwards, and running and shooting jump shots can also be used. The signs identify the hustle activity students are to perform as they approach a cone.

During the hustle, faster moving students should pass on the outside of the hexagon.

Change directions at times to keep students spaced out properly.

Lesson Focus -- Volleyball Skills and Drills (2)

Skills
Review the skills learned last week. Use some of the drills introduced in the previous lesson to practice the skills.
    a. Underhand serve
    b. Overhand pass
    c. Serving
    d. Setup
Introduce a new skill.
Blocking

    A member of the defensive team forms a screen by extending hands and arms straight up while jumping straight up. The ball is not struck, but rebounds from the blocker's stiffened hands and arms.

Blocking involves one or more members of the defensive (receiving) team forming a screen of arms and hands near the net to block a spike. At the elementary school level, a single individual usually does blocking, and little attention is given to multiple blocking. To block a ball, a player jumps high with arms outstretched overhead, palms facing the net, and fingers spread. The jump must be timed with that of the spiker, and the blocker must avoid touching the net.

Drills

Leave time for playing volleyball lead-up games.

Station (Small Group) Instruction

Divide the class into four equal groups. Set up a system of rotation that assures all stations will be covered.

Station 1 - Individual Volleying

1. Volley the ball directly overhead and catch. Try to consecutive volleys before the catch. Next, alternate a bump with an overhand pass before the catch. Finally, try to keep the ball going five or six times in a row with one kind of volley; alternate kinds of volleys.

2. Volley the ball 15 feet overhead, make a full turn and pass the ball again. Vary with other stunts (i.e., touching the floor, a heel click, clapping the hands at two different spots).

Station 2 - Volleying with a Partner

Players are 10 feet apart. One player tosses the ball to the other, who volleys it back to the first player, who catches it. After several volleys by one player, exchange tossers. Players can try to keep the ball going back and forth with a designated number of volleys before one player catches the ball.

Station 3 - Serving to a Partner

One partner serves to the other, who volleys the ball back. Exchange responsibilities after several serves and return volleys.

Station 4 - Setting and Blocking

For blocking, three players are positioned alongside the net, each with a ball. The players take turns on the other side of the net, practicing blocking skills. Each spiker tosses the ball to himself for spiking. A defensive player moves along the line to block consecutively a total of three spikes. The next step is to have two players move along the line to practice blocking by pairs.

The ball is not struck but rather rebounds from the blocker's stiffened hands and arms. Students should know about blocking even if it is used infrequently in elementary play.

Station work is facilitated if signs are made directing students what to do at each station. List key points and how to do the drills. Signs allow students to work independently

Many of the drills can be done without a net. This allows better use of space since nets restrict how much of the area is used.

Game Activity - Lead-Up Games

Mini-Volleyball

See the Lesson Plan, Volleyball Skills (Week 30) for a complete game description.

Regulation Volleyball

See the Lesson Plan, Volleyball Skills (Week 30) for a complete game description.

Three and Over Volleyball

Supplies: A volleyball

Skills: All volleyball skills

The game Three and Over emphasizes the basic offensive strategy of volleyball. The game follows regular volleyball rules with the exception that the ball must be played three times before going over the net. The team loses the serve or the point if the ball is not played three times.

Rotation Mini-Volleyball

Supplies: A volleyball

Skills: All volleyball skills

If four teams are playing in two contests at the same time, a system of rotation can be set up. Divide the available class time roughly into three parts, less the time allotted for logistics. Each team plays the other three teams on a timed basis. At the end of a predetermined time period, whichever team is ahead wins the game. A team may win, lose, or tie during any time period, with the score determined at the end of the respective time period. The best win-loss record wins the overall contest.

Dynamic Physical Education for Elementary School Children
Rhythmic Movement (4)
Level III – Week 32

Objectives:
To jump a self-turned rope for an extended period of time To develop an appreciation of folk dances and their respective cultures
To cooperate in a social setting (folk dancing)

Equipment Required:
Music for Continuity Drills
One individual jump rope for each student
15 scooters and cageball
Small object for Touchdown game

Instructional Activities	Teaching Hints

Introductory Activity -- Group Over and Around

One half of the class is scattered. Each is in a curled position. The other half of the class leaps or jumps over or moves around the down children. On signal reverse group roles quickly. In place of a curl, the down children can bridge and make other shapes.

The down children can move slowly around the area.

Emphasize controlled movement.

Fitness Development Activity -- Continuity Drills

Rope jumping—forward	25 seconds	
Double Crab Kick	30 seconds	
Rope jumping—backward	25 seconds	
Knee Touch Curl-Up	30 seconds	
Jump and turn body	25 seconds	
Push-Ups	30 seconds	
Rocker Step	25 seconds	
Bend and Twist	30 seconds	
Swing -Step forward	25 seconds	
Side Flex	30 seconds	
Free jumping	25 seconds	

Relax and stretch for a short time.

Make a tape with music segments (25 seconds) alternated with silence segments (30 seconds). When the music is playing, students jump rope; when silence occurs, students do a flexibility and strength development exercise.

Exercises can be done in two-count fashion. Exercises are done when the leader says "Ready." The class answers "One-two" and performs a repetition.

Allow students to adjust the workload to their level. This implies resting if the rope jumping is too strenuous.

Lesson Focus -- Rhythmic Movement (4)

Make dances easy for students to learn by implementing some of the following techniques:
Rhythms should be taught like other sport skills. Avoid striving for perfection so students know it is acceptable to make mistakes. Teach a variety of dances rather than one or two in depth in case some students find it difficult to master a specific dance.

1. Teach the dances without using partners.
2. Allow youngsters to move in any direction without left-right orientation.
3. Use scattered formation instead of circles.
4. Emphasize strong movements such as clapping and stamping to increase involvement.
5. Play the music at a slower speed when first learning the dance.

Jiffy Mixer

Music Source: WWCD-FDN
Formation: Double circle, partners facing.
Directions: The Windsor record has an introduction. Directions are for partners A; B's actions are opposite.

Measures	Introduction---use with Windsor record only
1--4	Wait, wait, balance apart (push away on the left foot and touch the right). Balance together (forward on the right and touch the left).

Measures	Action
1--4	Strike the left heel diagonally out and return to touch the toe near the right foot. Repeat. Do a side step left with a touch. (Heel, toe; Heel, toe; Side, close; Side, touch)
5--8	Repeat while moving in the opposite direction, beginning with the right foot. (Heel, toe; Heel, toe; Side, close; Side, touch)

| 9--12 | Take four chug steps backward clapping on the up beat. (Chug, clap, chug, clap, chug, clap, chug, clap) |
| 13--16 | Starting with the left foot, take four slow, swaggering steps diagonally to the right, progressing to a new partner. (Walk, 2, 3, 4) |

The chug step is done by jumping and dragging both feet backward. The body is bent slightly forward.

Horse and Buggy Schottische (American)

Music Source: WWCD-1046

Formation: Couples in sets of four in a double circle, facing counterclockwise. Couples join inside hands and give outside hands to the other couple.

Directions:

Measures Action

| 1--2 | Moving forward, perform two schottische steps. (Step, step, step, hop; Step, step, step, hop) |
| 3--4 | Progress in line of direction performing four step-hops. (Step-hop, 2-hop, 3-hop, 4-hop) |

During the four step-hops, either of the following patterns can be done.

1. The lead couple drops inside hands and step-hops around the outside of the back couple, who move forward during the step-hops. The lead couple then joins hands behind the other couple, and the positions are reversed.

2. The lead couple continues to hold hands and move backward under the upraised hands of the back couple, who untwist by turning away from each other.

Alunelul (Romanian)

Music Source: WWCD-TC1; WWC-TC1

Formation: Single circle, hands on shoulders to both sides, arms straight ("T" position)

Directions: The Romanians are famous for rugged dances. This dance is called "Little Hazelnut." The stomping action represents the breaking of the hazelnuts. The title is pronounced "ah-loo-NAY-loo."

Measures Part I Action

1--2	Sidestep right, step left behind right, sidestep right, step left behind right, sidestep right, stomp left foot twice. (Side, back, side, back, side, stomp, stomp)
3--4	Beginning with the left foot, repeat the action but with reverse footwork. (Side, back, side, back, side, stomp, stomp)
5--8	Repeat the action of measures 1--4.

Measures Part II Action

9--10	Sidestep right, left behind right, sidestep right, stomp. (Side, back, side, stomp)
11--12	Sidestep left, right behind left, sidestep left, stomp. (Side, back, side, stomp)
13--16	Repeat the action of measures 9--12.

Measures Part III Action

17--18	In place, step right, stomp left; step left, stomp right; step right, stomp left twice. (Side, stomp, side, stomp, side, stomp, stomp)
19--20	In place, step left, stomp right; step right, stomp left; step left, stomp right twice. (Side, stomp, side, stomp, side, stomp, stomp)
21--24	Repeat action of measures 17--20. Teaching suggestions:

The stamps should be made close to the supporting foot. In teaching the dance, scatter the dancers in general space so they can move individually.

Korobushka (Russian)

Music Source: WWCD-572; WWC-572

Formation: Double circle, partner A's back to the center, with partners facing and both hands joined. A's left and B's right foot are free.

Directions:

Measures Part I Action

1--2	Take one schottische step away from the center (partner A moving forward, partner B backward) starting with A's left and B's right foot. (Out, 2, 3, hop)
3--4	Repeat the pattern of measures 1 and 2, reversing direction and footwork. (In, 2, 3, hop)
5--6	Repeat the pattern of measures 1 and 2, ending on the last count with a jump on both feet in place. (Out, 2, 3, jump)
7--8	Hop on the left foot, touching the right toes across in front of the left foot (count 1). Hop on the left foot, touching the right toes diagonally forward to the right (count 2). Jump on both feet in place, clicking the heels together (count 1), pause, and release the hands (count 2). (Across, apart, together)

Measures Part II Action

9--10	Facing partner and beginning with the right foot, take one schottische step right, moving sideways away from partner. (Side, back, side, hop)
11--12	Facing and beginning with the left foot, take one schottische step left, returning to partner. (Side, back, side, hop)
13--14	Joining right hands with partner, balance forward and back: Step forward on the right foot (count 1), pause (count 2), rock back on the left foot in place (count 3), pause (count 4). (Forward, hop, back, hop)

15--16	Take four walking steps forward, starting with the right foot, and change places with partner. (Walk, 2, 3, 4)
17--24	Repeat the pattern of measures 9--16, returning to place.

Oh Johnny (American)

Music Source: WWCD-05114; WWC-57
Skills: Shuffle step, swing, allemande left, do-si-do, promenade
Formation: Single circle of couples facing inward with partner B on the right
Directions: A shuffle step is used throughout this dance.
Action
All join hands and circle for eight steps.
All stop and swing with partner.
A's turn to their left and swing the corner B.
Swing with partner again.
As turn to their left and do an allemande left with their corner.
As turn to their right and do a do-si-do with their partner.
As promenade with the corner B, who becomes the new partner for the next repetition.
Teaching hint: To simplify the dance, begin in scattered formation and teach each call with students changing from partner to corner using any nearby person. Since this is a fast-moving dance, the music should be slowed down until students can successfully complete the dance.

Virginia Reel (American)

Music Source: WWCD-05114
Skills: Skipping, arm turn, do-si-do, sliding (sashay), reeling
Formation: Six couples in a longways set of two lines facing. Partners on one end of the set are designated the head couple.
Directions:

Measures	Call	Action
1–4	All go forward and back.	Take three steps forward, curtsy or bow. Take three steps back and close.
5–8	Right hands around.	Move forward to partner, turn once in place using a right forearm grasp and return to position.
9–12	Left hands around.	Repeat measures 5–8 with a left forearm grasp.
13–16	Both hands around.	Partners join both hands, turn once in a clockwise direction, and move backward to place.
17–20	Do-si-do your partner.	Partners pass each other right shoulder to right shoulder and then back to back and move backward to place.
21–24	All go forward and back.	Repeat the action of measures 1–4.
25–32	Head couple sashay.	The head couple, with hands joined, takes eight slides down to the foot of the set and eight slides back to place.
33–64	Head couple reel.	The head couple begins the reel with linked right elbows and turns one and one-half times to face the next couple in line. Each member in the head couple then links left elbows with the person facing and turns once in place. The head couple meets again in the center and turns once with a right elbow swing. The next dancers down the line are turned with a left elbow swing and then the head couple returns to the center for another right elbow turn. The head couple thus progresses down the line, turning each dancer in order. After the head couple has turned the last dancers, they meet with a right elbow swing, turn halfway around, and sashay (slide) back to the head of the set.
65–96	Everybody march.	All couples face toward the head of the set with the head couple in front. The person on the right turns to the right while the person on the left turns to the left and goes behind the line followed by the other dancers. When the head couple reaches the foot of the set, they join hands and make an arch, under which all other couples pass. The head couple is now at the foot of the set and the dance is repeated with a new head couple.

The dance is repeated until each couple has had a chance to be the head couple.

Trio Fun Mixer (American)

Music Source: WWC-FFD

Skills: Walking, Do-si-do, star

Formation: Lines of three facing lines of three in a large circle

Directions:

Measures	Action
1-4	Facing threesomes (six dancers) join hands and circle left one time around back to place. (circle, 2, 3, ... 16)
5-6	Center student in each threesome does a do-si-do with each other. (Do-si-do, 2, 3, ... 8)
7-8	Right youngsters in each threesome move diagonally to do-si-do with each other. (Do-si-do, 2, 3, ... 8)
9-10	Left youngsters in each threesome move diagonally to do-si-do with each other. (Do-si-do, 2, 3, ... 8)
11-12	Center person in each threesome faces the person on the right and turns that person with a right hand star and then turns the person on the left with a left hand star and goes back to place. (Star, 2, 3, 4; Left, 2, 3, 4)
13-14	Lines of three go forward 4 counts and back 4 counts. (Forward, 2, 3, 4; back, 2, 3, 4)
15-16	Lines of three walk forward passing right shoulders and move forward to the next group of three (Forward pass, 2, 3, ... 8)

Repeat to the end of the music.

Game Activity

Scooter Kickball

Supplies: A cageball, gym scooters for active players

Skill: Striking with various body parts

Divide each team into active players (on scooters) and goal defenders. Active players are seated on the scooters and goal defenders are seated on the goal line with feet extended. The object of the game is to kick the cageball over the goal line being defended by the opposite team. The players are positioned as shown above. The game starts with a face-off of two opposing players on scooters at the center of the court. Active players on scooters propel the ball with their feet. Touching the ball with the hands is a foul and results in a free kick by the opposition at the spot of the foul. A player can use the head and body to stop and propel the ball.

Players defending the goal are seated on the goal line and may not use their hands. Use of the feet, body, and head is permitted. (If scoring seems too easy, the defenders can be allowed to use their hands.) Defenders are restricted to the seated position at the goal line and are not permitted to enter the field of play to propel or stop the ball.

Touchdown

Supplies: A small object that can be concealed in the hand

Skills: Running, dodging

Two parallel lines are placed at each end of the playing area. The class is divided into two teams with one team on each of the two lines. One team (offensive) huddles, placing their hands in the center. Players choose one player to carry the object to the opponents' goal line. The offensive team moves out of the huddle and spreads out along the line. On the signal "Hike," the offensive players move toward the opponents' goal line holding their hands closed so it is impossible to tell who is carrying the object. On the charge signal, the defensive team runs forward and tries to tag all the players. When tagged, players must freeze immediately and open both hands to show whether they have the object. If the player carrying the object reaches the goal line without being tagged, she calls "Touchdown" and scores 6 points. The defensive team now becomes the offensive team and vice versa.

Chain Tag

Supplies: None

Skills: Running, dodging

Two parallel lines are established at opposite ends of the playing area. Two groups of three players form a chain with joined hands and occupy the center. The players with free hands on either end of the chain do the tagging. All other players line up on one of the parallel lines. The players in the center call "Come on over," and children cross from one line to the other. The chains try to tag the runners. Anyone caught joins the chain. When the chain grows to six players, it divides into two groups of three players.

Dynamic Physical Education for Elementary School Children
Frisbee Skills
Level III – Week 33

Objectives:
To learn the unique throwing style required with frisbees
To learn the rules of frisbee golf
To play a round of frisbee golf in a cooperative manner

Equipment Required:
Moving to Music tape
Music cones, and signs for Squad Leader
  Exercises
Frisbees (one for each pair of students)
Scorecards and clipboards
Hoops, bowling pins, and cones

Instructional Activities	Teaching Hints
Introductory Activity -- Moving to Music	
Use different types of music to stimulate various locomotor and non-locomotor movements. Dance steps such as the polka, two-step, schottische and grapevine could be practiced.	If youngsters have trouble sensing the rhythm, use a tom-tom or tambourine to accentuate the beat

Fitness Development Activity -- Squad Leader Exercises with Task Cards

Suggested exercises to be placed on task cards:

Sitting Stretch
Push-Up challenges
Body Circles
Jumping Jack variations
Crab Kick combinations
Abdominal challenges
Treadmills
Toe Touchers
Leg Extensions

If there is a delay in starting an exercise, the squad should walk or jog.

The class is divided into groups of four to five students. Each group is given a task card that lists eight to ten exercises. One of the group members begins as the leader and leads the group through an exercise. Each time an exercise is completed, the card is passed to a new leader.

Use alternating intervals of music to signal exercising (30 seconds) with silence (5-8 seconds) to indicate passing the card.

Lesson Focus -- Frisbee Skills

Throwing the Disk
Backhand Throw
  The backhand grip is used most often. The thumb is on top of the disk, the index finger along the rim, and the other fingers underneath. To throw the Frisbee with the right hand, stand in a sideways position with the right foot toward the target. Step toward the target and throw the Frisbee in a sideways motion across the body, snapping the wrist and trying to keep the disk flat on release.
Underhand Throw
  The underhand throw uses the same grip as in the backhand throw, but the thrower faces the target and holds the disk at the side of the body. Step forward with the leg opposite the throwing arm while bringing the Frisbee forward. When the throwing arm is out in the front of the body, release the Frisbee. The trick to this throw is learning to release the disk so that it is parallel to the ground.

Catching the Disk
Thumb-Down Catch
  The thumb-down catch is used for catching when the disk is received at waist level or above. The thumb is pointing toward the ground. The Frisbee should be tracked from the thrower's hand. This clues the catcher about any tilt on the disk that may cause it to curve.
Thumb-Up Catch
  The thumb-up catch is used when the Frisbee is received below waist level. The thumb points up, and the fingers are spread.

Throwing and Catching Activities:
a. Throw the Frisbee at different levels to partner.
b. Throw a curve--to the left, right and upward. Vary the speed of the curve.

Use the following instructional cues to improve skill performance:

a. Release the disk parallel to the ground. If it is tilted, a curved throw results.

b. Step toward the target and follow through on release of the disk.

c. Snap open the wrist and make the Frisbee spin.

If space is limited, all Frisbees should be thrown in the same direction. Students can line up on either side of the area and throw across to each other.

Most activities are best practiced by pairs of students using one disk.

c. Throw a bounce pass--try a low and a high pass.
d. Throw the disc like a boomerang. Must throw at a steep angle into the wind.
e. Throw the Frisbee into the air, run and catch. Increase the distance of the throw.
f. Throw the Frisbee through a hoop held by a partner.
g. Catch the Frisbee under your leg. Catch it behind your back.
h. Throw the Frisbees into hoops that are placed on the ground as targets.
    Different-colored hoops can be given different values. Throw through your
    partner's legs.
i. Frisbee bowling--One partner has a bowling pin which the other partner
    attempts to knock down by throwing the Frisbee.
j. Play catch while moving. Lead your partner so he doesn't have to break stride.
k. See how many successful throws and catches you can make in 30 seconds.
l. Frisbee Baseball Pitching--Attempt to throw the Frisbee into your partner's
    "Strike Zone."

Youngsters can develop both sides of the body by learning to throw and catch the disk with either hand. The teacher should design the activities so that youngsters get both right-hand and left-hand practice.

Since a Frisbee is somewhat different from the other implements that children usually throw, devote some time to teaching form and style in throwing and catching. Avoid drills that reward speed in throwing and catching.

Game Activity

Frisbee Keep Away

Supplies: Frisbees

Skills: Throwing and catching Frisbees

Students break into groups of three. Two of the players in the group try to keep the other player from touching the Frisbee while they are passing it back and forth. If a defensive player touches the Frisbee, the person who threw the Frisbee becomes the defensive player. Begin the game by asking students to remain stationary while throwing and catching. Later, challenge can be added by allowing all players in the group move.

Frisbee Golf

Supplies: One Frisbee per person, hoops for hole markers, cones

Skills: Frisbee throwing for accuracy

Frisbee Golf or disk golf is a favorite game of many students. Boundary cones with numbers can be used for tees, and holes can be boxes, hula hoops, trees, tires, garbage cans, or any other available equipment on the school grounds. Draw a course on a map for students and start them at different holes to decrease the time spent waiting to tee off. Regulation golf rules apply. The students can jog between throws for increased activity.

Disk golf is played like regular golf. One stroke is counted for each time the disk is thrown and when a penalty is incurred. The object is to acquire the lowest score. The following rules dictate play:

Tee-throws: Tee-throws must be completed within or behind the designated tee area.

Lie: The lie is the spot on or directly underneath the spot where the previous throw landed.

Throwing order: The player whose disk is the farthest from the hole throws first. The player with the least number of throws on the previous hole tees off first.

Fairway throws: Fairway throws must be made with the foot closest to the hole on the lie. A run-up is allowed.

Dog leg: A dog leg is one or more designated trees or poles in the fairway that must be passed on the outside when approaching the hole. There is a two-stroke penalty for missing a dog leg.

Putt throw: A putt throw is any throw within 10 ft of the hole. A player may not move past the point of the lie in making the putt throw. Falling or jumping putts are not allowed.

Unplayable lies: Any disk that comes to rest 6 ft or more above the ground is unplayable. The next throw must be played from a new lie directly underneath the unplayable lie (one-stroke penalty).

Out-of-bounds: A throw that lands out-of-bounds must be played from the point where the disk went out (one-stroke penalty).

Course courtesy: Do not throw until the players ahead are out of range.

Completion of hole: A disk that comes to rest in the hole (box or hoop) or strikes the designated hole (tree or pole) constitutes successful completion of that hole.

Dynamic Physical Education for Elementary School Children
Gymnastics Skills (4)
Level III – Week 34

Objectives:
To understand the principles of stability and balance
To control the body weight in a variety of tumbling and stunt activities
To participate in "one on one" competition and accept the outcome
To play group games and cooperate with teammates

Equipment Required:
Music for Parachute Fitness
Parachute
Tumbling mats
15-20 foam balls (8") or playground balls
12-16 bowling pins

Instructional Activities	Teaching Hints

Introductory Activity -- Personal Choice

Students select any type of activity they wish to use to warm up. They may use one they have previously learned in class, or they may create one of their own. Emphasis should be on a balanced approach that works all major muscle groups.

If desired, students can work with a partner and share ideas with each other for desired activities.

Fitness Development Activity -- Parachute Fitness

1. Jog in circle with chute held in left hand. Reverse directions and hold with right hand.
2. Standing, raise the chute overhead, lower to waist, lower to toes, raise to waist, etc.
3. Slide to the right; return slide to the left.
4. Sit and perform curl-ups with a twist.
5. Skip.
6. Freeze, face the center, and stretch the chute tightly with bent arms. Hold for 8-12 seconds. Repeat.
7. Run in place, hold the chute at waist level, and hit the chute with lifted knees.
8. Sit with legs under the chute. Do a seat walk toward the center. Return to the perimeter. Repeat four to six times.
9. Place the chute on the ground. Jog away from the chute and return on signal. Repeat.
10. On sides with legs under the chute. Perform Side Flex and lift chute with legs.
11. Lie on back with legs under the chute. Shake the chute with the feet.
12. Hop to the center of the chute and return. Repeat.
13. Assume the push-up position with the legs aligned away from the center of the chute. Shake the chute with one arm while the other arm supports the body.
14. Sit with feet under the chute. Stretch by touching the toes with the chute. Relax with other stretches while sitting.

Tape alternating segments (25-30 seconds in length) of silence and music to signal duration of exercise. Music segments indicate aerobic activity with the parachute while intervals of silence announce using the chute to enhance flexibility and strength development.

Space youngsters evenly around the chute.

Use different grips (palms up, down, mixed).

All movements should be done under control. Some of the faster and stronger students will have to moderate their performance.

Lesson Focus – Gymnastics Skills (4)

Five groups of activities in this lesson ensure that youngsters receive a variety of experiences. Pick a few activities from each group and teach them alternately. For example, teach an individual stunt or two, then a tumbling skill or inverted balance, followed by a balance stunt, etc. Give equal time to each group of activities

Review activities taught in previous gymnastics lesson plans.
   a. Tumbling and Inverted Balances
   b. Balance Stunts
   c. Individual Stunts
   d. Partner and Group Stunts
   e. Combatives

Game Activity

Pin Knockout
   Supplies: Many 8" foam balls or playground balls, 12 bowling pins
   Skills: Rolling, dodging

   Divide the team in half and give each team many playground balls and six bowling pins. A court with a centerline is needed. The size of the court depends on the number of children in the game. The object of the game is to knock down all of the opponents' bowling pins. The balls are used for rolling at the opposing team's pins. Each team stays in its half of the court. A player is eliminated if any of the following occurs:

1. He is touched by any ball at any time, regardless of the situation (other than picking up a ball).

2. She steps over the centerline to roll or retrieve a ball. (Any opposing team member hit as a result of such a roll is not eliminated.)

3. He attempts to block a rolling ball with a ball in his hands and the rolling ball touches him in any manner.

A foul is called when a player holds a ball longer than 10 seconds without rolling at the opposing team. The ball must be immediately given to the opposing team. The bowling pins are placed anywhere in the team's area. Players may guard the pins, but must not touch them. When a pin is down, even if a member of the defending team knocked it over unintentionally, it is removed immediately from the game. The game is over when all pins on one side have been knocked down.

Over the Wall

Supplies: None

Skills: Running, dodging

Two parallel goal lines are drawn about 60 feet apart. Two additional parallel lines about 3 feet apart are laid out parallel to the goal lines in the middle of the game area. This is the wall. Two or 3 players are it and stand on the wall. All of the other players are behind one of the goal lines. The tagger calls "Over the wall." All of the players must then run across the wall to the other goal line. The taggers try to tag any crossing player. Anyone caught helps catch the others. Players also are considered caught when they step on the wall. They must clear it with a leap or a jump and cannot step on it anywhere, including on the lines. After crossing over to the other side safely, players wait for the next call. The game can be made more difficult by increasing the width of the wall. Taggers can step on or run through the wall at will.

Dynamic Physical Education for Elementary School Children
Softball Skills (1)
Level III – Week 35

Objectives:
To throw and catch a softball
To hit a softball
To be able to field softball grounders and fly balls
To know the basic rules of softball
To understand the roles of different positions in softball

Equipment Required:
Music, cones, and signs for Squad Leader Exercises
Station 1: Two batting tees, 4 balls, & 2 bats
Station 2: Four balls
Station 3: Four bases and 4 balls
Station 4: Four balls and 2 bats

Instructional Activities	Teaching Hints

Introductory Activity -- Personal Choice

Students select any type of activity they wish to use to warm up. They may use one they have previously learned in class, or they may create one of their own. Emphasis should be on a balanced approach that works all major muscle groups.

If desired, students can work with a partner and share ideas with each other for desired activities.

Fitness Development Activity -- Squad Leader Exercises with Task Cards

Suggested exercises to be placed on task cards:

Sitting Stretch
Push-Up challenges
Body Circles
Jumping Jack variations
Crab Kick combinations
Abdominal challenges
Treadmills
Toe Touchers
Leg Extensions

The class is divided into groups of four to five students. Each group is given a task card that lists eight to ten exercises. One of the group members is leader and leads the group through an exercise. Each time an exercise is completed, the card is passed to a new leader.

Use alternating intervals of music to signal exercising (30 seconds) with silence (5-8 seconds) to indicate passing the card.

Lesson Focus -- Softball Skills (1)

Skills
Practice the following skills:
1. Overhand Throw

In preparation for throwing, the child secures a firm grip on the ball, raises the throwing arm to shoulder height, and brings the elbow back. For the overhand throw, the hand with the ball is then brought back over the head so that it is well behind the shoulder at about shoulder height. The left side of the body is turned in the direction of the throw, and the left arm is raised in front of the body. The weight is on the back (right) foot, with the left foot advanced and the toe touching the ground. The arm comes forward with the elbow leading, and the ball is thrown with a downward snap of the wrist. The body weight is brought forward into the throw, shifting to the front foot. There should be good follow-through so that the palm of the throwing hand faces the ground at completion of the throw. The eyes should be on the target throughout, and the arm should be kept free and loose during the throw.

2. Pitching

Official rules call for the pitcher to have both feet in contact with the pitcher's rubber, but few elementary schools possess a rubber. Instead, the pitcher can stand with both feet about even, facing the batter, and holding the ball momentarily in front with both hands. The pitcher takes one hand from the ball, extends the right arm forward, and brings it back in a pendulum swing, positioning the ball well behind the body. A normal stride taken toward the batter with the left foot begins the throwing sequence for a right-handed pitcher. The arm is brought forward with an underhanded slingshot motion, and the weight is transferred to the leading foot. Only one step is permitted.

Whiffle balls and plastic bats are a much safer alternative for children this age. It is easier for them to swing plastic bats and the fear of getting hit by a softball will not be an issue.

Instructional cues for **throwing** are:
1. Place the throwing arm side of the body away from the target.
2. Step toward the target with the foot opposite the throwing hand.
3. Bend and raise the arm at the elbow. Lead with the elbow.

Instructional cues for **pitching** are:
1. Face the plate.
2. Keep your eyes on the target.
3. Swing the pitching arm backward and step forward.

3. Fielding Grounders

To field a grounder, the fielder should move as quickly as possible into the path of the ball and then move forward and play the ball on a good hop. The eyes must be kept on the ball, following it into the hands or glove. The feet are spread, the seat is kept down, and the hands are carried low and in front. The weight is on the balls of the feet or on the toes, and the knees are bent to lower the body. As the ball is caught, the fielder straightens up, takes a step in the direction of the throw, and makes the throw.

4. Batting (Right-Handed)

The batter stands with the left side of the body toward the pitcher. The feet are spread and the weight is on both feet. The body should be facing the plate. The bat is held with the trademark up, and the left hand grasps the bat lower than the right. The bat is held over the right shoulder, pointing both back and up. The elbows are away from the body. The swing begins with a hip roll and a short step forward in the direction of the pitcher. The bat is then swung level with the ground at the height of the pitch. The eyes are kept on the ball until it is hit. After the hit, there must be good follow-through.

Instructional cues for **fielding** are:
1. Move into line with the path of the ball.
2. Give when catching the ball.
3. Use the glove to absorb the force of the ball.
4. For grounders, keep the head down and watch the ball move into the glove.

Instructional cues for **batting** are:
1. Keep the hands together.
2. Swing the bat horizontally.
3. Swing through the ball.
4. Hold the bat off the shoulder.
5. Watch the ball hit the bat.

Station (Small Group) Instruction

The teacher should instruct at a different station each day. Start at the station that demands the most instruction. Set up a system of rotation that assures all stations will be covered during the unit.

Station 1 - Batting

Use a batting tee. For each station, two tees are needed, with a bat and at least two balls for each tee. Three to five children are assigned to each tee. There should be a batter, a catcher to handle incoming balls, and fielders. When only three children are in a unit, the catcher should be eliminated. Each batter is allowed a certain number of swings before rotating to the field. The catcher becomes the next batter, and a fielder moves up to catcher.

Station 2 - Throwing and Catching

Work with a partner and practice some of the following throwing drills:

a. Throw back and forth, practicing various throws.

b. gradually increase the distance of the throws.

c. focus on accuracy; if the throws are not caught, reduce the distance between players

Station 3 - Pitching

Students find a partner and pitch and catch with each other. Set out a number of bases at each station so pitchers can pitch and catch using a base as a target (home plate).

a. Pitch to another player over a plate.

b. Call balls and strikes. One player is the pitcher, the second is the catcher, and the third is the umpire. A fourth player can be a stationary batter to provide a more realistic pitching target.

Station 4 - Fielding

Players find a partner and practice throwing grounders and fly balls to each other.

a. One partner throws a grounder or fly ball, the other partner fields the ball and throws it back to the other. Reverse roles.

b. Do the same thing above except use a bat to hit the balls.

Hitters should avoid the following: lifting the front foot high off the ground, stepping back with the rear foot, or bending forward.

Stand about 7 to 10 yards apart when practicing throwing.

For youngsters who are afraid of the ball, use a whiffle ball.

Face the batter, both feet on the rubber and the ball held in front with both hands. One step is allowed, and the ball must be delivered on that step.
Ball must be pitched underhanded.
No motion or fake toward the plate can be made without delivering the ball.

Show form for high and low catch.

Move into the path of the ball.

Game Activity

Batter Ball

Supplies: A softball, a bat, a mask

Skills: Slow pitching, hitting, fielding, catching flies

Batter Ball involves batting and fielding but no base running. It is much like batting practice but adds the element of competition. A line is drawn directly from first to third base. This is the balk line over which a batted ball must travel to be fielded. Another line is drawn from a point on the foul line 3 feet behind third base to a point 5 feet behind second base and in line with home plate. Another line connects this point with a point on the other baseline 3 feet behind first base. The shaded area in the diagram is the infield.

Each batter is given three pitches (by a member of his own team) to hit the ball into fair territory across the balk line. The pitcher may stop any ground ball before it crosses the balk line. The batter then gets another turn at bat.

Scoring is as follows:

1. A successful grounder scores 1 point. A grounder is successful when an infielder fails to handle it cleanly within the infield area. Only one player may field the ball. If the ball is fielded properly, the batter is out.

2. A line drive in the infield area is worth 1 point if not caught. It can be handled for an out on any bounce. Any line drive caught on the fly is also an out.

3. A fly ball in the infield area scores 1 point if not caught. For an out, the ball must be caught legally by the first person touching it.

4. A two-bagger scores 2 points. Any fly ball, line drive or not, that lands fairly in the outfield area without being caught scores 2 points. If it is caught, the batter is out.

5. A home run scores 3 points. Any fly ball driven over the head of the farthest outfielder in that area scores a home run.

Three outs can constitute an inning, or all batters can be allowed one turn at bat and then the team changes to the field. A new set of infielders should be in place for each inning. The old set goes to the outfield. Limit pitchers to one inning and assure they take a turn at bat.

Tee Ball

Supplies: A softball, a bat, a batting tee

Skills: Most softball skills (except pitching and stealing bases), hitting a ball from a tee

This game is an excellent variation of softball and is played under softball rules with the following exceptions.

1. Instead of hitting a pitched ball, the batter hits the ball from a tee. The catcher places the ball on the tee. After the batter hits the ball, the play is the same as in regular softball. With no pitching, there is no stealing. A runner stays on the base until the batter hits the ball.

2. A fielder occupies the position normally held by the pitcher. The primary duties of this fielder are to field bunts and groundballs and to back up the infielders on throws.

Teams can play regular innings for three outs or change to the field after each player on the batting team has had a turn at bat.

Scrub (Work-Up)

Supplies: A softball, a bat

Skills: Most softball skills

The predominant feature of Scrub is the rotation of the players. The game is played with regular softball rules, with individuals more or less playing for themselves. There are at least two batters, generally three. A catcher, pitcher, and first-base player are essential. The remaining players assume the other positions. A batter who is out goes to a position in right field. All other players move up one position, with the catcher becoming the batter. The first-base player becomes the pitcher, the pitcher moves to catcher, and all others move up one place.

Dynamic Physical Education for Elementary School Children
Softball Skills (2)
Level III – Week 36

Objectives:
To throw and catch a softball
To hit a softball
To be able to field softball grounders and fly balls
To know the basic rules of softball
To understand the roles of different positions in softball

Equipment Required:
Music, cones, and signs for Squad Leader
  Exercises
Station 1: One bat and 4 balls
Station 2: Three home plates and 3 balls
Station 3: Four bases, balls and bats
Station 4: One bat and 4 balls

Instructional Activities	Teaching Hints

Introductory Activity -- Personal Choice

Students select any type of activity they wish to use to warm up. They may use one they have previously learned in class, or they may create one of their own. Emphasis should be on a balanced approach that works all major muscle groups.

If desired, students can work with a partner and share ideas for new ideas.

Fitness Development Activity -- Squad Leader Exercises with Task Cards

Suggested exercises to be placed on task cards:

Sitting Stretch
Push-Up challenges
Body Circles
Jumping Jack variations
Crab Kick combinations
Abdominal challenges
Treadmills
Toe Touchers
Leg Extensions

If there is a delay in starting an exercise, the squad should walk or jog.

The class is divided into groups of four to five students. Each group is given a task card that lists eight to ten exercises. One of the group members begins as the leader and leads the group through an exercise. Each time an exercise is completed, the card is passed to a new leader.

Use alternating intervals of music to signal exercising (30 seconds) with silence (5-8 seconds) to indicate passing the card.

Lesson Focus -- Softball Skills (2)

Skills
Review skills learned last week:
1. Overhand Throw
2. Pitching
3. Fielding Grounders
4. Batting
Introduce new skills:
Fielding Fly Balls

    There are two ways to catch a fly ball. For a low ball, the fielder keeps the fingers together and forms a basket with the hands. For a higher ball, the thumbs are together, and the ball is caught in front of the chin. The fielder should give with the hands, and care must be taken with a spinning ball to squeeze the hands sufficiently to stop the spinning. The eye is on the ball continually until it hits the glove or hands. The knees are flexed slightly when receiving and aid in giving when the ball is caught.

Station (Small Group) Instruction
The teacher should instruct at a different station each day. Start at the station that demands the most instruction. Set up a system of rotation that assures all stations will be covered during the unit.

Station 1 - Outfield Practice
One player in the group hits fly balls. The others field and practice using the sure stop when the ball is not caught on the fly. Rotate batters after 8 fly balls have been hit.

Whiffle balls and plastic bats are a much safer alternative for children this age. It is easier for them to swing plastic bats and the fear of getting hit by a softball will not be an issue.

Sure Stop for Outfield Balls
    To keep the ball from going through the hands and thus allowing extra bases, the outfielder can use the body as a barrier. The fielder turns half right and lowers one knee to the ground at the point toward which the ball is traveling. The hands catch the rolling ball, but if it is missed, the body will generally stop the ball.

If youngsters are not able to hit the ball, they can catch and throw it to the fielders.

Station 2 - Pitching and Umpiring

Students find a partner and pitch and catch with each other. Set out a number of bases at each station so pitchers can pitch and catch using a base as a target (home plate).
1. Pitch to another player over a plate.
2. Call balls and strikes. One player is the pitcher, the second is the catcher, and the third is the umpire. A fourth player can be a stationary batter to provide a more realistic pitching target.

When umpiring, strikes are called by raising the right hand and balls require raising the left hand.

Station 3 - Infield Practice
1. Throw around the bases clockwise and counterclockwise.
2. Throw grounders to infielders and make the play at first. After each play, throw around the infield.
3. If students have enough skill, bat the ball to the infielders in turn.

While having infield practice, one person at the station can run the bases and try to complete a circuit around the bases before the ball does.

Station 4 - Batting Practice

Each batter takes six swings and then rotates to the field. Catcher becomes batter and pitcher moves up to catcher.

Have more than one ball at the stations so the pitching can continue when a ball is hit or not caught.

Game Activity

Scrub (Work-Up)

See the Lesson Plan, Softball Skills (Week 35) for a complete game description.

Slow-Pitch Softball

Supplies: A softball, a bat
Skills: Most softball skills

The major difference between regular softball and Slow-Pitch Softball is in the pitching, but there are other modifications to the game as well. With slower pitching, there is more hitting and thus more action on the bases and in the field. Outfielders are an important part of the game because many long drives are hit. Rule changes from the game of official softball are as follows.
1. The pitch must be a slow pitch. Any other pitch is illegal and is called a ball. The pitch must be slow, with an arc of 1 foot. It must not rise over 10 feet from the ground, however. Its legality depends on the umpire's call.
2. There are ten players instead of nine. The extra one, called the roving fielder, plays in the outfield and handles line drives hit just over the infielders.
3 The batter must take a full swing at the ball and is out if he chops at the ball or bunts.
4. If a pitched ball hits the batter, she is not entitled to first base. The pitch is merely called a ball. Otherwise, balls and strikes are called as in softball.
5. The runner must hold base until the pitch has reached or passed home plate. No stealing is permitted.

Babe Ruth Ball

Supplies: A bat, a ball, four cones or other markers
Skills: Batting, pitching, fielding

Four cones separate the three outfield zones--left, center, and right field. It is helpful if foul lines have been drawn, but cones can define them. The batter calls the field to which he intends to hit. The pitcher throws controlled pitches so that the batter can hit easily. The batter remains in position as long as he hits to the designated field. Field choices must be rotated. The batter gets only one swing to make a successful hit. He may allow a ball to go by, but if he swings, it counts as a try. There is no base running. Players rotate.

Three-Team Softball

Supplies: A mask, a ball, a bat
Skills: All softball skills

Three-Team Softball works well with 12 players, a number considered too few to divide into two effective fielding teams. The players are instead divided into three teams. The rules of softball apply, with the following exceptions.
1. One team is at bat, one team covers the infield (including the catcher), and the third team provides the outfielders and the pitcher.
2. The team at bat must bat in a definite order. This means that because of the small number of batters on each side, instances can occur when the person due to bat is on base. To take a turn at bat, a player not on base must replace the runner.
3. After three outs, the teams rotate, with the outfield moving to the infield, the infield taking a turn at bat, and the batters going to the outfield.
4. An inning is over when all three teams have batted.
5. The pitcher should be limited to pitching one inning only. A player may repeat as pitcher only after all members of that team have had a chance to pitch.

Dynamic Physical Education for Elementary School Children
Fundamental Skills Using Climbing Ropes
Level III – Alternate Lesson Plan

Objectives:
To be able to recite safety rules for rope climbing
To be able to hang on a climbing rope for 5 seconds
To be able to hang and swing on a climbing rope

Equipment Required:
Climbing Ropes
Tumbling mats placed under ropes
Benches or Jumping Boxes

Instructional Activities	Teaching Hints

Introductory Activity

Substitute from a selected Lesson Plan

Fitness Development Activity

Substitute from a selected Lesson Plan

Lesson Focus – Fundamental Skills Using Climbing Ropes

Supported Pull-Ups

In supported Pull-Up activities, a part of the body remains in contact with the floor. The Pull-Up is hand-over-hand and the return is hand-under-hand.
1. Kneel directly under the rope. Pull up to the tiptoes and return to kneeling position.
2. Start in a sitting position under the rope. Pull up; the legs are supported on the heels. Return to sitting position.
3. Start in a standing position. Grasp the rope, rock back on the heels, and lower the body to the floor. Keep a straight body. Return to standing position.

Hangs

In a hang, the body is pulled up in one motion and held up for a length of time (5, 10, or 20 seconds). Progression is important.
1. From a seated position, reach up as high as possible and pull the body from the floor, except for the heels. Hold.
2. Same as the previous stunt, but pull the body completely free of the floor. Hold.
3. From a standing position, jump up, grasp the rope, and hang. This should be a Bent-Arm Hang with the hands about even with the mouth. Hold.
4. Repeat the previous stunt, but add leg movements---one or both knees up, bicycling movement, Half Lever (one or both legs up, parallel to the floor), Full Lever (feet up to the face).

Pull-Ups

In the Pull-Up, the body is raised and lowered repeatedly. The initial challenge should be to accomplish one Pull-Up in the defined position. The number of repetitions should be increased with care. All of the activities described for hangs are adaptable to Pull-Ups. The chin should touch the hands on each Pull-Up.

Swinging and Jumping

For swinging and jumping, a bench, box, or stool can serve as a takeoff point. To take off, the child reaches high and jumps to a bent-arm position. Landing should be with bent knees.
1. Swing and jump. Add half turns and full turns.
2. Swing and return to the perch. Add single- and double-knee bends.
3. Jump for distance, over a high-jump bar or through a hoop.
4. Swing and pick up a bowling pin and return to the perch.
5. Carry objects (e.g., beanbags, balls, deck tennis rings). A partner, standing to the side away from the takeoff bench, can put articles to be carried back on the takeoff perch by placing each article between the knees or feet.
6. Run toward a swinging rope, grasp it, and gain momentum for swinging.

Teaching Hints:

1. Mats should be placed under all ropes.

2. The hand-over-hand method should be used for climbing and the hand-under-hand method for descending.

3. Caution the children not to slide; sliding can cause rope burns on the hands and legs.

4. A climber who becomes tired should stop and rest. Proper rest stops should be taught as part of the climbing procedure.

5. Children also should be taught to leave enough margin for a safe descent. No children should go higher than their strength allows.

6. Spotters should be used initially for activities in which the body is inverted.

Climbing the Rope

1. *Scissors Grip.* For the Scissors Grip, approach the rope and reach as high as possible, standing with the right leg forward of the left. Raise the back leg, bend at the knee, and place the rope inside the knee and outside the foot. Cross the forward leg over the back leg, and straighten the legs with the toes pointed down. This should give a secure hold. To climb using the Scissors Grip, raise the knees up close to the chest, the rope sliding between them, while supporting the body with the hand grip. Lock the rope between the legs and climb up, using the hand-over-hand method and stretching as high as the hands can reach. Bring the knees up to the chest and repeat the process.

2. *Leg-Around Rest.* Wrap the left leg completely around the rope, keeping the rope between the thighs. The bottom of the rope then crosses over the instep of the left foot from the outside. The right foot stands on the rope as it crosses over the instep, providing pressure to prevent slippage. To provide additional pressure, release the hands and wrap the arms around the rope, leaning away from the rope at the same time. To climb using the Leg-Around Rest, proceed as in climbing with the Scissors Grip, but loosen the grip each time and re-grip higher.

Descending the Rope

There are four methods to descend the rope. The only differences are in the use of the leg locks, as the hand-under-hand is used for all descents.

1. *Scissors Grip.* From an extended scissors grip position, lock the legs and lower the body with the hands until the knees are against the chest. Hold with the hands, and lower the legs to a new position.

2. *Leg-Around Rest.* From the leg-around rest position, lower the body until the knees are against the chest. Lift the top foot, and let the feet slide to a lower position. Secure with the top foot and repeat.

3. *Instep Squeeze.* Squeeze the rope between the insteps by keeping the heels together. Lower the body while the rope slides against the instep.

4. *Stirrup Descent.* Place the rope on the outside of the right foot and carry it over the instep of the left. Pressure from the left foot holds the position. To get into position, let the rope trail along the right leg, reach under, and hook it with the left instep. When the pressure from the left leg is reduced, the rope slides smoothly while the descent is made with the hands.

Stunts Using Two Ropes

Two ropes hanging close together are needed for the following activities.

Straight-Arm Hang. To do the Straight-Arm Hang, jump up, grasp one rope with each hand, and hang with the arms straight.

Bent-Arm Hang. Perform as for the Straight-Arm Hang, but bend the arms at the elbows.

Arm Hangs with Different Leg Positions

  a. Do single- and double-knee lifts.

  b. Do a Half Lever. Bring the legs up parallel to the floor and point the toes.

  c. Do a Full Lever. Bring the feet up to the face and keep the knees straight.

  d. Do a Bicycle. Pedal as on a bicycle.

Pull-Ups. The Pull-Up is the same as on a single rope, except that each hand grasps a rope.

Inverted Hangs.

  a. Hang with the feet wrapped around the ropes.

  b. Hang with the feet against the inside of the ropes.

  c. Hang with the toes pointed and the feet not touching the ropes

Skin the Cat. From a bent-arm position, kick the feet overhead and continue the roll until the feet touch the mat. Return to the starting position. A more difficult stunt is to start from a higher position so that the feet do not touch the mat. Reverse to original position.

7. Rosin in powdered form and magnesium chalk aid in gripping. It is particularly important that they be used when the rope becomes slippery.

8. Children swinging on the ropes should be instructed to make sure that other children are out of the way.

9. Marks to limit the climb can be put on the rope with adhesive tape. A height of 8 to 10 feet above the floor is reasonable until a child demonstrates proficiency.

10. If the ceiling is higher than 15 or 16 feet, a bright piece of tape should be wrapped around the rope to limit climbing height.

Climbing Two Ropes

1. Climb up one rope, transfer to another, and descend.
2. Climb halfway up one rope, cross over to another rope, and continue to climb to the top.
3. Climb both ropes together without using the legs. This is difficult and requires the climber to slide one hand at a time up the ropes without completely releasing the grip.
4. Climb as on a single rope, with hands on one rope and feet on the other rope.

Game Activity

Substitute from a selected Lesson Plan

Equipment and Supplies for Physical Education

The following list identifies the equipment and supplies needed to teach a quality physical education program. The items are listed by priority in two categories—materials and supplies and capital outlay. Priority is based on cost, need, and versatility of the equipment. The first piece of equipment listed (playground balls) can be used to teach the most units making it the highest priority. The quantity of equipment is also listed to assure that the proper amount of equipment is ordered to facilitate a normal class size. Some of the equipment can be constructed (See Chapter 10 of *Dynamic Physical Education for Elementary School Children, Thirteenth Edition*) for specifications and construction tips.

The majority of listed equipment is available from **The Robert Widen Company, P.O. Box 2075, Prescott, AZ 86302**. The author has worked closely with this company in an attempt to assure that only quality equipment that is durable and reliable is shipped. Equipment is shipped quickly and is guaranteed for one year from the date of shipment against defects in workmanship and materials. For a current price list or more information, call toll free at (800) 862-0761 or FAX at (520) 776-8742.

Priority	Material and Supplies	Quantity
1	8½" inflatable rubber playground balls	36
1a	8" foam balls (can be substituted for playground balls)	36
1b	8" polyurethane coated foam balls (a substitute for playground balls; they are much more durable and give a true bounce. They can be used for all types of sport activities)	36
2	6" x 6" beanbags, assorted colors	72
3	Jump Ropes (plastic segments for beginners and speed ropes for experienced jumpers)	
	7 ft length	36
	8 ft length	36
	9 ft length	18
	10 ft length	12
	16 ft length (long rope jumping)	12
4	Game Cones (12" bright orange vinyl)	20
5	Tambourine, single head double ring	1
6	Hoops (solid or segmented)	
	30" diameter	36
	36" diameter	36
7	Wands (36" length, ¾" diameter hardwood)	36
8	Plastic racquets (sized for elementary children)	36
9	Foam balls for racquet skills (2½")	36
10	Fleece Balls (3-4" diameter)	36
11	Floor Hockey Sticks and Pucks - 36 of each	36
12	Whiffle Balls (use for throwing, hockey, softball, etc.)	36
13	Individual Mats (23" x 48" x ½")	36
14	Partner Tug-of-war Ropes (handles on both ends made with nylon webbing or garden hose and 1/4" nylon rope)	18
15	Juggling Scarves	108
16	Beachballs (18' to 20" diameter)	36
17	Soccer Balls (junior size or trainers)	18
18	Basketballs (junior size)	18
19	Footballs (Junior size or foam rubber)	18
20	Volleyballs (lightweight trainer balls)	18
21	Softballs (whiffle or extra soft)	18
22	Softball Bats (plastic or aluminum)	3
23	Frisbees, 9" to 10" diameter	36
24	Tinikling poles and riding boards (2 per set)	9 sets
25	Magic Stretch Ropes	12
26	Cageball (24")	1
27	Pinnies (twp colors - 18 each)	36
28	Ball Bags (nylon see-through mesh)	12
29	Team Tug-of-War Rope (¾"x50 ft nylon with sealed ends)	1

Priority	Material and Supplies	Quantity
30	Scoops	36
31	Stopwatches (digital)	6
32	Batons (for track & field relays)	12
33	Scooterboards, 12" with handles	18
34	Bowling Pins	24
35	Lummi Sticks	72

Priority	Capital Outlay Items	Quantity
1	Tumbling Mats (4 ft x 8 ft x 1¼" thick; Velcro fasteners on all sides)	12
2	CD/Cassette Tape Player	1
3	Parachute and Storage Bag (28 ft diameter)	1
4	Electric Ball Pump	1
5	Heavy Duty Equipment (Ball) Carts	4
6	Balance-Beam Benches (12 ft length)	6
7	Jumping Boxes (8" height)	6
8	Jumping Boxes (16" height)	6
9	Audiovisual Cart with Electrical Outlet (for tape player, etc.)	
10	Utility Gym Standards (for volleyball nets etc.)	4
11	Field Marker (for chalking lines)	1
12	Sit and Reach Box (measure flexibility)	4